PARTY POLITICS

VOLUME I

APPEAL TO THE
PEOPLE

Parliament
Cabinet Government
The British Constitution
The Approach to Self-Government

PARTY POLITICS

BY

SIR IVOR JENNINGS

K.B.E., Q.C., Litt.D., LL.D., F.B.A.
Master of Trinity Hall, Cambridge
Bencher of Gray's Inn

VOLUME I

APPEAL TO THE PEOPLE

CAMBRIDGE
AT THE UNIVERSITY PRESS
1960

PUBLISHED BY
THE SYNDICS OF THE CAMBRIDGE UNIVERSITY PRESS

Bentley House, 200 Euston Road, London, N.W. 1
American Branch: 32 East 57th Street, New York 22, N.Y.

©

CAMBRIDGE UNIVERSITY PRESS

1960

Printed in Great Britain at the University Press, Cambridge
(Brooke Crutchley, University Printer)

CONTENTS

CONTENTS

CONTENTS

PREFACE

The survey of the British Constitution begun in 1936 with *Cabinet Government* and continued in 1938 with *Parliament* was to have been completed about 1942 with *Party Politics*. It was hoped that *Party Politics*, like *Cabinet Government*, would deal with developments since 1832 and would be complete in one volume. Further research suggested that, though the Conservative party acquired its name in 1832 and the foundation of the Liberal party (though not its name) could be dated from 1830, there was no fundamental change in ideas and attitudes in the period of the first Reform Bill. Emphasis on the 'structure' of politics, in Sir Lewis Namier's sense, suggested the date 1783, or perhaps Burke's 'party political' defence of the Rockingham whigs in 1770. It proved, however, impossible to explain the ideas of Pitt and Fox except in relation to the Revolution of 1688. In the realm of ideas—by which I mean not political theories but the more pragmatic ideas which produce political decisions—the essential element is that of continuity. Each generation inherits and adapts the ideas of its predecessors. Among the electors of 1959 were a few who voted for (or against) Home Rule in 1886, and others who have a vague recollection that their fathers turned out Winston Churchill in 1945. So in 1640 there were voters who remembered the Spanish Armada; in the '45 there were supporters of George II who remembered James II; after Peterloo there were people who remembered the French Revolution. Our memories are lengthened by conversations with our parents and grandparents. Many of us now living have been told how Disraeli dished the whigs in 1867 and how votes were cast on the hustings in 1868; Queen Victoria was told by the Duke of Wellington what William Pitt had said; Pitt must have met people who had been involved in the Glorious Revolution of 1688; and some of the supporters of Bonny Prince Charlie had had first-hand descriptions of the execution of the first of the Charlies.

In the third volume of *Party Politics* it is hoped to illustrate the perpetuation of political ideas; but it is surely impossible to doubt that in the general election of 1959 there were faint echoes of the Civil War of 1641. On the other hand the difficulty of interpreting party politics in the light of three hundred years of political history will be appreciated, especially in an age when history is being reinterpreted. This difficulty will be more pronounced in the second and third volumes. For the moment it is enough to explain that my decision to consider developments since the Stuarts was one of the main causes of the postponement of *Party Politics* (the other was my preoccupation with other matters) and also the cause of its conversion into three volumes.

The main difference between the lawyer's and the historian's view of history is that the former is more concerned with 'subjects' than with events. A Representation of the People Act, for instance, is a lawyer's solution to a collection of political difficulties which have arisen at different periods of British history. His task is, therefore, to ascertain what those difficulties were and what attempts were made to solve them. When he drafts an election law for a different environment (as I have had to do) he can consider how much of the lengthy British experience is relevant to that environment. It is the historian's task to find out what happened at the general election of 1784 and the lawyer's to draw conclusions from those events. This is, of course, to draw a contrast more precisely than is possible in practice: the lawyer may interpret events and the historian may draw conclusions: but this is simply an aspect of the unity of knowledge. In the main the historian uses primary sources, as well as his own imagination, and the lawyer uses secondary sources: but each has to check the other because the one knows more history than law and the other knows more law than history.

Accordingly, I have not provided a lawyer's attempt at connected history (as, for instance, Sir Erskine May did in his *Constitutional History of England*). Professor Maitland's device of division into 'periods' was at first sight more attractive: but the assumption behind the third volume is that there are no 'periods' and that ideas are carried on from generation to generation in layers melting into a more or less consistent 'philosophy' of politics which can be called Whiggism, Toryism, Conservatism, Liberalism or Socialism as interpreted for the time being. The subject therefore falls into three parts each of which, as experience has shown, requires a separate volume. The first deals with elections in law and practice under the title *Appeal to the People*; the second deals with the composition and operation of parties under the title *The Growth of Parties*; the third deals with a number of leading political ideas under the title *The Stuff of Politics*. Some overlapping is unavoidable in this scheme, but I believe that each volume can be read separately. Since the other volumes are in typescript I have been able, I hope, to ensure consistency.

The volume was in typescript in January 1959 and in proof by October 1959. Except in Chapter x, few amendments have been made to take account of the general election of 1959.

I am indebted to Dr G. Kitson Clark, Fellow of Trinity College, for the loan of some of the material quoted in this volume. Dr G. F. S. Best, Fellow of Trinity Hall, has been good enough to read several chapters in draft, and has offered valuable suggestions. The London School of Economics and Political Science and the Hansard Society have given me permission to use some of the material quoted in Chapter x. I am especially indebted to my daughter, Mrs Claire Dewing, for undertaking the typing of the several chapters as they were written, and again as they were corrected.

W. I. J.

TRINITY HALL
CAMBRIDGE
30 January 1960

INTRODUCTION

'There may be occasions,' said William Pitt on 21 April 1800, 'but they will ever be few, when an appeal to the people is the just mode of proceeding on important subjects.' Seven years later Canning said: 'I defy you on this motion and on all other motions which you may make: I defy your majorities. I stand by the Crown and shall appeal to the people.' But the cynical Creevey in 1810 reminded the House of Commons that they were elected under 'Old Corruption'. 'To talk of a dissolution of Parliament as an "appeal to the people",' he said, 'was mere mockery and imposition. It was perfectly well known that a dissolution of Parliament was not an appeal to the people, but to the Treasury.'

Oddly enough, they were all correct. The British Constitution was, as usual, in a state of transition. In the first decade of the nineteenth century an election was both an appeal for 'popular' support and an occasion for the use of all the electioneering devices of the eighteenth century. The 'people' were, of course, very few, except in a few towns a small class, rather like the English-educated class in a Commonwealth country of Asia or West Africa. But on the one hand Pitt or Canning could appeal for the support of the independent country gentlemen and other electors on the ground of political principle; on the other hand somebody in the Treasury had to organise the election, with a view to a Government majority, by mobilising the men of influence in the counties and the patrons of boroughs, by looking for likely men who by reason of their local influence or well-filled pockets could hope to win county or borough seats, by using the Treasury or Admiralty influence wherever it existed in spite of the legislation of 1782, by using a little money to help to purchase a borough or to subsidise a candidate who lacked money enough to fight a contested election, by the exercise of judicious patronage or the promise of a step in the peerage or a ribbon, and generally by assuming that political principle was a matter of no importance.

The two styles of electioneering, the old and the new, went on together. The old style was not due only to an assumption that every man had his price, even when it could not be expressed in money (and usually it could not); it was also due to an assumption that a man was elected to Parliament to exercise his independent judgment on the measures to be submitted to Parliament and on the policies of His Majesty, and not to carry out a policy approved by his electorate. Even on those assumptions, it could not be expected that an influential landowner or a borough patron would secure the election of a person who was known to support Ministers of whom the landowner or the patron disapproved. Even John Robinson, the Secretary to the Treasury who managed the elections of 1774, 1780 and 1784,[1] had to consider the 'politics' of a borough patron before he classed the borough as for or against the Government or as doubtful. If, however, we go back to 1761, the last election managed by the fourth Duke of Newcastle, it is difficult to find any evidence of political principle. If we go forward to 1831, we find the electorate returning a House of Commons pledged to parliamentary reform. This bald comparison exaggerates the degree of the change. In 1761 there was no great issue dividing the politicians; and when there was such an issue, like the American war in 1780, we find something like 'party politics'. In 1831 there was a great political issue, but in 1835 there was not. The Reform Act had modified the technique of electioneering, but 'old style' electioneering was still in use in some constituencies in 1880, when Gladstone undertook the greatest of his 'pilgrimages of passion' in order to persuade electors to vote Liberal.

Even so, there was a change between 1760 and 1830, to which the Reform Act gave impetus. It should first be noticed that Burke in 1770 gave a theoretical justification for party politics.[2] His pamphlet was what we should now describe as 'party political', a defence of the connexion to which Burke belonged as 'man of business' to the Marquis of Rockingham and holder of one of the Marquis' boroughs. Nevertheless, Burke's party 'literature' was always important because, unlike his patron, he had a remarkable facility for finding some principle to justify his political actions. What Burke justified was the existence of a 'party'

[1] Though he did it unofficially in 1784.
[2] *Thoughts on the Cause of the Present Discontents.*

based upon 'particular principles' and operating as a 'formed opposition'. We do not get 'His Majesty's Opposition' until 1806, and even
then it was a bit of a joke;[1] but there was a 'formed Opposition' to the
American War in 1780. It was not yet a party Opposition, based upon
the acceptance of a common leadership for the advancement of a
common policy, but something very like it began to develop when
Fox led the attack on Pitt after 1783. The development of the party
system from Pitt and Fox is studied in the second volume: but some
aspects are relevant here. In 1780 George III dissolved Parliament,
on the advice of the Cabinet, in order to strengthen Lord North's
Government. The Parliament had lasted since November 1774, and so
a dissolution was necessary before November 1781; but the opportunity to dissolve earlier was seized because of a slightly favourable turn
in the American War, in the belief that at the moment, as Lord Sandwich
(a member of the Cabinet) put it, 'Government both personally and
politically stands very high': this 'popular favour', he added, would
gradually evaporate.[2]

This anxiety to 'cash in' on a temporary rise in popularity did not
prevent Lord North and John Robinson from organising the election
as if public opinion was a matter of little importance:

Public opinion was something intangible and incalculable; in any case, in
more than half of the constituencies it had no importance whatsoever. They
were concerned with the hard facts of the electoral system, much of them
readily ascertainable and reducible to methodical analysis. What was the
state of opinion among the hundred or so patrons of parliamentary boroughs?
How many were friendly, how many definitely adverse? Reckoning up in
advance what changes they were likely to make in their disposition of the
seats which they controlled, how would the balance of parties be affected?
Where, in the open constituencies, was there a likelihood of finding wealthy
candidates prepared to stand a contest, with or without assistance from the
Government?[3]

Thus, the politicians at the centre and their advisers regarded the
election both as an appeal to the people and as an exercise in the art of

---

[1] John Cam Hobhouse, 15 *Hansard Debates*, 135: 'It was said to be very hard on His
Majesty's Ministers to raise objections to this proposition. For his own part, he thought
it more hard on His Majesty's Opposition (*a laugh*) to compel them to take this course.'
[2] I. R. Christie, *The End of North's Ministry, 1780–82*, p. 31.   [3] *Ibid.* pp. 35–6.

political management. Exactly what happened in the constituencies can never be determined. It may be true that elections in Oxford were decided by 'beer and mob rule', and elections in Cambridge by 'oligarchy and wine' ('excellent wine', said an unregenerate alderman, 'and plenty of it'):[1] but this does not mean that the vote of the President of Magdalen, if he had one, was bought by beer or forced from him by the mob surging down the High. It is a little more credible that excellent wine would make the Master of Trinity Hall (if he were a freeman) favourably inclined—though he would have a higher standard of excellence than an unregenerate alderman—but he had prejudices in politics as well as a palate derived from long practice. In a contested election the candidate or his agent had to use the argument which persuaded: it might be beer or wine, or pressure from a landlord or employer, or a bribe, or an appeal to snobbery, or an opinion on the American War. Most elections were not contested, but this was not necessarily because the seats were owned or controlled by anybody. As Sam Long discovered in Cambridge after the Reform Act, a person who could dispose of two hundred votes was in a very strong position. Sam Long paid his disciplined cohort, but before the Reform Act this was not the usual method. A peer or a great landowner had 'influence' in a county because his nominees were usually accepted by his social inferiors, or by a sufficient number of them to make it unprofitable to oppose him. In few counties was the influence so strong that it could not be challenged: but challenges were few because a contested election was expensive not only to the great landowner but also to his supporters, who would expect to bring in their own supporters, usually at their own expense. If, therefore, influence was divided, it was better to divide the representation, or to do a deal which covered a neighbouring borough as well as the county. Moreover contested elections put country gentlemen to the choice between the candidates of two great landowners or groups, created bad blood, and upset 'the peace of the county'. Similarly, though there were 'proprietary boroughs' absolutely controlled by their patrons, in most boroughs the patronage depended on the influence exercised by the patron over the corporation

---

[1] F. W. Maitland, *Township and Borough*, p. 95, quoted by E. and A. G. Porritt, *The Unreformed House of Commons*, I, p. 70.

or the freemen. That influence could be contested, and quite often was.

Even where there were no contests, John Robinson had to consider the political prejudices of the patrons and their nominees. One of the characteristics of the 1780 election, when compared with that of 1761, was that certain patrons could be classed as 'opposition';[1] it was then necessary to consider whether it was practicable to get Government supporters to stand in opposition to the prevailing interest.

In 1780 there were contests in only eighty-six constituencies—sixty-eight in England:[2] but this was partly because the intention to dissolve was kept secret until the very last moment and little time was available to organise contests. The figures are, however, a little misleading. A candidate would not go to the poll unless he conceived that he had a chance of winning, and he might not know until he had completed his canvass of the influential people. Hence a good deal of electioneering was done even in uncontested elections. In that electioneering, as in the elections which went to the poll, political opinion undoubtedly played a part.[3] What part depended on local circumstances. At the one extreme was Yorkshire (eventually uncontested) where Sir George Savile breathed fire and brimstone against the Government in the style of the dragons of the nineteenth century.[4] Like Yorkshire was the great open borough of Westminster, where Charles James Fox declared that the contest was not between Lord Lincoln and him, 'but between Lord North and the electors of Westminster'.[5] On the other hand, even in the open borough of Newcastle the main points were 'at best local and personal issues, at worst hard cash';[6] and this was even more true in many of the smaller boroughs. The conclusion produced by Mr Christie's detailed examination of the election of 1780 is that in the counties 'a swing against the Government...was faithfully reflected in the returns of their representatives'; but that no such trend was discernible in the big urban constituencies.[7] On the other hand, there was political agitation in many of the boroughs. Even in the counties, however, the member of Parliament was not a

[1] See the list in I. R. Christie, *The End of North's Ministry, 1780–82*, pp. 54–7.
[2] *Ibid.* pp. 117–18.   [3] *Ibid.* pp. 120–63.   [4] *Ibid.* p. 122.
[5] *Ibid.* p. 135.   [6] *Ibid.* p. 143.   [7] *Ibid.* p. 156.

representative of the political opinion of his constituents, as he is—or thinks he is—now. After election he voted for or against the Government as his views or his interests dictated. This was part of the tradition, supported by the supposition that the Parliament of 1780 could last six years and that new circumstances would arise before 1786.

In fact, however, the next election was held in 1784, and it was again a deliberate attempt to strengthen the Government. Indeed, this was a much stronger case, for young Pitt had no means of strengthening himself in Parliament against the combined opposition of Fox and North. He had therefore to 'appeal to the people' to give the King and himself a majority.[1] The election of 1784 has not been studied in such detail as Mr Christie has studied that of 1780, and the historians dispute as to what happened. For those who thought of Wilberforce's victory in Yorkshire and Pitt's in the University of Cambridge, or Fox's narrow victory at Westminster and the rejection of so many of 'Fox's Martyrs', it was a great triumph for public opinion. For those who have seen John Robinson's careful calculations at the Treasury, it was merely another example of expert management of an election on behalf of the King. In all probability both are correct. If George III had not been able to win the election there would have been a constitutional revolution, for he always won elections. On the other hand, public opinion could not have played a smaller part than in 1780; and indeed there was in 1784 a major issue which was both political and personal. To put it into Government terms, should the King be forced, by an unprincipled coalition between Fox and North, to accept Ministers whom he did not want and to assent to policies with which he did not agree? Was not this an innovation on the Constitution, an infringement of the prerogative of the Crown? What is more, Fox himself attacked the prerogative as he saw the dissolution coming. These were matters which even the forty-shilling freeholders of the counties and the scot and lot electors of Westminster could understand: the country gentlemen, and their ladies, evidently felt strongly about them. Wilberforce

[1] This was, apparently, the point at which the idea of the appeal to the people developed; see the Speech from the Throne, 1784: 'I have the greatest satisfaction in meeting you in Parliament at this time after recurring, in so important a moment, to the sense of the people': Halévy, *History of the English People in the XIX Century*, I, p. 189.

did not win Yorkshire by corrupt methods; and Fox had to use all the arts of old-style electioneering to win second place at Westminster. These great constituencies did not set the pace; they merely indicated how opinion had swung where opinion mattered; and, since opinion had mattered in 1780, strong evidence of a change of electioneering practice would be needed before one could regard as an illusion the contemporary belief that the unpopularity of the coalition was a major factor in producing Pitt's majority.

Pitt and Fox were not aristocratic leaders depending on social prestige and their family connexions, but professional politicians putting forth competing arguments. This does not mean that Pitt neglected all the arts of political management; for though places, contracts and pensions began to disappear as major political instruments, peerages, baronetcies and ribbons played an even more important part. Nor did the appearance of Fox as Leader of the Opposition—we may surely use that term—involve the disappearance of the country house intrigues of the great whig families. The French Revolution and the Terror gave the development a twist without hindering it. The general election of 1790 strengthened Pitt's hold on the House of Commons; and in the course of that Parliament the Opposition became so weak that it almost disappeared. Partly the fault lay with Fox himself; he regarded the election of 1784 not as a swing of opinion but as an example of the excessive power of the King, and placed his hopes, so far as he had any, on the accession of the Prince of Wales. The main causes, however, were the French Revolution and the French Wars, which united the greater part of the governing class, with Burke as the new apostle of an English conservatism which was in due course to become Conservatism. English liberalism was kept alive by the Opposition whigs, but only just alive. The general election of 1796 was a wartime election, and as in 1790 there were no 'issues' to influence public opinion. Nor was there any real conflict of opinion in 1802. It is true that from the Government's most important pocket borough, Scotland, Dundas reported that 'the democratic interest had been more alive and active than he had known for many years past';[1] but from John Bull's other island Castlereagh was able to report that 'the

[1] *Life of Lord Sidmouth*, II, p. 72.

individuals chosen were perfectly proper, both in principles and property'.[1]

It will be noted that, except in 1784 (and in a measure 1780), Parliaments were normally dissolved after six full sessions, this being a convenient arrangement when the maximum duration of a Parliament was seven years. In 1806 this tradition was broken by the Ministry of All the Talents, with the deliberate intention of strengthening the Government and especially the Grenville whigs. Lord Hawkesbury (afterwards Earl of Liverpool) protested to the King against this misuse of the prerogative, which would 'have the inevitable effect of throwing the whole influence of Government in the borough elections into the hands of the present Administration'.[2] The King thought it unwise to refuse a dissolution which would precipitate a resignation of Ministers, but no royal funds were made available for the election, which appears generally not to have been managed efficiently, though the Government gained seats.[3]

However, when the Ministry went out in 1807 over Roman Catholic relief and the Duke of Portland became Prime Minister with Lord Hawkesbury as Home Secretary, the boot was on the other foot. It was decided to dissolve Parliament 'before the country had time to cool'.[4] There was, however, some justification for this step. The idea that there was anything improper in a 'formed opposition' had disappeared. We may almost say that, His Majesty's Government having resigned owing to a difference of opinion with the King, His Majesty's Opposition had been requested to form a Government. Having accepted the commission, it was reasonable that the latter should seek a working majority by appealing to the people. Indeed, the King's prorogation speech stated that 'His Majesty is anxious to recur to the sense of his people, while the events which have recently taken place are fresh in their recollection'.[5] In other words, the new Government proposed to appeal to the people on the question of supporting the King against Roman Catholic relief: and Spencer Perceval, in his election address to his constituents, emphasised this issue.[6] Mr Michael Roberts says that the election was fought on the issue of 'No Popery' in England and

[1] *Life of Lord Sidmouth*, II, p. 72.
[2] *Life of Lord Liverpool*, I, p. 219.
[3] *Life of Spencer Perceval*, I, p. 210.
[4] *Life of Lord Liverpool*, I, p. 237.
[5] *Life of Spencer Perceval*, I, p. 250.
[6] *Ibid.* pp. 251–2.

'King and Constitution' in Scotland.[1] The whigs complained that the King was corrupting the electorate, but no extraordinary efforts appear to have been made and the election seems to have been a genuine appeal to the people so far as that was practicable under the electoral system then prevailing.

Parliament was again dissolved in 1812, after only five years. Lord Liverpool had succeeded Spencer Perceval on the latter's assassination, the Duke of Wellington had had great success in Spain, Napoleon was in trouble in Russia, and the harvest was good in England. It was therefore a convenient opportunity for a new Prime Minister, with a weak Treasury Bench in the House of Commons, to strengthen his position. The electoral authority of the Treasury had been weakened in 1809 by Curwen's Act, which forbade the public sale of seats:[2] and it is plain that Government influence had progressively declined since 1780. Nevertheless, the Government gained some sixty seats, and the Parliament thus elected lasted the full six sessions—there was no 'khaki election' after Waterloo.

If the 'people' had been anything more than a small section of the population, there might have been a change of Government in 1818. There had been underground political movements, strong both in Nonconformist and in industrial areas, which had been barely represented in Parliament by a few eccentric Radicals. We shall see that modern electioneering technique had been begun in Westminster in 1807; there was great discontent among the labouring classes which led the Government of 1819 to impose the notorious 'Six Acts'; and yet this movement of opinion was almost unrepresented in Parliament. The Whig Opposition was divided, had not yet made up its mind about parliamentary reform, and had no leader. As the industrialisation of England and Scotland developed, the 'appeal to the people' became, at best, a polite fiction. The whigs won some thirty seats at the general election of 1818, but it can hardly be said that they deserved them.

Peterloo and the Six Acts did not affect the general election of 1820, necessitated by the death of George III. The Parliament then elected lasted the full six sessions. Canning had had the dissolution postponed

---

[1] Michael Roberts, *The Whig Party, 1807–1812*, p. 229.
[2] *Life of Lord Liverpool*, I, p. 444.

from 1825 to 1826 because of public excitement over 'No Popery' on which the Government was divided. In the interval there was an economic crisis which would, under a reformed Constitution, have turned out the Government. There was much distress and some disorder, but the unrepresented populace had no political leader. The election of 1826 was riotous in many of the towns and in urbanised counties; in the great open boroughs candidates won seats by promising reform of the Corn Laws. In other constituencies in which issues mattered, however, the battle was fought over Roman Catholic relief, an issue on which those dissenters who had votes joined with the country gentlemen against the whigs. On the other hand, the whigs gained seats in Ireland, where the Roman Catholics had votes but could not stand for election. Since a party label was still the exception, the election was indeterminate. In any case, what was tory policy and what was whig was still uncertain. Canning, who led the House of Commons and was soon to be Prime Minister, opposed the prejudices of most of the Government supporters against Roman Catholic relief and the reform of the Corn Laws.[1]

The resignation of Lord Liverpool in 1827, through ill health, brought in Canning as Prime Minister and ended an epoch. Though party lines were still very fluid, it could be said that there was a tory Government and a whig Opposition. On the other hand, there were no fixed party principles. Canning could support reform of the Corn Laws against his 'party'; Lord John Russell could split the whigs and obtain some tory support for a modest proposal of parliamentary reform; Roman Catholic relief was generally a whig policy but was supported by Canning. John Cam Hobhouse went so far as to say that the real Opposition to the Government was behind the Treasury Bench;[2] Canning's tory Government had whig support but tory opposition.

The death of Canning later in the year brought in (after a short interval) the Duke of Wellington with a more tory Government. The principal Canningites remained in office; but only for a short period, because they voted against the Government, and crossed the floor, on the question of disfranchising corrupt boroughs. This weakened the

[1] Halévy, *History of the English People in the XIX Century*, II, pp. 240–2.
[2] *Ibid.* p. 242.

Government considerably; and it was weakened still more by the passing of Roman Catholic relief in 1829, for it was carried with whig support and against the votes—and still more the opinions—of many tories. O'Connell's election for County Clare in 1828 had convinced Wellington and Peel: but if 'the country' was against Roman Catholic relief in 1826 it was still against it in 1829. There was, too, a good deal of economic distress in 1829–30, not handled so efficiently as Canning had handled it in 1825.

These facts are important because the death of George IV in 1830 compelled a dissolution, and it was taken early to enable Wellington to strengthen his Government in the House of Commons. For the first time since the Union with Scotland the King (William IV)—or his Government—lost an election. It is commonly said that parliamentary reform 'swept the country': but that is an exaggeration. Some of the early calculations suggested that the Government had won twenty seats. They certainly gained seats in Ireland, where the forty-shilling freeholders had been disfranchised as the price of Roman Catholic relief; they won every seat in Scotland; and they had the usual quota of safe borough seats.[1] There is little evidence about Government 'management',[2] and there were a great many uncontested elections.[3] There was the usual Radical agitation for parliamentary reform at the outset, but it could hardly be said to be an 'issue' until the Revolution in France aroused opinion just as the borough elections were being held, and before the county elections. Where public opinion was an important element in gaining votes—and it was so only in a few of the counties and in most of the open boroughs—candidates of all parties had to pledge themselves to parliamentary reform. Forty-seven knights of the shire were returned in opposition to the Government, including the *parvenu* Henry Brougham in the great constituency of Yorkshire.[4] The result was still doubtful, but Wellington made it certain by pledging himself against Reform. When an amendment was moved in the House of Commons on the Civil List proposals, the

[1] E. Halévy, *History of England in the XIX Century*, III, p. 4.
[2] J. R. M. Butler, *The Passing of the Great Reform Bill*, p. 83.
[3] Only nine of the forty English counties were contested: D. C. Moore, 'Politics of Deference', p. 38.
[4] *Ibid.* p. 88.

Government was defeated by twenty-nine and resigned. Even so, the second reading of the first Reform Bill was carried by one vote only,[1] and the whig (and Canningite) Government was beaten by eight votes on General Gascoyne's instruction not to decrease the number of members for England and Wales.

The dissolution of 1831, which followed this defeat, was not the first example of an appeal to the people against the House of Commons. The first was the dissolution of 1784. In 1831, however, the Parliament had lasted less than six months. Lord Grey was able to cite the precedent of the dissolution of 1807, which had occurred only five months after the meeting of Parliament.[2] He justified a dissolution, as in 1807, on the ground that 'this Government is now without its natural support, the Parliament having been *chosen by the late Ministers*, and all the seats usually at the command of the Ministers being now filled by their bitterest opponents'.[3] The King, too, was familiar with 'Old Corruption', for his main objection was that he had 'considered the period of general election to have been, at all times and under all circumstances, a period of disorder, of general relaxation, and more or less of outrage';[4] and he feared that the excitement engendered by the Reform Bill would cause widespread disorders with which the troops would be unable to deal. In the end, however, the King gave way rather than suffer the consequential resignation of Ministers.

There was no doubt, this time, that the Government was appealing to the people on a question of policy: but other methods also had to be used. Edward Ellice, Secretary to the Treasury, had John Robinson's former job of managing the election. Whig patrons of boroughs, even boroughs doomed by the Reform Bill, had to be persuaded to pledge their candidates to support for the Bill.[5] Ellice 'collected large sums from the leading whigs, with which he purchased several of the nomination boroughs, previously represented by tories, and he aided many of the party in expensive contests which, so soon after a general

---

[1] D. C. Moore, 'Politics of Deference', p. 208. England and Wales voted against, but only because of the members for close boroughs. Scotland was against, but the Irish majority enabled the whigs to win.

[2] *Correspondence of Earl Grey with King William IV*, I, p. 198.

[3] *Ibid.* pp. 186, 198. Present writer's italics.   [4] *Ibid.* p. 189.

[5] Porritt, *The Unreformed House of Commons*, I, p. 322.

election, they could not have undertaken without a liberal subscription'.[1] The tories, on the other hand, are said to have spent over £400,000. 'The excitement enabled the notorious freemen of Sudbury to raise their figure to £10 a head.' Even Scotland went wild. In Ireland Dublin Castle was accused of bringing pressure to bear on half-pay officers. Oddly enough, rioting was rare.[2]

The University of Cambridge distinguished itself by rejecting Lord Palmerston and a Cavendish and electing two tories; but elsewhere those who had supported General Gascoyne's motion went down like ninepins. Mr Molesworth[3] has a long list of the distinguished tories who suffered defeat, even in seats which had been considered to be safely under influence. The second reading of the second Reform Bill was carried by 367 votes to 231, thus showing that Ministers had gained 135 seats since the second reading of the first Bill.[4]

The first Reform Act made no fundamental difference, though it accelerated the changes which had begun in 1780.[5] First, the old form of 'close borough' disappeared, partly by the extinction of boroughs, partly by extending borough boundaries, and partly by swamping the old electorate by the new ten-pound occupiers. There were, however, still many small boroughs in which 'influence' could play a predominant part. In the medium-sized boroughs, which were usually freemen boroughs in 1831, the number of freemen electors was reduced by the requirement of residence, and the ordinary qualification became that of the £10 occupier, though in some boroughs the freemen were still numerous. In the great open constituencies the popular element was reduced by the abolition (after existing lives) of scot and lot and potwalloper qualifications, so that electoral power was transferred to the £10 occupiers. In the counties the £10 copyholders, £10 leaseholders, and £50 tenants at will were added to the forty-shilling freeholders. This addition to the electorate swamped the urban electors in a rural county, and indeed a forty-shilling freeholder in a borough could not vote in the county if he had a qualification in the borough, e.g. if he were a £10 occupier. Also, there were more county constituencies

---

[1] *Life of Viscount Althorp*, p. 319.   [2] J. R. M. Butler, *op. cit.* pp. 221–7.
[3] W. N. Molesworth, *History of the Reform Bill*, pp. 196–7.
[4] *Ibid.* p. 205.   [5] See generally Norman Gash, *Politics in the Age of Peel*.

because some counties were divided; and more agricultural constituencies because many urban areas, formerly in the counties, were converted into boroughs or added to existing boroughs. Since the copyholders and leaseholders generally deferred to the choice of the great landowners, as the forty-shilling freeholders had done, the first Reform Act greatly increased the influence of landowners. This influence did not begin to disappear until the interests of landlords and tenants began to diverge after 1874. It was practically destroyed by the Reform Act of 1884 and the Redistribution Act of 1885.

Secondly, the more corrupt forms of electioneering—though 'corrupt' is a little tendentious when applied to the saturnalia of free beer, bands, ribbons and processions—probably increased, especially in the boroughs where a couple of hundred voters, or even less, made all the difference. It is unnecessary to blame the freemen, though their practice of regarding an election as an opportunity for profit is commonly said to have corrupted the £10 occupiers. If a hundred votes would sway an election there was a great temptation to bless both him that gave and him that received. There was, however, a gradual diminution of both treating and corruption as 'political education' and Evangelical morality began to assert themselves, though the process was not accelerated until the Ballot Act of 1872 made it difficult to discover whether the candidate was receiving value for his money, and was not complete until 1885.

Thirdly, the process of registering electors made it desirable to have a permanent local organisation to make certain that the right people were put on the registers and the wrong persons kept off. The job of election agent—undertaken in Westminster in 1807 by Francis Place and continued by Joseph Parkes and his pupils—thus became professional; and some local body, the registration society, the Reform association, or the Constitutional club, was set up to become, in due course, the Liberal or Conservative association. There was, however, little local organisation in the agricultural counties until 1886, and even in the boroughs both Conservative and Liberal organisation was poor until after 1868.

Central organisation developed more slowly, though the Carlton Club and the Reform Club, established soon after 1832, provided a sort of exchange for political information and party candidates. What became the Liberal Central Association was, however, established in 1860 and the Conservative Central Office in 1870. Meanwhile, 'political education' had proceeded apace, mainly through the spread of the reading of newspapers which were concerned very largely with politics. This development had begun long before 1832, but larger circulations were attained after 1832, partly through the general spread of political interest, partly through the invention of mechanical methods of printing, and partly through the relaxation of restrictions on newspaper production, ending with the repeal of the paper duty in 1861. The leading politicians helped, at first by subsidising newspapers, and subsequently by supplying information. Moreover the practice of 'mob oratory', developed on the hustings and at corporation or constituents' dinners, and used extensively by the Catholic Association, the Protestant Association and the Anti-Corn Law League, came to take an increasing part of the politicians' time, leading eventually to Gladstone's 'pilgrimages of passion' in 1868 and 1879. The development was associated with the spread of newspaper reading, for until nearly the end of the nineteenth century a political leader could hope to be reported verbatim, a lesser light to receive a column, and even a third-rate politician to have a 'stick' or a paragraph. On the other hand, the formal 'party manifesto' had not yet appeared because the party, as such, had no policy. Peel's Tamworth Manifesto of 1834 was not a party manifesto but a statement of Government policy, approved by the Cabinet. In opposition, however, the party had no policy, though very often the leader of the Opposition consulted his principal colleagues—not yet the 'Shadow Cabinet'—before he issued his election address to his own constituents. Nor was Peel's example followed by other Governments until 1874, when Gladstone had to quote Peel's precedent to defend himself against a probable accusation from the Queen of subverting the Constitution.

The various methods of 'political education' became even more important when the Reform Act of 1867 gave the vote in boroughs to resident and rate-paying householders, many of whom were working men. The large increase in the borough electorates which resulted made candidates appreciate the advantages of a method which cost little and could be erected into a virtue by the obvious necessity of 'educating our masters'. A frontal attack on old-style electioneering had already been made by the Corrupt and Illegal Practices Act, 1854, though the methods adopted by that Act were not very effective. The extension of the franchise in 1867, the transfer of jurisdiction over election petitions in the same year from House of Commons committees to unsympathetic Queen's Bench judges, and the reduction of bribery and undue influence brought about by the ballot after 1872, enabled the destruction of old-style electioneering to be virtually completed by the Corrupt and Illegal Practices Act, 1883, which came into operation in 1885 simultaneously with the great extension of the county electorates under the Reform Act of 1884 and the creation of large single-member constituencies by the consequential legislation. Gladstone's new version of 'mob oratory' was generally not followed by Disraeli; but the 'cult of the individual' was firmly established and political conflicts became personal or party disputes rather than conflicts over policy—the elector was 'for' a party in the same way as, a little later, he was 'for' Tottenham Hotspur or Woolwich Arsenal.[1]

With larger constituencies, however, a more intense local organisation was necessary, especially in the large towns where, between 1868 and 1884, a device of the House of Lords designed to put Conservative horses into Liberal camps compelled the Liberals to organise themselves to repel invaders.[2] In a three-membered constituency each elector was given only two votes, so that three Liberals could not be elected unless the Liberal electors were organised and disciplined to distribute their votes. William Harris invented the 'Birmingham plan', involving an organisation into wards even more highly developed than Francis Place's ward organisation in Westminster in 1807. The device was successful only in Birmingham in returning three Liberals; but Liberals in other towns saw the advantages of the 'Birmingham plan', which could be used for borough council elections and school board elections as well as for parliamentary elections, and thus required a

[1] Football teams.
[2] The same device was applied to three-membered counties: but there it became usual to nominate two Conservatives and one Liberal, or two Liberals and one Conservative, so as to avoid a contest.

permanent organisation, with a subscription income, functioning at frequent intervals.

The Conservatives followed the Liberals with proper conservative caution, especially because the snob appeal, which had formed a large element in the landowners' influence, was still a potent Conservative weapon. In a Conservative association due attention had to be paid to the hierarchy of rank and class, and it was not at this stage practicable to claim, as the Radicals claimed—or rather pretended—that it was founded on democratic elections. Indeed, the snob appeal was deliberately organised in the Primrose League (founded on the model of the Orange League, but essentially upper and middle class, unlike the Orange Lodges) from 1883. Even so, there was from 1868 a more intensive organisation of Conservative associations, federated into the National Union of Conservative and Constitutional Associations. The National Union never became a very effective body. Lord Randolph Churchill and the 'Fourth Party' tried to make it so after 1880, but Lord Salisbury managed to send it back into decent obscurity, where it has remained ever since, in spite of television. Nevertheless, the permanent office of the National Union, which was shared after 1870 with the Conservative Central Office so as to prevent the former going off on a frolic of its own, became a centre of Conservative propaganda, particularly in the form of 'literature', meaning pamphlets and leaflets, most of which had no literary merits but had considerable utility in the days before the popular newspaper gave every household much more exciting reading-matter.

Joseph Chamberlain, who virtually controlled the Birmingham Liberal Association from 1876, saw that an organisation like the National Union could be used to forward his own political ambitions and the policies which he favoured. He therefore founded, with Gladstone's blessing, the National Liberal Federation, which was organised from Birmingham by Schnadhorst, secretary to the Birmingham association. It was used for the propagation of a new electoral device, the party programme, which appeared in 1885 as the *Radical Programme*, though it was called the 'Unauthorised Programme' by the whig section of the Liberal party. Chamberlain, like most politicians, was a little out-of-date in his appreciation of party strategy. He did not realise that Liberals voted for Gladstone and not for Liberal policy. But, by producing a policy when the Liberals had none—for Home Rule was produced *ad hoc*—it gave some indication that the Radicals, at least, were thinking in terms of politics for the working class.

Chamberlain's difficulty was that, having worked out this quite sensible programme, he was compelled by Gladstone's adoption of Home Rule to cross the floor. The National Liberal Federation did not follow him, and Schnadhorst moved to London so as to put the Federation under the influence of the whips. Nevertheless, the Federation proceeded to adopt the Chamberlain technique by producing a programme in a series of debates and resolutions. The collected works, having been completed in Newcastle in 1891, were known as the Newcastle Programme. Their principal characteristic was that, having been compiled in order to induce as many people as possible to vote Liberal, they provided something for everybody and had little relation with practical politics. The Newcastle Programme was indeed an embarrassment to the Liberal Government of 1892.

The Conservatives, by luck or good management, had a better view of electoral strategy, and never descended to the ignominy of having a programme, except of course the perpetual programme of preserving everything which ought to be preserved, but changing anything if it was thought that votes could thereby be won. Really, however, they required no policy at all. The spirit of the time favoured a moderate imperialism, and people voted Conservative while the trade unions fought their battle with the employers. The Liberals had the support of organised labour in 1906 and 1910, but meanwhile a new party had appeared.

The extra-parliamentary organisations of the Conservative and Liberal parties were developed to give aid, comfort and sustenance to parties already established in Parliament. The Labour party was established as, and still is, an extra-parliamentary party designed to produce and maintain the parliamentary Labour party. That party was intended to be a parliamentary pressure group capable of helping the trade unions to obtain better conditions for their members and for the working class generally. The miners were sufficiently concentrated geographically and sufficiently well organised to secure representation through the Liberal party. Elsewhere, the middle-class committees which controlled the Liberal associations usually managed to keep out working-class candidates. The attack on the trade unions through the machinery of the courts, which began after the trade union successes in 1889–90, led the Trades Union Congress to believe that a separate organisation, independent of the Liberal party, was necessary to support the trade unions in their efforts to have the law amended. The Independent Labour party and the National Democratic Federation, too, were anxious to organise the working class politically. The former society was, for the most part, socialist; the latter was Marxist: but though the trade unions contained socialist members, the purpose of the nascent Labour party was not socialism but working-class representation. Hence the Labour Representation Council, formed in 1900 with a very simple organisation and very little money, was representative of those trade unions and socialist societies which chose to affiliate. Its local organisation was usually the trades council (representing the local trade unions and the local branches of larger trade unions), the local branch of the Independent Labour party, or a committee representing both. Only in two constituencies was a local association, similar to those in the Conservative and Liberal parties, established before 1914.

The Liberal party, which had been out of office since 1895, was anxious not to split the potential Liberal vote, and accordingly a secret arrangement was made between the chief whip, Herbert Gladstone, and the secretary to the L.R.C., Ramsay MacDonald, whereby opposition between Liberal and Labour candidates was so far as practicable avoided. The L.R.C. thus secured the election of twenty-nine Labour members in 1906 and promptly converted itself into the Labour party. Though it lost seats in 1910, it was strong enough to be represented in the Lloyd George coalition from 1916 to 1918.

By the latter date, the Labour party's ambitions had developed. It was reorganised by Arthur Henderson, with the assistance of Sidney Webb, and was given a socialist objective set out in a party manifesto, *Labour and the New Social Order*. The new organisation involved the creation of local and divisional Labour parties in the constituencies and their representation at the annual conference together with the representatives of the trade unions and other affiliated organisations. For reasons which will need to be explained, the Labour party supplanted the Liberal party as His Majesty's Opposition and therefore formed minority Governments in 1924 and 1929. Except in 1931, its voting support increased progressively until a Labour Government, with a majority, was formed in 1945; and indeed it went on increasing until the Labour Government was defeated in 1951, by which time the Liberal party, even in the constituencies, was a small minority party whose candidates could rarely secure election unless they had Conservative or Labour support.

The development of the party system must be explained more fully in the second volume, and the fundamental ideas, or prejudices, of the parties in the third. The present volume is designed to explain the nature and composition of the electorate, the instruments by which the ideas of the parties are propagated, and the technique of electioneering. The whole purpose of a complicated electoral organisation and vast effort, both paid and voluntary, is to produce a Government whose actions are reasonably consonant with public opinion, or in other words to enable fifty million people to govern themselves freely. The relation between the individual and the Government is necessarily remote. To the citizen the Government is a vast bureaucracy controlled by persons of no very unusual merit whose actions often seem to be dictated by a desire for public applause. Nobody accuses British Ministers of feathering their own nests or promoting the interests of their families; but when persons of ordinary (or even extraordinary) ability and normal human failings are placed in positions of great power they are apt to forget Oliver Cromwell's injunction to think it possible in the bowels of Christ that they might be mistaken. Fortunately the British Constitution, with the infinite wisdom produced by centuries of experience, has provided Opposition parties to tell Ministers that, at least in respect of the matters under debate, they are wrong. The result is often an exercise in self-deception on both sides and, perhaps more often still, an exchange of uncomplimentary remarks in parliamentary language in which both sides emit fragments of truth embedded in a lot of 'party political' nonsense. It is not the function of the Opposition to oppose, but to find ideas or actions which they can oppose and then oppose. No doubt their purpose is to obtain office for themselves, the sense of power which office brings, the applause which half the population produces, though not always very enthusiastically, and the deference which everybody properly gives to Her Majesty's Ministers. In the process, however, they do seek out and expose grievances, challenge the ideas upon which governmental action is based, and remind Ministers that they are neither infallible nor immortal. It is not necessarily true that power corrupts; but in a world thirsty for 'news' and amply supplied with enough goblets to wet the driest, there is a temptation for Ministers to believe that everything they do is right if what they say is good enough to satisfy an obedient parliamentary majority. What the Opposition does is to remind them that, in less than five years, they must appeal to the people.

This does not mean that there is something called public opinion which is always right. Usually there is nothing which can be called public opinion. Only occasionally is there a sweep of emotion in the pub and the club, the restaurant and the canteen, the board room and the 'shop', which indicates a broad trend of opinion, and then it is as likely to be wrong as to be right. Nevertheless, once at least in every five years Her Majesty's Ministers have to leave their thickly carpeted offices and their deferential officials and to go back to their constituencies to ask Bill Bloggs for his vote. Bill Bloggs and his like can turn them all out and send them to the Opposition benches or the House of Lords. On most political issues Bill Bloggs has come to no rational conclusion at all, though sometimes he thinks he has. What he knows is that this lot is a pretty good lot or a pretty bad lot, and votes accordingly. On the whole Bill Bloggs is as likely to be right as anybody else, not because he has given any serious thought to the problems of public policy but because people whose actions are subjected to persistent and public criticism have to look before they leap, or at least to think what the House of Commons will say if they land themselves (and other people) in the mire. The process of government in public, subject to public criticism, means that every action is examined not only by Bill Bloggs (in so far as his newspaper can find space for it after adequate treatment has been given to football, women, crime and catastrophes), but also by every expert and would-be expert outside Whitehall. A single decision which seems to be bad may lose a few votes, but a series of such decisions convinces Bill Bloggs that this is a bad lot. The result sometimes is that no decision is taken because the alternatives are unpleasant; but more often the better alternative is chosen because the decision has to stand up to public criticism. Bill Bloggs is not the most expert judge of what is right and what is wrong, but the verdict of the ballot box is more likely to be right than the verdict of the bench of bishops or a bevy of economists.

The student who describes the working of institutions as he sees them and the behaviour of politicians as they appear to him in retrospect, has some difficulty in avoiding the appearance of being patronising. It must not be assumed, however, that the observations of a zoologist on the animals in his zoo imply that he would behave more intelligently if he were the elephant in the enclosure.

CHAPTER I

THE CONSTITUENCIES

I. BEFORE 1832

Though unlike the animals of the Ark they were all male, the knights and burgesses went to Westminster two by two. The County of York and the County of Rutland were each represented by two knights, while the city of Bristol and the borough of Gatton were each represented by two burgesses. It is not quite correct, as Professor Pollard alleges,[1] that the 'commons' were *communes* or *communitates*. There was equal representation for counties and boroughs, irrespective of population; and occasionally *communitates* in the plural was used;[2] but generally in the French form the word was singular, *la commune* or *la communauté*. During the short period when both French and English were used *la commune* was translated as 'commons'; and 'by assent of the commons' was 'par l'assentement de la commune'. Evidently the commons is singular and means the common people, who are distinguished from the archbishops, bishops, abbots, priors, earls and barons.

In another sense, however, the commons were communities. Feudal England was organised in communities, vills and towns, because the population was small and communications were difficult. The towns were often seaports or inland ports because the distribution of commodities was easier by water than by land. Around the vill was usually a large expanse of waste, traversable by those who possessed horses, but not by those who did not. Until the Black Death most people were tied to the soil; and even afterwards mobility was necessarily limited by poor communications. The county was the largest unit of administration and it was controlled by a royal officer, the sheriff, who had among his duties that of securing the representation of the county and its boroughs. It was not possible to enfranchise the vill unless it was important enough to be incorporated as a borough. The men of the

[1] Pollard, *Evolution of Parliament*, p. 12.
[2] E.g. Stubbs, *Select Charters*, p. 443.

county—which means the important men of the county—were accustomed to visit the county town to do business there, both public and private.

Since Wales and Monmouthshire and the Counties Palatine of Chester and Durham had not been enfranchised, there were at the accession of Henry VIII thirty-seven counties required and entitled to elect members to Parliament. There were also 110 boroughs entitled to elect two members each, though London elected four and the boroughs of Weymouth and Melcombe Regis were combined to elect four members. These boroughs were for the most part county towns, inland ports on navigable waterways, and seaports. Though no attempt was made to secure representation by population, an idea which was in any case unknown, the prosperous south was much more strongly represented than the wide open spaces of the north.[1] The six northern counties (excluding the County Palatine of Durham, which was not represented at all) contained only six boroughs, and Lancashire contained none at all. If we take the midlands to include the whole area bounded by Lancashire and Yorkshire on the north, Wales on the west, and Somerset, Wiltshire, Berkshire and Middlesex on the south, they contained only thirty boroughs. The remaining seventy-four boroughs were spread from Cornwall to Kent.[2] This distribution could not have been accidental. The counties with the largest representation were Wiltshire, Sussex, Devonshire, Kent, Cornwall and Dorset. Though many allowances must be made for political influences, these were the counties which included the main centres of the woollen industry, the tin mines, and the ports. In other words, the system of representation in operation in 1509 accorded reasonably well with prevailing social and economic conditions. It was balanced both in relation to classes and in relation to the distribution of economic activity.

There was, however, a great economic change in process. That England's atrocious weather produced luscious green fields on which cattle and sheep would fatten, and on which the latter would grow

[1] The boroughs were by origin those townships which had from time immemorial sent a jury of twelve instead of a reeve and four men in answer to the King's writ. Generally, they were fortified places, ports or county towns: Pollock and Maitland, *History of English Law*, I, pp. 635–6.

[2] See Appendix IV.

magnificent wool, had already been discovered. The manorial system of
the champion counties of the great midland plain was, however, adapted
to an economy of subsistence farming. To make the best use of the land
it was necessary to inclose the common fields and to incorporate them,
with or without portions of the waste, into fields owned and exploited
in severalty. The wool trade, having developed in the south, spread to
the midlands and East Anglia. Some of the boroughs created or
revived under the Tudors and the Stuarts were obviously the product
of these economic changes.[1] Under Henry VIII there were Buckingham, Lancaster, Preston and Thetford; under Edward VI, Boston, Lich-
field, Liverpool, Peterborough, Thirsk and Wigan; under Mary, when
political conditions were favourable to the more conservative midlands and north, most of the new boroughs were in that area; under
Elizabeth I we note especially Clitheroe, East Retford, Richmond
(Yorks), Sudbury and Tamworth; under James I and Charles I, again,
most of the boroughs revived were midland and northern towns.

It is not suggested that there was any conscious planning of representation in consequence of economic changes. To secure representation somebody had to initiate action. The borough itself might petition
the Crown or, under the Stuarts, the House of Commons. To secure
representation by resolution of the House of Commons, it was necessary
to show that the town had been represented in early Parliaments but
that representation had lapsed through desuetude. To secure representation from the Crown was easier, apparently, when the Crown held
the lordship. The representative history of Cornwall is obscure, but
during the Tudor and Stuart reigns the number of boroughs within
the Duchy increased from six to twenty-one. Towns within the
jurisdiction of the Duchy of Lancaster, too, were favoured. The
enfranchisement of three boroughs in the Isle of Wight under
Elizabeth I was effected at the election next after the Queen's relative,
Sir George Carey, assumed office as Captain-General or Governor,
and it is clear from the documents that the enfranchisement was at his
request.[2]

It would seem, in fact, that the initiative usually came from some

[1] See Appendix III.
[2] Neale, *The Elizabethan House of Commons*, p. 145.

great lord who wished to increase his power and prestige by increasing the number of seats subject to his influence. The power and prestige of a feudal lord depended upon the extent of his lands and the number of knights and retainers whom he led in the feudal array. The neo-feudalism of the Lancastrian period had virtually disappeared with the extinction or impoverishment of the lords. The great men of the Tudor period, the products of the more extended money economy, obtained prestige by putting their relatives and friends into the House of Commons. Here was the beginning of party, the foundation of the great whig connexion or, perhaps more accurately, whig connexions. 'Influence' arose from the social stratification of Tudor England, which had replaced the feudal hierarchy. It was not, as the whig historians themselves seemed to think, due exclusively to the control which a great landowner could exercise over his tenants and servants, the parishioners of his livings, and the shopkeepers and artisans who profited by his patronage. These things were of course important, but few needed to be forced to defer to a great lord: deference was in the natural order of creation, a tribute to great estate. Even today, after two centuries of individualism, it is far from true that in a Cabinet, a committee, a university or a church power depends upon the counting of noses. The views of those in authority properly receive consideration and even deference. So in Tudor England, the eighteenth century, and even well into the nineteenth century, deference was paid to rank and estate.

Deference to the great was therefore the evidence of greatness and, ambition not being a sin, it was the ambition of most, but especially of the newly great of the Tudor reigns, to extend their influence. The true test of greatness was to be able to nominate one's relatives to the two county seats, which had a prestige greater than the borough seats. If there were two great lords in a county, it was usually more convenient, and invariably less expensive, tacitly to divide the seats between them. Contests arose because there was competition for influence or power. My lord X was not prepared to defer to my lord Y, or my lord Z would not agree that my lords X and Y were entitled to dispose of a county by agreement. Failing influence over a county, my lords would wish to be able to nominate their relatives, retainers, subordinates and hangers-on to borough seats. In many cases influence in boroughs was of long standing. In the days when the burgesses sent to Westminster had to be paid 'wages' and travelling allowances, and when the cost of elections fell on candidates, it was convenient to accept the nominee of my lord, at least for one of the borough seats. Accordingly in many boroughs there had grown up a connexion which was maintained by the weight of tradition as well as by the deference due to rank and wealth. The greater and wealthier cities actually sent citizens to represent them. Smaller places allowed the nomination of at least one of the seats to rest with the neighbouring landowner; and he would generally nominate what a later generation called a 'carpet-bagger', a 'foreigner' whose only connexion with the borough was his acceptance of my lord's bounty.

Sir John Neale[1] gives a map showing the distribution of local residents, county residents, and 'foreigners' among the borough seats at the election of 1584. By relating this map to the lists on pages 140 and 141 of that book[2] it will be seen that 'foreigners' represented most of the boroughs created since 1509. This is not entirely conclusive, for the nominee of a borough corporation was often a lawyer or other 'carpet-bagger' whose candidature was not supported by a noble lord, just as, two centuries later, the independent city and county of Bristol achieved distinction both by electing Edmund Burke and by rejecting him. Nevertheless, it is plain from Professor Neale's researches that the enfranchisement of boroughs was often sought by landowners anxious to increase their own power and prestige by extending their 'influence'; and that the grateful boroughs were generally willing to accept the nominations of their patrons.

The causes of enfranchisement were therefore mixed. The results were of great importance. At the accession of Henry VIII in 1509 the House of Commons contained 296 members. The Long Parliament of 1640 contained 507.[3] This was due in part to the enfranchisement of

[1] *The Elizabethan House of Commons.*

[2] Or Appendix III of the present.

[3] Only 506 members were actually elected. Newport (Cornwall) was entitled to elect two burgesses but elected only one. For the development, see Appendix III, which is based mainly on Neale, *The Elizabethan House of Commons* and Brunton and Pennington, *The Members of the Long Parliament.*

Cheshire and Chester, Monmouthshire and Monmouth, and the Welsh counties and boroughs by Acts of Parliament of 1535. The number of members for English boroughs, however, increased from 222 in 1509 to 401 in 1640. Except for the enfranchisement of the county of Durham, the city of Durham, and the borough of Newark under Charles II, there were no further changes until the Act of Union with Scotland. Table 1 therefore tabulates the distribution of seats at the accession of Henry VIII, in the Long Parliament, and at the accession of Queen Anne.[1]

	1509	1640	1702
Northern Counties	22	66	70
Eastern Counties	34	50	50
Midland Counties	62	99	101
Home Counties	40	48	48
South and West	138	213	213
Wales and Monmouthshire	—	27	27
Totals	296	503	509

TABLE I

It will be noted that redistribution was effected not by disfranchise-ment but by enfranchisement. There had been disfranchisement in the middle ages because boroughs which could not or did not want to sustain the cost of what today would be called travelling and subsistence allowances permitted themselves to be disfranchised: but when once it became an object of ambition to nominate members of Parliament no further disfranchisement occurred. All the boroughs represented in the Parliaments of Henry VIII were also represented in the Parliament which passed the Reform Bill three hundred years later. Only one borough, Grampound, of all those created during the later Tudor and the Stuart reigns had been disfranchised before 1832. A right of representation—as the duty to be represented had become by 1509— was a form of property, which was sacrosanct to whig and tory alike.

[1] The universities (four in 1640 and 1702) are omitted. The distribution is different from that given in Brunton and Pennington, *The Members of the Long Parliament*, Appendix V, pp. 200–24.

The disfranchisement of Grampound for corruption in 1820 was an example of confiscation, the first swallow of the radical summer, the first bird to rise after the French Revolution, the dove that preceded the Reform Act of 1832.

Even so, there was no question of representation in proportion to population, or even in relation to economic importance. Between 1509 and 1603 Cornwall's representation increased from fourteen seats to forty-four seats, while that of Norfolk and Suffolk together rose from fourteen seats to twenty-four, in spite of the increased economic importance of East Anglia. Norfolk and Suffolk had increased to twenty-eight seats by 1640; but the part which East Anglia played in the Civil War was not due to a large number of seats in the Long Parliament. Some of the boroughs in existence in 1509 were, or became, 'pocket boroughs'; of the fifty-six boroughs disfranchised in 1832, thirty-one were created by the Tudor monarchs; and most of them were 'pocket boroughs' from their creation.

After 1640 there was no change, except the enfranchisement of County Durham (four seats) and Newark under Charles II, until the Act of Union with Scotland. That Act brought in forty-five members, and the Union with Ireland Act, 1801, brought in no less than one hundred members, sixty-four for counties, thirty-five for boroughs, and one for Trinity College, Dublin. The total number of members thus became 658, and it remained at that figure until 1885, but subject to redistribution in 1832 and 1868.

Though the total representation for Scotland was fixed at forty-five by the Act of Union, the distribution and the franchise were determined by an Act of the Parliament of Scotland,[1] which provided that thirty should be elected by the shires or stewartries, and fifteen by the burghs. There being thirty-three counties in Scotland, Bute and Caithness, Nairn and Cromarty, and Clackmannan and Kinross were combined, so that in each group the counties chose alternately. The fifteen burgh seats were divided among the sixty-six burghs by giving one member to Edinburgh and placing the other sixty-five burghs in fourteen groups, each burgh in a group choosing a delegate who met with the delegates from other burghs to elect a member. The distribution so

[1] Act 1706, cap. 8.

arranged was more logical than that in operation in England. Moreover the sizes of the shires and the densities of their populations gave something approaching representation by population. On the other hand, the franchise and the other conditions of election were so fixed by the Parliament of Scotland that nothing like popular election was practicable. While the franchise of the forty-shilling freehold in England enabled the great landowners to control county elections by 'influence', the Scottish representative system enabled elections to be 'managed' on behalf of the Crown. Further, it was plain both in 1706 and 1801, when the first census was taken, that in terms of population Scotland was under-represented. It was not thought, however, that population was a valid test; for it was argued that the produce of taxation was much heavier per head of population in England than in Scotland. If this argument had been logically applied, Cornwall would not have had four times as many members as Gloucestershire. The answer is that one must not try to discover principles in the British system of representation before 1885. Disraeli blessed it because it was 'mixed', which perhaps meant logically indefensible.

In the Irish House of Commons before 1801 there were sixty-four members representing thirty-two counties and 236 members representing 118 boroughs. The main problem at the Union was to reduce the representation to 100. It was at first proposed to follow the Scottish plan, giving one member for each county and grouping the boroughs so as to have election by rotation among them. This proposal could not be carried, however, because the counties were controlled by influence, most of the boroughs were pocket boroughs, and the patrons were not prepared to have their interests 'confiscated'. It was therefore decided to have two members for each county—which would enhance the value of influence because a seat at Westminster was worth more than a seat at Dublin—to give Dublin and Cork two members each and the University one, and to give one member to each of the thirty-one boroughs which contributed the most to the Exchequer by reason of the hearth money and the window tax. Since this would disfranchise eighty-five boroughs and reduce the representation of thirty-one, it was necessary to compensate the patrons, thus for the first and only time admitting by statute that the right to nominate for election was a species of property.[1] It will be noted, too, that the boroughs selected to send members to Westminster were selected not on the basis of population but on that of wealth, as shown by the combined effect of the hearth money and the window tax. Five of the boroughs[2] would not have secured representation if population had been selected.

2. THE REFORM OF 1832

While the Scottish system could be criticised because of the narrowness of the franchise and the Irish system because Roman Catholics could not be elected until 1829,[3] the English system could be criticised because of the franchise, the inequitable distribution of seats and the cost of contested elections. There was, however, not much criticism of the counties. The county members, whether whig or tory by conviction, had kept an independent position for most of the eighteenth century. Since the secession of the Portland whigs after the French Revolution most of the county members were regarded as tories and, indeed, they were the 'country party' which Disraeli was to lead (as second-in-command) with such skill after 1846. This secession of so many of the great landowners to the tory party was, however, not a problem of representation. As the industrialisation of England developed, there was a case for giving, say, Lancashire and Durham (Yorkshire already had four members after 1820) higher representation than Rutland or Bedfordshire; but in the Reform Bill the proposal to that end was simply a means of achieving a balance.

The borough representation, on the other hand, could not easily be defended on any basis except that a borough was 'property' which could not properly be 'confiscated', whether it was in the hands of a corporation or of a private patron. There were, of course, other arguments. What Disraeli called 'this respect for Precedent, this clinging to Prescription, this respect for Antiquity', which he contrasted with 'the abstract rights of subjects',[4] appealed to those of a

---

[1] The compensation was about £2000 per seat: i.e. £1,400,000 divided by 201 (= 85 × 2 + 31).

[2] Ennis, Dungannon, Portarlington, Enniskillen and Carrickfergus: see Porritt, II, p. 517.

[3] When large numbers of Roman Catholics were disfranchised by the raising of the property qualification.   [4] B. Disraeli, *Whigs and Whiggism*, p. 124 (written in 1835).

conservative cast of mind, especially to those who had been bred in the shadow of the French Revolution. The Duke of Wellington's famous declaration of October 1830 was an extreme expression of this point of view:

I have never read or heard of any measure, up to the present moment, which could in any degree satisfy my mind that the state of the representation could be improved, or be rendered more satisfactory to the country at large than at the present moment. I am fully convinced that the country possesses, at the present moment, a legislature which answers all the good purposes of legislation, and this to a greater degree than any legislature ever has answered in any country whatever. I will go further and say that the legislature and the system of representation possess the full and entire confidence of the country, deservedly possess that confidence, and the discussions in the legislature have a very great influence over the opinions of the country. I will go still further, and say that if at the present moment I had imposed upon me the duty of forming a legislature for any country, and particularly for a country like this, in possession of great property of various descriptions, I do not mean to assert that I would form such a legislature as we possess now—for the nature of man was incapable of reaching it at all—but my great endeavour would be to form some description of legislature which would produce the same results. The representation of the people at present contains a large body of the property of the country, in which the landed interests have a preponderating influence.[1]

The last sentence of the quotation now reads like an anticlimax, if not a sudden collapse of the whole argument. It is, however, an essential part of the story. The fact that the Duke of Norfolk returned eleven members, Lord Lonsdale returned nine, Lord Darlington returned seven,[2] and many peers returned two or three, was a mere illustration of the Duke's thesis, that the Constitution was founded on property, which was adequately and not more than adequately represented.

Probably the best defence of the system as it existed in 1831 was given by Sir Robert Inglis, who represented, very appropriately, the University of Oxford, 'an elegant scholar, a thorough gentleman, a worthy and honest man; he admirably represented the opinions and prejudices of the country gentlemen and clergy of the day'.[3] In his

---

[1] W. N. Molesworth, *The History of the Reform Bill of 1832*, pp. 59–60.
[2] C. Seymour, *Electoral Reform in England and Wales*, p. 51.
[3] W. N. Molesworth, *op. cit.* p. 119.

view, the member of Parliament was sent not to represent a particular place, but to consider the affairs of the country and the good of the church. Representation was not founded on population and taxation. A town was not created a parliamentary borough because it was populous, nor excluded from representation because it was small. The purpose of the Reform Bill was not to restore purity of representation, because it never had been any better; it was a revolution which would overthrow 'all the natural influence of rank and property'. The great benefit of the system as it existed in 1831 was that it represented all interests and admitted all talents. 'If the proposed change takes place, it will be almost entirely confined to one interest, and no talent will be admitted but the single one of mob oratory.' Lord Chatham first sat for Old Sarum, Pitt for Appleby, Fox for Midhurst, Burke and Canning for Wendover. It was only by means of what Lord John Russell called 'close and rotten boroughs' that young men who were unconnected by birth or residence with large towns could hope to enter the House unless they were 'cursed with that talent of mob oratory which is used for the purpose of influencing the lowest and most debasing passions of the people'.[1]

Sir Robert Peel[2] elaborated the argument about the representation of all classes which Disraeli defended with such zeal after his rejection as a Radical by the reformed 'close borough' of Chipping Wycombe.[3] In substance it was that the variations in the borough franchises, from Gatton and Old Sarum to Preston and Westminster, enabled all classes to be represented, not in accordance with population or taxation, but with due regard to rank and property. It was a representation of interests, and what the Reform Bill was proposing to do was to dis-franchise all interests—including the potwallopers of Preston and the scot and lot electors of Westminster as well as the burgage tenants of Old Sarum—save the £10 householder. Sir Robert also emphasised the argument that the close boroughs enabled those who, in Lord Plunkett's phrase, possessed 'that buoyancy of genius which would float them down the stream of posterity' to enter Parliament and, he added, to return there when rejected for popular seats 'by caprice, or

[1] *Ibid.* pp. 119–23.   [2] *Ibid.* pp. 137–42.
[3] *Whigs and Whiggism*, pp. 148–69.

want of money or otherwise'. He gave as examples Sheridan at Ilchester, Wyndham at High Ferrers, Lord Castlereagh at Orford, Tierney at Knaresborough, and Lord Grey at Tavistock.

Other arguments developed as the debate proceeded.[1] The whigs were not proposing to enfranchise the people, though they sometimes used arguments which suggested that they were. They were not very clear what they were trying to do; but it became evident that they were producing a new balance between the landed interest and the urban middle class. This was shown not only by the enfranchisement of the £10 householders in the towns and the extension of the county franchise to copyholders and leaseholders but also by their redistribution proposals. To the tories this was to disturb a Constitution which was already admirably balanced because the monarchy, the aristocracy and the commonalty each played its appropriate part. The extension of the power of the commonalty was therefore subversive of constitutional principles. It would weaken the monarchy as well as the aristocracy. On tory principles they were of course right; nor on whig principles were they far wrong, because that balance had been struck by the Glorious Revolution of 1688.

The whigs were not in fact enunciating new constitutional principles; they enabled the Radicals both to enunciate them and to carry them out in the next half-century. It was evident from the initial speech of Lord John Russell[2] that the whigs were merely attempting to correct anomalies in the representative system. He said that there were three grievances: 'First, the nomination of members by individuals; second, the election by close corporations; third, the expense of elections.'[3] Lord Palmerston made the grievances five in number: nomination by patrons, gross corruption among the lower classes of voters, inadequate representation of the larger manufacturing and commercial towns, the expense of elections, and the unequal and inequitable distribution of voting power between the middle and lower classes.[4]

Redistribution was thus a comparatively minor aspect of Reform as originally conceived, since emphasis was laid on the franchise and the

---

[1] Norman Gash, *Politics in the Age of Peel*, ch. 1.
[2] W. N. Molesworth, *op. cit.* pp. 103–19.
[3] *Ibid.* p. 105.　　　　　　　　　　[4] N. Gash, *Politics in the Age of Peel*, p. 13.

diminution of corruption. It was, nevertheless, on the redistribution provisions of the Schedules to the Reform Bill that the battle of Reform was fought. The scheme evolved in successive drafts. In the final draft, which became the Representation of the People Act, 1832, the representation of England and Wales was reduced from 513 members to 500, but the extra thirteen seats were given to Scotland and Ireland by the Scottish and Irish Acts, eight to Scotland and five to Ireland. The English Act completely disfranchised fifty-six boroughs returning 111 members (since Higham Ferrers had had only one member). The combined boroughs of Weymouth and Melcombe Regis lost two seats; and thirty two-member boroughs were each deprived of one seat. It had originally been intended to disfranchise or deprive on the basis of population, as shown by the census of 1821, alone. It was however found that in some cases the census district did not coincide with the parliamentary borough. Also, when the census figures of 1831 became available it was feared that they had been deliberately inflated by temporary residents in some of the threatened boroughs, and accordingly the final list was based partly on inhabited houses and partly on taxation.[1] Buckingham, which would have been disfranchised, retained both members; seven boroughs which would have been disfranchised retained one member; four boroughs which would have lost one member lost both; twenty-four boroughs which would have lost one member kept both members; and three boroughs which would have kept both members lost one.

Of the 130 seats available for distribution in England and Wales, sixty-six were given to new boroughs (including Merthyr Tydfil and Swansea District) and sixty-four to the counties (including those in Wales). Table 2 shows the changes in distribution, including the representation of Scotland and Ireland.[2] These figures by themselves show that the redistribution was not based on the principle of representation according to population. There was recognition of the movement of population to, and the economic importance of, the

[1] Seymour, *Electoral Reform in England and Wales*, p. 58.
[2] The representation of England and Wales in 1831 differs from that in 1702, *ante*, p. 6, because Grampound was disfranchised in 1820 and its two members transferred to Yorkshire.

commercial and industrial areas of the North and the Midlands, but the ten counties of the South and West still had nearly a quarter of all the members. Nor was there any substantial increase in the representation of Greater London. To the eight members for London, Westminster and Southwark were added ten members for Finsbury, Greenwich, Lambeth, Marylebone and Tower Hamlets: but Middlesex and Surrey

	1831	1832
Northern Counties	72	105
Eastern Counties	50	47
Midland Counties	101	117
Home Counties	48	53
South and West	211	142
Wales and Monmouthshire	27	32
Scotland	45	53
Ireland	99	103
Universities	5	6
Totals	658	658

TABLE 2

Electorate	Number of boroughs
Less than 300	30
300 to 500	42
500 to 1000	60
1000 to 5000	56
More than 5000	12

TABLE 3

did not receive additional county members, while Cornwall and Devonshire did. Nor was any breach made in the tradition that a borough should not receive more than two members. Birmingham was given two, while Buckingham, which had been listed for disfranchisement in the first Reform Bill, retained two. There were still many boroughs with very small electorates. Table 3 shows Professor Seymour's classification[1] of the boroughs according to electorate after 1832.

The effect of the changes on influence is less easy to determine,

[1] In *Electoral Reform in England and Wales*, p. 78.

chiefly because the alterations in the franchise increased the electorate (except in some of the boroughs where many of those entitled to the franchise of ancient right were not placed on the registers). The disfranchisement of many small boroughs necessarily diminished the power of patrons. Also, the areas of many boroughs were increased either by the addition of urban population or by bringing in large tracts of agricultural land.[1] Some of the boroughs were in fact rural districts with a village centre. There were, however, many boroughs in which a particular family was able to nominate candidates who were invariably successful. It is generally thought, too, that both redistribution and the changes in the franchise increased the influence of landlords in the counties. In order to diminish expense, especially the expense of transporting electors to the poll, the counties which after 1832 had four seats (or, in the case of Yorkshire, six) were divided into electoral divisions returning two members each, thus bringing the seats more closely under the landlords' control. Also, it was generally assumed that the £50 leaseholders, tenants at will, and copyholders enfranchised by the Reform Act were more subject to influence than the forty-shilling freeholders. This was due mainly to the belief that influence was due to the power of the landlord to terminate tenancies or otherwise. As will be suggested later, this may be a misinterpretation of the nature of influence. What in fact the Reform Act did, in relation to the counties, was to segregate the agricultural interest from the urban population. Before the Reform Act the forty-shilling freeholders in the boroughs, except those in the counties of towns (e.g. Bristol and Norwich), had had votes in the counties. Their weight was in 1832 reduced by three changes. First, a forty-shilling freeholder who had the borough franchise (e.g. because he was a £10 occupier) lost his county vote. Secondly, many urban areas in counties (e.g. Birmingham and Manchester) became boroughs and the forty-shilling freeholders who were £10 occupiers lost the county vote. Thirdly, many urban areas, especially suburban areas, were included in the boundaries of existing boroughs, and again the £10 occupiers, if forty-shilling freeholders, lost the county vote. Since at the same time the rural electors

[1] The borough area in 1831 was 500 square miles; in 1833 it was 2500 square miles: Seymour, *op. cit.* p. 98.

were increased in number through the enfranchisement of the copyholders, leaseholders and tenants at will, the general effect was to
increase the agricultural vote and to decrease the urban vote. The leaseholders and the tenants at will were generally in the inclosed parishes,
which were under the strong influence of the local landowners. Hence
the landowners' influence was at least as strong after 1832 as it was before.
That influence did not disappear until 1885.

Clearly the great change effected by the English Reform Act of 1832
was to enable the urban middle class to share political power with the
owners of land. This was done not merely by swamping the borough
constituencies with £10 householders but also by transferring the
control of boroughs from landowners to the urban middle class. Some
famous boroughs disappeared—Wendover in Buckinghamshire,
thirteen of the Cornish boroughs, Okehampton in Devon, New
Romney in Kent, Orford in Suffolk, Old Sarum in Wiltshire, Gatton
in Surrey, and many more—but some famous names were also brought
in, like Birmingham, Leeds, Bradford, Manchester and Sheffield. There
was some adaptation to the new economic order. Though the trend
was not really noticeable until 1867, the champion counties which rose
under the Tudors were declining in the nineteenth century; and what
was noticeable was that coal, iron and textiles were crashing into
Parliament. The trend favoured the whigs, though that was not the
intention, for the enfranchisement of the industrial towns was accom-
panied by a large increase in county representation; even so, Victorian
politics depended upon the supremacy of heavy industry, the railway
boom, and the growth of banking and finance. One must not, however,
place too much emphasis upon mere economics, which is but a branch
of politics. By enfranchising the middle classes the Reform Act of 1832
also brought 'chapel' into balance with 'church' and at the same time
gave scope to the 'Godless' Radicals.

The changes made in Scotland in 1832 need be mentioned only in
passing. In respect of the franchise the system had to be altered fundamentally.[1] Scotland 'resembled one vast, rotten borough'.[2] If the
franchise were changed, however, the distribution would be not un-

---

[1] *Post*, pp. 53–4.
[2] N. Gash, *Politics in the Age of Peel*, p. 36.

reasonable. It was decided to retain the arrangement whereby the thirty-three counties were represented by thirty members, and the only change made in this respect was to substitute three pairs of counties, each pair voting together as a single constituency, for the three pairs in which each county voted at alternate elections. For this purpose the pairs had to consist of contiguous counties: Elgin and Nairn, Ross and Cromarty, Clackmannan and Kinross. Accordingly, one seat was given to each pair and one seat to each of the remaining counties.

The device of combining burghs into burgh districts for purposes of elections, too, was not unreasonable, though the method of election, whereby each burgh council elected a commissioner to a meeting of commissioners, at which the member was chosen, necessarily led to corruption. The Scottish Reform Act followed the English plan in giving two members each to Edinburgh and Glasgow and one member each to Aberdeen, Paisley, Dundee, Greenock and Perth. Peebles, Selkirk and Rothesay were withdrawn from their respective burgh districts and thrown into their respective counties in order to enlarge the county electorates. The remaining burghs were combined into fourteen burgh districts, each district voting as a separate constituency for one member. This arrangement, combined with a £10 occupation franchise in the burghs and a £10 ownership or long leasehold franchise in the counties, produced the result that the burgh electorates were larger than those of the counties.[1] The reformers did not assume that the more popular the constituency the better it was; they had by no means broken with the tradition that property, not people, was in need of representation. The change made in 1832 was conservative in respect of distribution but radical in fact, for it transferred the franchise to the middle class of Scotland.

In Ireland, too, the problem was one of the franchise. The distribution of seats made in 1800 was not inequitable, but the raising of the franchise in 1829, as part of the price for enfranchising Roman Catholics, had disfranchised the Irish peasantry and created a number of very small constituencies which ought, on whig principles, to be eliminated. It being politically impracticable to reduce the number of constituencies, battle was joined over the franchise, and the constituencies

---

[1] *Ibid.* pp. 42–3.

remained unaltered, though an additional member was given to each of four boroughs, Belfast, Limerick, Waterford and Galway, and to the university constituency of Dublin.

3. THE REFORM OF 1867

As the tories so frequently emphasised in 1831, parliamentary reform, once undertaken, could not be stopped short of complete democracy, then a *terminus ad quem* which nobody except wild Radicals wanted to reach. If there was a case for giving representation to the £10 house-holders of Birmingham, Leeds and Manchester, there was also a case for enfranchising the £5 householders of those cities. If there was a case for giving two members to each of the larger towns and one member to each of the smaller towns, there was also a case for giving three or four members to the great provincial cities and very sub-stantially increasing the representation of Greater London. If it could be said, and undoubtedly it could, that property in the form of factories and machinery was as useful to the country as property in the form of land, there was little to be said for basing the franchise on the occupa-tion or ownership of land. At a given moment there might be more property in the Royal Exchange than in the whole county of Cornwall. The balance of monarchy, aristocracy and commonalty had been over-thrown. The monarchy was now part of the bourgeoisie and the aristocracy followed the price of railway shares as eagerly as it had once followed the price of corn. The commonalty were not, however, merely the ironmasters, the textile manufacturers and the linen drapers, but all the £10 householders, who included the overseers, clerks, skilled workers and many unskilled workers. If these were capable of exer-cising the franchise there was no reason why other workers should not. In short, the argument was unlikely to stop until the principle of 'one man, one vote, one value' was reached; and meanwhile argument might start over the enfranchisement of the monstrous regiment of women.

There was one strong argument for an early measure of reform after 1832. The convincing election of 1831 had been won by the whigs with the active support of the urban workers. Though they had no votes they had voices, and they raised them. Hardly anybody has ever voted, at any election, on the basis of pure reason; nor has any successful candidate been unaffected by the atmosphere of his own election. When, as in 1831, public opinion has been vocal it has affected politicians' minds even when many if not most of the voices were as unsubstantial as the grin of the Cheshire Cat, because they had no votes behind them. The workers expected to benefit by parliamentary reform, and they did succeed in persuading their betters to approve what was thought to be, in the context of the thirties, a very radical measure. It was soon seen, however, how much froth there is on a turbulent electoral sea. Before the end of the thirties the 'People's Charter', demanding adult suffrage, annual parliaments, and the secret ballot, had been adopted. It was a period of great economic distress, with much unemployment, low wages and relatively high prices. In such conditions the typical poise of the British people becomes disturbed. In this instance the Charter obtained wide support among the unenfranchised and, by its extreme, if not revolutionary, radicalism led to reaction among the middle-class electorate. No doubt the Charter, by asking too much, delayed a further instalment of parliamentary reform, but it made more inevitable the ultimate passing of that instalment.

The difficulty was, as in hire-purchase arrangements, to determine the sizes and the periods of the instalments. There was no agreement about these matters even in the Liberal party, and not much was likely to be done while Lord Palmerston was powerful. By 1866 it was clear that there must be an instalment, but the question of its size remained. Because of the confused political conditions of the time, it is difficult to find a rational explanation for the scheme adopted. Indeed, it was not a scheme. Disraeli wanted to produce a better Bill than that which his party had rejected, with the aid of the 'Cave of Adullam',[1] in 1866. 'Better' is perhaps a tendentious word; rather it should be said that it had to be popular without conceding too much. It had to be acceptable to a majority drawn from both parties; and it had to show that the Conservative party was the friend of the urban workers. Disraeli's first effort was a series of resolutions containing 'fancy franchises'. The Bill which replaced these resolutions, said Disraeli,[2] had no tendency in

---

[1] See I Samuel xxii. 1, 2: 'David departed thence, and escaped to the cave Adullam....'
[2] W. Heaton, *The Three Reforms of Parliament*, p. 196.

the direction of democracy, but proposed on conditions to enfranchise all householders in the boroughs and all occupiers of land rated at £15 in the counties. The 'fancy franchises' were also introduced. This scheme would prevent the preponderance of any class and give representation to the nation.[1] Gladstone was disposed to a procedure which would have wrecked the Bill, but a combination of his supporters, taking Disraeli's measure, decided to take such action in committee as would produce a Bill acceptable to Liberal opinion. When the Bill emerged what was left was household suffrage in the boroughs, a lodger franchise (£10 rent), and a £10 rateable value franchise in the counties.[2]

The Representation of the People Act, 1867, disfranchised four boroughs for corruption, and two (St Albans and Sudbury) had already been disfranchised. Thirty-eight two-member boroughs were deprived of one seat, on the basis that they had less than 10,000 population at the census of 1861. Six popular boroughs were to have an additional member each; one two-member borough (Tower Hamlets in Middlesex) was converted into two two-member boroughs (Tower Hamlets and Hackney); one new two-member borough (Chelsea, also in Middlesex) was created; and nine new single-member boroughs, all industrial towns, were created. The counties were not affected, except that the larger and more populous counties were divided into two-member divisions. There were, too, curious provisions, insisted upon by the House of Lords in order to provide for minority representation, that in the City of London, which was entitled to four seats, each elector should have only three votes, and that in the constituencies which had three members each elector should have only two votes. Also, the University of London was enfranchised.

There followed the Representation of the People (Scotland) Act, 1868, and the Representation of the People (Ireland) Act, 1868. The former alone affected distribution. Glasgow was given an extra seat, making three; but no elector might vote for more than two. Dundee was given two seats in place of one. Three counties were divided, each into two divisions, and each division having one seat. Two counties were united to return one member, and a new borough district (the

<hr />

[1] Heaton, *op. cit.* p. 197.   [2] See *post*, pp. 55–9.

Hawick District) created. The Scottish universities were divided into pairs, each of which was given one seat. To provide for all the extra seats so required, seven English boroughs having a population of less than 5000 were disfranchised.[1]

The changes so made, which did not take full effect until after the general election of 1868, slightly improved the position of Wales, Scotland and Ireland at the expense of England; but, as in England, they favoured the urban and industrial population at the expense of the rural population. Table 4 shows the effect, best indicated by groups of counties, as before.[2]

	1832	1869
Northern Counties	106	120
Eastern Counties	47	43
Midland Counties	116	112
Home Counties	53	60
South and West	142	120
Wales and Monmouthshire	32	33
Scotland	53	58
Ireland	103	103
Universities	6	9
Totals	658	658

TABLE 4

It will be seen that, in spite of an increase of nearly a million, or 88 per cent, in the electorate, the changes in distribution were small. The number of borough electors in England was more than doubled, but the number of borough members was reduced from 323 to 286, while the number of county members was increased from 144 to 172. Moreover, though the fact does not appear from the Table, there was a significant change in the balance between town and country. In the process of redefining borough boundaries a great many urban areas in the counties were transferred to the boroughs. In those areas persons did not have the county vote if they had the borough vote, and usually they had. Hence the redistribution provisions of the 1867 Act, unimportant though they appeared to be, in fact strengthened the

[1] See Appendix IV.   [2] *Ante*, p. 14.

agricultural interest which gave such support to the Conservative party because the rural electors still deferred to rank and station. Disraeli had 'dished the whigs'. He had given his party such a predominance in the counties that it could, by winning a few of the borough seats, win an election, as it did in 1874. Nevertheless, it was obvious that the Acts of 1867 and 1868 were such a tentative and partial adaptation to the process of industrialisation that a new reform would soon be demanded. Lancashire had eight county members, whereas Kent had four; Durham had four county members, but so had Cornwall. As in 1832, London suffered particularly from under-representation. In Middlesex the four members for Chelsea and Hackney were added to the fourteen members for London, Finsbury, Marylebone, Tower Hamlets and Westminster; but this increase in representation bore little relation to the great increase in population. In Surrey there was no increase, in spite of the fact that the population of Greater London south of the river had increased substantially. What had been done was to bring the representation of the counties and boroughs into some sort of balance. Eight hundred thousand county electors were represented by 172 county members; and 1,200,000 borough electors were represented by 286 borough members. A balance in respect of population had still not been obtained, for there were 11,500,000 people in the county areas and 9,000,000 people in the boroughs.

4. THE REFORM OF 1884

The enfranchisement of householders and lodgers in the boroughs but not in the counties was so obviously unjust that a further instalment of reform could not be long delayed. This having been done by the Representation of the People Act, 1884, a very large redistribution was effected by the Redistribution of Seats Act, 1885. There was no longer any justification for giving greater weight to the boroughs than to the counties: but in 1884 a county population of 13,700,000 was represented by 187 members while a borough population of 12,300,000 was represented by 297 members. Within the boroughs, too, there was great variation. In Calne there was one seat for 5000 people and in Liverpool one seat for 185,000. Similarly an industrial county division of Lanca-

shire had one seat for 150,000 people, while a rural borough of the
South-West (i.e. an ancient borough whose boundaries had been extended to bring in a large rural population) had one seat for 12,000.[1]

The pretence that the system of representation was carefully designed
to achieve a balance of interests could no longer be maintained. Nor
was it to the interest of either political party to maintain it. It had been
shown in 1874, when the Conservatives benefited, and again in 1880,
when the Liberals benefited, that the result of a general election depended more on hazard than on opinion. The homogeneity of British
opinion began with the building of the railways, but for its full development it required the invention of the internal combustion engine and
broadcasting. In 1884 it was still not possible to speak of a 'swing' of
opinion, except in very general terms. In 1874 the Conservatives
polled 30,000 more votes than the Liberals, but gained eighty-two more
seats, while in 1880 the Liberals polled 177,000 more votes than the
Conservatives but gained 127 more seats.[2] This looks to modern eyes
like the exaggerated effect of a 'swing'. There was, however, nothing
like a general 'swing'; it was far more variable from place to place than
it became in the twentieth century. Professor Seymour has shown that
a swing of two thousand electors in 1880, in the right places, would
have produced a Conservative Government.[3]

Moreover Disraeli's assumption when he 'dished the whigs' in 1867,
that manual workers could be induced to vote Conservative, had
proved to be correct. Though logic had suggested to the Liberals that
the workers would go with 'chapel' rather than with 'church' and with
industry rather than with the country party, they had forgotten two
emotional factors; the persistent respect for rank and station and
especially for the jolly, hard-riding and hard-drinking squire (unlike
the frock-coated merchant or banker of the late Victorian period); and
the nascent opposition between masters and men. One must not
generalise too readily, because local factors were still predominant: but
it had become plain by 1880 that the Conservatives would not necessarily lose if they adopted the principle of representation according to
population or 'one man, one vote, one value'. The secret ballot had

[1] C. Seymour, *Electoral Reform in England and Wales*, pp. 490–1.
[2] *Ibid*. p. 492.　　　　　　　　　[3] *Ibid*.

been introduced in 1872, and the Conservatives had little fear that employers would be able to coerce their employees.

These arguments seem to suggest that opposition to reform should come from the Liberals. The Radicals, led by Joseph Chamberlain, Sir Charles Dilke and G. O. Trevelyan, were now powerful in the Liberal party, which was pledged to reform. It was therefore comparatively simple, as soon as Gladstone could be induced to get off his high horse, for the parties to reach agreement on a large measure of redistribution. Two boroughs, Beverley and Bridgwater, had been disfranchised for corruption in 1870 and two others, Macclesfield and Sandwich, were similarly to be disfranchised; these four boroughs released eight seats. There were seventy-two boroughs with a population below 15,000, and seven of them had two seats each; thus another seventy-nine seats were released. There were thirty-six two-member boroughs with populations below 50,000; and this released another thirty-six seats. The City of London was now over-represented while Greater London was under-represented; the City therefore lost two seats. In Wales, Haverfordwest District was combined with Pembroke, giving one more seat. Two counties only were over-represented, Rutlandshire and Herefordshire, and they lost one seat each. This gave 140 seats to be distributed, though actually 142 were distributed. These were distributed almost equally between counties and boroughs. The counties secured sixty-eight seats so as to give them roughly representation according to population; and seventy-four seats were given to existing boroughs or new boroughs, including thirty-nine seats to metropolitan boroughs.

Moreover it was decided to divide all counties and nearly all boroughs into single-member constituencies, only those boroughs which had two members both before and after redistribution being excepted. The traditional representation of 'communities' by two knights or burgesses had almost disappeared, though in a few places the two burgesses continued until 1945. The Conservatives had hoped to save the agricultural interest, in spite of the urbanisation of the population, by grouping small towns into electoral districts, as in Wales and Scotland. This device the Liberal Government refused to accept. Towns with less than 15,000 inhabitants were thrown into the counties. Since the

24

average population of a single-member constituency was in the neighbourhood of 50,000, the urban and suburban population could play a large part in a county election. It was indeed said that the Acts of 1884 and 1885 'annihilated the agricultural interest'.[1] That interest was, however, disappearing as an economic fact. So long as traditional farming methods were used, the parish or manor formed a community in which the interests of lord of the manor, tenants and labourers were identical and the leadership of the landowner was accepted as a matter of course. When it became necessary to employ capital on improvements, stock and machinery in order to make the land pay, these interests diverged. The tenant-farmer needed security of tenure, low rents and a low level of wages. The landlord had to treat the land as a commodity which could be bought, sold, charged or mortgaged; and he expected to receive in rent the sort of income which he would have received had the capital been invested in industry. The Settled Land Act, 1882, provided the necessary flexibility even where the land was settled—and two-thirds of the land was settled; and the Agricultural Holdings Act, 1883, protected the rights of tenants against the landowners. The social hierarchy of the English village continued in many places, but they rapidly became fewer as lords of the manor removed into the cities.

The Redistribution Act applied to Scotland and Ireland as well as to England and Wales. Two of the burgh districts, Haddington and Wigtown, were thrown into the counties. Aberdeen's representation was increased from one to two, Edinburgh's from two to four, and Glasgow's from three to seven. Among the counties, Argyll's representation was reduced from two to one, Ayr's was raised from one to two, Lanark's from two to six, Perth's from one to two, and Renfrew's from one to two. Thus, Scotland's representation was raised from sixty to seventy-two.

Two of this increase were drawn from Ireland. The county representation was increased from sixty-four to eighty-five, but the borough representation was reduced from thirty-nine to sixteen. Adding the two university seats, the total representation of Ireland was reduced from 105 to 103.

[1] D. C. Moore, 'Politics of Deference' (unpublished thesis), p. 602.

It will be convenient at this stage to show, in Table 5, how the representation of the several parts of the United Kingdom had changed between 1831 and 1885.

	1831	1832	1869	1885
Northern Counties	72	106	121	154
Eastern Counties	50	47	43	36
Midland Counties	101	116	111	90
Home Counties	48	53	60	99
South and West	211	142	120	77
Wales and Monmouthshire	27	32	33	34
Scotland	45	53	58	70
Ireland	99	103	103	101
Universities	5	6	9	9
Totals	658	658	658	670

TABLE 5

This does not adequately represent the extent of the change. For instance, the representation of Lancashire increased from fourteen to fifty-eight, while that of Cornwall diminished from forty-four to seven. Middlesex increased its representation from eight to forty-seven, thus absorbing all the seats released by Cornwall. Similarly, though the Midlands showed a decrease since 1832, this was mostly in the agricultural counties: Derbyshire, Leicestershire, Staffordshire and Warwickshire showed increases. Most of the changes, evidently, were consequences of the Industrial Revolution. Even London had at last been given adequate representation, though for electoral purposes it was still treated as parts of the counties of Middlesex, Surrey, Kent and Essex. Moreover England and Wales, Scotland and Ireland were represented roughly in proportion to population.

There were still anomalies. The average population per constituency in England and Wales was 52,000, but a borough with more than 15,000 inhabitants had one seat, and a borough with more than 50,000 inhabitants had two seats. This was a compromise, for the Conservatives had wanted minima of 25,000 and 80,000 while the Liberals had asked for minima of 10,000 and 40,000.[1] The tradition that the small borough was Liberal changed, however, in the next decade. The great

[1] C. Seymour, *op. cit.* p. 540.

industrial constituency became the preserve of the Liberal party until the Labour party came along to oust it.

One change made in 1885 needs to be emphasised. Not only was the principle of representation according to population accepted, but also the principle was adopted of the single-member constituency. All the counties were so divided, except Rutlandshire, which had only one member. All the boroughs were similarly divided except where they had two members both before and after the coming into operation of the Redistribution of Seats Act. Hence all constituencies were single-member constituencies except the two-member constituencies of Stockport, Derby, Devonport, Plymouth, Sunderland, Portsmouth, Southampton, Blackburn, Bolton, Oldham, Preston, City of London, Marylebone, Norwich, Northampton, Newcastle-on-Tyne, Bath, Ipswich, Brighton, Halifax, York, Merthyr Tydfil, Dundee and Cork. There was little discussion of this decision. It had important consequences, for it prevented any kind of proportional representation and encouraged the two-party system. Indeed, it encouraged the candidatures of orthodox party men. A Radical would tend to lose Liberal votes and a 'die-hard' to lose Conservative votes. The local party organisation would probably be orthodox—though in the Liberal party there were two views of orthodoxy, that of Gladstone and that of Joseph Chamberlain, the defection of Chamberlain in 1886 solved that problem. Indeed, the defection of Chamberlain and the organisation of the Liberal Unionists illustrates this particular consequence. In a two-member constituency it was possible to have as candidates a Conservative, a Liberal Unionist and two Liberals. The Conservatives could then hope either to elect two Unionists, or to win enough Liberal votes for the Liberal Unionist to enable him, with Conservative votes, to capture one seat. In a single-member constituency the Unionists had to decide whether to nominate a Conservative or a Liberal Unionist.

This particular consequence was of course not foreseen, but the party leaders who agreed to the compromise in the 1885 Act had had much experience of the two-member and three-member constituencies, and in the latter the Lords' bright idea of a three-member constituency with each elector having two votes had been tried. From the point of view of the party politician, the single-member constituency is much the easiest to organise. 'Our men' can simply be told to vote for 'our man', there is no temptation for the party supporter to vote for one of the other side because he is 'a decent sort of chap'; the process of putting one cross on a ballot paper (which had been introduced in 1872) was easier than the process of putting two crosses on one paper; and it was cheaper and easier to get electors to the poll in a small single-member constituency than in a larger two-member constituency. No doubt the old two-member boroughs were retained because of tradition and because they were comparatively small in area. In short, the party managers decided for single-member constituencies because they were party managers; and they helped to perpetuate the two-party system, in spite of Joseph Chamberlain, by so doing. It was a curious way of deciding, almost by chance, one of the cardinal features of the British Constitution.

5. THE REFORM OF 1918

Parliamentary reform ceased to be a political issue after 1885, except in relation to plural voting and the enfranchisement of women. The former was a minor aspect of political controversy and the latter cut across party lines. The need for a Reform Bill, or at least for a Redistribution Bill, became evident as economic development changed the distribution of the population; but the war of 1914–18 prevented the enactment of such a Bill until 1918. There being a Coalition Government in office, it was easy for the parties to agree to a conference under Mr Speaker. On behalf of the Conference, Mr Speaker reported to the Prime Minister in January 1917.[1] In respect of redistribution the principal recommendations were:

(1) The number of members for Great Britain[2] should remain substantially as it then was.

(2) For this purpose the standard unit of population for each member should be 70,000.

(3) A county or borough (other than the City of London) with a population of less than 50,000 should cease to have separate representation.

(4) A county or borough with a population of 50,000 but less than 70,000 should continue to have separate representation.

[1] Cd. 8463 of 1917.　　[2] The representation of Ireland was not considered.

(5) A municipal borough or urban district with a population not less than 70,000 should become a separate parliamentary borough.

(6) A county or borough returning two members should not lose a member if the defect in the population was 20,000 or less.

(7) A member should be given for 70,000 and for every multiple of 70,000 and an additional member for any remainder which was not less than 50,000.

(8) The boundaries of parliamentary constituencies should, as far as practicable, coincide with the boundaries of administrative areas.

(9) The City of London should continue to return two members.

(10) Existing boroughs entitled to return two members should not be divided.

So far the Conference had accepted what may be called the principles of 1885. There was, however, a further recommendation for the use of proportional representation by means of a single transferable vote in a borough returning not less than three nor more than five members, or in contiguous boroughs which could be combined into such a constituency. For this purpose the Metropolis (excluding the City of London) was to be treated as a single area and divided into constituencies returning not less than three nor more than five members. Further, there was a recommendation, by a majority only, that in single-member constituencies the alternative vote should be used.

The proposals relating to the delimitation of constituencies proved to be unduly restrictive and eventually the Boundary Commissioners were, by resolution of the House of Commons, given a greater latitude as to population and directed that electorate, rather than population, was to be the determining factor.[1] The proposals relating to proportional representation and the alternative vote were incorporated in the Representation of the People Bill and were left to free votes of the House of Commons. They proved to be controversial and led to conflict between the House of Commons and the House of Lords.

To rewrite history on the foundation of hypotheses is always difficult, but we can make some guess at what would have been the political developments if the proposals of the Speaker's Conference had been enacted. There were in 1918 four political groups. The Conservative

[1] See the Reports of the Boundary Commissioners, Cd. 8576, 8585, 8670, 8756, 8757, 8758, 8759 and 8880 of 1917.

party had joined the Asquith Government in 1915, had followed Bonar Law into the Lloyd George Government of 1916, and had kept its organisation intact. The Liberal party had been divided by the events of 1916 and was in two groups, the Coalition Liberals led by Lloyd George and the Independent Liberals (or 'Wee Frees') led by Asquith. The Labour party had accepted Lloyd George's Coalition but regained its freedom of action at the general election of 1918. No doubt the Coalition would have won that election, but afterwards the Conservatives would either have absorbed the Coalition Liberals or have repudiated them. The alternatives to a Conservative Government would be a Labour or Liberal Government or a Coalition. Since the strength of the Labour party lay in London and the large towns, to which proportional representation would have applied, the scheme would have strengthened the Liberal party, or both sections of it. The alternative vote in single-member constituencies would also have favoured the Liberal party as the party of the middle way. Thus the Liberal party would have been strengthened and it might have survived the economic difficulties of the twenties and thirties. Whether the two-party system would ever have been restored is doubtful. Probably there would have been a three-party or four-party system.

These speculations are perhaps idle because the proposals for proportional representation and the alternative vote were eventually rejected. Except for a few two-member constituencies, the principle of single-member constituencies was accepted. In a single-member constituency the candidate who had a 'plurality', i.e. the candidate with the largest number of votes whether or not he had a majority, received election. The Liberal party, being the middle party, was forced out of existence; and the two-party system was restored with the Conservative party forming His Majesty's Government and the Labour party His Majesty's Opposition—or vice versa.

The economic and social changes since 1885 had been so great that the redistribution in 1918 was considerable. Table 6 shows the effect.

The pace of development in the North had become slower, though the representation of the Northern Counties did not reach the peak until 1945. While the rural counties of the Midlands lost seats, the industrial counties gained rather more. The Eastern Counties and the

South and West lost more seats. The great development of Greater London was, however, taking place. The County of London, which had become an administrative unit in 1889, had 62 seats in 1918, whereas in 1885 the five Home Counties had together had only 99; nevertheless it still had fewer seats than Lancashire. Even more noticeable was the shift to the great towns. Table 7 provides a comparison between 1885 and 1918 which is again instructive.

	1885	1918
Northern Counties	154	171
Eastern Counties	36	27
Midland Counties	90	92
Home Counties	99	126
South and West	77	69
Wales and Monmouthshire	34	35
Scotland	70	71
Ireland	101	101
Universities	9	15
Totals	670	707

TABLE 6

	1885	1918		1885	1918
London	70[1]	62	Bristol	4	5
Birmingham	7	12	Bradford	3	4
Liverpool	9	11	Hull	3	4
Manchester	6	10	Glasgow	7	15
Sheffield	5	7	Edinburgh	4	5
Leeds	5	6			

TABLE 7

Thirty-two English boroughs disappeared in 1918. In fact, of the 102 English boroughs in existence in 1831, only thirty-five remained after 1918.[2] Twelve boroughs, Blackburn,[3] Bolton,[3] Brighton,[3] Derby,

[1] Included in Kent, Middlesex and Surrey in 1885. The movement from the County of London to the suburbs had reduced the number of seats.

[2] Reading, Cambridge, Carlisle, Derby, Exeter, Plymouth, Bristol, Gloucester, Portsmouth, Southampton, Hythe, Rochester, Liverpool, Preston, Wigan, Leicester, Grimsby, Lincoln, London (City of), Westminster, Norwich, Great Yarmouth, Northampton, Morpeth, Nottingham, Oxford, Bath, Newcastle-under-Lyme, Ipswich, Southwark, Hastings, Coventry, Worcester, Kingston-upon-Hull and York.

[3] Enfranchised in 1832.

Norwich, Oldham,[1] Preston, Southampton, Stockport,[1] Sunderland,[1] the City of London and Dundee,[1] which had had two members before 1885 and retained two members in 1918, continued to be two-member constituencies. All the other constituencies, except some of the universities, had one member each.

The Government of Ireland Act, 1920, reduced the number of Irish members in the House of Commons from 106 to forty-six, since it was intended to set up separate legislatures for Northern and Southern Ireland. Of the forty-six members, thirty-three were to represent constituencies in Southern Ireland and thirteen to represent constituencies in Northern Ireland. The establishment of the Irish Free State in 1921 rendered this provision inoperative in so far as it applied to Southern Ireland; and it was provided in the Irish Free State (Agreement) Act, 1922, that after 31 March 1922 no writ should be issued for the election of a member for a constituency in Ireland other than a constituency in Northern Ireland. For the first time since 1509, therefore, the size of the House of Commons was reduced by the Acts of 1920 and 1922. Table 8 shows the numerical effect of the change.

	1918	1922
Northern Counties	171	171
Eastern Counties	27	27
Midland Counties	92	92
Home Counties	126	126
South and West	69	69
Wales and Monmouthshire	35	35
Scotland	71	71
Ireland (Northern Ireland only in 1922)	101	12
Universities	15	12
Totals	707	615

TABLE 8

The House of Commons had not been so small since the Act of Union with Ireland, 1801. The disappearance of the 'irrepressible Irish' (a term never applied to dour Ulstermen) had a profound effect upon parties. In 1885, 1892 and 1910 the Irish Nationalist party had held

[1] Enfranchised in 1832, but Dundee had only one member until 1868.

the balance of power, and Liberal Governments had been able to remain in office only with Irish votes. Except in 1906, the Liberal party had not held a majority of seats in Great Britain since 1885. The effect of the Acts of 1920 and 1922 was to add at least ten solid Unionist votes to the Conservative party in Great Britain, and virtually to deprive the Liberal and Labour parties of Irish support. After 1918 the Liberal party would have had a hard struggle even if it had been reasonably unanimous, for it would have had to capture Conservative seats and at the same time to keep down the progress of the Labour party. The Labour party, too, had not merely to capture Liberal seats, but also to fight a Conservative party which began with at least twenty safe seats—ten from Ulster and the rest from the universities of Great Britain.

Women of the age of thirty and upwards had been enfranchised in 1918. In 1929 the franchise was made identical for men and women. Since the increase in the number of electors in each constituency was roughly proportionate, no redistribution was effected: and in fact there was no redistribution until 1945.

6. THE REFORM OF 1945-8

The changes made in anticipation of the general election of 1945 do not deserve the name of 'reform' because they were temporary measures consequential upon the suspension of party activities during the war. No registers of electors had been compiled since 1939, and in 1942 a committee recommended[1] that, since there had been and would be vast movements of population during the war, and since a new elector would not be able to vote until $16\frac{1}{2}$ months after the end of six months' residence in a constituency, it was impracticable to use the pre-war registration system for a wartime or post-war election; hence the National Register should be used as a basis for the compilation of new registers. Redistribution should be effected at frequent intervals by a permanent boundary commission: but this was impracticable during the war and the next election should be fought on the existing distribution, subject to a redistribution where there was a considerable divergence from the quota.

[1] Report of the Committee on Electoral Machinery: Cmd. 6408 of 1942.

33

The former recommendation was carried out by the Parliament (Election and Meeting) Act, 1943, as amended by the Parliamentary Electors (War-Time Registration) Act, 1944. Consideration of the proposal about redistribution was postponed pending a report by a Speaker's Conference set up in 1944.[1] This Conference, which as in 1917 was representative of all parties and, so far as possible, of all sections of opinion, decisively rejected proposals for proportional representation and the alternative vote. It then agreed that there ought to be permanent machinery for redistribution. There should be separate boundary commissions for England, Wales, Scotland and Northern Ireland, presided over by the Speaker. Each commission should make a general review of boundaries at intervals of not less than three nor more than seven years. Scotland and Wales should not have their numbers reduced, and the representation of Northern Ireland should remain at thirteen. The total number of seats should remain substantially unchanged. The total electorate should be divided by the number of seats, and in general no constituency should have a population more than 25 per cent above or below the quota so obtained. There should be no change in the university constituencies, the two-member seats should be divided, but the City of London should continue to have two members. It was, however, impracticable to effect a redistribution on these lines for the next election, and accordingly the larger seats, those which had grown by 1939 to more than 190 per cent of the average, should be divided. This would involve a temporary addition of twenty-five extra seats.

These recommendations were carried out by the House of Commons (Redistribution of Seats) Act, 1944, though with slight modifications. Twenty constituencies with a 1939 *electorate* of over 100,000 each were divided into forty-five constituencies. The list, which is classified in Table 9, gives some indication of the changes in population between 1918 and 1939. The list shows the main areas to which the population had moved, but not the areas from which it had come. The changes were approved by a Coalition Government, and the Labour party was not anxious for alterations which would enlarge small constituencies.

[1] Speaker's Conference on Electoral Machinery and Redistribution of Seats: Cmd. 6534 and 6543 of 1944.

Most such constituencies were in areas which had been heavily industrialised and were therefore safe Labour seats. Nevertheless, permanent

Counties	No. of new constituencies
Northern Counties	
Cheshire	1
Lancashire	1
Eastern Counties	Nil
Midland Counties	
Buckinghamshire	1
Hertfordshire	1
Warwickshire	3
Home Counties	
Essex	6
Kent	2
Middlesex	7
Surrey	2
South and West	
Sussex	1
Total	25

TABLE 9

Boundary Commissions were set up, as recommended by the Speaker's Conference, with terms of reference including the following:

(1) Wales was to have not less than thirty-five constituencies and Scotland not less than seventy-one, while Great Britain as a whole was to have not substantially more or less than 591.[1] Northern Ireland was to have twelve. The Act had no application to university constituencies. In effect, therefore, the 1918 figure of 615 seats was being retained, but with the proviso that Wales (including Monmouthshire), Scotland and Northern Ireland were not to lose seats.

(2) Speaking generally, a two-member seat was to be either divided or allocated one seat, but the Boundary Commission was permitted, after holding a local inquiry, to retain it as a two-member seat if it was large enough.

(3) So far as practicable, a single-member constituency was not to be greater or less than the quota by more than 25 per cent.

[1] Altered to 613 by the Act of 1948: see House of Commons (Redistribution of Seats) Act, 1949, 2nd Schedule.

(4) The City of London was to remain a constituency, returning either two members or one member.

(5) So far as practicable, the boundaries of constituencies were to follow local government boundaries.

(6) The Commissions were to report at intervals of not less than three years nor more than seven years, and their recommendations could be carried out (with or without modifications) by Order in Council approved by resolutions in both Houses of Parliament.

These terms of reference were modified by the House of Commons (Redistribution of Seats) Act, 1947. The margin of 25 per cent mentioned in paragraph (3) above was removed, so as to provide greater elasticity in the adaptation of constituencies to local government areas. The Commissions reported at the end of 1947 and their reports formed the basis of the redistribution clauses of the Representation of the People Act, 1948. The only major changes originally proposed were, first, that university representation should be abolished and, secondly, the City of London should be joined with the City of Westminster to return one member. This latter alteration was due to the Labour Government's decision to abolish the business premises qualification, which had been limited but not extinguished in 1944. In Committee, however, the Government moved amendments to divide the eight proposed constituencies with more than 80,000 electors and to add one member to each of the nine largest boroughs in England. These proposals were violently opposed by the Conservative Opposition as examples of 'gerrymandering'. On the other hand, there was a case for allowing an increase in the number of seats in order to prevent large constituencies; and the new boundaries were drawn by the Boundary Commission.

The Acts of 1944 and 1947, with the amendments of 1948, were consolidated in the House of Commons (Redistribution of Seats) Act, 1949, and the first general review of boundaries was completed before the general election of 1955.[1] Table 10 gives the changes made in 1945, 1950 and 1955.

It will be seen that the Northern Counties reached their peak in 1945.

---

[1] By an amendment made in 1958, the next review will be conducted between 1964 and 1969: see House of Commons (Redistribution of Seats) Act, 1958. Paragraph (6) above now reads: 'not less than ten nor more than fifteen'.

The heavy increase in the representation of the Home Counties in 1945 was due to the arbitrary method of redistribution adopted, because of war conditions, in 1944; and in fact the representation of Greater London has, apart from that instance, been steadily increasing. This is shown not only by the higher representation of the Home Counties, but also by higher representation in Bedfordshire, Hertfordshire and

	1922	1945	1950	1955
Northern Counties	171	173	170	167
Eastern Counties	27	27	26	26
Midland Counties	92	97	104	107
Home Counties	126	143	132	136
South and West	69	70	74	75
Wales and Monmouthshire	35	35	36	36
Scotland	71	71	71	71
Northern Ireland	12	12	12	12
Universities	12	12	—	—
Totals	615	640	625	630

TABLE 10

Sussex, which in some measure provide 'dormitories' for London. The South and West, after a steep decline in the Victorian era, are now rising slowly in political importance. The increasing importance of the Midlands is due mainly to Staffordshire and Warwickshire.

7. THE PRESENT ARRANGEMENTS

Before 1832 there was little connexion between the franchise and the distribution of seats, and up to 1884 the connexion was not close. In 1885 the principle of 'one vote, one value' was accepted with minor modifications. The formula was completed in 1948, when university representation and the business premises qualification having been abolished, 'one man (or woman), one vote' became the law of the United Kingdom. There are, however, still qualifications to the formula 'one vote, one value'. First, Scotland and Wales have their minimum representation fixed by a 'gentlemen's agreement' of 1948, Scotland at seventy-one and Wales at thirty-five, while Northern Ireland has its representation fixed at twelve because it has its own Parliament. Table 11 gives the relation of seats in 1959 to population in 1951.

There is, accordingly, a bias in favour of Wales and Scotland and a bias against Northern Ireland, the latter being due to its quasi-federal status.

Secondly, though the universal use of the single-member constituency makes more or less artificial units essential, some attempt is still made to delimit constituencies along local government boundaries. This has two objectives. The major objective is to give unity to a constituency, to make it something of a 'community', and so to make certain that the members of Parliament represent not merely 50,000 electors but a section of the population with interests and perhaps ideas

	Population	Seats	Population per seat
England	41,148,000	511	80,500
Wales and Monmouthshire	2,597,000	36	72,100
Scotland	5,096,000	71	71,800
Northern Ireland	1,371,000	12	114,250

TABLE II

and emotions of their own. The growing homogeneity of the population of the United Kingdom due to ease of communications, the mobility of unskilled and clerical labour, common newspapers, and common broadcasting and television, makes this less important than it was, especially in the suburbs of Greater London and the great cities where so many constituencies are 'dormitories'. Moreover frequent alterations of boundaries, as now required by the House of Commons (Redistribution of Seats) Acts, 1949 and 1958, necessarily hinder the development of a local political tradition and obstruct the development of close relations between a member and his constituents. It is indeed reasonably certain that the Labour Government went too far in 1948 in its anxiety to carry out the principle of 'one vote, one value'—though it should be remembered that the recommendation was made by the Speaker's Conference of 1944: the general effect has been to encourage the 'carpet-bagger', who knows little about the constituency, and to base elections more than ever on the party label. The second objective in following local government boundaries is purely one of machinery, to make easier the provision of common registers for parliamentary and local government electors.

The result in any case is to produce considerable variations in the sizes of constituencies. The 511 English constituencies in 1959 are classified in terms of electorates in Table 12.

Electorate	No. of con- stituencies
35,000–40,000	8
40,000–45,000	28
45,000–50,000	65
50,000–55,000	121
60,000–65,000	112
65,000–70,000	80
70,000–75,000	37
75,000–80,000	9
Over 80,000	3

TABLE 12

These figures give an inadequate picture of the extent of the variation. In England in 1959 it was between the 87,544 of Hornchurch and the 37,320 of Battersea South; in Wales between the 71,342 of Newport and the 26,435 of Merioneth; in Scotland between the 66,351 of Aberdeen North and the 25,178 of the Western Isles; and in Northern Ireland between the 93,634 of South Antrim and the 48,663 of Belfast East. Except in Northern Ireland, the largest constituency is at least twice as large as the smallest, in spite of the intention in 1944 (subsequently given up) of allowing only a 25 per cent variation from the average. It is therefore far from true that 'one vote' has 'one value'.

Thirdly, the vote that counts is the vote that wins. In most constituencies at most elections the result is as certain as the time of sunrise, because the candidate of a specified party is bound to win. It cannot be said that a vote for a successful candidate in a safe seat is wasted: it is a safe seat because people do vote. It is nearer the truth that a vote for an unsuccessful candidate for a safe seat is wasted, because that candidate never had a chance of being elected. Elections are won and lost in the marginal constituencies, because both parties have a considerable number of safe seats. A system of proportional representation on a national list would result in the number of members from each party being proportionate to the number of electors, and every vote would then have the same value. With straight voting in single-member constituencies the value of the vote depends upon the narrowness of the potential margin. A party may win a majority of the votes at a general election and yet lose the election, because the votes cast for it are not of equal value.

The essential characteristic of the present British system is that it minimises the risk of 'gerrymandering'. A Boundary Commission is a permanent body, consisting of the Speaker of the House of Commons, a Judge, the Registrar-General of Births, Deaths and Marriages in the part of the United Kingdom in which the Commission has jurisdiction, the Director-General of Ordnance Survey (or in Northern Ireland the Commissioner of Valuation) and two other persons appointed by the Government. Members of Parliament are disqualified for appointment. Provisional recommendations by a Commission must be advertised and any representations made must be considered. The rules for redistribution are laid down in a Schedule to the Act. They give considerable discretion to the Commissions; and though the Secretary of State has power to make modifications in their recommendations he must lay before Parliament a statement of his reasons for them. In any case a draft order requires the approval of both Houses. It will be seen that there is room for 'gerrymandering'; but it is unthinkable that Mr Speaker would have any part in it; and if it was done by modifying the recommendations of a Commission it would be obvious to the world. The fierce attack on the Labour Government in 1948—when the Government was undoubtedly maladroit—shows how easy it would be to damage the prestige of a Government which tried to gerrymander.

The Commissions explained in 1953 that they were impressed by criticism of reviews at comparatively short intervals, and suggested for consideration the lengthening of the periods. They also felt that they should be allowed to retain the *status quo* where it appeared to be desirable and such action was not inconsistent with the rules in the Second Schedule to the Act of 1949. It cannot be doubted that they were right. Given the principles upon which distribution is founded and the rapidity of changes in the distribution of population, frequent alterations of boundaries are necessary. To make such alterations in every Parliament was, however, to weaken the relations between members and prospective candidates, on the one hand, and constituencies on the other, and accordingly the law was changed in 1958 so that at least two, and possibly more, Parliaments will be elected for virtually the same constituencies. Electors are necessarily more concerned with parties than with candidates, but it is undesirable to have the choice of candidates wholly in the hands of local parties. There is a greater chance of having good candidates, and therefore of having good members, if the electors are encouraged to exercise their votes in a discriminating manner and if the local party committees are aware that good candidates attract votes while bad candidates repel them. When the elector does not know, from one election to another, in which constituency he is to vote, he is discouraged from finding out about the candidates who hang the respective party labels around their necks.

CHAPTER II

THE ELECTORS

The idea that the elector is the average man, the common man, the ordinary reasonable man, the man on the Clapham omnibus, the plain citizen, and his female equivalent, is a recent innovation, born of the homogeneity of the British peoples in the twentieth century. It is indeed possible to exaggerate that homogeneity. In spite of the British Broadcasting Corporation, English is still spoken in a variety of accents, and there are British electors who prefer to speak Welsh or Gaelic, or even Polish or Hebrew. The man from Hoxton may take a job in Huddersfield or the Gorbals, but in the pub he is recognised as a foreigner. Though the man who pays surtax has not much more net income than the man who does not pay income tax, there are class distinctions based upon differences of income. Some people read *The Times* and some the *Daily Mirror*, though it must be confessed that the best people read both. Not only is there a difference between the public bar and the saloon bar, but also there is still a difference between church and chapel. Everybody rides in the buses, but not everybody has joined the Automobile Association. Some wear old school ties and some do not, though not many dispense with ties altogether. The female electors all wear the same sort of clothes, but somehow they wear them differently. The Bar Council has not been affiliated to the Trade Union Congress, nor have the members of the British Medical Association joined the Transport and General Workers Union. The Federation of British Industries has not yet absorbed, apparently, the industry which provides the football pools. The homogeneity of the British electorate, like every other aspect of the British Constitution, must be accepted with the customary qualifications, limitations and exceptions.

This homogeneity is, however, a very recent development. Medieval England was a congeries of local communities, and Wales, Scotland and Ireland were essentially foreign to England and to each other. The task of knitting them together was begun with the canals, the turnpike roads and the stage-coaches, developed with the macadamised roads and the railways, and continued even more rapidly after the invention of the internal combustion engine, the electric telegraph, the telephone, and the wireless valve. Other developments have helped. The medieval agricultural system was static, and the vill or manor was an almost isolated community. The shortage of labour caused by the Black Death, the development of wool-farming, and the introduction of a money economy permitted of and required greater mobility. The invention of printing, the consequent spread of literacy in the sixteenth and seventeenth centuries, the translation of the Bible and the prayer book into English, were factors of the utmost political importance whose consequences seem never to have been fully investigated. The armies of the Civil War, even though small on modern standards, must in some measure have broken down local isolation and spread common opinions. The great economic developments in the eighteenth century, commonly called the Industrial Revolution, collected men and women into towns and created a public opinion among all classes which could gradually be unified in the nineteenth century. The movements for parliamentary reform, the People's Charter, and the repeal of the Corn Laws, were the first genuinely national movements, though as one might expect they were strongest in the towns.

In the process the character of representation in the House of Commons has changed. Though, as has been suggested already, the commons was the commonalty, representation in Parliament was essentially local and communal. Burke's notion that members were elected to express opinions on national policies could not have been formulated much before 1600 and would have been rudely contested by the Stuarts. It was indeed contested by the patrons of boroughs and even by the great majority of the members, reformers and anti-reformers alike, in 1830. The division of the adult population into more or less equal 'constituencies', in order that each person might be 'represented' by a member of Parliament, would have been incredible before the second half of the nineteenth century. It was one of the six points of the People's Charter,[1] and indeed something like it had been suggested by the Council of the Army in 1647;[2] but the authors were wild men,

[1] Howell, *The Chartist Movement*, p. 2.
[2] Gardiner, *Constitutional Documents of the Puritan Revolution* (3rd ed.), p. 317.

43

and even John Stuart Mill had other ideas.[1] The idea of 'one man, one vote, one value' is comparatively new in practical politics, not a perfect and happy conclusion of a long and inevitable development since the beginning of time.

I. BEFORE 1832

What the franchise was in the fourteenth century nobody knows because nobody thought about it and therefore nobody put it on record. If Robert Braunch, Master of Trinity Hall when Parliament was summoned to meet in Cambridge in September 1388, had been asked who was entitled to elect the knights and burgesses, he would probably have hedged as carefully as the present incumbent of his office. He would have said that they had to be returned by the sheriffs in response to the King's writs (though in this case, as it happened, the Parliament was summoned not by Richard II but by the commission of government) and their duty was determined by the form of the writs. These insisted that the election be in full county court and by assent of the same. It was not, however, very clear what a 'full county court' meant. It was probably the regular court, held every three weeks or a month, and not the full court summoned to meet the justices twice a year. At a regular court, however, there would be only the suitors, and anyhow the Statute of Merton, 1235, allowed any free man to appear by attorney. It would seem, therefore, that the sheriff could and should afforce the county in order to secure an election: indeed he would probably have to do so in order to secure a couple of knights willing to undertake the onerous journey to Cambridge and risk the agues of the fens for wages of four shillings a day. On the question of the persons bound to elect the citizens and burgesses there was no authority at all. Presumably the sheriff simply ordered the mayor or bailiff to impress a couple of citizens or burgesses.

The problem had not arisen because representation was a duty, not a privilege, and it was more important to be exempted from the levy necessary for the payment of wages than to be permitted the doubtful honour of riding to the county town to take part in the election. It was only in the fifteenth century that the Commons began to take an interest

---

[1] *Representative Government*, ch. III.

in elections. In 1406 it was laid down by statute[1] that, at the next meeting of the county court after the receipt of the writ, proclamation be made in full county (i.e. in open court) of the day and place of the parliament, and that all those present, as well those summoned for that cause as others, await the election of their knights, and that they proceed to the election freely and indifferently, notwithstanding any prayer or command to the contrary. This did not determine who should attend, though the further requirement that those present seal an indenture giving the names of those elected suggests that only those with seals were expected to be present. In another statute in 1413[2] it was provided that the knights elected and the 'knights, esquires and others' who were electors should be residents in the counties. This statute also required that the burgesses elected should be resident but did not specify that the electors in boroughs should be resident.

In fact, the borough electors were never determined by statute until 1832; but the famous Act of 1430[3] ordered that in future the knights of the shire be elected in each county by the people resident therein, of whom each should have a free tenement of the value of forty shillings a year at least above all charges. The preamble indicates that people were becoming interested in elections, for it recites that the elections of knights in several of the counties had been made by an excessive number of people, of whom the greater part were people of little property and no value, each of whom claimed to have an equal voice with the most worthy knights and esquires, whence homicides, riots, batteries and divisions among the gentry and other people would very likely arise if a suitable remedy was not found.

The county elector had by the statutes of 1413 and 1430 to be resident within the county and by the statute of 1430 he had to have a freehold worth forty shillings a year within the county. How soon the requirement of residence fell into desuetude is not known,[4] but it was consistently ignored long before it was abolished in 1774.[5] The other

[1] 7 Hen. IV, c. 15; Lodge and Thornton, *English Constitutional Documents, 1307–1485*, p. 162; and see 11 Hen. IV, c. 1, *ibid.* pp. 164–5.
[2] 1 Hen. V, c. 1; Lodge and Thornton, p. 165.
[3] 8 Hen. VI, c. 7; Lodge and Thornton, p. 167.
[4] See Porritt, *The Unreformed House of Commons*, I, p. 24.
[5] 14 Geo. III, c. 58.

qualification, a freehold worth forty shillings, remained the sole county qualification until 1832 and one of the county qualifications until 1918. In the course of four hundred years, however, it took on a new meaning. Sir William Blackstone, who was good at inventing explanations, tells us[1] that the sum of forty shillings was adopted in 1430 because 'that sum would then, with proper industry, furnish all the necessaries of life, and render the freeholder, if he pleased, an independent man'. The leaseholders and the copyholders were excluded because those tenures were not known in 1430, and freeholders holding lands not worth forty shillings would be tempted to dispose of their votes 'under some undue influence or other'. Blackstone adds that land worth forty shillings in 1430 would be worth £20 in his day, though he did not say that those not holding land worth £20 disposed of their votes 'under some undue influence or other'.

The depreciation of sterling increased the number of county electors. There were, however, other methods of manufacturing votes, which eighteenth-century legislation sought to regulate. A person was qualified if he had 'frank tenement' of the value of at least forty shillings a year above all charges. Whatever this was intended to mean, it did not necessarily mean seised of an estate in land in fee simple of that value in possession. It was enough if the tenant had a life estate, or held a charge on land, or was trustee or mortgagee, or held in right of his wife's dower, or held a freehold office. Indeed, it was enough if he was seised at the time of the election on trust to reconvey the tenement after the election. The manufacture of 'faggot votes' was thus easy and began at least as early as 1628.[2] The statute 10 Anne, c. 23 (1712) forbade fraudulent conveyances designed to create votes, provided that no person might vote unless in actual possession of the lands, or in receipt of the rents or profits, for one year before the election (unless the lands came to him by descent, marriage, marriage settlement, devise, presentation to a benefice, or promotion to an office), and deprived of the franchise any person who did not pay the public taxes, church rates and parish duties. This arrangement continued until 1781, when the Act 20 Geo. III, c. 17 substituted the requirement that the forty-shilling freeholder be assessed to the land tax in his own name within six

---

[1] 1 Bl. Comm. 173.   [2] Porritt, *op. cit.* p. 22.

months before the election. The land tax register thus became an embryo register of electors.

The borough franchise was not regulated by statute until 1832. Unless there was a charter or a custom to the contrary, the franchise was vested in all the inhabitant householders of the borough.[1] This usually meant all 'potwallopers', i.e. all heads of families who boiled their own pots; but it might mean all who paid the local taxes, scot and lot. In any case, the king having the prerogative of creating parliamentary boroughs,[2] the franchise might be determined by charter. Strictly speaking, the franchise could not be determined by custom, because no parliaments were summoned before the beginning of legal memory in 1189; but the lawyers assumed that parliaments had existed before the beginning of legal memory, and in any case a custom beginning after 1189 would be evidence of a lost grant and would therefore found a claim by prescription. Under a charter or by prescription, the franchise might be vested in all who held lands by burgage tenure, or in the corporation, or in the freemen. Porritt[3] divided the 203 boroughs in existence in 1831 as follows:

Scot and lot	59
Burgage	39
Corporation	43
Freemen	62
Total	203

[1] 4 Com. Dig. 288.

[2] Chitty, *Prerogatives of the Crown*, pp. 67–8. Chitty's view was that the prerogative, though not exercised since 29 Car. II, had not been abrogated by the Acts of Union.

[3] *The Unreformed House of Commons*, I, p. 30. Professor Seymour has a different classification as follows:

Scot and lot and potwallopers	66
Burgage tenure	27
Corporation boroughs	30
Freemen	107
Freeholders (i.e. counties of towns)	17
Total	247

See Seymour, *Electoral Reform in England and Wales*. There were in fact 203 boroughs, and no doubt Professor Seymour includes some boroughs twice because two qualifications were accepted in those boroughs.

These are generic terms, and within the groups there were variations due to local usage. There were, as Sir William Blackstone says with unusual exaggeration, 'infinite disputes'.[1] Since the House of Commons claimed privilege in these matters, judicial legislation by a series of binding precedents was not practicable. It was enacted in 1729 by Grenville's Act, 2 Geo. II, c. 24, that the last determination by the House of Commons should be conclusive. This applied only to determinations before the date of the Act; but the Act 28 Geo. III, c. 52, in effect enabled a committee on disputed elections to make a binding decision which was conclusive for future elections. Generally decisions of this character favoured the narrowing of the franchise, since borough patrons had influence in Parliament and honest freemen had not.

The borough seats in the last Parliaments of England numbered 417 out of 513. Since Scotland could be managed for the Crown and most of the Irish seats were in the hands of patrons, the English boroughs played a predominant part in the politics of Great Britain and the United Kingdom of Great Britain and Ireland. In the middle of the eighteenth century nobody was prepared to defend the borough franchises. Sir William Blackstone's defence[2] ended with the assertion that the Constitution was 'not quite so perfect' as he had described it; and if any alteration might be wished or suggested 'it should be in favour of a more complete representation of the people'. After the French Revolution, however, the realisation that Britain had avoided both the Terror and Napoleon by reason of its admirable Constitution settled all the doubts which Blackstone's admission might have raised. The system of representation, as he pointed out, steered a middle course between vesting power in the rich and vesting power in numbers. On the one hand were Preston and Westminster, where numbers alone counted; on the other hand were Old Sarum and Gatton, which were virtually private property. On the one hand, too, were the counties, representing the landed interest; on the other hand were the boroughs, representing the mercantile interest. Thus all points of view and all interests were represented in the House of Commons, without giving any section of opinion or any interest a dominating influence.

[1] 1 Bl. Comm. 174.   [2] 1 Bl. Comm. 172.

The weakness of this line of defence was that it ignored the degree to which representation had fallen into the hands of patrons and the degree to which the Crown could manage elections with the co-operation of one or more of the political groups. This is a matter to be discussed in connexion with parties. At this point, however, a caveat must be entered against the extreme radical criticism. Power depends not only on the persons who exercise it but also on the manner in which it is exercised. Most of the county seats were within the influence of great landowners, for reasons already explained. On the other hand the county members had throughout the eighteenth century a great reputation for independence. Most of them had no political ambitions; they could be neither bribed nor bullied; they decided public questions on the arguments put before them. Nor were they mere representatives of their class, the landed gentry. *Noblesse oblige* was a good eighteenth-century tradition. The forty-shilling freeholders voted for the nominees of the great landowners because the great landowners were the leaders of the community; the members so elected were in Parliament not to vote for their patrons but to represent the people. When industrialisation developed, the 'bosses' could not represent the workers; but in the hierarchy of the English countryside of the eighteenth century the squire was not a 'boss' but a *parens patriae*, as natural a representative as the chief of a tribe or the father of a family.

The boroughs were more varied. Some were mere 'pocket boroughs' returning as a matter of course the nominees of their patrons. Others were wide open to corruption. Most were in the intermediate group, returning by deliberate choice the nominees of their patrons, or perhaps one nominee of a patron and one local man. The borough member might be a careerist on the make, but he might instead be a young man of good family and excellent prospects who proposed to devote his life to public service, the same sort of man as the young Liberal or young Conservative of the nineteenth century. There is not very much difference between the nominee of a borough corporation and the nominee of a Conservative or Liberal caucus or a trade union. The only difference, in fact, is that the man on the Clapham omnibus can reject the nominee but does not, while his predecessor had no choice. The nominee of a caucus has to pay attention to public opinion, even in the safest seat, because there is a chance of his being rejected at the next election; but the nominee of a patron had to pay attention to public opinion also, because usually his patron's power depended mainly on the ready acquiescence of the electors, whether they were corporators, burgage tenants, freemen or potwallopers. Whig history has exaggerated the instruments of power. It is true enough that many electors were paid, but usually at the standard rate. It is true that a landlord could eject his tenants, but one must not assume that Bill Bloggs voted for his landlord because Bill was a tenant at will. It is true that Lady Blarney could withdraw her custom from Grimes the grocer; but Mr Grimes thought it a great honour to be invited to vote for Lord Blarney's candidate; it was indeed very gracious of milady to ask him. Of course the scion of 'the big house' was elected; in the scale of values adopted by Messrs Bloggs and Grimes it was incredible that anybody should even dare to stand against so worthy a representative of so worthy a family.

The truth is that the Industrial Revolution gradually shifted the balance. The suggestion that the workers of Birmingham were represented by the members for Warwickshire was almost as ridiculous as the suggestion[1] that the American colonies were represented by the members for Kent because the colonies were held as of the manor of Greenwich. John Wilkes, Member for Middlesex, was the portent, if not the omen. It was difficult to allege that the forty-shilling free-holders of Middlesex, the scot and lot electors of Westminster and Southwark, and the all-comers in Preston, could adequately choose for the workers of Birmingham and the industrial North. The anti-reformers' arguments broke down because the stannaries of Cornwall could not be said to represent the coal mines of Durham or South Wales. The Constitution was still 'mixed' but it was the wrong mixture. It provided too much representation for the herbage and too little for the garbage.

2. THE REFORM OF 1832

The Representation of the People Act, 1832, added to the forty-shilling freeholder (a) the copyholder and the leaseholder for a term of sixty

---

[1] Made by Sir James Marriott, M.P., Master of Trinity Hall: but he said it during a filibuster.

years or more, of £10 clear yearly value above charges; (*b*) the lease-holder for a term of twenty years or more, of £50 clear yearly value above charges; and (*c*) a person in actual occupation as tenant and liable to a rental of at least £50 to the same landlord, and the sub-lessee and the assign of any such person similarly qualified. This last qualification was the famous 'Chandos clause', carried against the Government on the motion of the Marquis of Chandos, the 'farmers' friend'. It was argued for the tories that the tenants at will in the counties ought not to be worse off than the £10 occupiers in the boroughs, who were given the vote. For the Government it was argued that a vote for a tenant at will was a vote for his landlord. The whig landlords voted with the tories because they supported the tenant farmers; the radicals voted with the tories because they favoured the extension of the franchise; and the Government was defeated. On the other hand, the forty-shilling freeholder in a borough retained a vote in the county, unless he was a £10 occupying freeholder, in which case he had a vote in the borough.

In the boroughs the franchise was given to any male person who for one year before registration had occupied as owner or tenant any house, warehouse, counting house, shop or other building, either separately or jointly with other land, of a clear yearly value of not less than £10. The occupier must have been rated to the poor rate and at the time of registration have paid all rates and taxes due from him the April preceding. An occupier who had received poor relief during the twelve months preceding the registration was disqualified. There was of course conflict over this enfranchisement of 'a vulgar, privileged pedlary' and 'the oligarchy of shopkeepers'; but the main battle was fought over ancient rights. None of those rights could after 1832 be exercised except by persons in residence in the boroughs and no new rights could be created. The freemen, if resident, continued to exercise their franchise, and in certain cases the rights of freeholders and burgage tenants were continued: but potwallopers and scot and lot voters were to continue only for their lives. In practice, of course, many of those with ancient rights would be ten-pound occupiers.

It has been estimated[1] that there were 435,000 electors in England and

[1] See Seymour, *op. cit.* pp. 78–100.

Wales before the Reform Act and 652,000 afterwards. On the basis of the population of 1831, this was an increase from 3·1 per cent to 4·7 per cent. Thus the Reform Act was revolutionary not in respect of enfranchisement but in respect of distribution. There were, however, considerable changes in the distribution and the character of the electors. The borough electors rose from 188,000 to 282,000, an increase of 50 per cent, and the county electors rose from 247,000 to 370,000, an increase of 49 per cent. In the counties, however, no electors were disfranchised, even if they were in new boroughs, though some forty-shilling freeholders, being ten-pound occupiers in new boroughs, were transferred from the counties to the boroughs. In the boroughs, on the other hand, some electors lost their voting rights, some because they were resident in disfranchised boroughs and some because they were not resident in their boroughs. The number of electors with ancient rights fell by no less than 108,000: but many of them became ten-pound occupiers.

In the counties, 70 per cent of the electors were freeholders, 10 per cent were copyholders and leaseholders, and 20 per cent were tenants at will enfranchised by the Chandos clause.[1] Some of the freeholders were urban electors, but it will be seen that the new electors did not swamp the old. There was some shift in the balance. The Chandos electors were more numerous in the agricultural counties, most of which would have been tory in any event. The freeholders were most numerous in the urban and industrial areas, and were generally whig or Radical. In the boroughs, on the other hand, the ten-pound occupiers swamped the electors with ancient rights, except in sixteen of the freemen boroughs, while in forty-eight boroughs the freemen were one-third of the electorate.[2] Taking the boroughs as a whole, 62 per cent of the electors were ten-pound occupiers, 22 per cent were freemen, and 16 per cent were electors with other ancient rights.

The ten-pound occupiers were mostly members of the commercial and industrial middle class. The disfranchisement of freemen and the prohibition against adding to the number of freemen operated against the working class. In many boroughs, especially where the apprenticeship system prevailed, many of the freemen had been artisans or

---

[1] Seymour, *op. cit.* p. 78. [2] *Ibid.* pp. 84–5.

'tradesmen' in the Army sense, i.e. skilled workers. Gladstone estimated that before 1832 the workers held a majority in sixty-five boroughs returning 130 members.[1] If so, their voting strength was much weakened by the Reform Act. In 1865 more than half the freemen were workers; but most of the middle-class freemen would of course be ten-pounders and registered as such. Generally the Liberals won where the ancient-right electors were strong, but these boroughs were often the most corrupt. There were sixteen elections avoided for corruption between 1832 and 1854, in sixteen ancient-right boroughs. Three of them, Beverley, Lancaster and Reigate, were eventually disfranchised, and the freemen were disfranchised in Great Yarmouth.[2] It will be seen, therefore, that the tory accusation that the new franchise was less representative than the old had some substance. What the Act had done was to enfranchise the commercial and industrial middle class, but to offset this by strengthening the power of the rural vote through redistribution.

It would not be unfair to assert that the Scottish constituencies before 1832 were all 'pocket counties' and 'pocket boroughs' and that the people of Scotland as such had no representation in the Parliament at Westminster. 'From the Tweed to John o' Groats', said Lord Brougham in 1832,[3] '...there is not within the memory of man, the knowledge of anything like a popular election.' The electors in the counties were the men who were in possession of property or superiority of forty-shilling land of old extent holden of the Crown or, where the old extent was not ascertainable, of land held of the Crown liable in public burden for £400 (Scots = £33. 6s. 8d. sterling) of valued rent.[4] The system of registration and election was complicated and gave ample opportunity for political manœuvre. In 1788 the electorate numbered 2662 and ranged from 205 in Ayr to 12 in Bute,[5] but faggot votes were easily created by splitting freeholds, and the electorate varied from election to election. In 1820 it was estimated that there were 2889 electors, and of these probably some 1200 were faggot voters.[6] When an application for compensation was made in 1832 it

---

[1] *Ibid.* p. 88.   [2] *Ibid.* p. 87.
[3] Porritt, *The Unreformed House of Commons*, II, p. 142.
[4] *Ibid.* p. 145.   [5] *Ibid.* p. 149.   [6] *Ibid.* p. 157.

was alleged that a 'naked superiority', i.e. in the terms of English law the estate of a mesne lord held of the Crown, which gave a right to vote if of the value of £400 Scots, was worth from £250 to £2500 sterling according to political conditions in the county.[1] The demand for compensation was resisted. Under the Representation of the People (Scotland) Act, 1832, there was no equivalent of the forty-shilling freeholder, but the vote was given to the £10 proprietor and the £50 leaseholder.

Before the Reform Act the burghs were represented in Parliament by an odd system of indirect election. The burghs were in groups; the municipal council in each burgh elected a commissioner to a convention, which then chose a member for the grouped burghs. Each commissioner had one vote, but the commissioner for the presiding burgh also had a casting vote; and the presiding burgh was the burgh next in the order of priority of creation as a burgh, starting with the oldest burgh in 1707. This system gave ample opportunity for factionalism and manipulation. The number of burgh councillors in 1831 was only 1303,[2] who were thus represented by fifteen members. Under the Representation of the People (Scotland) Act, 1832, the burgh franchise was virtually the same as the borough franchise in England and Wales. The result of this change, together with that in the counties, was that while Scotland was represented by forty tories and five whigs in 1831, it was represented by forty-four whigs and nine tories afterwards.[3] Indeed, Scotland only once failed to have a Liberal majority between 1832 and 1910, and that was at the khaki election of 1900.

The county franchise in Ireland, as in England, was based on the forty-shilling freeholder, though after 1795 he had to be in occupation if the annual value was less than £20. The borough franchise was as confused and as confusing as in England. In 1783, only eleven out of 117 boroughs were not under the control of patrons.[4] Some of the worst of the pocket boroughs disappeared at the Union, but it is said that in 1820 the election was really open only in four boroughs.[5] In 1829, as the price of Catholic emancipation, the county franchise was

---

[1] Porritt, *The Unreformed House of Commons*, II, p. 158.   [2] *Ibid.* p. 128.
[3] *Ibid.*; but some accounts make it forty-three whigs and ten tories.
[4] *Ibid.* p. 296.
[5] McDowell, *Public Opinion and Government Policy in Ireland, 1801–1846*, p. 44.

raised to £10 freehold, thus disfranchising the great mass of Irish peasants. The Representation of the People (Ireland) Act, 1832, extended this £10 freehold qualification to the leaseholders and copy-holders and gave the Irish boroughs the same £10 occupation qualification as in England. Though the electorate was even then still under 100,000, Ireland returned a majority of Liberals until 1859.

3. THE REFORM OF 1867

By 1866 the total electorate for the United Kingdom had risen to 1,136,000. Since the population in 1861 was 28,900,000, it followed that 3·9 per cent of the population had the vote. The Reform Acts of 1867 and 1868 raised the number of electors to 2,468,000, or 8·5 per cent of the population in 1861. This was due in the main to an increase in the number of borough electors, which was more than doubled, as the following figures, for England and Wales, testify:[1]

	Population	Electors 1865	Electors 1868
Counties	11,400,000	542,000	789,000
Boroughs	8,900,000	514,000	1,210,000

It will be seen that, while in the boroughs the percentage of electors was 13·6, in the counties it was only 7·0. This anomaly was to some extent offset by the redistribution provisions of 1868 which, as we have seen, decreased the representation of English boroughs and increased the representation of the English counties and of Scotland. The boroughs had, however, been seriously over-represented in 1866, having one seat for 26,000 population, while the counties had one seat for 70,000 population.[2]

In the English boroughs the £10 occupation franchise was abolished and replaced by two franchises, an occupation franchise and a lodger franchise. For the occupation franchise it was necessary to be, for the whole of the twelve months preceding 31 July, an inhabitant occupier, as owner or tenant, of any dwelling-house within the borough. For

[1] Seymour, *Electoral Reform in England and Wales*, p. 286. The population figure for boroughs is taken as half that of 1865 and 1868 added together.
[2] *Ibid.* p. 320.

the lodger franchise it was necessary to have occupied in the same borough separately and as sole tenant, for the twelve months preceding 31 July, the same lodgings, such lodgings being part of one and the same dwelling-house, and of a clear yearly value, if let unfurnished, of £10 or upwards. It was, however, necessary to make a specific claim for the lodger franchise.

In the English counties the vote was given to a man who was seised at law or in equity of lands or tenements, freehold, copyhold or otherwise, of the clear yearly value of not less than £5. Since the forty-shilling freehold franchise was retained, this in effect meant that the limit for copyholders was reduced from £10 to £5. Further, if a man held under a term of years originally created for sixty years or more, he could vote if the yearly value was £5. In addition there was an occupation franchise of £12. The provisions of the 1832 Act relating to leaseholds and tenants at will were left outstanding, but many who would have qualified under those provisions now qualified as £5 lease-holders or £12 occupiers. That some were still qualified under the 1832 Act above was shown by the 1883 figures given by Professor Seymour.[1]

Owners	514,226
£12 occupiers	356,344
£50 leaseholders	92,934
Total	963,504

In Scotland the same franchise was provided for burghs as for English boroughs. In the counties, too, the franchise was virtually the same as under the English Act of 1867, though the occupation franchise was fixed at £14.

In Ireland the franchise had been lowered in 1850, because so many of the Irish seats were still won by influence and corruption. An occupation franchise of £8 had then been given in the boroughs, and by the Act of 1868 it was lowered to £4. The Act of 1868 also gave a £10 lodger franchise, as in England. In the counties an occupation franchise of £12 had been introduced in 1850, and this was not altered in 1868.

[1] *Op. cit.* p. 286.

The general effect of these changes was to enfranchise the working-class householder in the towns but not in the counties, where £12 a year (£14 in Scotland) was still a high rent even for an urban cottage or tenement-house. Since there were many urban areas in the counties, it was difficult to justify this anomaly, even if it was just to distinguish between the urban worker and the rural worker on the assumption that the former was more likely to be literate and less under the control of a landlord. In most of the towns the workers were now in a clear majority. In the counties, on the other hand, the electors were mainly small farmers and the shopkeepers and wealthier artisans of the urban areas. It may be noted, too, that most of those who, under the Act of 1832, were not qualified in the towns but were qualified in the counties as forty-shilling freeholders were now qualified in the towns as occupiers, and were therefore no longer qualified as county electors.

For Disraeli and the Conservative party the Acts of 1867 and 1868 were more than a 'leap in the dark'; they were in fact a gamble. It was, however, not an unreasonable gamble. The party gained in the counties and did not lose much in the English boroughs. It lost more seats in Wales, Scotland and Ireland and therefore lost twenty seats between 1865 and 1868. On the other hand, it lost only three seats in England, while the Liberals gained five. In 1874, however, there was a violent swing in England, and moderate gains in Wales and Scotland, so that the Conservative party won a majority for the first time since 1841. The Conservatives were able to win every county seat in which the freeholders were swamped by the twelve-pound occupiers, even in industrial areas. The Conservatives also gained substantially in Greater London and in some of the medium-sized towns. The large towns, the county towns, the cathedral towns, and the smaller towns remained predominantly Liberal. These movements must not, however, be ascribed only to the Reform Acts. There was a general movement of opinion towards Conservatism in the second half of the nineteenth century.[1]

[1] See generally Seymour, *op. cit.* pp. 300–7.

4. THE REFORM OF 1884

The reform of 1867–8 was clearly an interim measure. It was difficult to draw a distinction between the urban worker and the rural worker, especially after literacy spread to the rural areas. Nor was the distinction between borough and county the same as the distinction between urban and rural. There were large rural boroughs in which 75,000 agricultural workers had the vote after 1868, and many urban areas in counties in which 400,000 tradesmen and artisans were not enfranchised.[1] Apart from one provision, of minor importance, relating to the boroughs, the Representation of the People Act, 1884, was designed to bring the counties into line with the boroughs and the burghs, and also to equate the franchise in all the countries of the United Kingdom. In effect, the main qualification became occupation of a dwelling-house for a period of twelve months preceding the qualifying date. The lodger franchise and the £10 occupation franchise (which would usually apply to a shop or office) were also extended to the counties.

The effect of the Act was to increase the electorate from 3,000,000 in 1883 to 5,700,000 in 1885, or from 8·6 per cent of the population in 1881 to 16·4 per cent. Table 13 shows the great increase in the counties (in England and Wales).[2]

	1883	1886
Owners	514,226	508,554
Occupiers	356,344	2,020,650
Leaseholders	92,934	—
Lodgers	—	8,973
Totals	963,504	2,538,177

TABLE 13

It will be seen that the owners (freeholders and copyholders) were still important, and this was so especially in thinly populated rural areas.

It may be a coincidence that there was a long period of Unionist rule, broken only by the short Liberal Governments of 1892 to 1895, from 1886 to 1906. As we shall see,[3] there are social, political and economic

[1] Seymour, *op. cit.* p. 462.   [2] *Ibid.* p. 479.   [3] Volume II.

reasons for that phenomenon, perhaps the most interesting in British politics. It is not entirely a coincidence, however, that in 1885 the counties and the boroughs were placed on an equivalent footing, so that the Conservative strength in the rural areas could compete with and actually win against the Liberal strength in urban areas. What happened in 1906 will need further investigation.

5. THE REFORMS OF 1918 AND 1928

Though in 1884 the electoral system went somewhere near the principle of 'one man, one vote, one value', near enough to allow the next generation to assume it as a major premise, it was not completely accepted. There were in 1891, in round figures, six million electors. The male population was then 18,300,000 and the adult males numbered nearly nine million. There were many electors with two votes because, in addition to the household franchise, there was in both counties and boroughs an occupation vote, applying particularly to business premises, and in the counties there was also an ownership vote. We may take it, therefore, that while there were nine million adult males, there were less than six million separate electors. Moreover no women were as yet enfranchised. There was much argument over the enfranchisement of women before 1914, but as often happens the argument had virtually disappeared by 1918.

The Representation of the People Act, 1918, was not designed to remove all these qualifications to the principle 'one person, one vote, one value'. It was a compromise among the parties and therefore a progressive measure, not a radical one. The conflict, which was not a conflict of parties, was over proportional representation and the alternative vote. Both were rejected, in spite of advocacy by the Liberal party and other 'cross-bench' members, who not only believed in them but stood to gain by them.

The Act of 1918 had two major objectives, to enfranchise all adult males, and to enfranchise all females aged thirty and above. Both objectives were attained by basing the franchise not on ownership or occupation but on residence. The occupation franchise of 1884 was, however, retained in the form of a 'business premises qualification', based upon the occupation of land or other premises of the value of no less than ten pounds for the purpose of business, profession or trade. This qualification had become slightly ridiculous: for since 1884 most businesses, though not most professions, had fallen into the hands—if they have hands—of limited liability companies. The village shop-keeper was enfranchised but not the multiple store; the stockbroker was enfranchised but not the bank; the 'doctor' was enfranchised but not the chemist's shop or the oculist; the accountant in private practice was enfranchised but not the railway accountants or the accountants to the Bank of England. The whole scheme was a compromise, and this particular arrangement helped the Conservative party, which dominated the Government after 1916, and with whom Lloyd George proposed to appeal to the country. Nor was it easy to justify the refusal of the franchise to the women under thirty, then known somewhat dis-respectfully as 'the flappers'. This particular limitation was however removed, rather unexpectedly, in 1928. The 'flappers' helped to bring in a Labour Government in 1929 and to destroy it in 1931.

The result of the 1918 Act was a very large increase in the electorate. In 1915 there were 8,400,000 electors; but in 1918 there were 21,400,000. Expressing these figures as percentages of the population in 1911, the electorate rose from 18·6 per cent to 47·3 per cent. In 1928 the electorate was 22,000,000; and in 1929 the addition of the 'flappers' made it 28,000,000. In terms of the population of 1921 it rose from 51·8 per cent to 65·4 per cent. It must be remembered that there was some duplication through the business premises qualification, though no person might exercise more than two votes, one of which must be the residential vote.

The number of persons registered for the business premises qualifi-cation in 1929 was 371,594.[1] The number of electors in 1929 was there-fore 27,600,000, or 64·3 per cent of the population in 1921. The effect of the 1928 Act, too, was to give the women electors a majority. They did not combine to turn out the men, and in fact the number of women members of Parliament rose very slowly.

[1] Butler, *The Electoral System in Britain, 1918–1951*, p. 147.

6. THE REFORMS OF 1945 AND 1948

The Speaker's Conference of 1944[1] recommended that the business premises qualification be retained, but that the wife or husband of the person so qualified should not have an extra vote. This recommendation was carried out by the Representation of the People Act, 1945. The business premises vote had been falling before the war; in 1945 it was only 48,974 and therefore insignificant.[2] The registers of electors were based on the National Registration and were very defective. Even so, they contained the names of 29,400,000 electors, or 58·5 per cent of the population in 1951.[3]

The business premises qualification was abolished by the Representation of the People Act, 1948, which also abolished the university seats. The principle of 'one adult, one vote' was thus at last carried out. The electorate in 1951 was 34,600,000 and the population 50,200,000, and so the electorate was 68·9 per cent of the population. The change since 1945 was due to more adequate registers: but the change since 1929 was due to the alteration in the balance in the population between minors and adults, due to the combination of a low birth rate and a low death rate.

[1] *Ante*, pp. 34–5.   [2] Butler, *loc. cit.*
[3] There was no census in 1941.

CHAPTER III

THE MACHINERY OF ELECTIONS

One of the polite fictions of electioneering is that everybody is anxious to vote but cannot make up his mind between candidates so worthy as Messrs Dodson and Fogg. Perhaps this derives from a period, not much more than a century ago, when the free and independent electors of so many famous boroughs required the touch of silver, or even of gold, to indicate to them which way to vote. These days being past, the assumption is that Messrs Dodson and Fogg have to tour the constituency, complete with rosettes and loudspeakers—bands and banners having been banned by law—in order to persuade the electors of their respective merits. The lesson which is taught in the schools for election agents is, however, or at least ought to be, that the great majority of the electors have no views on the respective merits of Messrs Dodson and Fogg and have no particular anxiety to acquire any. Messrs Dodson and Fogg are symbols, representing Mr Macmillan or the Labour party (the one party adopting the cult of the individual and the other not). The real task of electioneering is not to persuade the elector which way he ought to vote, but to persuade him to vote, or not to vote, as the case may be. Messrs Dodson and Fogg have to 'get out the vote'. Apathy in the west end or the east end, though distressing to both gentlemen as a matter of general principle, wears a different complexion as a matter of practical politics. According to Mr Dodson, apathy in the west end is to be deplored as indicating lack of patriotism, while apathy in the east end shows the extent to which Mr Fogg's party has lost popular support; to Mr Fogg, on the other hand, apathy in the west end shows that Mr Dodson's party has lost the support even of its friends, while apathy in the east end lets the workers down.

I. BEFORE 1832

Perhaps this has always been so, *mutatis mutandis*, since the beginning of the fifteenth century. Certainly elections have since then been organised on the assumption that Messrs Dodson and Fogg have wanted to be elected to Parliament and not many people wanted either of them. When elections began, and for most of the fourteenth century, representation was a burden, not an honour, and knights or burgesses were elected with as great reluctance as other commands in the King's writs were obeyed. The writs were sent to the sheriffs (including the sheriffs of towns which had them);[1] but they were so sent not because the sheriffs were impartial returning officers but because they were royal officers bound to execute the royal commands. The changes in the writs in the fourteenth century[2] were due mainly to an anxiety to get better representatives; but in the fifteenth century the changes were due to Acts of Parliament, and there was evidently an anxiety to prevent the elections from being manipulated, either by interested parties getting the writs into their own hands or by the sheriffs themselves.

The Act of 1406 to which reference has already been made[3] required that the election be held in the next county court, that those present proceed to the election freely and indifferently 'non obstant aucune prier ou comaundement au contrarie', and that the return be made by an indenture sealed by those present. This was presumably designed both to prevent royal interference and to provide for a genuine election. It did not, however, prevent the writ's being obtained by interested parties, who could then get an indenture sealed and return it with the writ.[4]

Complaints by the Commons in 1445 that election law was not being observed resulted in the lengthy statute 23 Hen. VI, c. 14. Having recited 1 Hen. V, c. 1, it added 'which citizens and burgesses have always... been chosen by citizens and burgesses and no other, and to the sheriffs of the counties returned'. It then recited 8 Hen. VI, c. 7 (the forty-shilling freeholder Act, 1430), and added that of late

divers sheriffs...for their singular avail and lucre, have not made due returns of the knights, nor in convenient time, nor good men and true returned, and sometimes no return of the knights, citizens and burgesses lawfully chosen...; but have returned such knights, citizens and burgesses

---

[1] For some of the earlier parliaments writs were sent to the mayors and bailiffs of towns, and this practice seems to be justified by the *Modus Tenendi Parliamenti*: but the fourteenth-century practice was to require the sheriff to return the elections of citizens and burgesses.   [2] Stubbs, *Constitutional History*, III, pp. 396–401.

[3] 7 Hen. IV, c. 15; *ante*, p. 45.

[4] Porritt, *The Unreformed House of Commons*, I, pp. 21–2.

which were never duly chosen, and other citizens and burgesses than those which by the mayor and bailiffs were to the said sheriffs returned; and sometimes the sheriffs have not returned the writs, but the said writs have imbeziled (embezzled); and moreover made no precept to the mayor and bailiff or to the bailiffs or bailiff where no mayor is. . . .

It was therefore enacted that the said statutes be duly kept in all points; that every sheriff issue a precept to the mayor and bailiff, or bailiffs or bailiff where no mayor is, commanding them to choose, by the citizens or burgesses, citizens or burgesses to come to Parliament; that the mayor and bailiffs, etc., lawfully return the said precept to the same sheriff, by indentures between them and the sheriff, with the names of the persons chosen; and thereupon that every sheriff shall make a good and lawful return of every such writ, and of every return by mayor and bailiff. Penalties for breaches of the statutes were added. It was further provided that an election of knights was to take place in full county court between 8 a.m. and 11 a.m.

The fifteenth-century procedure, therefore, was to have an election between 8 a.m. and 11 a.m. at the next ordinary meeting of the county court, all forty-shilling freeholders being entitled to the vote. In the case of a borough, the sheriff sent a precept to the mayor (or bailiffs) and the mayor held an election among burgesses whose qualifications were prescribed by local custom. The mayor (or bailiffs) returned the names under indenture; and the sheriff returned the writ with an indenture sealed by those present at the election in county court. It will be noticed that there was no statutory provision for a poll but it seems to have been the practice, at least in the counties. Coke says[1] that if one be demanded the sheriff cannot deny the scrutiny, 'for he cannot discerne who be freeholders by the view'. The same argument would apply to a borough election unless it was either a close borough, in which the corporation alone elected, or an open borough, in which everybody could vote. If election was by scot and lot, or by freemen, or by persons holding by burgage tenure, a scrutiny would be needed. There were, however, no registers of electors.

The process of election began again to be regulated by statute after the Revolution of 1688. By the statute 7 & 8 Will. III, c. 25 (1696), it

[1] 4 Inst. 48.

was provided that there should be forty days between the *teste* (i.e. the issue of the writs) and the return of the writs of summons. The writs should be issued to the officer concerned with execution, and nobody else, and the date of receipt must be endorsed on the back. The person concerned (usually the sheriff) was required forthwith to make out a precept for each borough and within three days to deliver it to the proper officer and nobody else; the proper officer must endorse the writ, give public notice of the election forthwith, and proceed to election within eight days. The Act further provided that upon every election for a knight of the shire the sheriff must hold his county court 'at the most publick and usual place of election, and where the same has most usually been for forty years, and shall there proceed to election at the next county court...and then shall adjourn the court to some convenient day, giving ten days notice of the time and place of election'. If the election was not determined upon the view of hands (or the hearing of voices) and a poll was required, the sheriff or the under-sheriff and his deputies must forthwith proceed to take the poll 'in some open place or places'. Clerks were to be appointed and sworn 'truly and indifferently to take (the poll) and to set down the names of each freeholder, and the place of his freehold, and for whom he shall poll, and to poll no freeholder who is not sworn, if required by the candidates'. Moreover the sheriff was to appoint persons, nominated by each of the candidates, to be 'inspectors' of every clerk. The county court was not to be adjourned to some other place without the consent of the candidates, but was to proceed from day to day.

The statute 10 Anne, c. 23 (1712) added that the polling clerk must take the address of each voter as well as his freehold, and that after the election the sheriff must deliver the poll-books to the clerk of the peace. It will be seen that the procedure might be slow and that an election might take a week or ten days. It was also expensive, for the freeholders had to be brought into the county town and entertained at the expense of the candidates or their friends. The statute 18 Geo. II, c. 18 (1744) tried to accelerate matters by requiring the sheriff to erect, at the expense of the candidates, such number of booths or places for taking the poll as any of the candidates should, three days at least before the commencement of the poll, require. There was, however, a limit of fifteen, or less if there were few rapes, wards, wapentakes, hundreds, etc. There was to be a clerk in each booth, who should be paid not more than a guinea a day, at the expense of the candidates. The rape, ward, etc., was to be marked in the booth, and the sheriff was required to compile a list, for each booth, of the towns, villages, parishes and hamlets lying wholly or partly within the rape, etc. The same Act allowed each 'inspector' to keep a 'check-book', i.e. to duplicate the poll-book as a check on the polling clerk.

There was other legislation relating to counties of towns and the City of London. In London, by the statute 11 Geo. I, c. 18, the poll had to be finished within seven days and the poll-books then sealed in the presence of the candidates. The seals were broken, and the number of votes declared, at the place of election (usually Guildhall). If a scrutiny was demanded it had to be granted, and the candidates nomi-nated scrutineers who went through the lists and checked the qualifi-cations of the electors against the lists of liverymen supplied by the Livery Companies.

It must be remembered that a great many elections were not contested, especially in the boroughs. Where the electors were few and influence strong, as was usually the case, it was useless to challenge a contest. The expense of a contested election was so heavy that nobody would spend money on a hopeless struggle, though it might be desirable to fight a losing battle in order gradually to build up a connexion which would oust the prevailing influence. Since polling was open and the 'inspector' had copies of the poll-books, it was known from hour to hour how the candidates were faring; and the losing candidates would probably concede the election unless they knew that they had substantial reserves ready to bring up. How the election went when it was fought to the bitter end may be judged from the by-election in Northamptonshire in 1730.[1] This was due to the death of Sir Justinian Isham, Bart., who had been a county member since 1698. Though a tory, he had managed to survive the Hanoverian Succession because of a division among the whigs. Since neither whigs nor tories had an unchallenged majority, a compact was arranged for the general elections of 1722 and 1727,

[1] E. G. Forrester, *Northamptonshire County Elections and Electioneering, 1695–1832*, pp. 46–59.

under which the county and the borough seats could be filled without contests. It was not so easy to reach agreement at a by-election, and in 1730 Mr William Hanley was put up as a whig candidate against Sir Justinian's son, also called Sir Justinian.

The sheriff published the date of the election and stated that it would take place 'on or near the Bowling Green on Northampton Heath'. It was then, apparently, adjourned for the poll. On 8 June Sir Justinian Isham proceeded to Northampton 'with a considerable Body of Gentlemen, Clergy and Freeholders'. Four booths were erected on the Market Hill and two out of the town 'for the convenience of those who were apprehensive of the smallpox'. Mr Hanley asked for another on Wood Hill, but this was not granted. On this first night Mr Hanley had a majority of above forty. On the ninth many were polled, Lord St John and Lucy Knightley, Esq., bringing in 'great Bodys of Men'. Sir Justinian had a majority of seventy-four. On the 10th Sir Justinian again had a majority, and he was chaired by the mob, though improperly because the poll had not closed. On the eleventh the poll was closed, Sir Justinian having a majority of 171. Mr Hanley demanded a scrutiny, which was refused, and Sir Justinian was chaired. There was a scrutiny, but perhaps only in case of an election petition. Lists of freeholders were made up and sent to landowners for checking, and copies of the poll-books were sent to Lords Northampton and St John. It appears that both candidates had some bad votes (e.g. copyholders), but eventually Mr Hanley acquiesced in the election. It will be noted that the arrangements contemplated by the Act of 1744 were in operation in the county, though that Act had not yet been passed.

The Act of 1712 required that the freehold be assessed to the 'public taxes, church rates, and parish duties', but this was sufficiently vague on the one hand to make it easy to challenge votes on a scrutiny and on the other hand to make it impracticable to use a taxation list as a register of electors. The Act 20 Geo. III, c. 17 (1781) altered the requirement into assessment to the land tax, so that the land tax registers became informal registers of electors. The Act 28 Geo. III, c. 36 (1788) in fact provided for registers of freeholders; but the cost proved to be so great that the Act was repealed in 1789.[1]

---

[1] 29 Geo. III, c. 13: see Porritt, *The Unreformed House of Commons*, I, pp. 27–8.

2. FROM THE REFORM ACT TO 1917

The absence of registers of electors and the complications of the franchise before 1832 gave great power to the returning officers, who could reject a vote on the ground that the voter was not qualified. In *Barnardiston* v. *Soame*,[1] where it was alleged that the sheriff had maliciously made a double return to the writ, the Court of Exchequer Chamber had held that the sheriff was a judge of the qualifications of the electors, and could therefore not be sued for damages, that in any event the proper remedy was in Parliament, and that in a doubtful case a double return was a lawful procedure. Moreover the statute 23 Hen. VI, c. 15, had provided a statutory remedy, so that no action lay at common law. Legislation was then enacted against false and double returns,[2] but this did not affect the ruling that the sheriff was not liable for maliciously refusing a vote. In *Ashby* v. *White*,[3] however, it was held that an action did lie. The plaintiff alleged that he was an elector of the borough of Aylesbury and that his vote had unlawfully and maliciously been rejected by the defendants, the constables of Aylesbury, to whom a precept for the election of two burgesses had been issued by the sheriff of Buckinghamshire. Verdict being given for the plaintiff, a motion to arrest judgment was moved in the Court of Queen's Bench and approved, Lord Holt C.J. dissenting. On a writ of error to the House of Lords this judgment was reversed on the grounds stated by Lord Holt. These were, in effect, that the constables were not judges but executive officers and could be sued, that the plaintiff had a right which gave him a remedy at law, that he had suffered damage, and that he was entitled to his remedy for that damage in the Queen's courts. This decision led to a conflict between the House of Lords and the House of Commons, the latter House claiming privilege. This is not a matter which concerns us: but the cases show the difficulties involved in giving the sheriffs and the officers of boroughs power to determine who might or might not vote at elections.

---

[1] (1644) 6 St. Tr. 1063. Affirmed in the House of Lords: see Broom, *Constitutional Law*, p. 839.

[2] 7 & 8 Will. III, c. 5; made permanent by 12 Anne st. 1, c. 15.

[3] (1704) 14 St. Tr. 695; 2 Lord Raym. 1105.

Another objection to the procedure in operation before 1832 was, as we have seen, that it involved lengthy and therefore expensive elections. One of the objectives of the Representation of the People Act, 1832, was to reduce the cost of elections. One solution was the division of large counties into two or three constituencies, and this was done with twenty-six counties. A second solution, also adopted by the Act, was to divide each county constituency into polling districts as provided by the 2 & 3 Will. IV, c. 64 (1832), subject to the proviso that there were not to be more than fifteen polling districts in any county constituency. In the case of a city or borough the returning officer was bound, if required to do so by any candidate, and in any case was enabled if he thought it expedient, to establish different polling booths for different parishes, districts, or parts of the city or borough. Each booth was to be divided into compartments, so that not more than 600 electors would be required to poll in one compartment. These booths might be at different places; and, if they were, the returning officer was authorised to appoint deputies to preside at each of them.

The main solution, however, was to provide for registers of electors and to take away from the returning officers the duty of holding a scrutiny. The duty of preparing the registers was placed upon the overseers of the poor. Applications for registration had to be made to them by fixed dates in each year and the overseers were required to publish lists of persons claiming. Objections might be taken to any names on the list, and such objections were to be heard by barristers appointed by the Judges of Assize or the Lord Chief Justice. The list of freemen in a borough was, however, compiled by the town clerk.

The provision of electoral registers enabled the period of the election to be cut down to two consecutive days, the poll being open for seven hours on the first day and eight hours on the second. At the close of the poll the poll-books were to be sealed and delivered by hand to the returning officer, who was to hold them sealed until the next day (not being a Sunday), when he might break the seals, count up the number of votes, openly declare the state of the poll, and make proclamation of the member or members chosen.

These provisions placed on the elector the duty of being registered, and in fact a charge of one shilling was made. A county elector had to claim once only, for he was retained on the register unless his qualification altered or he changed his residence. A borough elector had, however, to apply every year. If an objection was made to a claim, the claimant had either to appear and defend his claim or have his claim disallowed. The anticipation, based upon the public agitation for reform, that everybody entitled would claim his vote and insist upon it, proved to be unjustified. Many persons qualified did not claim; it was easy to get valid claims struck off because claimants could not be bothered to attend before revising barristers; and many claims were struck out on technical grounds—for instance, that the claimant had moved house since he made his claim, though still resident in the constituency, or that he had not paid his rates in time. What is more, many persons who were otherwise qualified were disqualified because they paid rent inclusive of rates (the so-called 'compounders'). On the other hand, it was still possible to create faggot votes, e.g. by creating £10 leaseholders or even forty-shilling freeholders.[1] Thus the provisions of the Reform Act provided ample scope for the new party organisations and the Anti-Corn Law League.

The provisions of the Representation of the People Act, 1832, relating to registration were repealed and re-enacted with amendments by the Parliamentary Voters Registration Act, 1843. The changes made were not, however, either numerous or important. The only clause designed to meet the inefficiency of the overseers merely provided that in a county the clerk of the peace and in a borough the town clerk should issue his precept and supply forms. The precepts gave instructions about the compilation of registers and probably improved administration. The duty of compiling lists in a borough was, however, now placed on the overseers, without claim by the elector, except where his name had been omitted or he desired to be registered for a different qualification. Moreover the overseers were to publish notices drawing attention to the date before which rates must be paid. The mere fact that a person had changed his address would no longer disqualify, since the revising barrister was empowered to insert the new address. The revising barrister was authorised to award costs to a person claiming or a person objecting and to fine overseers for neglect

[1] See Seymour, *Electoral Reform in England and Wales*, pp. 116–24.

of duty. Finally, the fee of one shilling for making a claim was abolished.

Some minor modifications were made before 1867. The Compound Householders Act, 1851, made it unnecessary for the 'compounder', who had claimed to pay rates personally in order to secure the franchise, to renew his claim annually. The County Voters Registration Act, 1865, provided that a notice of objection, other than a notice to overseers, must specify the grounds of the objection.

The Representation of the People Act, 1867, sought to remove the difficulty over 'compounding' by abolishing it, but this caused immediate difficulties. In some boroughs the Act was ignored and compounding continued, with the result that in some boroughs the tenants got the vote and in others they did not. The Poor Rents Assessment Act, 1869, therefore allowed compounding, but provided that the names of compounders should be entered on the registers. In other respects the difficulties remained, and indeed were increased by the need to claim for the lodger franchise. Minor modifications, directed mainly to getting the initial lists more accurate and avoiding frivolous or malevolent objections, were made in 1878 and 1885.[1] Generally, however, the system became more efficient after 1885 not by changes in the law but by improved administration. Under the Local Government Act, 1888, the Crown was empowered to alter the instructions, precepts, notices and forms under the Registration of Electors Acts. A comprehensive order, known as the Registration Order, 1895, was issued under this power and set out in great detail the procedure to be observed by overseers in accordance with their precepts. In effect, the Home Office had taken over the responsibility for supervising elections, though technically the precepts still went from the clerks of the peace and the town clerks. The procedure thus became uniform throughout the country and the machinery of registration efficiently run. So the law remained up to 1917.

It has been thought desirable to continue the story of registration from 1832 to 1917 without reference to parallel changes in other branches of election law. The registration provisions of the Reform Act were sufficiently successful to enable borough elections to be cut

[1] Parliamentary and Municipal Registration Act, 1878; Registration Act, 1885.

down to one day by the Parliamentary Elections Act, 1835. By the Parliamentary Elections Act, 1853, the ancient practice of including in the writs to the sheriffs a direction to elect citizens and burgesses for cities and boroughs was at last changed. Henceforth writs were to issue direct to the returning officers of cities and boroughs and to the vice-chancellors of the universities. They were to make returns in accordance with the directions of the writs (i.e. direct to the Chancery). Incidentally in respect of boroughs this abolished the form of election in the county court, which had long been extinct in practice because sheriffs, unless diligent antiquarians or learned lawyers, probably did not even known that they were sitting in county court.[1]

The greatest change, however, was the enactment of the Ballot Act in 1872, as a temporary measure which was not made permanent until 1918.[2] The main purposes of the Act were to substitute written nominations for oral nominations at the assembly in the county court or other place determined by statute or custom, and to substitute a poll by secret ballot for a poll on the hustings (technically the polling booths) by oral declaration to the polling clerk. The ballot had been proposed in the report of the Cabinet Committee which prepared the first Reform Bill, but the proposal was rejected by the Cabinet.[3] It was one of the points of the People's Charter. The proposal had been brought forward almost annually. The main objection to it was inarticulate, that members elected, by influence and otherwise, without a poll or on the hustings, could not be sure that they would be re-elected if there were a secret ballot. There were, however, articulate objections, formulated by John Stuart Mill.[4] The vote was a trust, which should be exercised in the public interest, not in the private interest of the elector. To vote was a duty, not a right. The elector's vote had no more to do with his personal wishes than the verdict of a jury. Mill was well aware that a vote in public might in practice be exercised not in the public interest but in the private interest of some person who had control over the

---

[1] The Sheriffs Act, 1887, section 18, made it unnecessary to hold a county court, except for an election or the execution of a writ.

[2] It was originally in force up to 31 December 1880, but was continued annually by Expiring Laws Continuance Acts.

[3] J. R. M. Butler, *The Passing of the Great Reform Bill*, p. 184.

[4] *Representative Government*, ch. x.

elector: but the power of coercing electors had declined and was declining, so that the elector had to be protected more against his own sinister interests and discreditable feelings than against influences from others. These and other arguments, added to the inarticulate objection of the member of Parliament to change a system which was so good that it had elected him, proved sufficiently convincing until 1867. The enfranchisement of the urban workers by the second Reform Act convinced the Liberal party that the ballot was needed to protect the electors against the pressure of landlords and employers. 'Experience showed that without secrecy in its exercise the suffrage was not free. The farmer was afraid of his landlord, and the labourer was afraid of the farmer; the employer could tighten the screw on the workman, the shopkeeper feared the power of his best customers, the debtor quailed before his creditor, the priest wielded thunderbolts over the faithful. Not only was the open vote not free; it exposed its possessor to so much bullying, molestation, and persecution, that his possession came to be less of a boon than a nuisance.'[1] If these arguments, expressed with Mr Morley's literary exaggeration, did not prevail, there was an inarticulate argument which became more convincing as the whigs turned Conservative, that influence was more likely to favour the Conservatives than the Liberals, and accordingly the ballot was more likely to favour the Liberals than the Conservatives. The House of Lords duly opposed the ballot as another attempt to subvert the Constitution and another danger to the monarchy. The usual attack on a hereditary peerage having developed, the peers came to the conclusion when the second Ballot Bill came up that it had been adequately discussed, and the Bill passed as a temporary measure.

The Ballot Act did not extinguish all the old law. The writ was still issued by the Clerk of the Crown in Chancery (who had replaced the Clerk of the Petty Bag), but a new form was prescribed by the Ballot Act, and the returning officer was directed to cause an election to be made not of knights for the shire or citizens for the city or burgesses for the borough, but of members or a member; and a separate writ was issued for every division of a county. Though 7 & 8 Will. III, c. 25 required the writ to be delivered to the proper officer, it did not say

[1] *Life of Gladstone*, II, p. 366.

how: but the 53 Geo. III, c. 89 provided that (except in London and Middlesex) the messenger or pursuivant of the Great Seal, or his deputy, should deliver the writ to the General Post Office, by which it was to be conveyed to the local postmaster, and he was to deliver it to the returning officer. Various precautions were laid down to meet the old difficulty that the messenger might be waylaid and a false return made.

By the 15 & 16 Vict. c. 23, thirty-five days were allowed for the return to the writ.[1] Within two days of the receipt of the writ in a county, and on the date of receipt or the following day in a borough, the returning officer was directed by the Ballot Act to give public notice between 9 a.m. and 4 p.m. of the day and place at which he would proceed to an election and of the time of the election, and of the day on which a poll would be taken in case the election was contested, and of the time and place at which forms of nomination papers might be obtained. His discretion in these respects was, however, strictly limited by the rules, and as to place his discretion was further limited by the Redistribution of Seats Act, 1885, as amended by the Local Government Act, 1888, which authorised the county council to fix the place in every county division.

At the place of election, within the times fixed, the returning officer was to receive nominations for election, in writing subscribed by two electors as proposer and seconder and by eight other electors as assenting to the nomination; and a nomination was to be delivered by the candidate or his proposer or seconder. No person was allowed to be present except the persons assisting the returning officer, the candidate, his proposer, his seconder, and one other person selected by the candidate. Detailed rules about nomination papers were laid down and objections could be made before the expiry of the time appointed for the election. Such an objection could be determined by the returning officer, but only if it was an objection to the nomination paper: he could not determine, for instance, whether the candidate was qualified for election. On receiving the nomination paper the returning officer was to publish the names of the candidate or candidates and his or their proposers and

---

[1] By ancient custom approved by 7 & 8 Will. III, c. 25, the period was forty days, but the Act of Union with Scotland allowed fifty days.

seconders, by placards outside the building. If at the expiration of one hour after the time appointed for election no more candidates had been nominated than there were vacancies to be filled, the returning officer was to declare them elected, make a return, and give public notice. If more candidates were nominated than there were places to be filled, he was to adjourn the election and take the poll, giving public notice of the date. The public concourse, the election by view (i.e. show of hands) or voice (i.e. shouts), and the demand for a poll, as required by the old law, were thus abolished.

Polling districts in county constituencies were provided for by the Reform Acts of 1832; and by the Reform Act of 1867 the justices in sessions had power to divide a county constituency. Later on the Corrupt and Illegal Practices Prevention Act, 1883, required that polling districts be so assigned that, so far as practicable, every elector resident in the county had a polling place within three miles of his residence, the division being made, after 1888, by the county council. There was no express power to divide a borough into polling districts until the Reform Act of 1867, which vested the power in the town council. It was enlarged by the Act of 1883.

Under the Reform Act of 1832, as already mentioned, the sheriff was empowered (and at the request of a candidate compelled) to set up polling booths. The term 'booth' was replaced by 'station' by the Ballot Act, and the returning officer was required, in a borough as in a county, to provide polling stations.[1] The change of name was due to the fact that, wherever practicable, the returning officer was to hire a building (or use a school) instead of erecting a polling booth. The cost of booths (or stations) was still charged to the candidates.[2]

The Ballot Act laid down in great detail the procedure at a poll. It has been found by experience to have been very well drafted, and for all practical purposes it is still in force. At each polling station there can be only the presiding officer and his clerks (under the Ballot Act appointed by the returning officer), the agents of the candidates, and

[1] The power in a borough was given by 9 Geo. IV, c. 59, where the number of electors exceeded 600. The Reform Act of 1867 required the provision of polling booths where a borough was divided into polling districts.
[2] Representation of the People Act, 1832, s. 71.

the constables on duty. All these are sworn. The agents of the candidates are there to watch the procedure and to challenge impersonators. The ballot box is sealed by the presiding officer, after demonstrating that it is empty, at the commencement of the poll, and the candidates' agents may affix their seals also. The elector's right to vote is determined by the register. He receives a ballot paper, giving the names of the candidates (but not their parties), which he marks in a compartment. This ballot paper is torn from a book and numbered on the back, and the elector's own number is marked on the counterfoil, but no mark may be made on the ballot paper to identify the elector. Before it is handed to him the ballot paper is stamped on both sides, usually by imperforation, and he must show the mark on the back when he drops the ballot paper, folded, into the ballot box. The fact that a ballot paper has been issued is marked on the register. If a ballot paper has already been issued in an elector's name, he receives a 'tendered ballot paper' of a different colour, which must be delivered to the presiding officer when marked, and kept in a separate packet. In no case can the presiding officer refuse a ballot paper (or a tendered ballot paper) unless it appears to him, after putting the statutory questions,[1] that the person who gives a name on the register is not that person, or has previously voted at that election, or refuses to answer either question, or refuses to take the oath or make the affirmation. The polling agent of a candidate can challenge a person for impersonation and require that the statutory oath (or affirmation) be put to him, but he cannot stop him from voting or insist that he be given a tendered ballot paper.

At the end of the poll the presiding officer must seal the ballot box so as to prevent the introduction of additional papers, and seal in separate parcels the unused and spoiled ballot papers, the tendered ballot papers, the marked copies of the register and the counterfoils of the ballot paper, and certain other documents. The candidates' agents may, if they wish, affix their seals also. The presiding officer must also prepare a statement accounting for the ballot papers delivered to him. All this must be delivered to the returning officer, who counts the votes in the presence of the candidates and their agents. The returning

[1] These were, in 1872, prescribed by 2 & 3 Will. IV, c. 45; 6 & 7 Vict. c. 18: see also 48 & 49 Vict. c. 23.

officer must open the boxes in the presence of the agents, take out the papers, count them, and record the number, and then mix them. During counting of the papers or the votes, the ballot papers must be kept face upwards, so as not to show the numbers on the backs. Tendered ballot papers are not counted and the sealed packages must not be opened. Nor must the other sealed packets be opened.

A ballot paper must be counted unless

(1) it has not the official mark on the back, or

(2) votes are given to more candidates than the elector is entitled to vote for, or

(3) anything except the number on the back is written or marked on the ballot paper by which the elector can be identified, or

(4) it is unmarked, or

(5) it is not certain for whom the elector intended to vote.

If this procedure is followed in detail (and it always is) the election is unimpeachable except for corrupt or illegal practices. In a single-member constituency the total number of votes counted should be equal to the total number of ballot papers counted, and this should be equal to the total number of ballot papers issued by presiding officers as recorded in their statements. It should also correspond (if a court order a scrutiny) with the number of marks on the registers, and should be the total number of ballot papers issued to returning officers less the unused ballot papers and spoilt ballot papers in the sealed packets. There is the additional check that every ballot paper must be stamped before issue, and every ballot paper counted must have the official mark so stamped.

Secrecy is maintained because the elector cannot be identified unless the sealed parcel of counterfoils is opened, and this cannot be done except on the instructions of a court.

3. SINCE 1918

The Representation of the People Act, 1918, completely recast the system of registration. The overseers and the revising barristers disappeared. There were to be two registers each year, compiled by a statutory registration officer, who was generally to be the clerk to the county council or the town clerk, though in certain cases he might be the clerk of an urban district council or a metropolitan borough, or the Secondary of the City of London.[1] The duty of compiling a register was placed upon the registration officer under the direction of the Home Secretary[2] and the details of procedure were laid down in an Order in Council usually known as R.P. 134. In effect the register was first compiled by canvass. Thereafter three electors' lists were published; the current register; the list of newly qualified electors; and the list of persons who had ceased to be qualified. This made it possible to see what names were being added and deleted. Claims and objections could then be made and were determinable by the registration officer, subject to an appeal to the county court. The lists were then combined into a new register.

The Ballot Act was made permanent and only minor modifications were made in its provisions. The dates for the specific steps in an election were, however, prescribed, and at a general election all polls had to be held on one day, thus avoiding the influence of one election on another and also the concentration of party effort at the later elections. A beginning was also made with a system of voting by post and by proxy in certain very limited cases. Finally, every candidate was required to deposit a sum of £150 with the returning officer. This deposit was to be forfeited if he was not elected and the number of votes polled by him did not exceed one-eighth of the total votes polled.

The returning officer was to be the sheriff in the case of a county or county of a city or a town having a sheriff, and the mayor or chairman of the district council in the case of every other parliamentary borough. The expenses of returning officers were charged on the Consolidated Fund.[3] Generally speaking, however, the duties of the returning officer were to be discharged by the registration officer as acting returning officer. New rules were laid down for the division of constituencies into polling districts and the provision of polling places 'in such manner as to give to all electors in the constituency such reasonable

[1] There has been only one register a year since 1926: see now Electoral Registers Act, 1949.

[2] Originally the Local Government Board; the function was transferred to the Home Office in 1921.

[3] After 1919: in 1918 they were payable out of moneys provided by Parliament.

facilities for voting as are practicable in the circumstances', and there was an appeal to the Home Office.

These provisions were modified for the general election of 1945 because, owing to the war, full registers could not be compiled; and we need note only the extension of postal voting and voting by proxy. The more permanent arrangement was made by the Representation of the People Act, 1948. The changes were, however, incidental and the Ballot Act, as amended, was continued. There was an extension of 'absent voters' sufficiently great to make an appreciable difference in some constituencies, and detailed rules were laid down for voting by post and by proxy.

Finally, the whole of the law relating to parliamentary elections was consolidated in the Representation of the People Act, 1949, which includes the provisions of and repeals the Ballot Act. It occupies 273 pages. Reference must also be made to the Electoral Registers Acts, 1949 and 1953.

CHAPTER IV

OLD CORRUPTION

I. EIGHTEENTH-CENTURY CONDITIONS

'Old Corruption' was William Cobbett's description of the British Constitution. It is, however, a little hard to judge one century by the standards of another. A Georgian gentleman, surveying the Conservative party through his eye-glass, would want to know how the whig lords came to nominate this distressing collection of tradesmen. Turning to survey the Labour benches, he would remark that nothing good ever came out of those popular constituencies. It would of course be pointed out to him that as a result of Burke's Economy Act it had become necessary to find places and pensions for all members of Parliament, so that they are all Treasury hacks. Even the peers are paid three guineas a day out of public funds. Nobody can get elected to the House of Commons unless he has either Treasury influence or the support of the mob. The days when freeholders elected independent country gentlemen and great landowners found seats for able young men are, alas, gone for ever. Nowadays, property is confiscated unless it is made by gambling in South Sea stock, the Duke of Norfolk has had to ask Parliament to break his entail, and the extent of the Bedford interest depends upon how many people order a dish of tea at Woburn.

Only for the last hundred years has a general election been regarded as an occasion for the electors to go to the poll. In the eighteenth century most elections were uncontested. In 1761 the electors went to the poll in only forty-eight out of 315 constituencies.[1] Between 1768 and 1818 there were fifty-three counties in England and Wales, but on the average only between six and seven went to the poll, the largest number being ten in 1818 and the smallest three in 1780. In the same period there were 217 boroughs in England and Wales, and on the average fifty-four went to the poll, the largest number being seventy-

---

[1] Namier, *The Structure of Politics at the Accession of George III*, 1, p. 196.

five in 1818 and the smallest forty-two in 1774.[1] In Scotland contests were as rare as the sunshine. There was greater electoral activity after the first Reform Act. In 1832, 1835 and 1837 a majority of the constituencies went to the poll, though in 1841 there were polls in only 188 of the 401 constituencies in the United Kingdom (146 out of 284 in England and Wales), and in 1847 there were polls in 164 out of 400 constituencies. There was again an increase after the second Reform Act (1867). In 1865 there were 293 uncontested elections and in 1868 only 130. In England and Wales in the latter year there were only seventy uncontested, whereas in 1865 there were 161.

Through the researches of Mr E. G. Forrester,[2] we have a record of all the county elections for Northampton from 1695 to 1832. Of the six elections between 1695 and 1705, inclusive, all but one were contested. From 1708 to 1832 inclusive, there were thirty-five elections: of these only four were contested, two of them at by-elections. The two general elections at which the seats were contested were significant. In 1806 party lines were becoming firmer and Lord Althorp's decision to break down what had been a tory monopoly for a century was due (only in part) to the fact that his father, Earl Spencer, had some influence in the county. From then until 1830 the county was shared by the whigs and the tories. In 1831, however, Lord Althorp was joined by a second Reformer. Northamptonshire was not a county in which there was any dominating influence. A substantial number of peers and gentry had some influence, and the county prided itself on its independence. The 'peace of the county', as the long period of electoral passivity was called, was due in part to the expense of county elections. Mr Forrester does not give the cost of the elections of 1806 and 1831, though in the former it was obviously heavy. In 1698 the cost to one successful candidate was less than £200.[3] In 1748, a sum of £1360 was raised by subscription. The sheriff's bill for customary fees and tips was £148 and was met by subscription. One supporter of the successful candidate spent £379. The candidate himself paid £689 for canvassing, and

---

[1] These figures are calculated from those given in Jephson, *The Platform, passim.* Jephson omits the elections of 1800 and 1807.

[2] *Northamptonshire County Elections and Electioneering, 1695–1832.*

[3] *Ibid.* p. 22, n. 5.

voters' expenses, the cost of polling booths, and other customary expenses. His bills for entertainment totalled £4176, but many of these were fraudulently inflated. One publican claimed for 409½ gallons of ale, though investigation showed that he had drawn only 195 gallons. There was similar overcharging for lodging, stabling and meals.[1]

Expenses of this order, and they probably grew during the second half of the eighteenth century, were conducive to 'the peace of the county', but that peace was also due to deliberate policy. A contested election involved battles among the noblemen and squires who had influence; and, since they would be in large measure personal owing to the weakness, if not non-existence, of the party system, they would interfere with the amenities of daily life. The modern Englishman's dislike of squabbles over religion or politics was shared by his ancestors, and in the eighteenth century it was impossible to fight an election without squabbles. There was much criticism of Lord Althorp's candidature in 1806, not merely because he was a whig and the scion of a noble house, but also because he upset the peace of the county.

In the middle of the twentieth century most of the candidates do not expect to get elected. Indeed, if there is a sudden swing of opinion, as in 1931, some of the successful candidates are embarrassed by their success. Most candidates are fighting 'forlorn hopes' with no hopes whatever, even forlorn. They are undergraduate members of the class of parliamentary candidates, hoping to graduate to more likely constituencies next time. They are supported, and indeed put forward, by the organised parties because in the long run no seat is safe. Even Merthyr Tydfil will go Conservative when the mines have been exhausted or the miners drive to the pits in their Bentleys. In any case the Conservative party must not admit that it has nothing to offer the miners except blood, tears, toil, sweat and pit-head baths. The chance that Cheltenham will 'go Labour' is even higher. Even if nobody puts an atomic energy pile in the constituency, the Labour party can claim to be the saviour of the new underdog, the salaried man and the pensioner. The Labour party, too, must claim the middle-class vote, for it will never win a general election without it. Moreover constituency boundaries are no longer permanent and a change may alter the

[1] Forrester, *op. cit.* pp. 68–9.

balance of parties. Even more important is the fact that electors are so mobile. The potential Conservative in Merthyr Tydfil or the potential Labour voter in Cheltenham may be registered in a marginal constituency next time. He must therefore be 'educated' to vote the right way. A contested election is the best type of propaganda, and in any event a constituency party must have the stimulus of a contest if it is to remain efficient as a propaganda machine.

We have, however, properly changed to twentieth-century concepts. In the eighteenth century nobody would be so stupid as to go to the poll and bear the enormous expense involved unless his canvass showed that he was likely to win—unless like Henry Brougham he decided to challenge the Lonsdale interest for the sake of the notoriety. The county seats, if contested, were usually the most expensive, not because of bribery, but because the inevitable costs became, as the century proceeded, very high. Everybody having an official part in the election, from the deputy sheriffs downwards, expected to be well paid for his services, and the customary charges tended to rise. Outvoters—i.e. freeholders who lived outside the county—expected to be brought in and lodged at the candidates' expense. Though the gentry would drive or ride to the county town and might even wish to bring in their tenants (i.e. freeholders who held of them in chief, and freeholders who were also copyholders, leaseholders, etc.) at their own expense in order to show the extent of their influence, a great deal of the expense of hiring carriages and horses and providing stabling would fall on the candidates. Part of the technique of electioneering consisted in convincing one's opponent that he was going to lose and so persuading him to 'decline the poll' (i.e. to use the Americanism, concede the election); and for this purpose it might be necessary to house large batches of electors while awaiting the psychological moment. In any case, there had to be substantial quantities of free ale and food, and not too many questions asked about the qualifications of the consumers or the quantities consumed. In the nineteenth century this was the corrupt practice of 'treating', but it was a necessary part of an eighteenth-century election. It did not affect votes unless it was omitted. Agreements among the candidates to limit expense by using voters' tickets entitling the electors to specified quantities were possible, but difficult to enforce, because there was always a suspicion that the other fellow was evading the agreement in order to curry favour.

Estimates of the cost are probably much exaggerated, since they usually come from recorded gossip. Professor Halévy noted that the Yorkshire election of 1807 was said to have cost the candidates £500,000,[1] while Professor Coupland quoted £200,000 as the reputed expenditure of Wilberforce's opponents, though Wilberforce himself spent less than £30,000.[2] Even so, £30,000 was a large sum even for the privilege—and it was a very great privilege—of being knight of Yorkshire. At the next election Wilberforce accepted a convenient nomination borough. Yorkshire was a very exceptional county and this was an exceptional election; but when Lord Howick sought to capitalise his father's (Earl Grey's) influence in Northumberland in 1826 and destroy the Duke of Northumberland's monopoly, his family spent £14,000 and the other whig candidate is reported to have spent £80,000.[3] In the two elections of 1776 and 1802 Sir William Geary spent £22,000 in Kent,[4] while as far back as 1754 the Oxfordshire election cost £40,000.[5]

It must be emphasised, however, that contested elections were exceptional. In a few counties for substantial periods one great land-owner, like Lord Lonsdale in Westmorland, controlled the election and nominated the candidates. More often several great landowners dominated their several parts of the county and could, if they agreed, control the election. In defence of their own pockets, if not for the peace of the county, a 'compact' was desirable. Since they probably had influence in a few boroughs also, the compact might cover borough seats as well as the county seats, thus maintaining everybody's prestige and, if necessary—and it tended to be necessary after 1784—providing for both whigs and tories. In other counties, like Staffordshire and Northamptonshire, this kind of 'aristocratical' dominance was regarded as objectionable and the freeholders prided themselves on being 'democratical'. Openly to announce a candidature before the nomi-

[1] *History of the English People*, I, p. 124.
[2] R. Coupland, *Wilberforce*, p. 352.
[3] G. M. Trevelyan, *Lord Grey of the Reform Bill*, pp. 199–200.
[4] Halévy, *op. cit.* p. 124.
[5] Namier, *England in the Age of the American Revolution*, p. 197.

nation meeting was regarded as an infringement of the freedom of elections: polite calls at which the forthcoming election happened to be mentioned were not objectionable, but open canvassing was. In fact, however, it was usually decided before the nomination meeting whether there was to be a contest. In some counties, apparently, the election took place at the nomination meeting. More often the election was adjourned so as to enable all important freeholders to take part. If it appeared from the nominations that there would be a contest, it was likely that, before the adjourned meeting, somebody would withdraw. A quick canvass of those having influence would show where the odds lay.[1] Also, neither the candidates nor the greater landowners would welcome a contest because of the expense. For the sake of their prestige the landowners would want to poll their tenants at their own expense, and anyhow a contested election, while providing excitement for the mob, would upset the social life of the gentry and be a confounded nuisance. Hence there would be a contested election only if some ambitious landowner was anxious to establish his own influence (with a view, perhaps, to political office or a step in the peerage) or (in the fifty years before the Reform Act) national politics were relevant and the whigs or the tories, as the case might be, saw a chance of winning a seat.

At a contested election each considerable landowner could, at least in the middle of the century when party politics were irrelevant, poll most of his tenants and neighbours. No doubt there was a sanction behind his power. If any of his tenants at will was also a freeholder and refused his vote he could terminate the tenancy; he could remove his custom from a tradesman; he could neglect to send an invitation to a recalcitrant freeholder and his ugly but ambitious daughter; there would be no jobs for the boys if the boys were naughty; and so forth. This obsession with sanctions is, however, a Radical characteristic. The man who refrains from breaking his grandmother's skull because he

[1] As Lord Stanley said: 'It was known that when any man attempted to estimate the probable result of a county election in England it was ascertained by calculating the number of the great landed proprietors in the county and weighing the number of occupiers under them': quoted by G. Kitson Clark, 'The Electorate and the Repeal of the Corn Laws', *Transactions of the Royal Historical Society*, 5th ser. 1, p. 112, from the *Leeds Mercury*, 8 July 1841.

fears the hangman is the exception, not the rule, though the rule applies to everybody. The fact that his University can deprive a Cambridge man of his degree does not stimulate an artificial interest in a boat race. In the eighteenth century there was due regard for rank, station and influence which later developments destroyed. The landowner himself would recognise that there were exceptions which justified a man in refusing a vote. A dissenter could not be expected to vote against occasional conformity; a freeholder could not vote against his brother's employer; a parson might be torn between his duty to his tory squire and his whig bishop and both, probably, would be very nice about it. These exceptions apart, the ordinary freeholder would support his squire for the same reason that an undergraduate would support his College; and the squire would welcome an opportunity to support his great neighbour's candidate as eagerly as he would welcome an invitation to dinner. There was nothing very nefarious about influence until the end of the century, when party politics began to interfere with personal loyalties and class consciousness began to develop. It then became a little ridiculous for a tory squire to expect the vote of a whig tenant and even more ridiculous for a whig peer to try to coerce a tory squire by social sanctions.

The position in the boroughs was different, but it is more difficult to generalise because so much depended on the nature of the franchise and the number of the electors. The tradition of 'Old Corruption' depends very largely on the statements made by the whigs during the Reform agitation of the eighteen-thirties; but they were taking care not to let the tory dogs have the best of it and accordingly were selecting their examples. Lord Brougham's language was the most extreme and picturesque, and may be quoted as such:

That a peer, or a speculating attorney, or a jobbing Jew, or a gambler from the Stock Exchange, by vesting in his own person the old walls of Sarum, or a few pigsties at Bletchingley, or a summer-house at Gatton, and making fictitious and collusive and momentary transfers of them to an agent or two, for the purpose of enabling them to vote as if they had the property of which they all the while knew they have not the very shadow, is in itself a monstrous abuse, in the form of a gross and barefaced cheat, and becomes the most disgusting hypocrisy when it is seriously treated as a franchise by virtue of property. I will tell these peers, attorneys, jobbers, loan contractors and the nabobs' agents, if such there be still amongst us, that the time is come when these things can no longer be borne....[1]

Gatton was a scot and lot borough containing only six houses,[2] quite unlike such populous scot and lot boroughs as Westminster, Southwark, Northampton and Preston. Old Sarum was a burgage borough without an inhabited house, and had seven electors;[3] and Bletchingley was another burgage borough:[4] but there were only thirty-nine burgage boroughs.[5] It was possible to buy burgage-rights; it was sometimes possible to persuade a corporation, for a consideration, to create freemen in freemen-boroughs; and if a scot and lot borough was small it was possible to put in one's own tenants.

Nevertheless, the position of a borough generally varied according to the number of the electors. Borough-mongers used to draw a distinction between 'nomination boroughs', in which the patron had an interest in the nature of property, which he could sell with reasonable assurance that the purchaser would be able to nominate his own members, and other boroughs under the influence of patrons. 'Influence' in a borough had a complex connotation. It might be merely the product of the deference properly shown, according to eighteenth-century ideas, to the neighbouring landowner. In a few cases he was allowed to nominate both candidates; in most he was allowed only one. In some cases he could effectively elect a member of his own family, but not a 'foreigner'. All this was easier in the corporation boroughs, where the mayor and corporation elected, because they were properly deferential to him, and anyhow his lordship spent a lot of money in the borough. In the freemen-boroughs it was not so easy. Sometimes the patron was allowed to nominate freemen, and so create voters; but generally his influence depended on the willing support of the freemen. In either case his lordship, and his lordship's candidates, had to treat the borough with due consideration. Like a county it had to be 'nursed'. In the course of the century many boroughs changed their allegiance, sometimes because the estate was sold—in which case

[1] G. J. Garratt, *Lord Brougham*, pp. 268–9.
[2] Porritt, *The Unreformed House of Commons*, I, p. 31.
[3] *Ibid.* p. 35. [4] *Laws of Election* (6th ed.), p. 129.
[5] Or thereabouts: Professor Halévy made it thirty-six.

the purchaser did not necessarily acquire the influence of the vendor—sometimes because some of the electors decided, either permanently or temporarily, to support somebody else.

Even the nominations in proprietary boroughs had to be treated with due consideration. If there were any independent electors at all—and corporations were always independent in this sense—money had to be spent in the borough, not necessarily by purchasing votes. A good election agent would know, from time to time, how much a candidate would have to spend. There were customary fees for all the officials concerned, and they might vary from a guinea to a couple of hundred guineas. If there was a poll, the cost of polling booths had to be met. Entertainment, especially ale and porter, would probably be expensive. Only in comparatively few of the more populous boroughs was there actual bribery, and these were generally freemen or scot and lot (or potwalloper) boroughs.

According to Sir Lewis Namier's researches,[1] in 1761 fifty-one peers had forty-one seats in nomination boroughs and sixty other seats in which they had influence. The other borough patrons numbered fifty-five, and they were able to nominate for forty seats and influence fifty-one more. This gives a total of 192 seats nominated or influenced by sixty-six patrons. This does not mean that other landowners had no influence. It means only that such other influence was not such that it gave a customary right to nominate. Obviously, when rank and status gave influence, whether out of loyalty or otherwise, the interest of any great man was worth cultivating. On the other hand, it must be remembered that most borough patrons wanted seats for themselves and their close relatives. Indeed, much influence depended on this very fact. If seats could be bought, the electors would probably prefer to do the selling; and if the patron acted as broker he, or his purchaser, had to pay the price to the principals. Actually, by the end of the eighteenth century very few boroughs could be bought; they were nearly all in the hands of patrons who wanted seats for themselves or their relatives, or of peers who desired to retain political influence.[2]

[1] *The Structure of Politics at the Accession of George III*, I, pp. 176–81.
[2] G. T. Garratt, *Lord Brougham*, p. 190.

In addition to these boroughs in which private patrons had influence, there were in 1761 some thirty-two seats, including three in boroughs pawned by Thomas Pitt, to which the Government could nominate candidates with a reasonable chance of success. Also, there were some boroughs in Cornwall and other western counties in which local patrons could nominate themselves or their relatives, but which became Government boroughs when they did not.[1] It is said that between 40,000 and 60,000 revenue officers had the franchise out of a total of about 300,000 electors, and that their votes were important in respect of some seventy seats.[2] This may be an exaggeration; but the revenue officers were certainly important electorally, they usually voted as they were instructed by the Treasury, and their disfranchisement by one of the Acts of 1782 weakened the Government.[3] There were also boroughs —included in the number given above—in which the Admiralty and the Ordinance had influence through the dockyards, navy and army stores, etc.

Sir Lewis Namier[4] concludes that in 1761 some 234 seats were under patronage, or nearly half the total representation (489) of the whole of England. There were others in which landowners had considerable influence, without being able to carry the seats except in combination. Most of the Welsh seats were similarly under patronage. The Scottish members were elected in such a manner that they almost invariably supported the Government for the time being.[5] After 1800 the Irish constituencies were small and added very considerably to the seats subject to patronage. Even so, one must not exaggerate. To use the modern terminology, very few of these seats were so 'safe' that the Government or a patron could secure the election of a nominee, no

[1] Namier, *The Structure of Politics at the Accession of George III*, I, pp. 174–5.
[2] Hammond, *Charles James Fox*, pp. 49–50.
[3] *Auckland Papers*, I, p. 12.
[4] *Op. cit.* I, p. 183.
[5] Dicey and Rait, *Thoughts on the Union between England and Scotland*, p. 263. 'The total number of freeholders on the rolls for 33 counties of Scotland (in 1831) is 3255. But of these not less than 700 or so are enrolled in two or three or four different counties, so that the total number of individuals is not more than about 2500....In the burghs, 66 in number, the only electors are the magistrates (who elected the burgh delegates to the convention), who annually re-elect each other without any control from the inhabitants. Their whole number is about 1440': Jeffrey to Grey, 27 September 1831, quoted by Trevelyan, *Lord Grey of the Reform Bill*, p. 273.

matter who he was or what policy he supported. Influence was dependent in part on the control which the landlord had over his tenants, the anxiety of tradesmen for the custom of the patron, and the money spent by the candidates: but it also depended in part on the ordinary elector's lack of interest in general politics. So long as England was mainly agricultural a man could leave politics to his betters: with the growth of urbanisation a public opinion began to develop outside the clubs and coffee-houses. It can almost be dated, for it first received publicity in the Middlesex elections of 1768–9, though Westminster had been the home of popular electioneering since 1741. At the time attention was concentrated on the behaviour of what was then called 'the mob'; but it was more significant that over a thousand forty-shilling freeholders stood by a scallywag like John Wilkes in order to demonstrate their opposition to the Crown and its advisers. George III learned the lesson, or at least William Pitt did; though all the methods of Old Corruption were used in the general election of 1784, there was also a definite appeal to public opinion to condemn the 'Unnatural Coalition' of Fox and North. The election was managed as those of 1774 and 1780 were managed, and by the same person, John Robinson. All the tricks of electioneering, presently to be described, were used, and the result accorded with John Robinson's forecast some months previously. It has accordingly been presumed by some historians[1] that public opinion played no part at all. The conclusion does not follow from the evidence. The story that a 'deep roar of public indignation' against Fox and North 'shattered the united Opposition' is obviously a fiction now that we have the materials. On the other hand, the Unnatural Coalition was unpopular; the delaying action which Pitt fought in the House of Commons, even if unconstitutional, did and does compel admiration; Fox's own fight at Westminster, where he was beaten into second place and saved his seat only by great efforts of electioneering; all this tends to the conclusion that some patrons of boroughs and some electors must have been swayed by emotion.

'This trade of politics', said George III,[2] 'is a rascally business. It is

---

[1] W. T. Laprade, *Public Opinion and the General Election of 1784*, 31 E.H.R. 224; C. E. Fryer, *The General Election of 1784*, 9 Hist. 221.

[2] Quoted by Sir G. O. Trevelyan, *The Early History of Charles James Fox*, p. 115.

a trade for a scoundrel, not for a gentleman.' The difference between George III and his predecessors and successors was that he kept the keys of the store in his own hands. Not until after Sir Robert Peel's victory in 1841 was it clearly understood that a dissolution was an appeal to the people not by the monarch but by the Government.[1] During the eighteenth century not only was it an appeal by the King, but also it was an important part of the Government's strength. There was always something discreditable about opposition to the King's Government, because it was opposition to the King himself. The idea began to weaken under George III because he was so obviously a partisan politician (though he thought he was precisely the opposite). John Wilkes had bought a good line and Charles James Fox lost credit not because he opposed the King but because, having opposed him, he took office with Lord North. The French Revolution and the Napoleonic Wars hindered the development of the idea that a 'formed opposition' was respectable. The Portland whigs joined with the tories and took with them their ablest pamphleteer, Edmund Burke. The opposition could then be branded by their opponents as friends of the Terror until, in due course, they became friends of Napoleon. There was, of course, something in this. Even in the twentieth century it is not plain how far an Opposition ought to oppose a Government which has, in the Opposition's view, got the country into a difficult international situation. During the Boer War the Liberal party split on this issue; in 1914 and 1939 Opposition virtually ceased, but there was no sub-stantial conflict over the declaration of war; in 1956 the Labour party was accused of 'friendship with Nasser' because it opposed the Con-servatives' Suez adventure—the party's duty, it was claimed, was to back up the men in the tanks. It is not surprising, therefore, that in the eighteenth century opposition was tinged with sedition if not tainted with treason. As late as 1807, when Sidmouth left the Grenville Ministry, he refused to go into opposition: 'It is the King's Govern-ment, and to a systematic opposition I will never be a party.'[2] On the other hand, Fox's abstention from Parliament after 1797 and Tierney's

---

[1] *Cabinet Government* (3rd ed.), p. 330.

[2] *Life of Lord Sidmouth*, II, p. 469. The Duke of Wellington said much the same in 1830, but he regarded himself as a soldier and therefore a servant of the Crown.

weakness created difficulties, because the vast movement of opinion which resulted in the Reform Act and the Liberal Governments of the nineteenth century was inadequately represented in the House of Commons. The French Revolution had not created 'the friends of Liberty' but it had given them great strength: they could hardly support Robespierre and Napoleon, however, and so the normal development of the two-party system, implicit in the great social and economic changes of the Industrial Revolution, was retarded. Even in 1830 both Reformers and Anti-Reformers used the King's name with the greatest freedom. On the one hand it was alleged that the King favoured Reform; on the other hand it was argued that the King must be saved from the Reformers, into whose pockets he had unfortunately fallen. Until 1841, therefore, a general election was an appeal to the country to support the King's Government and nobody appealed to the country to provide His Majesty with a strong Opposition, or even an alternative Government. The revolution could be carried through by the Conservatives after 1832, mainly because it was implicit in the new political conditions, but partly also because in election cant the tories had always been the 'honest men' who supported the monarchy, whereas the whigs were corrupt seekers after patronage. This tradition, which derives from the independent country gentlemen who dominated so many of the counties (other than those which had fallen into the hands of whig magnates) has continued into the twentieth century: 'respectable' people always vote Conservative.

How, then, did the King's Government win an election? They did not, of course, formulate a 'programme', print thousands of posters with the Prime Minister's most fetching portrait on them, or do anything else that might spell 'faction'. The cult of the individual started very modestly with Pitt and Fox but did not reach national proportions until, after 1868, Gladstone and Disraeli went to the tops of the respective bills.

In the eighteenth century the majority of the counties and the popular boroughs could be left to themselves. There seems no reason to doubt the assertion that the independent county members normally supported the King's Government because they thought it proper so to do. They were independent, however, because they did not and would not take office. They were not so independent as to refuse all minor patronage for their families and constituents; nor were they immune from the temptations of 'honours'. Baronetcies were especially favoured,[1] perhaps because baronies went to Ministers and borough-mongers, and perhaps because baronies tended to upset the peace of the county by creating difficulties over the succession to county seats. The history of the popular boroughs has not been written, but the Government had not the means for organising them and they required a great deal of money, which the Government did not possess.

In the main, however, the process of electioneering was a process of mobilising influence, in the counties so far as they were subject to it, but especially in the boroughs. To return a number of members to Parliament was a certain way to the House of Lords, but most of the patrons were already there. This was necessarily so because, though in some of the counties there was opposition to 'aristocratical' domination, influence depended primarily on rank and station: the Duke of Omnium was necessarily a greater man than a plain squire, however ancient the lineage of the latter might be. In 1761, as we have seen,[2] fifty-one peers were able to return 101 members. When Canning was forming his Government in 1827 Croker reminded him 'how impossible it is to do anything satisfactory towards a Government in this country without the help of the aristocracy'.[3] His lists showed that the tory peers returned ninety-six members and the whig peers returned fifty-four. Canning replied that he would not act 'as the tool of any confederacy'. Croker retorted that 'the old tory and the steady whig aristocracies have at least 150 members in the House of Commons, not by influence of connection, but by direct nomination, and that no Government which did not divide them could stand for any length of time'.[4] This was explained by Croker in a later note, in which he brought up the total to 203 tory seats and seventy-three whig seats, these including seats gained by influence as well as nomination seats, and commoners as well as peers.[5] Croker was an Anti-Reformer and was not

[1] There were seventy-three baronets in the House of Commons in 1701: R. Walcott, *English Politics in the Early Eighteenth Century*, p. 32.
[2] *Ante*, p. 88; see Namier, *The Structure of Politics at the Accession of George III*, 1, pp. 176–82. [3] *Croker Papers*, 1, 367.
[4] *Ibid.* p. 309. [5] *Ibid.* p. 372.

trying to make a case for Reform, as the whigs of 1830 were. Canning was not convinced: 'Your list is good for nothing without commentary. Add, therefore, if you can, to these names the *price* that Government pays for their support, in Army, Navy, Church, and Law, Excise, Customs, etc. And then calculate what number of unconnected votes the same price distributed amongst others would buy in the market if the Crown were free.'[1]

Canning was a little unkind. Most of these noble lords placed their seats at the King's disposal, at least when he was served by the appropriate Ministers. Naturally they expected some recognition of this complaisance. Normally, and especially after 1783, a step in the peerage was enough, at least for one generation. The growth of the peerage between 1702 and 1830 (Table 14) is significant.[2]

	1702	1830
Dukes	17	23
Marquesses	1	18
Earls	70	110
Viscounts	9	21
Barons	65	153
Totals	162	325

TABLE 14

This does not record the titles which became extinct. There were, for instance, thirty-one Dukes in 1727. Nor does it record Scottish and Irish peerages—the latter could be created after 1800, but subject to limitations.

It is however true that patrons expected patronage also. The whole of the public service, military, civil and judicial, was filled by nomination, and it was inevitable that nominations should go to the relatives of those who supported the Government and their friends—who of course included their prominent constituents. Moreover the system of primogeniture under strict settlement required it. When in each generation the estate was again settled, charges would normally be provided for sons and daughters: but these could never be sufficient to maintain them at the standard to which they were accustomed if there was a

[1] *Croker Papers*, I, p. 370.   [2] *Constitutional Yearbook* for 1938, p. 94.

large number of such charges surviving in each generation, even allowing for the coming in of marriage portions. So long as land was the main source of wealth it was necessary to provide other incomes for younger sons, and until late in the eighteenth century the Church and the public services were almost the only sources. Moreover the maintenance of influence in a county, a corporation borough, a freeman borough, or a large burgage or scot and lot borough was an expensive business.

Some of the 'placemen' were in the House of Commons itself. In the Parliament of 1701 there were forty-eight officers of the army and navy and 105 holders of various offices, some of which remained after the end of 'Old Corruption' as political offices.[1] In 1742 there were 124 'placemen' supporting the Government in the House of Commons,[2] including twenty-two army and navy officers,[3] and five merchants holding Government contracts.[4] In 1761, sixty-four army officers were elected to the House of Commons,[5] and Sir Lewis Namier gives a remarkable list of the admirals who had served or were serving in that House.[6] Twenty-one naval officers were elected in 1761.[7] For the rest, Sir Lewis puts the matter negatively: 'Of the 558 members returned in 1761, about 300 seem to have held no place, office, contract or pension from the Government.'[8] These figures clearly suggest that there was a considerable increase in the higher patronage under the Duke of Newcastle's management. It must also be remembered that there were a great many lawyers in the House—sixty-two in 1701 (including some 'placemen'),[9] twenty-three in 1742[10] and some forty practising lawyers in 1761:[11] many of these were genuinely independent, and indeed in 1701 those who supported the Crown were a minority, but judicial preferment usually came to those with political influence.

There was in addition a considerable quantity of minor patronage

[1] R. Wolcott, *English Politics in the Early Eighteenth Century*, pp. 165, 171.
[2] John B. Owen, *The Rise of the Pelhams*, p. 47.
[3] *Ibid.* p. 50.   [4] *Ibid.* p. 53.
[5] Namier, *Structure of Politics at the Accession of George III*, I, pp. 32, 33.
[6] *Ibid.* pp. 38–9.
[7] Namier, *England in the Age of the American Revolution*, p. 256.
[8] *Ibid.* p. 257.   [9] Walcott, *op. cit.* p. 168.
[10] Owen, *op. cit.* p. 59.
[11] Namier, *The Structure of Politics at the Accession of George III*, I, p. 56.

designed not for members but for their relatives and supporters. Some of it was in the hands of members who held sinecures, since they appointed and paid their deputies. Most was in the hands of Ministers who were expected to 'do favours' for patrons and members. These 'favours' might, however, include Government contracts, especially contracts for loans, which in turn could be sub-contracted. There was usually a handful of Government contractors in the House of Commons, but membership was not necessary if one held influence in a borough. Nor must one forget the Church, where the patronage varied from the rich bishoprics and deaneries to some 900 other livings vested in the Crown.

The political importance of this patronage must not be exaggerated. It was less a bait or bribe for future services than a reward for past services. It does not appear that there was any general purge on a change of Ministers,[1] and in any case many of the persons appointed had freehold offices. The King took a personal interest in the royal forces and would not allow an excess of 'politics' in appointments and promotions. The lords Stair and Cobham and William Pitt, the future Earl of Chatham, were dismissed from the army in 1736,[2] but Walpole probably lost more than he gained.

If a borough patron could not be persuaded by loyalty to the Crown or by favours past and favours to come, he might be persuaded by a contribution towards election expenses or by a promise that Government influence be used, either with public officers who had votes in the borough (or perhaps some other borough in which he was interested) or with other persons who had influence. Lord X might not be able to win Muddleton unless he had the support of Messrs A, B and C, all of whom had obligations to Ministers or hoped for favours from them. Some borough seats might have to be bought outright, though a bargain price might be obtained if there were a promise, express or implied, of a peerage, a baronetcy or a red ribbon of the Order of the Bath. Money would be needed for this purpose, and some would come (under George III) from the King, some from the Ministers themselves, and some from the Secret Service Fund. Sir Lewis Namier has shown

---

[1] But see the purge of 1762: G. O. Trevelyan, *Early Life of Charles James Fox*, pp. 28–33.
[2] B. Williams, *The Life of William Pitt, Earl of Chatham*, I, p. 67.

that the amount spent from the last source was not large. In 1754 it was in the neighbourhood of £30,000[1] and it was paid in respect of twenty-four candidates, except as to £1000 for Scotland.[2] There were also small annual subsidies for maintaining the Government interest in Government boroughs.[3] No secret service money was spent on the general election of 1761.[4]

It cannot be pretended that Old Corruption was democratic, in the twentieth-century sense of that term. The 'democratical' part of the Constitution, as the eighteenth century understood it, was in the independent counties where the freeholders, under the leadership of the squires, genuinely chose independent representatives. In the view of the eighteenth century, the peasants and landless labourers were represented by their squires. The urban workers, 'the mob', had their representatives in the open boroughs, like Westminster and Preston, but nobody thought very highly of those boroughs, or of the methods used by Charles James Fox and his leading ladies (especially Georgiana, Duchess of Devonshire) to win Westminster. Even in 1784 England was still an agricultural country, Wales was feudal territory, and Scotland was only just starting an interest in politics. Public opinion was to be found mainly in the London coffee-houses and in quarter sessions. To that opinion Parliament was very responsive. The idea of a party Government, opposed by His Majesty's alternative Government, had not developed. The executive authority was vested in the King, though he had to have Ministers to win elections for him and to get his measures through both Houses. Members supported or opposed the King's measures without reference to party, which existed only in embryo. Many of them owned, or at least influenced, the boroughs which they represented, and influence depended, in part at least, on their being in tune with their constituents. Only a few boroughs sold themselves without reference to men and measures, and no county ever did. Members were not bound even to their own patrons, though there was a sort of understanding that a member would resign if he found himself in fundamental disagreement with his patron.[5]

---

[1] Namier, *The Structure of Government at the Accession of George III*, I, p. 251.
[2] *Ibid.* p. 252.   [3] *Ibid.* pp. 252–3.   [4] *Ibid.* p. 258.
[5] Creevey's *Memoirs*, II, p. 166.

2. THE DECLINE OF OLD CORRUPTION

Old Corruption never died; it only faded away. Even in its heyday it had its critics, though not because it was not 'popular' but because, according to the whigs, it gave too much power to the Crown. Dunning's famous resolution of 1780, that the influence of the Crown had increased, was increasing, and ought to be diminished, was good whig doctrine. Sir William Anson[1] occupies three pages with a list of the statutes which in 1922 disqualified various officials for membership of Parliament. It begins with 5 & 6 Will. & Mary, c. 7, which disqualified farmers, collectors and managers of money duties or other aid; and 12 & 13 Will. III, c. 10, which disqualified farmers, managers and collectors of customs. It was not complete because it did not include repealed Acts: 11 & 12 Will. III, c. 2, disqualified commissioners or farmers of the excise. In 1694 both Houses passed a Bill to prohibit all members from accepting office under the Crown, but William III refused the royal assent.[2] Parliament tried again in 1700, and the Act of Settlement, 12 & 13 Will. III, c. 2, provided that after the accession of the House of Hanover no person who had an office or place of trust under the King, or received a pension from the Crown, should be capable of serving as a member of the House of Commons. This provision, which would have made the development of Cabinet Government impossible, was however repealed by 4 Anne, c. 8. That Act provided instead that the holder of a new office created after 25 October 1705 should be incapacitated from sitting in Parliament, while members of Parliament appointed to old offices should vacate their seats but be capable of re-election. This requirement held no terrors for those sitting for nomination boroughs, though it became important in the nineteenth century. The Act 1 Geo. I, c. 56, disqualified pensioners for terms of years; but, since most pensions were granted at pleasure or for life, its effect was extremely small. Deputies or clerks in the Treasury, Exchequer, Admiralty, the Departments of the Secretaries of State, and certain other Government Departments,

---

[1] *Law and Custom of the Constitution* (5th ed.), I, pp. 101–4.
[2] Erskine May, *Constitutional History of England*, I, p. 307. For the protest of the Commons, see E.H.D. VIII, pp. 181–2.

were disqualified by the House of Commons Disqualification Act, 1741.

Dunning's resolution of 1780 was followed by a wholesale attack on Old Corruption by the Rockingham Ministry. In rapid succession Acts were passed excluding Government contractors, disfranchising revenue officers, disfranchising the borough of Cricklade for corruption, and, finally, Burke's Economy Act. Burke's Act was limited by the hostility of George III, but it abolished some forty sinecures, provided that the pension list be reduced to £90,000, and limited the secret service money to £10,000 a year.[1]

It is evident from John Robinson's proceedings at the general election of 1784[2] that the process of electioneering was not at first hampered seriously. No doubt the loss of the Treasury boroughs and the Crown influence through the revenue officers was serious eventually. The effects of the Act could, however, be seen only in the long term. Treasury influence could not be traded for patron's influence; the means for gratifying members of parliament with places and pensions were much reduced; there was less money for election expenses. Mr Eden (Lord Auckland) said that 'Burke's foolish Bill has made it a very difficult task for any set of men either to form or maintain an Administration'.[3] Pitt further limited his power in 1784 by putting the Funding Loan out to tender and thus depriving himself—and, since this became a precedent,[4] future Prime Ministers—of a juicy piece of patronage. There were, too, administrative reforms over the next few years. In 1799 there were 747 fewer excise officers than in 1784; eighty-five sinecures were abolished in the Customs; Army and Navy contracts were put out to tender.[5] On the other hand, Pitt increased the number of peerages, and quite a number of noble lords owe their status to borough-mongering under Pitt.[6]

Curwen's Act of 1809 (49 Geo. III, c. 118) imposed heavy penalties upon corrupt agreements for the return of members, whether for

---

[1] The £10,000 a year was not abolished until 1886.
[2] *Ante*, p. 90.   [3] *Auckland Papers*, I, p. 12.
[4] Stanhope, *Life of Pitt*, I, pp. 219–20, 223.   [5] *Ibid.* IV, pp. 416–17.
[6] One example will suffice. In January 1799 the Earl of Ely denounced the proposal for union with Ireland as a 'mad scheme'. In 1800 he and his six borough members voted for union. The noble earl was given an Irish marquisate and an English peerage.

money, office or other consideration, and deprived the member returned of his seat. While it had little effect on private agreements, it did limit the older form of electioneering by the Crown. In 1812 Lord Liverpool said that the Treasury had only one seat which could be obtained free of expense, and private friends had put two more at his disposal. Curwen's Act 'has put an end to all money transactions between Government and the supposed proprietors of boroughs. Our friends, therefore, who look for the assistance of Government must be ready to start for open boroughs, where the general influence of Government, combined with a reasonable expense on their own part, may afford them a reasonable chance of success.'[1] What in fact the Act did was to compel the Government to rely heavily on the proprietors of boroughs. A good example is the way in which Charles Wynne entered the Cabinet in 1821. 'That Mr Wynne should ever have been thought of as a Cabinet minister was a singular instance of the way in which the crafty possessor of borough influence can at times employ it to gain his ends. For he was a man of the most ordinary capacity, and remarkable indeed for nothing but a ridiculously thin squeaking voice, and the same overweening idea of his own importance which had distinguished every member of the house of Grenville for two generations.'[2] It was, however, essential to secure the Grenville influence. Mr Wynne was not the only beneficiary. The Marquis of Buckingham was offered a dukedom and one of his brothers was sent as envoy to Switzerland.[3]

Opinion was, however, changing slowly. Napoleon having been defeated, for the last time, in 1815 the more permanent effects of the French Revolution became noticeable. The stream of political literature became a flood and swamped all efforts to dam it. Peterloo and the six Acts, and still more the raising of the populace in support of Queen Caroline, showed the unrepresentative character of the House of Commons. The death of George IV removed the obstacle to the accession of the whigs, and Reform became inevitable.

Althorp told his colleagues that, after only a few weeks in office [he led the House of Commons as Chancellor of the Exchequer], his experience of the

[1] *Life of Lord Liverpool*, I, p. 444. [2] *Ibid.* III, p. 156.
[3] *Ibid.* III, p. 158.

corrupt pressure of the borough-owners on the Government was such that he would no longer tolerate any vestige of a system which left seats in the hands of individuals—no, not even to give able young lawyers and budding Burkes, Cannings and Macaulays a better chance of being put early and easily into the House by their patrons, nor even to find new Ministers a sure place of refuge in taking office under the Crown [and seeking re-election under the Act of 1704].[1]

The effect of the Reform Act of 1832 was to abolish all the proprietary boroughs, to widen representation in smaller boroughs and in many cases to extend their boundaries, to convert all more or less closed boroughs to semi-open boroughs by enfranchising the £10 householders, severely to limit the number of out-voters in boroughs but not in counties, to convert some of the wide open boroughs into semi-open boroughs by limitations on the ancient franchises, to create many new boroughs as semi-open boroughs, to give free elections to Scotland, to add considerably to the county electorate, to divide twenty-six counties, and to add sixty-five county seats.

We may take the counties first. The freeholders were not swamped because, taking the country as a whole, they still held seventy per cent of the votes.[2] The Chandos voters (i.e. the tenants at will) were particularly strong in the purely agricultural divisions, where there were large estates farmed by tenants. The freeholders dominated in the industrial divisions.[3] The immediate effect was to increase 'influence'. Great landowners who could not sway a whole county could sometimes sway a county division. For instance, the Grey interest had twice fought and lost against the Duke of Northumberland's influence in Northumberland, but could influence two seats when the county was divided. It was generally thought, too, that the Chandos voters voted with their landlords, though it must be remembered that many Chandos voters were also freeholders. On the whole it would seem that the Reform Act did not have much effect on the influence of the landowners, except in the growing industrial divisions, and in the smaller towns not separately enfranchised, which were in effect much the same as the smaller boroughs.[4] There were, however, many more

[1] G. M. Trevelyan, *Lord Grey of the Reform Bill*, p. 268.
[2] Seymour, *Electoral Reform in England and Wales*, p. 78.
[3] *Ibid.* p. 80.   [4] Gash, *Politics in the Age of Peel*, pp. 94–5.

OLD CORRUPTION

contests, especially in 1832, partly because there were sixty-five extra
county seats, and partly because in 1832 the division of counties
altered the balance of interest and because subsequently influence
began to decline as the industrialised areas expanded.

In the boroughs the situation was fundamentally changed. There
were no proprietary boroughs which could be bought and sold, but
there were still boroughs in which the interest of a great landowner
predominated. Calne in Wiltshire 'belonged' to Lord Lansdowne
until it was disfranchised in 1885. John Bright said in 1857 that Robert
Lowe, then the member, 'was merely the nominee of an influential
nobleman who could, had he chosen, have sent his butler or groom into
Parliament';[1] but probably Bright exaggerated. Dudley in Worcestershire was another pocket borough in the fifties, 'owned' by Lord Ward.
Sir Stafford Northcote was member in 1857, and Lord Ward wanted
him to vote for Lord Palmerston's Government. Sir Stafford refused
and at the next election changed his constituency.[2] Lord Ward also
'owned' Kidderminster, where he had provided funds for the conversion
of the carpet industry from hand-looms to steam.[3] It is not surprising
that Lord Ward became Earl of Dudley, because he had an income of
£100,000 and 'considerable influence bearing upon the return of
members for two or three seats'.[4] Marlborough was a Liberal borough
'owned' by the Bruce family until it was disfranchised in 1885.[5]
Woodstock in Oxfordshire was the pocket borough of the Churchills
until 1885. In 1844 it was held by the Marquis of Blandford, heir of the
Duke of Marlborough, who owned the borough. When the Marquis
became a free-trader he applied for the Chiltern Hundreds and a
protectionist was elected. The protectionist was succeeded by Lord
Arthur Churchill. In 1846 the Marquis settled his difficulties with his
father and again became member in 1847, continuing as such until he
succeeded his father in 1857. Lord Arthur Churchill then became
member but during 1860 he allied himself with Lord Palmerston.

[1] *Life and Letters of Robert Lowe, Viscount Sherbrooke*, II, pp. 175–6.
[2] *Life of Sir Stafford Northcote*, pp. 87, 92.
[3] *Life of Robert Lowe, Viscount Sherbrooke*, II, pp. 43–4.
[4] Bell, *Lord Palmerston*, II, p. 158.
[5] *Life of Lord Long of Wraxall*, p. 67; Sir Charles Petrie, *Walter Long and his Times*,
p. 28.

After discussion with the Duke, it was agreed that he stay as member until the election, but no longer. The Duke's nominee was elected in 1865 and again in 1868, retiring in 1874. Lord Randolph Churchill was then candidate, but the Ballot Act had altered the situation. 'With the ballot one can tell nothing—one can only trust to promises, and I have no doubt a good many promises will be broken.' Lord Randolph did not in fact trust to promises, for he hired the three principal hotels, leaving the Radical candidate 'nothing except a wretched, low, miserable pot-house to stay in'. The resident of the miserable pot-house secured 404 votes out of 973, but that was almost the end of Woodstock's electoral history, for it was disfranchised in 1884.[1]

These are exceptional cases, but they show that in the small boroughs influence was still strong in the middle of the nineteenth century.[2] It had to compete, however, with three forces. The first was the rapid development of public opinion as the fundamental factor in electioneering. The public agitation over Queen Caroline was followed by the Reform movement, the agitation for the People's Charter, and above all the work of the Anti-Corn Law League. The whigs got carried along with Reform. The Charter was outside the party conflict because it was opposed by both parties, but it formed the basis of much Liberal policy in later decades. The League was annexed to the Liberal party because the Conservative party became the country party which repudiated Sir Robert Peel's repeal of the Corn Laws, and the Liberal party became the party of free trade. The Platform, the Press and the Party became the instruments of electioneering.[3]

In the second place, in urban areas where books were read and even in rural areas where men went to chapel, influence became an outmoded concept which people could not quite comprehend. Liberty, equality and fraternity were red flags to Conservatives, but to ordinary people in the towns they rapidly became major premises which needed no proof. Why anybody should be followed merely because he owned

---

[1] *Life of Lord Randolph Churchill*, I, pp. 18–21, 52–6. For the election of 1880, when Lord Randolph Churchill won by only sixty votes, see *ibid.* pp. 114–17.

[2] Mr Gash gives a list of 'proprietary boroughs' after 1832, including forty-two probables and ten possibles, returning seventy-three members: *Politics in the Age of Peel*, pp. 438–9. The propriety of 'proprietary' is doubtful.

[3] See Chapters V, VI and VIII, respectively.

a lot of land became quite incomprehensible to a large section of the population. The Earl of Derby was no doubt an important person, and he had plenty of urban rents as well as much land: but were not the Lancashire mill-owners important people? The landed interest was pushed into the agricultural counties, which became of increasingly less importance as industrialisation developed. On the other hand, most of the mill-owners and the industrialists generally were not at this stage 'gentry'. At this stage they were 'masters' working in their shirt-sleeves among the 'men'. The second generation went to the public schools and the universities, built houses in the suburbs or migrated to the country, and paid their tribute to respectability by attending Church, or at least subscribing to it. The 'masters', on the other hand, lived by the factory or mine and went to chapel with their 'men'. The parson might be one of the evangelicals and go into the East End; but he was more likely to be, as in private duty bound, a supporter of the established order which was already being under-mined. The minister, on the other hand, was almost invariably an urban product who had taken religion, and he probably knew as much about land as the average parson knew about machinery. Even the urban worker had respect for his 'betters', but he had not been taught to take orders about voting. He might well be loyal to the 'master', self-interest might suggest that he vote the same way, but he agreed with the minister and the 'master' that bread ought to be cheap. He was in any case set free of undue influence by the Ballot Act, which came into operation, at least in the newer towns, before the 'master' had been succeeded by his expensively educated son. It must be remembered, too, that the 'men' had no votes until 1868, unless they were £10 occupiers or (in the counties) forty-shilling freeholders. The £10 householders were the respectable people who sat behind the 'master's' pew in the chapel and, like him, contributed to the chapel funds, though perhaps not much.

In the third place there was still money. Indeed, there was much more of it because the commercial and industrial classes were becoming interested in politics, or at least in representation which would help them to keep down costs of production, improve the roads, build railways. The rise and fall of the railway interest would make an interesting chapter. In those boroughs in which landowners still had influence they would probably have to fight to keep it, for some Liberal carpet-bagger would probably turn up with lots of money in the bag, ready to spend it on entertainment, bands and banners, bribes, and all the ballyhoo of Eatanswill as described by that son of the people, Mr Charles Dickens. The city of St Alban supplies a good example. It was said in 1840 to 'belong' to the Earl of Verulam, but his tory nominee lost the seat to a whig in 1841 owing to bribery;[1] and St Albans was disfranchised for corruption in 1852. Horsham provides another example.[2] Before 1832 it was a burgage borough in which most of the burgages had been bought up by the Irwin family of Temple Newsam, though that interest was contested by the Duke of Norfolk, eventually successfully. The price of a seat was £4000 or £5000, though there was a risk of an election petition.[3] In 1832 its boundaries were enlarged and the franchise was in effect vested in the £10 householders, who numbered less than 300. Until 1847 it was represented by a Reformer or whig. In 1847, however, it was contested by a Conservative and a Radical, both with plenty of money; and forthwith it became first cousin of Eatanswill. Liquor was free for all for six weeks, the favourite election brew being lemonade and brandy, an invention of a waiter at the 'Black Horse'. This made it a Radical drink, but it seemed to be equally popular among Conservatives. It was also potent, for 'most of the male population of Horsham was frequently drunk, many were continually drunk, and some were continuously drunk, for the whole six weeks....'.[4] The cost of liquor at two Conservative hotels was £1590, and at two Radical hotels £1218;[5] but this must indicate the cubic capacity of the respective electors, for there is no evidence that treating affected votes. In the end the candidates—or, strictly speaking, their agents—had to resort to bribery and kidnapping: and, since the latter was prevalent, it was thought necessary to protect the voters. A van-load of Conservative electors, for instance, was driven to Brighton, where they were fed and kept until polling day, when they were driven back to vote

[1] *Life of Lord Clarendon*, I, p. 219.
[2] See W. Albery, *A Parliamentary History of Horsham, 1295–1885*.
[3] *Ibid.* p. 250.   [4] *Ibid.* p. 353.   [5] *Ibid.*

Conservative. One elector promised his vote to both sides, but was captured by the Radicals and lodged at a Radical inn. He was rescued by the Conservatives, recaptured by the Radicals, given £40, and driven off drunk for a quiet trip into the country.[1] The cost to the Conservative candidate is put at various figures between £60,000 and £100,000; and the Radical candidate probably did not spend much less.[2]

It seems probable, though the assertion cannot be proved, that there was more bribery and other forms of corruption in the boroughs immediately after 1832 than there had been before. The Parliament elected in 1841 has been called the 'Bribery Parliament'. Probably this was a whig explanation for a tory victory. There were in fact fewer contested elections than in 1832, 1835 and 1837,[3] and fewer election petitions than in 1837 and 1852.[4] Only six elections were avoided, though eleven returns were amended by the substitution of other names. The fact that there were contests in only about 190 constituencies (146 in England and Wales, or slightly more than half) is probably to be explained by the expense of elections. This was the fourth election in nine years and it must have been difficult to find candidates willing to put up the money. In any event the political tendencies of most constituencies under the reformed system were known, and the parties were not yet so highly organised that they could afford to fight forlorn hopes.

The Reform Act had made some provision for the reduction of expenditure—counties were divided and polling districts established in county divisions; a contested election could not last more than two days at first and thereafter (1835 in boroughs, 1853 in counties) only one day. On the other hand, the increase in the electorate required more expenditure on customary fees, entertainment and, where necessary, bribes. It is impossible to say whether elections cost more or less after 1831 than they did before 1832, because it is impossible to compare like with like. The figures given by Mr Gash[5] for the 1841 elections are below the highest figures for 'Old Corruption', but this does not prove very much. Those given by Robert Lowe in 1866[6] are much the same

---

[1] W. Albery, *A Parliamentary History of Horsham*, p. 366.
[2] *Ibid.* p. 410.   [3] Gash, *Politics in the Age of Peel*, p. 441.
[4] *Ibid.* p. 431.   [5] *Ibid.* p. 130.
[6] *Life of Viscount Sherbrooke*, II, pp. 295–6.

as those for 1841 when allowance is made for the fact that they cover all candidates, though Lowe added 'all legitimate expenses but by no means the whole expense'. There is not the slightest doubt that legitimate expenses did increase until 1885, but it is probable that illegitimate expenses declined. An experienced electioneer[1] says that there was very little corruption after the Ballot Act. It had always been rare in the counties because the electorate was too large to be corrupted. It had been common only in the pocket boroughs, 'where freemen looked on a contested election as shareholders'. This allegation against the freemen is common form, and it probably was true that the freemen, having been used to bribery before the Reform Act, contaminated the new electorate. On the other hand Mr Gash's list of corrupt boroughs[2] does not accord with Professor Seymour's list of boroughs with large freemen electorates.[3] This is not conclusive, but Professor Seymour's other figures suggest qualifications. In Cambridge the famous Sam Long controlled two hundred votes by bribery and was therefore able to elect whom he chose from 1839 to 1852. 'The freemen were the same class which had been accustomed to bribery as one of the privileges of their position; the £10 householders were sometimes more corrupt than the freemen, and in general they were dependent upon the good will of the rich, and therefore easily influenced'.[4] At the election at St Albans in 1841, 270 out of 354 householders, thirty-one out of sixty-three freemen, and sixty-four out of sixty-six scot and lot electors were bribed:[5] but the eighty-four honest householders were not necessarily those who resisted the temptations held out by thirty-one freemen, to which 270 householders succumbed. We must merely take it that in some boroughs there was bribery, large contributions to municipal charities, corrupt loans, and intimidation. Old Corruption was an unconscionable time a-dying, and yet it had almost faded away by 1885. Professor Seymour asserts that direct bribery had died out by 1860, but that indirect corruption and intimidation continued.[6] Intimidation

[1] J. A. Bridges, *Reminiscences of a Country Politician*, p. 41.
[2] Warwick, Penryn and Falmouth, Hull, Ipswich, Lewes, Liverpool, Nottingham, Norwich, St Albans, Stafford, Sudbury, Totnes, and York: *op. cit.* p. 154.
[3] *Electoral Reform in England and Wales*, pp. 84–5. Norwich, Stafford and York are common to the lists.
[4] *Ibid.* pp. 170–1.   [5] *Ibid.* p. 171.   [6] *Ibid.* p. 232.

virtually disappeared in 1872 with the Ballot Act.[1] Indirect corruption continued for some time, but most of it had disappeared by 1885. Partly, this was due to the Corrupt and Illegal Practices Act, 1883, which replaced the ineffective Act of 1854. In the main, however, it seems to have been due to better enforcement. From 1672 to 1770 election petitions were virtually decided by the House of Commons itself, often on partisan grounds.[2] From 1770 to 1839 they were heard by a Select Committee, but the elections to that Committee were generally partisan.[3] After 1839 the committees were small bodies of six members chosen by the committee of selection, and the quality of the decisions at once improved. The Parliamentary Elections Act, 1868, transferred the jurisdiction to a judge of the Court of Queen's Bench, and in 1879 it was provided that there should be two High Court judges. 'Excessive leniency' was then replaced by 'rigorous severity',[4] and this had a marked effect on the purity of elections, though indirect corruption continued. 'The great weapon of parliamentary warfare is beer.'[5] In one town in 1879, no less than 2281 electors went on a treat and returned 'firm and enthusiastic supporters of Mr Disraeli's policy'.[6]

Old Corruption was fading away, except at Oxford, where the cost rose from £2310 in 1868 to £3275 in 1880.[7] Public opinion, in Cambridge and elsewhere, was now against these practices, and the general election of 1880 produced the Corrupt and Illegal Practices Act, 1883, which in all its essential principles is still in force. It repeated the definitions of the Act of 1854 and increased the penalties. It also introduced a new idea, the limitation of expenditure according to detailed schedules. Every candidate had to have an election agent, who would be solely responsible for all payments, and who was required to submit a statement of expenses within a short period after the election. Pay-

---

[1] It was alleged in 1885, when the agricultural labourers were first enfranchised, that the landowners tried to maintain their control of county elections by requiring the labourers to sign written undertakings to vote Conservative. Tuckwell, the Radical parson, advised them to sign, so as to avoid intimidation, but to vote Liberal. This led to a correspondence in *The Times* on the ethical principles involved: see W. Tuckwell, *Reminiscences of a Radical Parson*, p. 42.

[2] Erskine May, *Constitutional History of England*, I, p. 302.

[3] *Ibid.* pp. 305–6.

[4] Seymour, *op. cit.* p. 426.   [5] *Ibid.* p. 437.

[6] *Ibid.* p. 438.   [7] *Ibid.* p. 441.

ment for transport, the hire of committee rooms in excess of the statutory number, the use of premises for exhibiting notices, etc., became illegal. This Act, like the Ballot Act, was neatly articulated and has proved to be one of the better examples of the draftsman's art.

Even so, legislation and the courts merely tolled the bell, for Old Corruption was already nearly dead. Members of Parliament even more than other people depend for their reputation upon public opinion; and it is as worth while to be a member without reputation as it is to be a doctor of a university which sells degrees to all comers. Membership of Parliament has been prized because it gives a sense of power and confers prestige. The power of the private members went into a rapid decline as the control of parties became strict. In modern times the member can make a nuisance of himself, but he obtains no power unless he is invited to join the Cabinet. A member who had purchased a seat by corruption would have as little prestige as a knight who had obtained a baronetcy by purchase. Corruption at elections is, however, not merely purchase; it is fraudulent and illegal. One of the merits of the Victorian era, due no doubt to its rather narrow conventions (for what is illegal is not necessarily immoral), was its condemnation of illegality. *Bonus paterfamilias* obeyed the laws with absolute rigidity. Hence a member of Parliament who acquired his seat illegally was not merely a doubtful character; he was a bit of a bounder, a cad, an outsider, the sort of man who could not be invited to take tea with one's daughters. There were and still are, and indeed ought to be, a few cads as well as a few eccentrics of other types in Parliament, for all politicians are a bit eccentric. In any case, an eccentric who acquired his seat by purchase would not be approved in chapel; and even in church the women would pass remarks about him. Queen Victoria and her people were not amused by what we now call 'spivs': not many of them have got into Parliament since 1868, and fewer still have stayed there.

In this hard, competitive world, nobody spends money except to put it to usury. What rate of interest could be obtained on money laid out in elections? After Sir Robert Peel there were no jobs for the boys. There were and still are baronies, baronetcies and knighthoods: but, as Mr Lloyd George discovered, generosity is not always a virtue.

Besides, it was easier to make a large contribution to party funds than to spend money on corrupting electors. The way to honour, metaphorical as well as real, was to convince an electorate by lawful means that Gladstone or Disraeli, as the case might be, was the saviour of the nation and the prophet of tomorrow.

It helped considerably that the nation divided itself into halves, Liberals and Conservatives, and took politics almost in the same spirit as it took the boat race, a test match or the cup final.[1] The better team ought to win, but according to the rules. The Conservative party has compensating advantages, but it suffers from the disadvantage of a suspicion of 'dirty play', though in fact the whigs were usually more corrupt. The verse of the royal hymn which ends:

> Confound their politics,
> Frustrate their knavish tricks,
> On Thee our hopes we fix,
> God save the Queen.

derives from 'Old Corruption'. Gladstone capitalised the Nonconformist conscience and only Conservatives appreciated Labouchere's remark that he did not mind Mr Gladstone having the ace of trumps up his sleeve; what he objected to was his assuming that God had put it there. Gladstone was, however, in a long tradition. Pitt's reputation is better than his practice and even Sir Robert Peel did not receive the approval of Disraeli; but it is true that much cleaning of political stables was done, by deliberate policy, between 1783 and 1846. As late as 1906 it was possible to throw mud, but it had to be done very surreptitiously indeed and it could not be approved by the party machines because a party would lose more votes than it gained if it did not 'play the game'. The hard-faced professionals in the central offices fought to win,[2] but

---

[1] For the benefit of foreign readers who have not studied the sociology of English sport it should be explained that (1) the boat race is a rowing match between crews representing the Cambridge University Boat Club and the Oxford University Boat Club, held annually on the Thames; (2) a test match is a cricket match between the Marylebone Cricket Club (which selects a representative team from the English and Welsh counties) and a team from another Commonwealth country, preferably Australia; and (3) the cup final is the last round in an annual eliminating contest among the professional football teams of England and Wales. Only a war takes precedence over these great events.

[2] See, for the Conservative party, P. G. Cambray, *The Game of Politics*.

officially they had to give the election agents, most of whom became professionals, such instructions about running elections as if the parties deserved their high reputations in academic circles.[1] With highly organised parties, staffed by professionals who wanted to keep their jobs, and assisted at election times by enthusiastic amateurs who would do the chores for the honour and the glory of the party, honesty became the best policy.

Thus, Old Corruption was cleaned up by a combination of methods. There was some deliberate policy at the centre, especially from Pitt, Sir Robert Peel and Gladstone. There was a changing climate of public opinion based mainly on the Nonconformist conscience (which in this respect was shared with the Church of England). With increased electorates corruption became too expensive unless serious steps to limit it were taken. The State assumed the responsibility of taking elections to the people and so deprived the candidates of the responsibility of taking the people to the elections. The secret ballot weakened the value of bribery and did not, owing to the climate of opinion, increase personation. A comprehensive and well articulated law was developed in great detail and its enforcement was transferred from committees of politicians to High Court judges, who applied their sanctions with great severity. Above all, a highly organised party which claims for its leading members the responsibility of Government has to proclaim all the political virtues and dare not practise secret vices. Today even abuse is a dangerous weapon.

[1] See G. G. Butler, *The Tory Tradition*; F. J. C. Hearnshaw, *Conservatism in England*; W. Lyon Blease, *A Short History of English Liberalism*; G. D. H. Cole, *A History of the Labour Party since 1914.*

CHAPTER V

MOB ORATORY

'Mob oratory' was the phrase used by the burgess for the University of Oxford in the debate on the first Reform Bill.[1] It was a little hard on those worthy Oxford men, John and Charles Wesley, and George Whitefield, who taught the politicians how to handle vast crowds, to play on their emotions, and to arouse their enthusiasm. Sir Robert Inglis of course had not the Methodists in mind. 'The mob' was political cant for the workers of the industrial towns, or industralised counties like Middlesex, who attended the most celebrated elections, like those of John Wilkes and Charles James Fox; and Sir Robert almost certainly had in mind 'Orator Hunt', the Radical member for the open borough of Preston, who spoke in the same debate. Macaulay's word was 'rabble': and, said Orator Hunt, 'when the honourable member for Calne (Macaulay) talked of the *rabble*, he looked very hard at me'.[2] The industrial workers, usually known as 'the poor',[3] were comparatively speaking a new phenomenon produced by the use of steam power. They had burst the bonds of the guild system even in the commercial cities, and that system never applied in the new industrial towns. In the open boroughs, however, many of them had the vote and a new technique had to be developed to persuade them, or at least to induce them, to vote for the right candidates. One method was bribery and treating, but the Radicals discovered that they could use the techniques of the Methodists in what are now called 'mass meetings'. Its use by other parties developed very slowly. Gladstone began his 'pilgrimages of passion' in 1862,[4] though Disraeli invented the phrase in 1866.[5] Even during the Midlothian campaign of 1879, however, Conservative critics declared that Gladstone's performances were an innovation on the Constitution and aggravated the evil tendencies of

---

[1] *Ante*, p. 11.
[2] Molesworth, *History of the Reform Bill*, p. 125.
[3] Lewis, *On the Use and Abuse of some Political Terms*, ch. XIII.
[4] A. Tilney Bassett, *Gladstone's Speeches*, p. 28.
[5] M. Corry, *Disraeli's Speeches on Parliamentary Reform*, p. 404.

democracy;[1] and the Conservative party did not take much part in 'public agitation' until the success of the Caucus in 1880 compelled them, in self-defence, to go and do likewise.

I. THE CANVASS

The old English method of electioneering was the personal canvass. In the counties it was attuned to the system of influence which could be maintained only if the person claiming to exercise it made a personal approach with the proper degree of condescension, but no more than was proper. Speaking generally, it was thought improper to canvass until the meeting of freeholders had been summoned by the sheriff, though necessarily there was some discussion with one or two of the leading men of the county to make certain of nomination. If it was found necessary to have a poll, canvassing was essential. It was, how-ever, normally done by, or in co-operation with, those who had or claimed influence, for it was their privilege as well as their duty to exhibit their power. A perfect system of influence would be much like a perfect feudal system—including the characteristic that it never existed. The noble lord who influenced the county would canvass the less noble lords who influenced the hundreds; those less noble lords would canvass the lords of the manors in their hundreds; the lords of the manors would canvass the freeholders who held of them, the shop-keepers in their villages, and so forth. Though this system never existed, it expresses the idea. There were, however, persons who could exercise some influence who held no land in the county. If there were revenue officers (and they had not been disfranchised) the assistance of the Treasury would be sought. The parson might be persuaded by the bishop, or even by his College; and he would probably include a few well-chosen words in his sermon. The squire might be friendly with a great man in another county; or possibly he was a connexion of some great house. 'Damn the whigs', said Lord Melbourne, 'they're all cousins': but cousins were useful in contested elections, for family was more important than policy, especially when there was no policy.

[1] *Life of Gladstone*, II, p. 589.

The boroughs, as usual, were more diverse. In a nomination borough there was nothing whatever to be done; it was not even necessary to visit the borough. In a corporation borough the mayor and corporation would expect to be entertained to dinner. In a smallish borough under influence the electors would expect to be both canvassed and entertained. Moreover the canvassing might have to be done by the patron, with or without his carpet-bagger candidates. The 'patriarch' of all canvassers, Thomas, Marquis of Wharton, who knew the electors and their children by their Christian names and could ask, 'Is not Jemmy breeched yet?', was a patron, not a candidate.[1] Similarly in the notorious 'Spendthrift Election' at Northampton in 1768 the real 'candidates' were the three Earls of Halifax, Northampton and Spencer, who were competing for the influence.[2]

Northampton was, however, a scot and lot borough with nearly a thousand voters and was therefore nearly within the class of the great open boroughs of the type of Eatanswill. The Westminster election of 1774 was a battle between the Percies and the Pelhams, with a Montmorres, a Stanhope and a Mahon joining in. Since both the Percy and the Pelham were elected, the House of Commons decided, with admirable discretion, that Lord Montmorres had not proved direct solicitation by peers, contrary to the sessional order.[3] Mr Grego says that the Westminster election of 1784 'must have been tame by comparison'.[4] It was, however, made memorable by the use of the most attractive ladies of fashion as canvassers. Charles James Fox was threatened with the defeat which attended 'Fox's Martyrs' in that election. Georgiana Spencer, Duchess of Devonshire, with her sister, the Countess of Duncannon, drove into the suburbs and canvassed the householders. 'The novelty of being solicited by two women of rank and remarkable fashion took the popular taste universally.'[5] The Foxite vote went up at once. The tories brought up reinforcements of the

---

[1] J. Grego, *History of Parliamentary Elections* (1892 ed.), pp. 69–70.
[2] *Ibid.* pp. 226–8. This was the occasion on which the Earl of Halifax ran out of port and had to produce his best claret, whereupon his guests left in a body, since they would not vote for a man who gave them 'sour port'.
[3] *Ibid.* pp. 237–9.
[4] *Ibid.* p. 237.
[5] Wraxall, *Posthumous Memoirs*, quoted by Grego, *op. cit.* p. 271.

same sex, but the tory ladies were neither so young nor so attractive as Georgiana Devonshire and her escorts of whig ladies.

> Sure Heav'n approves of Fox's cause
> (Tho' slaves at Court abhor him);
> To vote for Fox, then, who can pause,
> Since *angels* canvass for him.[1]

There were, however, other canvassers. The Prince of Wales appeared with Fox's badge, laurel and a fox's brush, and an escort of prize-fighters.[2] The poll was closed on the fortieth day and Fox was chaired in a huge procession ending, appropriately enough, with the 'State Carriages of their Graces, the Duchesses of Portland and Devonshire, drawn by six horses, superbly caparisoned, with six running footmen attendant on each'.[3] This was by no means the end of the rejoicing, for the Prince of Wales gave a fête and Mrs Crewe gave a feast, at which everybody, including the Prince, wore the party colours, buff and blue. The Prince toasted 'True Blue and Mrs Crewe', while Mrs Crewe replied with 'True Blue and all of you'.[4]

This kind of thing converted contested elections into sporting contests in which the emotions of the participants were strongly engaged. Georgiana Devonshire's efforts were not a mere friendly gesture to Fox: they were a constitutional rebellion against the King because his powers had increased, were increasing, and ought to be diminished. It was a contest between Pitt and Fox, but on public issues. Though the Duchess did not know it, she helped to found the Liberal party. The 'friends of Mr Fox' supported the 'principles of Mr Fox'; and though Opposition languished during the French Wars, there always was an Opposition, which took office in 1830, passed the Reform Bill, and dominated politics for most of the nineteenth century.

Mr Fox's methods, too, were copied. Princess Lieven described an election in Brighton in 1820:

Everything is turned to account, women and children, too; there is a whole technique of attack, defence and knock-out; there is systematic bribery and, in the midst of it all, a regular saturnalia. The proud aristocrat shakes the

---

[1] Grego, *op. cit.* p. 279.
[2] Lascelles, *The Life of Charles James Fox*, p. 153.
[3] *Ibid.* p. 155.　　　　　　　　　[4] Grego, *op. cit.* pp. 285–6.

butcher by the hand, gives sweets to his wife, and ribbons to the whole family, and so on, down to the dead animals—for the butcher is careful to decorate his meat with pink ribbon. There are probably eight thousand cockades of that colour in Brighton. Everything which displays them is greeted with cheers, everything which does not—with mud and boos. Cheers and insults follow one another and are mingled in the oddest way. What a strange country! What a strange and beautiful thing its Constitution is![1]

There were relics of these picturesque methods in the early years of the twentieth century. Many still living will remember the red and blue cockades of 1910 and the processions of children singing the naughty verse which began (comparatively discreetly):

> Vote, vote, vote for Mr Dodson,
> Turn old Foggy out the land.[2]

This technique was, however, on the way out. Its efficacy had been limited by the growth of the population, the extension of the franchise, the abolition of treating and bribery, the secrecy of the ballot, and the restriction of polling to one day. Canvassing was still the major instrument of the nineteenth century, though after 1868 the election meeting competed with it. The job was taken over and organised by the registration societies from which the local parties developed. It was particularly necessary after 1868 because of the rule that where there were three seats (e.g. in Birmingham) each elector could cast only two votes. This gave the Conservatives one seat unless the Liberal electors were so carefully organised that votes were distributed among all three Liberal candidates, and this was done by the Birmingham Association. As the century developed, too, it became obvious that the real purpose of canvassing must be not to persuade electors to change their allegiance but to 'get out the vote'. If an elector said that he proposed to vote Liberal the Conservative canvasser would strike him off. If he said

---

[1] *The Private Letters of Princess Lieven to Prince Metternich*, p. 23. Somebody ought to write a thesis on the constitutional importance of butchers. There was a story that Georgiana Devonshire kissed a butcher to obtain his vote. Presumably the butcher was the lowest form of shopkeeper, i.e. elector.

[2] Cf. the politer version, supposed to have been sung by the Glee Club of the Conservative Women's Association in R. J. Cruickshank's novel *The Double Quest*, quoted by H. G. Nicholas, *To the Hustings*, p. 323.

he intended to vote Conservative his name would be noted; and if he needed transport a carriage or car would be sent for him. The registered numbers of the persons voting were noted by agents outside the polling stations and conveyed to the committee rooms. In the evening there would be a check on all those who had not voted and canvassers would go forth to get in the laggard voters.

There appears, however, to have been some diminution of canvassing in the present century. Enthusiastic canvassers are not found so easily, people do not like to be dragged from the wireless or television set to answer the door-bell, and there is a general distrust of politicians. It is therefore difficult to get canvassing well done, and if it is done imperfectly it is not very useful.

2. THE PUBLIC MEETING

Meanwhile the public meeting had gained in popularity and then lost. The election dinner, with speeches, is of course an old institution, but it usually came after the election. At county elections, and in boroughs where meetings of electors were called, it was customary for the proposers and seconders of the candidates to extol their virtues. In the popular constituencies, especially those in or near London, the practice of making speeches from the hustings developed late in the eighteenth century. Generally, however, public meetings were discouraged because, in the absence of a professional police force, they so easily got out of hand and led to rioting. It is true that rioting was a recognised election technique, because it kept respectable electors away from the poll, but it was safer for the candidate to appear to have nothing to do with it. The public meeting at which the candidate explained his policy, or that of his party, was a late development because candidates were not supposed to have policies or parties. They were, in theory, elected as independent persons to represent the free and independent electors of the county or borough and to apply their minds to the questions submitted to them by the King. To lecture the country gentlemen on political matters was to try to teach grandmother to suck eggs. Indeed, the attitude was the same as that of the middle-class elector today. It is very helpful for Colonel Dodson, the Conservative candidate, to go along to the factory to explain to the men the connexion between high wages and a high cost of living; but you and I know a good deal more about it than Colonel Dodson, who is quite a decent chap but not very strong on economics, and anyhow he is only going to tell them what he has in the 'Notes for Speakers' compiled in the Central Office. Colonel Dodson's predecessors had no 'Notes for Speakers'; but they could not tell the country gentry anything about the price of corn that they did not know already, and indeed they would not dare: it was the job of the electors to tell the Colonel about the price of corn. The election speech was in fact a device to enable the candidate to harangue the lower orders. Free speech was a long way behind free beer as an election device, but it was discovered late in the eighteenth century that 'the mob' included people who thought, or at least felt. The public agitation which followed the decision to seat Colonel Luttrell after John Wilkes's fourth election in 1768 startled the House of Commons by its novelty, for it had not the support of the respectable classes and was disapproved of by the whig leaders.[1] If the forty-shilling freeholders in the urban areas of Middlesex could be organised to support a demagogue like Wilkes the popular electorates in the towns could similarly be organised.

When Edmund Burke was nominated for Bristol in 1774 he made a speech from the hustings and also made the famous 'Speech at the Conclusion of the Poll'. This was the first example of the 'frank and unrestrained use of the election platform by a great orator and states-man'.[2] They were quite short speeches, and a person of Burke's eminence could make them to 'the worthy freemen, and this corporation'.[3] The whig leaders took charge of the Economy agitation in 1779 and Charles James Fox and others actually addressed public meetings. Fox remarked that his speech in Wiltshire was the first he had addressed to 'an uncorrupt assembly'.[4] This early enthusiasm for speech-making was, however, very considerably damped by the Gordon Riots of 1780, which grew out of a public meeting to present a petition; while the French Revolution put 'respectable classes' in terror of 'the mob' and

[1] H. Jephson, *The Platform*, I, p. 71.
[2] *Ibid.* I, p. 94.
[3] Burke, *Works* (1834 ed.), I, pp. 176–80.
[4] Jephson, *The Platform*, I, p. 105.

led to legislation against 'seditious meetings' in 1795. Even so, there were many public meetings, some of them even organised by the Foxite leaders. There was, too, some speech-making at the general election of 1802: and in 1804 Sir Francis Burdett, candidate for Middlesex, made a speech from the hustings on every day of the poll for nearly three weeks.[1] When Henry Brougham was a candidate at Liverpool in 1812 he made 160 speeches to clubs, etc., and Canning's speeches were at least as numerous.[2] Even so, public meetings as such were still not 'respectable', nor were they made more respectable by the collaboration of the whigs in the agitation of 1820 in support of Queen Caroline, though that agitation was a great demonstration of the power of popular disapproval.

The Irish agitation for Catholic emancipation from 1823 to 1829 was important because it was the first in which speech-making on a large scale was organised. There were weekly meetings in Dublin and parish meetings in every parish, speakers being sent down from Dublin. The Catholic Association also organised conventions, 'the father of all conventions',[3] in different towns, each town vying with the others to make its convention a more emphatic success. Candidates were put up at the election of 1826, and a number of candidates pledged to emancipation were successful.[4] 'The nation had become a nation of politicians, not a single chapel which had not its lecture, not a single lecture which had not thousands for its audience.'[5] O'Connell won County Clare in 1828 by a highly organised campaign of speech-making, in which the priests took an active part.[6] His victory was

[1] *Ibid.* I, p. 309.   [2] *Ibid.* I, p. 348.   [3] *Ibid.* II, p. 14.

[4] R. B. McDowell, *Public Opinion and Government Policy in Ireland*, pp. 104–5.

[5] T. Wyse, *Historical Sketch of the late Catholic Association of Ireland*, I, p. 340; quoted by Jephson, *op. cit.* II, p. 18.

[6] According to an adverse but Irish critic, they used other methods also: 'One hundred and fifty priests, very many of them clergymen of saintly lives, watched all the avenues to the polling. The peasantry were adjured to give their votes to O'Connell "for God and the country". The voters of his opponent were denounced by priestly lips as "renegades to God". It was the era of open voting, and if an elector was observed going to vote against O'Connell, a priest rushed to intercept, and making the sign of the Cross with his consecrated hand upon the peasant's forehead, turned him back from his purpose. A forty-shilling freeholder who had voted for O'Connell's rival was announced to the crowd by a priest as having dropped dead, and the awed multitude were asked to go on their knees "and beg God for mercy on his soul"': F. H. O'Donnell, *History of the Irish Parliamentary Party*, I, p. 22.

the most significant single event in the history of electioneering. 'O'Connell's election challenged not only the Protestant ascendancy but the great landed interests' traditional control over county politics, and provided a disturbing illustration of the power wielded by a popular organisation managed by middle-class liberal politicians. No longer, as an indignant Conservative put it, were elections to be decided by freeholders voting as directed by "generous benefactors, steady friends, extended information and superior judgment".[1] That goes a little too far: generous benefactors, steady friends, extended information and superior judgment won a great many elections after 1828; but it is true that the importance of organisation and agitation was demonstrated. The Duke of Wellington's remark, 'The Irish gentlemen have at present none of the influence which belongs to men of property in a well-regulated society',[2] was ominous for England as well as for Ireland. Influence could be destroyed by organising public opinion on great issues.

The lesson was indeed learned in England. 'Agitation and organisation' on the Irish model could be used to secure reform.[3] It was, however, much easier to organise the Catholic freeholders of County Clare than it was to organise the independent electors of England and Wales. The Parliament of 1830 was due not to organisation and agitation but to spontaneous combustion, though in the middle of it a spark flew from another French Revolution and the newspapers were not slow to blow on all the flames they could find. Ministers lost only some twenty or thirty seats, but members in all sections had felt the heat. The Duke of Wellington admitted, with some exaggeration, that 'there was scarcely an election, even in a corrupt borough, in which the candidates were not called upon to give pledges, and did not pledge themselves to vote for Reform'.[4]

The general election of 1831 was better organised, of course on a local basis, the Political Unions, where they existed, taking the lead.[5] There was real electioneering throughout England and Wales and

[1] R. B. McDowell, *Public Opinion and Government Policy in Ireland*, p. 106.
[2] Quoted *ibid*.
[3] Jephson, *The Platform*, II, p. 38.
[4] Quoted by J. R. M. Butler, *The Passing of the Great Reform Bill*, pp. 97–8.
[5] *Ibid.* pp. 221–5.

influence virtually disappeared.[1] Even Scotland, which had never had the hustings, took a hand, though the Reformers could not do much.[2] In the House of Commons there was a majority of 367 to 231 for the Reform Bill. The rejection of the Bill by the House of Lords started a great spate of public meetings, and the Political Unions secured a great accession of strength.

From this period, too, came the practice of public speaking by Ministers. Lord Liverpool, though Prime Minister for nearly fifteen years, never made a public speech outside Parliament[3]—though perhaps his was not such a good record as that of the Duke of Portland, Prime Minister from 1804 to 1807, who never spoke in the House of Lords either.[4] The Duke of Wellington rarely spoke outside Parliament, and never on political subjects.[5] Lord Althorp spoke at a public dinner in September, 1831; Earl Grey and Lord Althorp were given the freedom of the City of London in July 1832. By the end of 1833 a newspaper could write of 'the customary ministerial dinner circuit'— Lord Brougham had spoken at York, Lord John Russell at Plymouth, Lord Stanley at Manchester, etc. In the autumn of 1834 Lord Brougham made a speaking tour of Scotland, while Earl Grey (after his resignation), Lord Brougham and the Earl of Durham spoke at a dinner in Edinburgh.[6] This led to the King's protesting:

His Majesty has...not ceased to deprecate the practice, which has more especially obtained lately, of giving great dinners, which are a sort of political assembly at which topics are introduced which necessarily lead to crimination and recrimination when parties are split as at present, and he also objects to 'itinerant' speechifying, particularly by individuals holding high offices.[7]

The King was following a royal tradition in resisting an inevitable trend; for though the growth of public opinion enabled the whigs (under a complaisant monarch) to reform the system of representation, the decision of so many electors to choose their members according to their political opinions necessarily compelled both members of Parliament and Ministers to keep turning their ears to find out what their constituents were saying and compelled Ministers to go into the

---

[1] Jephson, *The Platform*, II, pp. 77–85. [2] Butler, *op. cit.* pp. 223–5.
[3] Jephson, *op. cit.* II, p. 162. [4] *Life of Lord Liverpool*, I, p. 228.
[5] Jephson, *op. cit.* II, p. 162. [6] *Ibid.* pp. 163–9.
[7] *Lord Melbourne's Papers*, p. 217.

country and defend themselves. Influence was still important, even as late as 1880, but Greville noticed the changed conditions in 1833, though he obviously did not appreciate their significance: 'every man is thinking of what he shall say to his constituents, and how his vote will be taken'.[1] What was lacking, at that time—and this was the burden of Greville's criticism—was organisation into parliamentary parties which would (though Greville did not go so far as this) be based upon local organisation in the constituencies. Then the party would be able to tell its members what to say in their constituencies. In due course Colonel Dodson would have his 'Notes for Speakers'.

Until party organisation and discipline provided stiffening, Governments tended to be weak in face of public opinion. Professor Yonge's comment, made in 1868, is exaggerated, but it expresses the view of a historian who had had exceptional opportunities for comparing the working of the Constitution before the first Reform Act and before the second Reform Act: Lord Liverpool was

the very last Minister who has been able fully to carry out his own political views; who has been so strong that in matters of general policy the Opposition could extort no concessions from him which were not sanctioned by his own deliberate judgment; the very last who, in the strict sense of the word, can be said to have governed England.... The Reform Bill...has unquestionably had the effect...of rendering the Government permanently and incurably weak; so that since his day there has been no Prime Minister who has not found himself compelled to consent to, and even at times to adopt and promote measures inconsistent with his previous professions, adverse to his notions of general policy and condemned, or at least dreaded, by his deliberate judgment.[2]

It may be doubted whether this correctly represents the attitudes of Sir Robert Peel, Lord Russell, Lord Palmerston and Lord Derby (or Disraeli): but undoubtedly the play of a fortuitous public opinion, acting upon members who had no strong local organisations, before the two-party system had been cemented by the rivalry of Gladstone and Disraeli, did introduce a measure of instability. The Government is not, however, 'permanently and incurably weak' because it can no longer be defeated in the House of Commons and is therefore safe for four

[1] *Journals of the Reigns of George IV and William IV*, III, p. 17.
[2] *Life of Lord Liverpool*, I, pp. 3–4.

years. On the other hand, the development has compelled every Minister and every member of Parliament to agree with his party and even to assert, with all the strength of the 'mob orator', that his party is wholly in the right and the other people wholly wrong. Since no sensible person can possibly believe that and politicians are usually quite sensible people, the result is that the 'mob orator' talks a lot of nonsense which he knows to be nonsense and most of his audience knows to be nonsense. This curious tradition may be on the way out: few electors go to election meetings now and it is very difficult to arouse enthusiasm over the sins of one's opponents when the wireless or television has to compete with little Johnny, who wants a glass of water, teen-age Margaret, who wants to switch to Luxemburg and have a dance, and grown-up Herbert who dislikes being told to do washing-up and is therefore doing it noisily. Father, expectorating into the fire, is apt to say 'them —— politicians'; and when Father swears we all swear.

The growth of organised parties is discussed elsewhere.[1] It was not, however, in the parties but in the agitation for the Charter and the activities of the Anti-Corn Law League that public opinion grew up. The Charter was backed mainly by working-class opinion; and, though it failed, it made almost inevitable the extension of the franchise to that class. The League was essentially middle-class, though the working classes joined in.[2] Its success was helped by two factors. First, the peripatetic 'lecturers' were able to travel by railway; secondly, its circulars could be sent by the penny post.[3] Since the League was against the landlords, its activities virtually spelled the end of influence except in the strictly rural areas. Its method was the public meeting, and indeed the mass meeting, for its leading members were Nonconformists who knew the contagion of mass emotion. Its precedents were the Catholic Association of the twenties and the Reform agitation; but, unlike them, it was a genuinely national organisation and went into every town and village:

The Political Unions had been a rough-and-ready combination, in a revolutionary crisis, to frighten the tories into surrender; and O'Connell banded

[1] Volume II.   [2] Cobden in 1842: Jephson, *The Platform*, II, p. 315.
[3] *Ibid.* p. 316.

together, under the hypnotism of his personality, an oppressed race, singularly homogeneous in its social and intellectual experience. The League, on the other hand, was a means of educating the very various classes and sects of English society in town and village, up to the point of uniting them all in a common enthusiasm for a proposition in economics.[1]

That proposition, if true, affected the lives of millions of men, but it was acceptable, at least at the outset, to neither of the great political groups. The constitutional machine had before 1832 been almost exclusively in the hands of the country landlords; after 1832 the urban middle class had received representation, but the increased representation of the counties had retained predominance in the landlords, and indeed the Parliaments of 1832, 1835, 1837 and 1841 were much like that of 1830. In the agitation against the corn laws the interests of the urban middle class coincided with those of the virtually unrepresented working class. As John Bright put it in his motion in 1846 for the suspension of the active operation of the League in view of the repeal of the corn laws, 'out of a machine especially contrived for the contrary, justice and freedom are at length achieved for the nation'.[2] As is usual in political speeches, Bright claimed rather more than his due, but it is undoubted that the League succeeded, by public agitation and otherwise, in changing British policy for nearly a century.

The League made the public meeting a normal and active part of political controversy. The lesson was not learned by the registration societies, however, until the foundation of the Birmingham Liberal Association in 1868 and that, as we have seen, had a particular objective, the organisation of the Liberal electors in such a manner that, though each had only two votes, all three of the Birmingham seats could be won by the Liberals, thus nullifying the minority clause of the Representation of the People Act, 1867. It was, however, not merely an electoral machine whose activities were suspended between elections. Being used for municipal politics also, it was constantly active. Moreover it was soon discovered that it was not enough to 'get out the vote' at a general election, it was necessary to win the electorate between elections and retain it. This process, called 'political education', implied

[1] G. M. Trevelyan, *Life of John Bright*, p. 91.   [2] *Ibid.* p. 151.

that the main function of a political association was not to make certain that its supporters were on the register and that they voted at the election, but to create a body of supporters. The function was of course particularly important after 1867 because the urban householders had to be 'educated' to vote the right way, and again after 1884 because the rural householders had similarly to be persuaded. Accordingly the seventies and eighties of the nineteenth century were the great days of the public meeting. The 'Birmingham plan' spread rapidly over the country and was copied by the Conservatives, though slowly and with great reluctance.

The public meeting was the principal device of the political association for several reasons. First, the personal canvass was no longer practicable as a means for political 'conversion', though it could be used to get out the vote when 'political education' had been completed and the party was cashing in at the election. The foundation of the personal canvass under Old Corruption had been the social subordination of the elector to the patron or the landlord. The Marquis of Wharton did not propose to discuss politics with 'Dick'. What he wanted was simply to 'drink a glass with him'. Similarly, Georgiana, Duchess of Devonshire, did not deliver lectures on the principles of whiggism. There was of course much of this social condescension in the late nineteenth century, and even now the 'Ladies' of the Conservative party are among its assets, particularly among the socially self-conscious middle classes. Attitudes in the working classes were changing in consequence of unemployment and trade union action in the eighties and nineties, but the principle that 'Jack is as good as his master' was not firmly and widely established before 1914. Even so, the Liberals could not play the picture cards after 1885 because most of them were in Conservative hands. They had to persuade, and with the large electorates created by the Reform Acts of 1867 and 1884 this could not be done by a personal canvass.

In the second place, though much use was made of 'literature' in the form of leaflets and pamphlets,[1] a substantial part of the electorate could not read and a much larger part did not read. One must not judge from the small circulations of newspapers, because they were comparatively

[1] Chapter VI.

expensive, and because modern methods of distribution depend on the rubber tyre and the internal combustion engine.[1] People who can read but have very little to read, because they cannot afford books and papers, do read leaflets and pamphlets which a more sophisticated generation spurns as boring. Nevertheless, there were electors who could not be converted in this way, and in any case the reading of pamphlets is a middle-class disease.

In the third place, the public meeting was much the quickest and cheapest method of getting at the electorate. There were few counter-attractions, and both the public house and the music-hall cost money, whereas the public meeting cost nothing and even, in the winter, saved heating and lighting. Provided that the organisers put up a show, an audience could be gathered without great difficulty, as the Anti-Corn Law League had shown.

In the fourth place, the public meeting had a contagious effect on the audience. The technique was that of the Nonconformists, as adapted by the Anti-Corn Law League, which was itself an emanation of the Nonconformist conscience. It was necessary to get a large, closely packed and enthusiastic audience, whose emotions were played upon by a skilled orator, preferably a player of tragedies like Gladstone or Bright, not a comedian like Disraeli, who was much more effective in the House of Commons. Even the inferior politicians soon picked up the tricks of the trade, especially the three-pronged sentence, still in vogue. 'I say this book ought never to have been written (*hear, hear*); it is trash (*cheers*); it is a disgrace to civilisation (*loud and prolonged applause*).' In other words, it is rather a feeble sort of book.

In the fifth place, frequent and successful meetings were 'good for the party'. It is not easy to get together a large voluntary organisation at each election. The volunteers have to be continuously employed, otherwise they will take up religion, or football, or gardening. Frequent committee meetings are very helpful. A political association is therefore given an unnecessarily complex structure, is associated with like-minded associations, and federated or united in a grand national

[1] It used to be necessary to send a boy down to the railway station—and he had no bicycle.

assembly. Everybody can then have a gay time sending resolutions up, down and sidewise and debating them at length at every level. They can eventually be disposed of by an agenda committee of hard-faced professionals, but meanwhile everybody has been happy to take such an active part in the formulation of national policy. This is the stuff of political life, but circuses also are necessary. Balls (mostly Conservative), dances (mostly Labour), whist drives (typically Liberal) and trips to Blackpool, Bournemouth, Eastbourne or Southend (according to party) are or were useful and among the major trials of a prospective candidate. To do a real job of work, however, one had to organise a meeting. It required a series of committee meetings and the allocation of jobs among the members—hiring a hall, getting a lord to preside, hiring furniture, printing tickets, organising stewards, arranging seats on the platform, selecting speakers, getting hospitality for visitors, and so forth. The more meetings there were, the more work had to be done, and the happier everybody was to be of service to the party and, by definition, to the country. The tram, the bicycle, the bus and the car helped, by enabling the politically-conscious towns to distribute their messages among the villagers.

This epidemic of public meetings has now died down, but it has left some legacies. Members still have to be oracles, though they need not be orators. The Governments of the eighteenth century saw to it that there were enough 'men of business' in the House of Commons to run public affairs. Not many are there now, though a great many more are wanted. This is not only because the late nineteenth century encouraged slick talkers with superficial minds, but it is one of the causes. Modern speeches have to be much shorter than they were in the great days, but each has still to make a point in as many different ways as possible, so as to get that point home. The art of political speaking is still the art of exaggeration.[1] Politics has to appear to be, not a choice between bad alternatives, but a choice between good and evil, so that every problem looks simple until one gets into office, and then it would be simple if it were not for the Opposition. Blackguarding the other side may be the

---

[1] 'The loose-tongued vituperation, the reckless use of second-hand facts, the appeals to every form of unthinking prejudice—the tools of Cobbett's trade' (and of the trade of many politicians since): Graham Wallas, *Life of Francis Place*, pp. 116–17.

mark of a bad lawyer, but it is the mark of a good politician. A passage, taken almost at random, will illustrate:

Gentlemen, I have come into this country [Scotland] to repeat, with your permission, the indictment which I have to the best of my ability endeavoured to make many times elsewhere against Her Majesty's Government. It is a very serious indictment. It is well in these things that men should be held to the words that they utter, should be made to feel that they are responsible for them, and therefore you will perhaps allow me to read a sentence, which I embodied in the letter written in reply to your most flattering and most obliging invitation. My sentence was this: 'The management of finance, the scale of expenditure, the constantly growing arrears of legislation, serious as they are, only lead up to still greater questions. I hold before you, as I have held in the House of Commons, that the faith and honour of the country have been gravely compromised in the foreign policy of the Ministry; that by the disturbance of confidence, and lately even of peace, which they have brought about, they have prolonged and aggravated the public distress; that they have augmented the power and influence of the Russian Empire, even while estranging the feelings of its population; that they have embarked the Crown and people in an unjust war [in Afghanistan], full of mischief if not of positive danger to India; and that by their use of the treaty-making and war-making powers of the Crown they have abridged the just rights of Parliament and have presented prerogative to the nation under an unconstitutional aspect which tends to make it unsecure.' Not from one phrase, not from one syllable of that indictment do I recede.[1]

This passage from one of Gladstone's speeches at Midlothian in 1879 is not typical of him because most of it comes from his election address, compresses a good deal of criticism into one paragraph in consequence, and does not illustrate his torrential eloquence with its vast verbiage and enormous sentences. On this Lord Morley, who was present, must be quoted:

It was Demosthenes, not Isocrates. It was the orator of concrete detail, of inductive instances, of energetic and immediate object; the orator confidently and by sure touch startling into watchfulness the whole spirit of civil duty in a man; elastic and supple, pressing fact and figure with a fervid insistence that was known from his career and character to be neither forced nor feigned, but to be himself. In a word, it was a man—a man impressing him-

[1] A. Tilney Bassett, *Gladstone's Speeches*, p. 563.

self upon the kindled throngs by the breadth of his survey of great affairs of life and nation, by the depth of his vision, by the power of his stroke. Physical resources had much to do with the effect; his overflowing vivacity, the fine voice and flashing eye and a whole frame in free, ceaseless, natural and spontaneous motion. So he bore his hearers through long chains of strenuous periods, calling up by the marvellous transformations of his mien a succession of images—as if he were now a keen hunter, now some eager bird of prey, now a charioteer of fiery steeds kept well in hand, and now and again we seemed to hear the pity or dark wrath of a prophet, with the mighty rushing wind and the fire running along the ground.[1]

The quotation from Gladstone's speech does, however, show how to criticise a Government. This being the indictment, one would like Lord Beaconsfield's defence; but he, as a peer, could not make election speeches; and, when the election was over, it was easier to attack the new Liberal Government for what it had done, or not done, in Ireland:

I do not know anything which would be more justifiable than an amendment on the Address, expressing our deep regret that measures for maintaining peace and order, for guarding life and property, and, let me add, liberty, which I think is equally in danger in Ireland, were not taken in time, and pointing out that if such measures had been taken in time an enormous number of terrible incidents might have been averted; that men would now have been alive who have been murdered; that houses would now have been in existence which have been burned; that cases of torture to man and beast would never have happened....[2]

In case this seems a feeble riposte, let us take a speech of 1872, when Disraeli was Leader of the Opposition and Gladstone was Prime Minister. Having said that the Administration was 'avowedly formed on a principle of violence' Disraeli mentioned Conservative policy in Ireland.

The policy of our successors was different. Their specific was to despoil churches and plunder landlords, and what had been the result? Sedition rampant, treason thinly veiled, and whenever a vacancy occurs in the representation a candidate is returned pledged to the destruction of the realm [i.e. Home Rule]. Her Majesty's new ministers proceeded in their career like a body of men under the influence of some delirious drug. Not satisfied with

---

[1] Morley, *Life of Gladstone*, II, pp. 593–4.
[2] *Select Speeches of the Earl of Beaconsfield*, II, pp. 227–8.

the spoliation and anarchy of Ireland, they began to attack every institution and every interest, every class and calling in the country.[1]

After explaining this last phrase, Disraeli came to a famous passage:

As time advanced it was not difficult to perceive that extravagance was being substituted for energy by the Government.... Their paroxysms ended in prostration. Some took refuge in melancholy and their eminent chief alternated between a menace and a sigh. As I sat opposite the Treasury Bench the ministers reminded me of one of those marine landscapes not very unusual on the coasts of South America. You behold a range of exhausted volcanoes. Not a flame flickers on a single pallid crest. But the situation is still dangerous. There are occasional earthquakes, and ever and anon the dark rumbling of the sea.[2]

Lord Morley called this 'one of the few classic pieces of the oratory of the century'. But when we of the next century admire the oratory of those great gladiators, and wish that we had been there to hear, we nevertheless ask ourselves what it was all about. Was Church and land reform in Ireland so very stupid? It did not, as Gladstone thought it would, provide an adequate substitute for Home Rule; but the Conservatives eventually conceded not merely Home Rule but Dominion status, a republic, and independence outside the Commonwealth. The Volunteers, whose establishment Disraeli attacked, fought quite well in South Africa and never menaced civil liberties. The Royal Navy, which Gladstone was said to be ruining, did not have to fight for more than forty years and then escorted the German Fleet into captivity. The 'extinct volcanoes' did not abolish the income tax, but neither did the Marquis of Salisbury, Bonar Law, Baldwin or Sir Winston Churchill. Was Disraeli wrong to sign the Treaty of Berlin, to acquire Cyprus and shares in the Suez Canal? Was the Afghan War a greater blunder than the Boer War? We may take sides on these matters, but we can no longer utter such philippics against either Government. They now seem to be neither better nor worse than most Governments.

We ask ourselves, therefore, whether party politics really requires such extravaganzas. In any case the quality deteriorated in the next generation. There are no purple patches in Joseph Chamberlain's speeches; there is hard hitting in plain, unadorned but translucent

[1] *Select Speeches of the Earl of Beaconsfield*, II, p. 513.   [2] *Ibid.* p. 516.

language, sometimes not in the best of taste.[1] Nobody nowadays can read the 'interminable repertory of damnable iterations'[2] of the Home Rule controversy without a sense of bewilderment. Evidently there were powerful passions engaged which, in so far as they affected Englishmen, nobody can now pretend to understand. The impression the speeches give is that both sides became punch-drunk, hitting they knew not whom or why. It was a battle fought for its own sake, and everybody seems to have forgotten that the whole purpose was to find a solution to the problem of governing Ireland.

Perhaps this struggle rose to the peak of intensity between 1909 and 1914. It was still about Ireland, but this time there was a more intelligible reason also. Joseph Chamberlain's defection probably prevented the enactment of Radical measures, but the Radicals at last assumed control in 1906. The old governing class, whom Chamberlain himself had asked to pay 'ransom' for their property, feared the sequel when the strength of their last bastion, the House of Lords, was seriously reduced. There was still the curious passion over Home Rule, but the two questions were mixed.

Since 1918 the bandying of insults has been much reduced, and we must ask why. There have been occasions, as over the invasion of Abyssinia by the Italian Fascisti, the Spanish civil war, and the Suez adventure of 1956, in which controversy has been fierce. In each case there was a moral issue, and honest men took opposite sides. There was no such issue in 1931, when MacDonald formed the so-called National Government. The passions of politicians were turbulent, and some of the nastiest insults of the century were bandied about: but looking back we can say with reasonable assurance that if all the politicians had advised the King to send for a sensible peer and commission him to form a non-party Government for six months the whole problem could have been solved with as much satisfaction to everybody as the circumstances allowed.

For the rest, the inter-war period was comparatively calm. A partial explanation is the ingrained respect of the Labour party for a majority

---

[1] *Life of Joseph Chamberlain*, I, pp. 467, 549; II, pp. 63, 71, 73, 303. For Mr Garvin's favourable verdict on his oratory, see *ibid.* I, p. 547.

[2] Mr Garvin's phrase, *ibid.* II, p. 303.

decision, which induced it to accept its defeats in 1924 and 1931 as the sort of thing that might happen to a constitutional party and to carry on as His Majesty's Opposition. Another partial explanation is that Baldwin's sentimentalism led him, especially after the General Strike of 1926, to adopt something of a cross-bench attitude. The principal explanation seems to be, however, the great social developments of the twentieth century. The middle classes took to their cars and the rest of the population to the cinema. The prima donnas were not politicians but film stars; the gladiators were footballers and cricketers; occasionally one had to turn aside to see what them politicians was a doing of; but nothing they could do would interfere with the excitement of a test match or a cup final. If one wanted to listen to anybody one did not go to a public meeting; one switched on the wireless. Newspaper proprietors discovered that women, crime and sport sold a newspaper, and that the quickest way to kill it was to put politics into it. Political broadcasts were accepted with great hesitation, but when they were the tub-thumpers came off very badly, for the essence of a political meeting is a vast, enthusiastic audience: and there is no vast, enthusiastic audience in the kitchen, when Father has his shoes off, Mother peels the potatoes, Marilyn is waiting for the boy-friend, and the kids are even more noisy than usual. If the politician wanted to get a hearing he had to drop his Town Hall tactics and be calm, cool and sensible. The public meeting became a dozen stalwarts and a couple of oddities in an uncomfortable schoolroom. The candidate had to go round the streets with a loud-speaker, in the forlorn hope that his voice would not be drowned by the wireless set. Not a single politician, except perhaps Sir Winston Churchill after 1945, could fill the Town Hall. Ministers still make public speeches, and in the expensive newspapers they may secure half a column.

Nevertheless, the politicians play the game as they have done for a hundred years. In public they slander each other according to the tradition of Joseph Chamberlain. It is an odd process, for nobody really believes that they are doing much more than secure publicity for themselves. Among the electors a scepticism has set in. The situation is of course dangerous. A Prime Minister is selected from among a miscellaneous collection of Old Etonians living on capital, retired service and professional men, journalists, broadcasters, lawyers, and trade union officials, all selected by self-selected and unrepresentative committees in the constituencies. They spend their time in shadow-boxing. They are quite sensible people; and at select committees and other bodies they make very sensible criticisms because they are then 'non-party'; but when speaking in the House of Commons or the constituencies they become 'party' and therefore talk a lot of stuff which they and the electors know to be extravaganzas. As Princess Lieven said in 1820: 'What a strange country! What a strange and beautiful thing its Constitution is!'

CHAPTER VI

GRUB STREET[1]

'If the world could be saved by sermons and pamphlets', says Professor Tawney about the sixteenth century,[2] 'it would have been a Paradise.' The flood was let loose by the invention of printing. It is probable that at the end of the fifteenth century half the population of England could read. There were few literates in the North and West, but many in the populous towns and the better populated countryside.[3] The books first produced were for the most part Bibles, breviaries, books of devotion and lives of the saints; and they were read by ordinary people who could not afford manuscript copies.[4] Religion never had been regarded as a mystery confided to the priests alone; and indeed the claim of the Church of Rome to the prerogative of exclusive inter-pretation of the scriptures was developed long after the Reformation. With cheap pamphlets and printed books every man who could read could be a theologian; and theology became not only the stuff of politics but the great national sport—until the 'saints' gave the country too much of it.

The richer and more intensive town life which Tudor prosperity had brought to London created a demand for something more, the sort of news and gossip which are now provided by the newspapers. In the proclamation suppressing, or intending to suppress,[5] Cowell's *Inter-preter*, James I complained of the insatiable curiosity abroad in the land and the itching of tongues and pens to leave nothing unsearched to the

---

[1] 'Originally the name of a street near Moorfields in London, much inhabited by writers of small histories, dictionaries, and temporary poems, whence any mean pro-duction is called *Grub Street*': Dr Johnson's *Dictionary*. Grub Street is now called Milton Street, after the poet; but it is commonly assumed to be a derisory name for Fleet Street, where the newspapers have tended to congregate. It suggests that journalists are impecunious hack writers.

[2] *Religion and the Rise of Capitalism*, p. 73.

[3] H. Maynard Smith, *Pre-Reformation England*, p. 102.

[4] *Ibid.* p. 425.

[5] It is not clear that it was suppressed. The most obvious place to look for copies was the Library of Trinity Hall. A copy of the 'suppressed' edition is still there, as well as one of the edition of 1727 which contains the text of the proclamation.

bottom both in talking and writing. 'Men in this age do not spare to wade in all the deepest mysteries that belong to persons or state of kings and princes that are gods upon earth.'[1] It was a heavy-handed rebuke for a Master of Trinity Hall who had merely tried to produce a law dictionary, but it conveys the sense of disquiet which the broadcasting of printed matter was creating. There were in fact many proclamations designed to suppress licentious speech and writing. They were enforced in the Star Chamber and the Council; and, though they did not suppress licentious speech, they did hinder the development of the newspaper. Under Charles I there were newsbooks giving news of events abroad, but no corresponding publications dealing with domestic affairs. The abolition by the Long Parliament of the jurisdiction of the Star Chamber and the Council, and the exciting events due to the conflict between King and Parliament, produced scores of newsbooks until Cromwell confined the press to two official publications, each issued once a week.[2]

The official newspaper, the *Oxford Gazette*, was founded in 1665, when the Court was in Oxford because of the plague, and it became the *London Gazette* in 1666.[3] There were, however, no reports of public meetings or parliamentary proceedings during the seventeenth century.[4] The privilege of freedom of debate, which the Parliaments of James I and Charles I had needed to protect them against the King, implied that proceedings in Parliament should be secret. The result was, however, that journalism played no part in the stirring events of the seventeenth century. Speeches were published as pamphlets, but there was no contemporary reporting. That two civil wars could be waged without a newspaper press shows that they were the concern of politicians and small armies, not of the people of England, who were affected only when one of the armies passed near by.

I. THE NEWSPAPERS

Political journalism began with the settled conditions of Queen Anne; and among the journalists were famous men, Jonathan Swift, Daniel

[1] G. Davies, *The Early Stuarts*, p. 409.   [2] *Ibid.* p. 410.
[3] J. B. Williams (or J. G. Muddiman), *History of English Journalism to the Foundation of the Gazette* (1908).   [4] J. Grant, *The Newspaper Press*, I, p. 34.

Defoe, Henry Bolingbroke and Pulteney. The first daily newspaper in the world was the *Daily Courant*, founded in 1702.[1] More important, perhaps, was the *Review*, founded by Defoe in 1704. It was not a daily, but it started the career of the political essay, which played a great part in the formation of public opinion until well into the nineteenth century. The 'versatile, speculative and impecunious Steele'[2] founded the *Tatler* in 1709, and Addison the *Spectator* in 1711. The *Craftsman*, to which Bolingbroke contributed, was started in 1726, and the *Gentleman's Magazine* in 1731. Politics were not the special concern of these periodicals. They provided general reading for cultured households. Their successors were the *Edinburgh Review* (1802) and the *Quarterly Review* (1809) of the nineteenth century, and by this time politics predominated. As communications improved and events moved faster, however, the monthly reviews lost their influence. The *Economist*, which was founded in 1843, indicated by its title the demands of a new class of readers and began the series of weekly reviews, which continues to the present day with the *Spectator* and the *New Statesman*.

The progress of newspapers was impeded by several factors. Professor Aspinall, writing of the period 1780–1850,[3] lists five causes. First, there were technical difficulties. Newspapers were printed by hand at the rate of about 250 sheets an hour. *The Times* used steam power from 1814 and could print 1100 sheets an hour. By 1824 printing at the rate of 4000 sheets an hour was practicable. Secondly, communications were so bad that distribution was difficult. From 1784, when the coach from London to Manchester was scheduled to complete the journey in twenty-four hours, the stage coaches could be used; but the problem of distribution was not solved until the railways were built. Even in the late nineteenth century, however, provincial readers had to buy their copies at the railway station; and the present system depends upon delivery to newsagents by railway, bicycle and delivery van. Thirdly, the great mass of the population was illiterate. In 1840 ten out of eleven persons were completely illiterate, and the situation

---

[1] J. Grant, *The Newspaper Press*, I, p. 87.
[2] Sir Leslie Stephen, *English Literature and Society in the Eighteenth Century*, p. 70.
[3] *Politics and the Press, 1750–1850*, ch. 1; see also A. Aspinall, 'The Circulation of Newspapers in the Early Nineteenth Century', *Review of English Studies*, XXII, pp. 29–43.

improved only very slowly until the end of the nineteenth century, when compulsory education began to take effect. Fourthly, the governing class was opposed to the circulation of newspapers among persons other than themselves, since they were thought to stimulate public agitation which, in an age in which the justice of the peace and the village constable represented public order, was dangerous to the stability of the country. Popular newspapers were as much disliked as mob oratory, and in fact there were none until the twentieth century. The newspapers dealt with politics in stodgy essays, designed for the respectable classes. Fifthly, there was heavy taxation. A stamp duty of $\frac{1}{2}d.$ a half sheet was imposed in 1712 at the same time as a tax of 1s. on every advertisement. In 1757 the advertisement duty was doubled and the newspaper tax raised to 1d. for a sheet or half a sheet. In 1776 the newspaper tax was raised to $1\frac{1}{2}d.$ a sheet and in 1780 the advertisement duty to 2s. 6d. In 1789, the year of the French Revolution, the rates were 2d. and 3s., and in 1797 the newspaper tax was $3\frac{1}{2}d.$ In 1815, the year of Waterloo, the rates were 4d. and 3s. 6d. There was also a duty on paper. The Times then cost 7d. a copy, of which $5\frac{1}{2}d.$ went on taxation, printing, and the discount on distribution.[1] In 1836 the tax was reduced to 1d., and the price of The Times then came down to 5d. In 1855 the tax was repealed; and the last of the 'taxes on knowledge', the paper duties, were repealed in 1861, though against the opposition of the House of Lords. Sixthly, though stamped newspapers were sent free of charge to any part of the British Isles, they could not be sent abroad unless franked by post office officials, who derived a lucrative revenue from the process.

In spite of these difficulties, the circulation of newspapers expanded enormously during the Industrial Revolution. In 1753, when the population was 6,200,000, the number of stamps sold was 7,400,000.[2] Table 15 shows the increase between that date and 1836 as given by Professor Aspinall.[3] In 1853, when the population was 27,725,000, the sale was 128,178,900.[4] Thus, in the hundred years between 1753 and 1853 the population had increased $4\frac{1}{2}$ times, but the sale of newspapers had increased 17 times.

---

[1] *History of The Times*, I, p. 332.　　[2] Grant, *Newspaper Press*, I, p. 172.
[3] *Politicians and the Press*, pp. 6, 350.　　[4] Grant, *op. cit.* p. 174.

For many years, however, the circulations of individual newspapers were very small. The great whig organ, the *Morning Chronicle* (founded 1769), had an average circulation of 2500 before 1820,[1] though by 1837 (when the newspaper tax had come down to 1*d.*) it had risen to 9000. The great Liberal daily, the *Morning Herald* (founded 1780), had a circulation of 1200 in 1820, though soon afterwards it took to reporting

	London	Provinces	Total
1776	—	—	12,230,000
1788	—	—	12,800,000
1801	7,000,000	9,000,000	16,000,000
1836	19,250,000	11,000,000	30,250,000

TABLE 15

crime and its circulation went up to 3000.[2] The principal tory paper, the *Morning Post* (founded 1772) sold 300 copies in 1795, 2000 in 1799, and 4500 in 1803, when it had the largest circulation of any newspaper.[3] Later, it was surpassed by the *Courier*, which was founded as a Liberal paper in 1792 but became tory in 1799. It was in close touch with the Foreign Office and its circulation rose to 12,000.[4] On the other hand the *Sun*, which was founded by William Pitt in 1792, had a circulation of less than 400 in 1825, when it turned Liberal.[5] It must however be remembered that the private purchase of newspapers was unusual before 1830.[6] Generally they were read in coffee-houses and taverns; and even in 1829 it was estimated that one copy was read by thirty persons.[7]

The reduction in the stamp duty in 1836 was a barely disguised attack on *The Times*, which had been founded in 1781 as the *Daily Universal Register*, and changed its name in 1785. It was then in competition with eight other daily papers and with nine evening papers published three times a week on 'post' days. Though, like other papers, subsidised by the Government from 1789, it supported Queen Caroline, and thundered for Reform. In 1834 it turned against the whigs, who

[1] *History of The Times*, I, p. 332. [2] *Ibid.* II, p. 234.
[3] Grant, *Newspaper Press*, I, p. 404. [4] *Ibid.* I, p. 355.
[5] *Ibid.* I, p. 333.
[6] *History of The Times*, I, p. 36.
[7] A. Aspinall, *Politicians and the Press*, p. 24.

bought the dying *Morning Chronicle* and reduced the stamp duty in the belief that the reduction would embarrass *The Times*. That paper had since 1822 provided gratis a supplement of four pages, and it was believed that it could not do so if the price was reduced. In fact, however, the change strengthened *The Times*. The penny stamp justified free transmission by post, and subscribers all over the country received a longer and better paper for 5*d.* than any other newspaper could provide. The supplement paid for itself by increased circulation, which rose from 11,000 in 1837[1] to something like 60,000 in 1855.[2] In that year the new *Saturday Review* alleged that 'this country is ruled by *The Times*'.[3]

In 1855 the newspaper tax was remitted and the privilege of free carriage by post abolished. Since *The Times* was heavier than other newspapers because of the supplement, its rates became 4*d.* unstamped or 5½*d.* stamped, while the price of its competitors became 4*d.* unstamped or 5*d.* stamped. Further, provincial newspapers could compete with the London papers more easily. The weekly *Manchester Guardian* (founded 1831) became a daily, and among the provincial newspapers established were the *Liverpool Post*, the *Sheffield Telegraph*, the *Birmingham Mercury*, and the *Scotsman* (Edinburgh).[4] These were 'quality' papers like the London papers, appealing to the members of the upper middle class.

The main purpose of the Radicals who initiated the removal of the 'tax on knowledge' was, however, to enable smaller and cheaper news-papers to be produced in London for what was called 'the million', the literate people, mostly of the lower middle class, whose members could not afford a 5*d.* newspaper. The *Daily News* was founded by Charles Dickens in 1846 but did not pay, and the management was taken over by Charles Wentworth Dilke,[5] who reduced the price from 5*d.* to 2½*d.* and took the circulation from 4000 to 22,000.[6] The *Morning Chronicle* then reduced its price to 4*d.*, and in 1848 the *London Telegraph* was founded at 3*d.*, though it lasted only five months. These efforts were

---

[1] *History of The Times*, I, p. 332.
[2] *Ibid.* II, p. 234.   [3] *Ibid.* II, p. 300.   [4] *Ibid.* II, p. 294.
[5] Grandfather of Sir Charles Dilke, the Radical politician.
[6] *History of The Times*, II, p. 195.

unsuccessful, the *Daily News* (which had raised its price to 3*d.*) being in financial difficulties and the *Morning Chronicle* losing readers. There was, however, an unsatisfied demand for a cheap newspaper within the reach of 'the million'. The remission of the newspaper tax produced immediately the *Daily Telegraph and Courier* (which soon dropped 'and Courier') at 2*d.*, though in a few months the price was brought down to 1*d.* At this price its circulation rose to 27,000. A few months later Cobden and Bright brought out two new penny papers, the *Morning Star* and the *Evening Star*. For the most part, these penny papers created a new readership among the poorer members of the literate classes, but they also took readers away from the *Morning Chronicle*, the *Morning Herald*, and the *Morning Post*. Further, the *Standard*, founded in 1821 as an evening paper, became a morning paper at 2*d.*, while retaining its size and quality. In 1858 it reduced its price to 1*d.*

The result of these changes was that the circulation of *The Times* came down to 50,000, while the *Daily Telegraph* and the *Standard* had about 30,000 each. In 1861, however, the paper tax was remitted. *The Times* came down to 3*d.*, and its circulation rose to 65,000.[1] Indeed, it ousted the *Morning Chronicle*, which in 1862 was absorbed in the *Daily Telegraph*, and the *Morning Herald*, which closed down in 1869.[2] This left *The Times* with only one rival in its own field, the *Morning Post*, but even that rivalry disappeared in 1881, when the price of the *Post* was reduced to a penny.[3] *The Times* had, however, failed to capture the new readers of a lower class. In 1870 the circulation of the *Daily News*, which had reduced its price to 1*d.* in 1868, rose to 150,000, and very soon the *Daily Telegraph* was claiming the 'Largest Circulation in the World', with a daily average issue of 200,000.[4]

There was, however, an increasing market in the working class, especially after the board schools established from 1870 produced a new generation of literates. In 1892 two halfpenny papers were founded, *The Morning*, afterwards the *Morning Herald*, which was

[1] *History of The Times*, II, pp. 298–9.
[2] *Ibid.* II, p. 303; Grant, *Newspaper Press*, I, pp. 312, 319.
[3] R. Lucas, *Lord Glenesk and the 'Morning Post'*, p. 285.
[4] *History of The Times*, II, pp. 307, 354.

absorbed into the *Daily Express* in 1900; and the *Morning Leader*, which survived until it was absorbed into the *Daily News* in 1912. The most successful halfpenny paper, however, was the *Daily Mail*, established in 1896. Though priced to catch the working-class reader, its tone was rather higher. A halfpenny paper relied on circulation to boost advertisement revenue, but advertisers wanted readers who spent money, preferably on luxury articles. Hence the *Daily Mail* became the business man's paper, the business man who voted Unionist but could not be bothered with stodgy politics and who wanted something to read in the train. Its success led to the foundation of the *Daily Express* in 1900. The opinion was growing that too much politics killed a newspaper; and the *Express*, even more than the *Mail*, concentrated on features and sport. It was not, however, a very flourishing newspaper until the war of 1914 to 1918, after most of the shares had been acquired (in 1913) by Lord Beaverbrook.

Meanwhile the other newspapers were feeling the competition. *The Times* remained at 3*d.* until 1912, but competition from the *Morning Post* and the *Daily Telegraph* had reduced its circulation to 40,000. In 1908 it had been secretly brought under the control of Alfred Harmsworth, afterwards Lord Northcliffe. In 1913 the price was brought down to 2*d.*, but the gain in readers was only 6000, insufficient to justify the reduction.[1] In the following year, the price came down to 1*d.* At this level, thought Lord Northcliffe,[2] *The Times* could attract advertisers from the *Morning Post* and the *Daily Telegraph* if it could attain a circulation of 120,000. Actually, the average sale after the reduction was 145,000,[3] and the outbreak of war in 1914 sent it still higher.

Northcliffe's view that the trade could not support four 'quality' papers proved to be correct, though three papers struggled on. *The Standard*, the fourth penny paper, ceased publication in 1917. It had long been supported by its faithful, but aging, readers. It was of this paper that Sir Arthur Pearson, who had become owner in 1904, remarked: 'Damn this east wind; six more readers gone.'[4] *The Morning*

---

[1] *History of The Times*, IV (1), pp. 130, 140.
[2] *Ibid.* IV (1), p. 146. [3] *Ibid.* IV (1), p. 154.
[4] Robertson Scott, *The Story of the Pall Mall Gazette*, p. 165.

Post put up its price to 2*d.* in 1916 and reduced it to 1*d.* again in 1926, but though it struggled nobly it was amalgamated with the *Daily Telegraph* in 1937. The *Daily Telegraph*, which had had 300,000 readers in 1888, was down to 84,000 in 1927. In 1930 its price (which had been raised to 2*d.*) was reduced to 1*d.*, and it secured a circulation of 200,000 which was raised to 750,000 by 1939.[1]

The competition of the *Daily Mail* and the *Daily Express* had forced the *Daily News* and the *Daily Chronicle* (founded 1869) to become halfpenny papers in the early years of the present century, but they became penny papers in 1918 and 1917. They survived until the Great Depression, but in 1930 they were amalgamated as the *News Chronicle*. By this time there were three other papers, deliberately appealing to the working-class market. The *Daily Mirror* was founded in 1903 as a pictorial paper appealing especially to women. It was a failure at first because its appeal was too exclusively feminine, but within a year its circulation had risen to 290,000 and by 1914 it claimed, correctly, that it had 'the world's largest sale'. It was, in fact, 1,210,000.[2] It suffered a set-back in the post-war depression, and its circulation was 987,000 in 1931. The *Daily Sketch* was founded in 1908 in imitation of the *Daily Mirror*, though it did not begin publishing in London until 1911. It absorbed the *Daily Graphic* in 1946 and took its name, but it has since reverted to the name *Daily Sketch*. The *Daily Herald* was a Labour weekly from 1912 to 1929, when it was taken over by Odhams Press Ltd to provide daily use for the machines of the *People* (a Sunday newspaper), though provision was made for the continued representation of the point of view of the Labour party.

The war of 1939–45 enormously increased the demand for newspapers, which had been stimulated by the spread of education. According to a UNESCO survey, made immediately after the war, the United Kingdom was second to the United States in the number of newspapers purchased daily per thousand population, the United Kingdom figure being 611.[3] Table 16 shows the circulations of the London dailies in 1947.[4]

[1] Lord Camrose, *British Newspapers and their Controllers*, p. 27.
[2] Hugh Cundlipp, *Publish and be Damned*, p. 22.
[3] Pitt Robbins, *Newspapers Today*, p. 5.
[4] Lord Camrose, *British Newspapers and their Controllers*, p. 100.

This list is arranged, so far as can be judged, in the order of the social classes. *The Times* is read, according to its own advertisements, by 'top people', i.e. the comparatively wealthy and the intellectuals, though the latter often have a preference for the (*Manchester*) *Guardian*. The less eminent read the *Daily Telegraph* or the *Daily Mail*. The lower middle class reads the *Daily Mail*, the *News Chronicle*, or the *Daily Express*. *Hoi polloi* read the *Daily Express*, the *Daily Herald*, or the *Daily Mirror*. These are, of course, generalisations to which there are many exceptions.

The Times	270,000
Daily Telegraph	1,016,000
Daily Mail	2,008,000
News Chronicle	1,623,000
Daily Express	3,857,000
Daily Herald	2,144,000
Daily Mirror	3,600,000
Daily Graphic	772,000

TABLE 16

2. THE NEWSPAPERS AND POLITICS

The notion that politics are the things that really matter is carefully fostered by the politicians, but it is not generally acceptable; and the excessive interest of editors in politics has sometimes caused newspapers to decline and die. It is necessary in the public interest that much space be devoted to politics, because politicians are not to be trusted with power unless they are carefully watched; and politicians like to have much space devoted to their actions because their reputations depend upon publicity. It is proper that successful politicians be given great honour, as an inducement to others to go and do likewise, though in fact the possession of power is usually its own reward: but it should not be thought that the hierarchy of honours, in the constitutional sense, has much to do with the hierarchy of merit, or even the hierarchy of interest among readers of newspapers.

It has been mentioned above that the demand for newspapers developed just before and during the Civil War, an unusual event which perhaps deserved more contemporary publicity—even the *Daily*

Sketch, had it existed, would occasionally have put Oliver Cromwell on the front page, and the Civil War was, after all, in the nature of a sporting event. The Augustan Age, during which newspapers developed, had its own scale of values, based upon the pursuits of a country gentleman of taste. His taste for politics was rather low, and Grub Street was regarded as a suitably named haunt for the hacks paid by Sir Robert Walpole and his political opponents. The owner of the *Free Briton* (founded 1730 or 1731) received £11,000 between 1735 and 1738, for support of the Government, and the Government spent some £50,000 upon authors and printers of newspapers.[1] The Letters of Junius, which appeared in the *Public Advertiser* between 1769 and 1772, mark a stage in the history of political journalism. 'For the first time in English journalism the influence of an independent writer was exerted upon discriminating readers, and the regularity of the articles, as much as their ability, was responsible for developing the factor in political society now known as "public opinion".'[2] Independence was due, however, to the invention of advertising, which gave the press the revenue needed to sustain itself without subsidies; and if Junius is credited with the fall of the Marquis of Grafton he must also be blamed for the accession to office of Lord North, and perhaps for the loss of thirteen of the American colonies. In any case, subsidised journalism did not cease with Junius. In 1789 *The Times* was offered and accepted £300 a year, though the fact that its proprietor was imprisoned for printing certain paragraphs at the request of the Government was perhaps an inducement to Barnes, the first of its great editors, to maintain its independence.[3] It was, however, not *The Times* but the Government which stopped the subsidy in 1799, because of alleged libels against the House of Commons.[4] The fact that *The Times* had taken a subsidy for ten years did not preclude that newspaper from taking a very high line when the Reform Ministry appointed J. S. Buckingham, at a salary of £500 a year, to arrange for the supply of articles to three newspapers, whose editors undertook to insert them as editorial articles and generally to adopt a friendly attitude towards

[1] *History of The Times*, I, pp. 17–19.
[2] *Ibid.* I, p. 21.
[3] *Ibid.* pp. 58–9.
[4] *Ibid.* I, pp. 58–9.

the Government. *The Times* called them 'Gatton and Sarum news-papers—nomination journals'.[1]

Subsidies had practically ceased in Great Britain in 1830, though the *Observer* received a subsidy in 1840 which was probably withdrawn in 1841.[2] They may have continued in Ireland until 1853;[3] but in Great Britain any subsidies came from party funds after 1841. By this time a newspaper of quality and experience could be a profitable investment. Though circulations were small, even after 1830, the number of readers was large and they were, generally, drawn from the leisured classes which frequented coffee-houses and the more genteel taverns. They thus had money to spend on the luxuries advertised in the newspapers. Proprietors and editors sought increased circulation in order to attract the advertisements and put up their advertising rates. The difficulty was that at any given time a party might find very little support in the newspapers because their proprietors supported the other side, or perhaps because the proprietors found it more profitable to support the other side. After 1830 the modern convention, that a party is always right and criticisms are due to the malevolence or incompetence of opponents, became firmly established—partly indeed because the newspapers gave publicity to parliamentary proceedings and political meetings, so that the party had to appear to do no wrong. Politicians had therefore to interest themselves in the purchase or foundation of newspapers; and, though it was easier to lose money on newspapers than to gain support from them, the belief that it was necessary only to start a newspaper to secure a platform for one's own views persisted until our own generation, when only a posse of Conservative million-aires or a group of trade unions could raise the necessary funds.

Newspapers are commercial enterprises, and if they are more interested in politics—or anything else—than their readers they decline and die. It was that rogue John Wilkes who first stimulated newspaper readers to take an interest in politics, and ever since they have been more interested in rogues than in less picturesque politicians. Politics can be made interesting to 'the million' if they take on the character of a sporting contest, as in the days of Pitt and Fox or Gladstone and

[1] *Ibid.* I, p. 61.   [2] *Ibid.* I, pp. 229–30.
[3] *Lord Melbourne's Papers*, p. 472; A. Aspinall, *Politicians and the Press*, p. 374.

Disraeli. Even then they must take second place to a boat race, a cup final, a test match or the Derby.

Nevertheless, politicians must secure publicity, not only to advance their own political careers, but also to bring their parties to office and keep them there. Since the Reform Ministry took office in 1830 the press has been the most important instrument of political propaganda, and accordingly for the next hundred years, at least, politicians tried to influence the press in their favour. Most of the devices of the Reform period have disappeared. Subsidies ceased when advertisement revenue made the press independent. Selective advertising by the Government became proportionately so little that it was not worth while to beg for it. The free circulation of selected newspapers became useless when the press attained circulations measured by tens of thousands. Places and pensions could not be found for enough journalists, though the process of 'honouring' proprietors continued. The preferences shown by 'clerks of the road' in the Post Office became of no value when, after 1855, the newspapers organised their own distribution by railway. There was no method left except the purchase of newspapers and the conveyance of advance confidential information, which enabled favoured newspapers to 'scoop' their rivals.

In 1762 Smollett started the *Briton* on behalf and at the expense of Lord Bute. Though it lasted only six months it had the distinction of encouraging John Wilkes' more famous *North Briton*.[1] The *Sun* was founded in 1792 by William Pitt,[2] though it was sold in 1825 and became Liberal. The *Anti-Jacobin* was founded by Canning in 1797 to support Pitt's Administration.[3] The *Morning Chronicle*, founded in 1769, was the great whig oracle, though in 1839 the Melbourne Government decided tentatively to cease giving it support and to start a new paper.[4] Within a few years it was sold to the Duke of Newcastle, Gladstone and Sidney Herbert and thus became Peelite and Puseyite. It lost money and was sold in 1854, though its Peelite and Puseyite character was retained by a subsidy.[5] In 1850 negotiations were

---

[1] Grant, *Newspaper Press*, I, pp. 161–2.   [2] *Ibid.* I, p. 330.
[3] *Ibid.* IV, pp. 2–3.   [4] *Lord Melbourne's Papers*, pp. 399, 400.
[5] Grant, *op. cit.* I, pp. 310–11.

started by the Conservatives to purchase *John Bull* and to start a new paper. *The Press* was then started in 1853, but it was sold by Disraeli when he took office in 1858 and it expired in 1866.[1] In 1900 Lloyd George arranged with a group of wealthy supporters for the purchase of the *Daily News* so that its politics should be changed from Liberal Imperialist to 'Pro-Boer'.[2] In 1918, when the *Daily Chronicle* was criticising Lloyd George, Frederick Guest was instructed to arrange for its purchase. After much negotiation it was purchased by supporters of Lloyd George and 'then gave political satisfaction to Downing Street'.[3] Since the cost was £1,000,000 and the *Daily Chronicle* was amalgamated with the *Daily News* twelve years later, the satisfaction was dearly bought.

Examples of the influencing of newspapers by personal interviews 'off the record' and by preferences in respect of news are so numerous as not to be worth quoting. *The Times* has been in a favoured position at least since Delane became editor in 1840.[4] So evident is this fact that the newspaper is often regarded as the organ of the Foreign Office; and when it criticises the Government it is frequently assumed either that the Government is flying a kite or that a change of policy is near at hand. It is, however, a wholly independent paper and its facts are sometimes wrong—though it usually corrects them by including a correct statement in a leading article a few days later. The *Manchester Guardian* under C. P. Scott had a similar direct approach to Ministers.[5] With Lloyd George in office, too, both the *Daily Express* and the *Daily Chronicle* had access to official sources: indeed it was sometimes difficult to decide which should have a 'scoop'.[6]

It is difficult to separate these cases of what may perhaps be called inspiration on behalf of a Government from inspiration on behalf of individual Ministers anxious to stand well before public opinion. Henry Reeve, who combined the office of Clerk to the Council with

[1] *Life of Disraeli* I, pp. 1306–21.
[2] *Life of Sir William Harcourt*, II, p. 526; S. Mills, *Sir Edward Cook*, ch. XI.
[3] *History of The Times*, IV (2), pp. 1076–7; H. A. Taylor, *Robert Donald*, ch. X.
[4] See, in addition to the *History of The Times*: Dasent, *John Delane*; J. E. Wrench, *Geoffrey Dawson and our Times*.
[5] J. L. Hammond, *C. P. Scott*.
[6] *History of The Times*, IV (2), p. 1077.

leader-writing in *The Times*, was in frequent contact with the Lord Clarendon of his time.[1] Perhaps Lord Clarendon learned the technique from his superiors, for in 1840 Lord Palmerston supplied information to the *Morning Chronicle* and Lord John Russell supplied it to the *Globe*.[2] In 1850, too, there was close contact between Lord Palmerston and the *Morning Post*, though that newspaper was generally against the whig Government; and that association continued for fifteen years.[3] Of the curious coalition of 1854 under Lord Aberdeen, Lord John Russell, who was a member, remarked: 'It is not the least of the disadvantages of my position that the two morning papers which have communications from the Government are personally hostile to me. Lord Aberdeen has only to bear the attacks of the Opposition, but I am attacked by Opposition and Government and have no defender in the press except the worthy old *Globe*.'[4] This was written to Lord Clarendon, who was in touch with *The Times* through Henry Reeve, while Lord Aberdeen was in touch through Delane. The other paper was probably the Peelite organ, the *Morning Chronicle*, since the *Morning Post* was in Opposition. No doubt Lord John took the necessary steps to keep the *Globe* in step with him, as he had done in 1840 and 1850.[5]

Conservative Governments were no less anxious to propitiate *The Times*,[6] while in Gladstone's Government of 1880 the Radicals kept up a regular barrage. Joseph Chamberlain was in touch with the *Birmingham Daily Post*, the *Standard*, the *Pall Mall Gazette*, and the *World*; Sir Charles Dilke's contacts were with the *Daily News*; and Forster was in touch with *The Times*, the *Standard* and the *Leeds Mercury*.[7] A particularly nasty example of communication by a Prime Minister is exhibited by Lord Salisbury's explanation to the *Pall Mall Gazette* of Lord Randolph Churchill's resignation, though

[1] See, e.g., *Life of Henry Reeve*, I, pp. 186, 257–60, 285ff., 289, 296, 325; *Life of Lord Clarendon*, I, p. 279.

[2] *Life of Lord Clarendon*, I, p. 213.

[3] H. C. F. Bell, *Lord Palmerston*, II, pp. 33–4; R. Lucas, *Lord Glenesk and the 'Morning Post'*, ch. IV.

[4] *Later Correspondence of Lord John Russell*, II, p. 171.

[5] *Ibid.* II, p. 75.

[6] E.g. *Life of Delane*, I, pp. 297–8 (1858); II, pp. 228, 229, 237, 243 (1868).

[7] *Life of Joseph Chamberlain*, I, p. 307; *Life of Sir Charles Dilke*, I, pp. 316–17, 442.

Lord Randolph himself had been forbidden to give any public explanation until Parliament met.[1]

Examples can be quoted from the twentieth century also.[2] It is probable, however, that the influence of the press was greatest during the war of 1914 to 1918. It was alleged that the resignation of Asquith in 1916 was forced by a press campaign, that Lord Haldane could not be employed because of the attitude of the press, and so forth. Mr Spender's explanation[3] was that, in the absence of an Opposition, three was no other way. The war went badly, the press looked for scapegoats, and changes of Ministers were engineered by intrigues in which the press lords, but especially Lord Beaverbrook, took an active part. As experience between 1939 and 1945 showed, this could not have been the whole explanation. It should be noted that the popular press had expanded rather suddenly. The *Daily Mirror* reached a circulation of a million copies in 1914 and the *Daily Mail* had lost its lead, while the *Daily Express*, which had come into Lord Beaverbrook's hands in 1913, was fighting hard (and successfully) to get a circulation. It is probable that both the press lords and the Ministers exaggerated the political importance of large circulations. The older newspapers, especially *The Times*, the *Morning Post* and the *Daily News*, had actually formed public opinion, or at least had appeared to form it, among a small but instructed circle of readers. It seemed credible that the popular press could do the same among 'the million' who were, by definition, less educated than the readers of the older and smaller papers—and most Ministers in those days would have added 'less intelligent'. Moreover as the examples quoted above show, the relations between the Government and the Press had not been formalised. It had been a practice since the time of Pitt for individual Ministers to have close relations with proprietors and editors, and even leader-writers; and some Ministers were capable of using these relations to advance their own careers as well as to strengthen the Government. If Asquith was supported by the *Daily News*, Lloyd George could (until 1918) rely on

[1] J. Saxon Mills, *Sir Edward Cook*, pp. 97–8.

[2] E.g. Fitzroy, *Memoirs*, I, p. 268; Countess of Minto, *India, Minto and Morley*, pp. 310–12; Spender, *Life, Journalism and Politics*, I, pp. 72, 89.

[3] *Life of Lord Oxford and Asquith*, II, pp. 242–4; Spender, *Life, Journalism and Politics*, II, p. 72.

the *Daily Chronicle* and Bonar Law on the *Daily Express*. Nobody could rely on the *Daily Mail*, because that was owned by Lord Northcliffe, who was capable of changing the paper's policy overnight. Even so, these relations gave ample scope for intrigue, which was fully exploited.[1]

Since 1922 the Government's relations with the press have been formalised. Lloyd George's 'garden suburb' in Downing Street was then pulled down and in due course the inspiration of the press was taken in hand not by Ministers but by public relations officers. The Minister is allowed to blow his own trumpet at a press conference; but if he does not there is a 'handout' or a press conference by an anonymous civil servant. Questions can be addressed over the telephone to the appropriate public relations officer, who will indicate whether he can be quoted or whether the information supplied must be treated as 'background information' given so that mistakes may be avoided. That selected editors still have private access seems clear both from Geoffrey Dawson's diary[2] and from the explanation given by Mr Macmillan in November 1957 of the manner in which the intention to restrict credit (simultaneously with the raising of the bank rate) was communicated.[3] Nevertheless, the present arrangements seem to minimise what may be called the journalism of the political backstairs.

The principal development is, however, the discovery that the newspapers are not as influential as was at one time thought. This discovery is not entirely new. Lord George Hamilton[4] pointed out that after 1867 *The Times* was not able to win elections because politics were no longer dominated by London. Mr Gladstone, in fact, paid very little attention to press opinion—not even, apparently, when the Radicals in his Government were doing their best to 'nobble' it.[5] He won the election of 1880 with most of the press against him, and the cynical comment of the owner of the *Pall Mall Gazette*, when he sold it in 1892, may be quoted:

As for the [Liberal] party, I feel no compunctions at all. They have never done anything for me, though I did a real service to them in 1880 by turning

---

[1] See Beaverbrook, *Politicians and the War*; and Tom Clarke, *My Northcliffe Diary*.
[2] J. E. Wrench, *Geoffrey Dawson and Our Times*.
[3] 577 H.C.Deb., 5 s., 964–9.
[4] *Parliamentary Reminiscences*, I, pp. 26–8.   [5] *Ante*, p. 148.

the paper round. They despise the press. Mr Gladstone might easily have kept the [Daily] Chronicle and probably the [Daily] Telegraph if he had baroneted Lloyd and Lawson [the respective proprietors]; and if they had ever done anything for me I don't suppose I should be selling now.[1]

The process of 'doing something for' newspaper proprietors was accelerated under Lloyd George. Table 17 shows the 'newspaper honours' for which he was responsible in six years:[2]

Viscounts	5
Barons	5
Baronets	11
Privy Councillors	1
Companions of Honour	1
Knights	6

TABLE 17

This average has not been maintained, perhaps because the number of press proprietors is limited. No doubt every little helps, and even a baronetcy may sway a marginal constituency. It is, however, plain from the rise of the Labour party before 1931 that an adverse press does not necessarily lose an election. In 1945, admittedly, the newspapers were, according to circulation, almost equally divided. The *Daily Herald*, the *News Chronicle* and the *Daily Mirror* had a total circulation for the Labour party of 6,000,000; the *Daily Mail*, the *Daily Express*, the *Daily Sketch*, the *Daily Telegraph* and *The Times* had a total circulation for the Conservative party of 7,000,000.[3] In 1950 the *Daily Herald* and the *Daily Mirror* had a combined circulation of 6,600,000, while the Conservative papers had a combined circulation of 8,100,000.[4] In 1951 there was no great change.[5] In 1955 the newspapers were nearly all very cool.[6]

It is true that in the post-war period the newspapers have had strong competition from broadcasting and television; but in the course of their

---

[1] J. Saxon Mills, *Sir Edward Cook*, pp. 115–16.
[2] *History of The Times*, IV (2), p. 1129.
[3] MacCallum and Readman, *The General Election of 1945*, p. 181.
[4] H. G. Nicholas, *The General Election of 1950*, p. 144.
[5] D. E. Butler, *The General Election of 1951*, pp. 129–30.
[6] D. E. Butler, *The General Election of 1955*, pp. 94–6.

battles for circulation they have discovered that the mass of the population is not interested in politics. The figures given by the Royal Commission on the Press, 1947–49 (Tables 18 and 19) show how little space is given to political, social and economic matters.[1] The percentages of editorial space are given in Table 18, of news space in Table 19.

Newspaper	Circulation (1947)	1927	1937	1947
The Times	270,000	20	18	38
Daily Graphic	772,000	—	—	15
Daily Telegraph	1,016,000	—	—	36
News Chronicle	1,623,000	—	—	29
Daily Mail	2,008,000	13	10	29
Daily Herald	2,144,000	—	—	34
Daily Mirror	3,600,000	5	4	16
Daily Express	3,857,000	—	—	28

TABLE 18

Newspaper	1927	1937	1947
The Times	27	22	49
Daily Graphic	—	—	30
Daily Telegraph	—	—	48
News Chronicle	—	—	37
Daily Mail	20	17	36
Daily Herald	—	—	47
Daily Mirror	16	8	30
Daily Express	—	—	35

TABLE 19

The conditions of 1947 were abnormal owing to paper rationing, which kept the newspapers to a wartime size. It will be noticed that in 1927 the percentages were much lower, for the three newspapers for which figures are given, than in 1947, and that the percentages were even lower in 1937 than in 1927. If figures could be given for 1957, they would probably be at least as low as in 1937. *The Times* and the *Daily Telegraph* would then stand out as 'political' papers with the *Daily Herald* (before its reorganisation late in 1957) a good third. Then come the *News Chronicle*, the *Daily Mail* and the *Daily Express*.

[1] Royal Commission on the Press, Cmd. 7700 (1949), pp. 249 ff.

Finally there are the picture papers, the *Daily Mirror* and the *Daily Sketch* (i.e. the *Daily Graphic* renamed). This is clearly a 'class' structure, except for the *Daily Herald*, which was (before October 1957) bound to give prominence to Labour party politics. In other words, it is assumed that four per cent of politics are enough for working-class women, ten per cent for the middle-class readers of the *Daily Mail*, and something like twenty per cent for the 'top people' who are alleged (by *The Times*) to read *The Times*.

Since editors may be presumed to know their job, this is probably a correct appreciation of public interest; but reading newspapers occupies only a small part of each week-day and the Sunday newspapers would show even less concern with politics. How far the hasty scanning of selected news and tendentious editorials affects the public mind cannot be determined. On particular questions, probably, that mind is very little affected. There is no evidence that the concern of the *Daily Express* with 'our Empire' has affected opinions or votes. Every reader recognises it as a personal idiosyncrasy of Lord Beaverbrook. The general tone, especially in the gossip columns, is probably more important and in recent years the more popular newspapers have been not merely critical but contemptuous of politicians. More important still, perhaps, is the extent to which notoriety is attached to particular persons, especially those in 'Society'. A daily reading of gossip columns over a lengthy period probably gives the impression that it is decadent if not corrupt. A staid party, a happy marriage, a hard-working peer, or a successful politician, is not news. Grub Street is more than ever among the grubs.

CHAPTER VII

INDIRECT PROPAGANDA

Politicians are, or ought to be, practical men whose job it is to find, with the assistance of their staffs and others, practical solutions to practical problems. They do not produce political theories, though it can be discovered, when their actions are studied over a fairly long period, that they are acting upon theories—or, more correctly, since theories imply formulation, upon ideas and emotions. These ideas and emotions rarely come from the politicians themselves. They are articulate people, but generally their ideas and emotions are created or stimulated by others. The 'movers and makers of the world forever' are the divines, the poets and dramatists, the scholars, the artists, the scientists, the historians, the lawyers. To take only one of the many factories of ideas and emotions, the Cambridge contribution to politics must be assessed not by listing the Cambridge politicians from Lord Burghley to Pitt, from Pitt to Lord Palmerston, and from Lord Palmerston to Baldwin and Nehru, but by listing the divines of the Reformation, the poets, philosophers and scientists. Similarly the Oxford contribution would be headed not by her galaxy of great statesmen, but by the Wesleys, because they helped to establish a movement which dominated politics for a century.

The material or stuff of politics therefore comes mainly from sources outside politics, in the narrower sense; and those who would write about it must step out cheerfully where specialist scholars fear to tread.[1] In so doing they follow the examples of the politicians themselves, for these handle the same material, though within a narrower band of time, with the glib assurance of the platform orator. The politician is the common man, slightly inflated. He propagates freely ideas which came to him from outside, but he is not the only propagandist, because the ideas are propagated by their inventors, glossators, commentators, critics and publicists. Gladstone's oratory in the Midlothian campaign did not win the general election of 1880, though no doubt it helped.

[1] See Volume III.

The Liberals won that election because the ideas and emotions propagated by them were sufficiently in tune with the minds and hearts of a sufficient number of electors in a sufficient number of constituencies. To explain how that happened would require research which would tax the ingenuity and the imagination of the ablest historian, for every consequence had a multitude of causes and every vote was a consequence. The best that can be done is to indicate the general characteristics of the major ideas and emotions which appear to dominate politics, and this is attempted in Volume III.

Since the ideas and emotions have their own propagandists, apart from the politicians who adopt them, it is necessary to say something about those whose connexion is closest. To go further would be to delve deeply 'into the dark backward and abysm of time', to show the connexion, for instance, between the publication of Newton's *Principia Mathematica* in 1687, and the conflict over rent policy at the general election of 1959. The main instruments of propaganda, apart from the press, the parties and the politicians, are the churches and chapels, broadcasting and television, clubs and trade unions, and general literature.

I. CHURCHES AND CHAPELS

Churches and chapels are obviously purveyors of political propaganda when religion is the stuff of politics, as it has been for long periods.[1] They are then vested interests fighting for power and influence, and often for property, as well as advocates of the truth as they see it. One does not always find, however, that the churches and chapels are lined up behind the parties that support their respective pretensions. Though this is an inevitable tendency, there are often differences of opinion about methods. The conflict between uniformity and toleration, for instance, was a conflict in which those within the established Church could take sides. The Quakers and the Methodists would disagree about methods, even when they agreed about objectives, which they rarely did.

The churches and chapels could, however, influence political opinions in three other ways; first, by direct contact between the clergy or

[1] Volume III, chapter II.

pastors and their parishioners or members; secondly by providing a forum in which political issues might be discussed; and thirdly by creating an emotional environment which influenced political opinion.

The first method took the form of preaching from the pulpit or (after Wesley) in the open;[1] and also of canvassing or advising parishioners or members. The clergy of the Church of England in the eighteenth century were members of the governing class. They were often wealthy, either through having wealthy livings or through having several livings *in commendam*. In the villages they were second in importance only to the squires and had influence among the freeholders, while the ministers of the free churches had influence among the small farmers, many of whom would be freeholders. In the towns the Church usually had the more influence in the corporation, but the chapel was often influential among the shopkeepers and artisans, many of whom would be freeholders, freemen or scot and lot electors.

This influence would be exercised by direct personal contact. It is not likely that much direct political propaganda was done by preaching, but examples are not unknown. One of the first devices of the Anti-Corn Law League was to send circular letters to dissenting ministers asking them to deliver sermons against the Corn Law and to persuade their congregations to send petitions to Parliament.[2] In the following year (1841) a conference of nearly seven hundred ministers of religion was assembled in Manchester and persuaded to condemn the Corn Law.[3] This was due to excellent 'management', but it had the desired effect of putting God on the side of the manufacturers and against the Corn Law. This practice of getting God on the right side had been used by both Charles I and Cromwell, but they had persuaded themselves; with the League it was, in part at least, a piece of cynicism. With Gladstone it was probably self-deception, because there is no evidence that he sought to use the clergy as electioneering agents: it just happened that, after the death of Palmerston, right and justice were always on the side of the Liberals. About Joseph Chamberlain's trade with the

---

[1] Preaching in public was, however, a Puritan practice, especially in the New Army of the Civil War and the Commonwealth.

[2] Norman McCord, *The Anti-Corn Law League*, p. 74.

[3] *Ibid.* p. 104.

Nonconformist conscience one cannot be so sure, for he never explained his motives. On the one hand he entered politics *via* Nonconformist agitation; on the other hand he used the Nonconformist ministers so long as they were useful to him. On the whole, however, churches and chapels have taken sides because of different interpretations of Christian duties and have not readily used their influence to advance the ambitions of cynical politicians.

Whatever views be expressed on religion or morality must, however, be coloured by the preacher's own prejudices as well as by the doctrines of his church or denomination. The Church of England is catholic in its doctrines and allows the Bible to be interpreted, to use political terms, from any point of view from extreme right to extreme left, though it has a strong preference for right centre. The free churches are sometimes more dogmatic in their views and feel strongly about what the Irish newspaper intended to say when it reported that there were 'sermons on temperance and other social evils'. Both the politician and the preacher are against sin and, since they try to cure it with words, they cannot help trespassing on each other's close. Both the politician and the preacher want to build the new Jerusalem, and they cannot avoid getting in each other's way. What is more, the preachers as well as the politicians differ among themselves.

Secondly, when people are gathered together to worship they are also enabled to talk among themselves. Indeed, both church and chapel have encouraged it so as to associate religion with daily life and daily life with religion. The vestry was once the meeting-place of the parish; the dissenters fortified themselves against oppressive uniformity in the chapel or the meeting-house. The whigs complained that the mass meetings of the Methodists encouraged 'the democratical spirit, the insubordination to authority, the tendency to republican sentiments, which they alleged to have gained ground among the people'.[1] This was when the Methodists were still very conservative. Church meetings, when the squire and the parson were present, should have been equally objectionable to the whigs, since they encouraged loyalty to Church and King, and that was the tory cliché. One must not assume, however, that people always talked politics. Political leanings are rarely the

[1] Jephson, *The Platform*, I, p. 8, quoting Hallam.

result of profound rationalisation. More often they are the unformu-
lated legacies of social inheritance, learned like religion and language in
the home, the school and the church or chapel. They are affected by the
environment in which men live, play and work. They are, too, the
product of intuition based upon personal experience, so that if religion
is changed either by the slow process of gradual conversion or by the
surge of emotion which the Methodists and the evangelicals learned to
create, other attitudes to life, including politics, will change also.
Moreover the environment of church or chapel had other, perhaps less
worthy, consequences. The Church was the handmaiden of the landed
gentry, a career for their relatives. It stood high in the social hierarchy.
The vicar, if resident, dined with the squire, hunted with the gentry,
took his wife and daughter to the hunt ball, sat in quarter sessions and
supported the squire at petty sessions. The chapel was the meeting-
place of the lower middle class, the shopkeepers, small farmers, artisans
and perhaps labourers. There was both merit and pleasure in being
powerful even in this small circle, to be a trustee of the chapel, to
contribute a substantial part of the minister's salary, to be able—in
some denominations—to dismiss him because his sermons lacked fire,
his private life was tainted, or he was not sufficiently appreciative of the
efforts of the leading members of the congregation. There was, however, a great temptation to leave these squalid surroundings, to get on
speaking terms with the squire or the mayor, to enable one's wife to
call and to receive invitations to dine. If the social attractions of the
established Church were not sufficient in the first generation they probably would be in the second. The son would probably be sent not to a
dissenting academy but to a school for the sons of gentry, where it
would be assumed that he was 'C. of E.' If he went to the university
he would be required to subscribe to the thirty-nine articles, though
Cambridge abolished this requirement for undergraduates in 1775. His
wealth would justify him in marrying into the lower ranks of the gentry,
and his wife would not wish to exhibit her degradation by attending
chapel. There was, in short, a constant seepage of the wealthier men
from chapel to church.

After the middle of the eighteenth century this was made easier by
the Methodists, who did not at first differ in doctrine from the Church,

did not set out to compete with the Church but to teach it to do its duty, and in the beginning could not communicate in their chapels if there was a church within access. Even when, being spurned by the Church, they set up house for themselves, it was permissible for a Methodist to attend a service in the Church of England, and it would be much like his own. Methodism thus provided a stepping-stone between dissent and conformity.

It must further be emphasised that the attractions of church and chapel varied considerably. The fire of Puritanism soon died after 1660, and the zeal of dissenters was maintained only by oppression and a sense of martyrdom. Even this ceased to be important as the casual and somewhat contemptuous toleration of the eighteenth century developed. The Methodists, though originally within the Church, stimulated the dissenters by their example; and, though after their severance from the Church they chose a middle way, they strengthened Nonconformity by their numbers and influence. The strength of Nonconformity was further increased in the second half of the eighteenth century by the Industrial Revolution, which increased the relative size of the lower middle class to which the free churches appealed, even though there was at the same time a process of disintegration by the creation of more sects. The evangelical movement, though primarily within the Church, stimulated both church and chapel. Politically, however, the Reform Act of 1832 strengthened Nonconformity especially, because the £10 leaseholder in the country or the £10 householder in the town was often a Nonconformist. This did not mean that Nonconformists elected Nonconformists. As we shall see,[1] the Nonconformist conscience was shared by many in the Church, and it was a series of ideas and emotions rather than a Nonconformist movement.

The Reform Acts of 1867 and 1884 had less effect than might be supposed. There were areas in England where Nonconformity was strong among the working class, particularly in some of the industrial towns of the North and in the West. In Wales and Scotland it was of course dominant. The phenomenon of the 'Celtic fringe' was thus produced, though it was not wholly Celtic and the more aggressive Celts in Ireland were Roman Catholics. Elsewhere, in southern and

[1] Volume III.

eastern England especially, the workers, though not particularly religious, tended to support the old order rather than the new. Indeed, Disraeli in 1867 gambled on their doing so, and won his gamble when the Liberals split over Ireland. The industrial workers did not begin to realise their strength until towards the end of the century. Their class-consciousness, too, developed late, so that they often preferred the gentry of the Church and the Conservative party to the bosses and shopkeepers of the Liberal party. Nor was the Liberal association with Nonconformity an attraction. The attack on 'temperance and other social evils' was, more often than not, an attack on the social habits of the industrial workers; it was a product both of high ideals and of Victorian distaste for the behaviour of the poorer neighbours in the back streets. In the agricultural counties the workers generally preferred the squire, the parson, and the other gentlemen to the small farmers who went to chapel, voted Liberal, and tried to keep down wages.

After 1914 religion as a direct political force disappeared. Nonconformity in alliance with the Labour movement won a spectacular triumph in 1906, but that was its swan-song. Except in the Celtic fringe, it was irrelevant after 1918, and the fringe was gradually cut back. The Church of England retains its political importance not because its direct political power is important but because it still creates a traditional atmosphere which favours moderate Conservatism.

2. LITERATURE AND POLITICS

When the memoranda, records of private discussions, correspondence, projects and speeches relating to any great reform are examined it is found that many of the arguments used to justify and criticise it are temporary and fugitive. The existing law is the subject of complaint by persons who are politically powerful. What changes can we make to meet those complaints? What will be the consequences of a particular measure of reform? Will there be complaints from other persons who are politically powerful? Would not a second proposal, removing some only of the grounds of the first set of complaints, also diminish the force of the second set of complaints? On the other hand, will it not antagonise the second complainants while not satisfying the first complainants? What arguments will the Opposition raise in criticism of either proposal? Will our own men be convinced by those criticisms even when they vote for us? Will either proposal tend to lose votes in the constituencies forthwith, or within a few years? To this extent the whole process is empirical. There are, however, 'principles' involved, either articulate principles like those set out in party programmes or inarticulate principles which can be discovered by the trend of the discussions, especially when a series of related problems is examined over a period of time.

It used to be assumed by theoretical writers that these principles were rational, and to some extent they are; but they must be founded on assumptions which are not rational but are matters of belief. One is not led straight back to religion, because only philosophers build systems out of first principles. The ordinary man—and the politician is an ordinary man—has a complex system of assumptions based upon his social inheritance and his own experience. The assumptions should be regarded as prejudices, because the ordinary man does not seek to prove them and he applies his reason so as to judge in their light. Many of them are inarticulate; indeed for busy practical men they are almost all inarticulate. They could be formulated if one took the trouble to analyse them; but the practical man cannot do that because while he made the attempt the files would accumulate on his desk and he would soon find himself turned out of office for incompetence. Young men and women of education and intelligence do try to formulate their prejudices when they have time and inclination; but even in the universities there is no time to do the thing properly. If one spent twelve months—and the process would certainly take longer—with one's feet up, thinking out one's prejudices or principles, one's tutor would politely suggest that it be done elsewhere. Wherever one is, a job has to be done.

In the main, every generation relies on the wisdom of its ancestors, and that wisdom is passed on in two ways, by direct personal contact and by reading. My political experience, derived by personal contact, goes back to 1868, because my grandfather was able to tell me how and why he voted for Disraeli's candidate on the hustings. If I live a few more years, I shall be able to pass on that experience to my grandson, though the first elections within my own recollection are those of 1910. There is thus a period in respect of which I am able to pass on experience by hearsay, and another period in respect of which I can rely on my own recollection of events. My grandson will, of course, acquire such direct experience from others besides me, more probably from his father's generation than from my generation. Since the whole period is roughly ninety or a hundred years, there is a sort of cycle in the centuries, though each person has his own century.

The illiterate elector takes his ideas from direct personal contact only. The semi-literate elector may add to them ideas derived from semi-literate papers, magazines and books. We who are fully literate have the whole world of literature open to us, though we can do no more than sample it, and in practice few do more than sample the literature in their own language and readily available in their own period. The sample is selective, too, in respect of subject-matter, depending on the reader's range of interests and the time at his disposal. It should be noted, too, that much of the experience which we derive from direct personal contact comes from literature at second or third hand and this is particularly true of politicians, who usually do not read much outside newspapers and official memoranda but are in personal contact with those who do.

Those who write in newspapers and other periodicals have the same background of direct and literary experience, but usually they read more. Those who write books tend to read more than those who do not. Thus the texture of opinion in any literate society is woven with literature of all kinds. Nor is that literature limited to 'information' and rational argument from stated or unstated premises. While there is a literature which conveys facts and arguments, most literature is read for amusement, recreation or enjoyment and helps to produce emotions of various kinds. The direct experience derived from personal discussion is also charged with emotion; and emotions are stimulated by art, music and the environment generally.

It follows that political decisions are not taken only by a process of rationalisation. Reason and emotion are inextricably confused. Political theories enunciated in books are no doubt of practical importance, but few practical politicians have much direct knowledge of them, and any indirect knowledge that they may possess lies confused in a mass of experience of all kinds. Since much of this derives from literature in all its forms, general literature, imaginative and otherwise, is continually involved in the propagation of politics, even when its connexion with politics is so remote that superficially it appears to have no connexion at all.

Let us take the example of a politician who was unusually well-read, of whose training we have more information than usual, and who failed to obtain the highest office only by an unhappy accident. Sir Charles Wentworth Dilke[1] was a descendant of two well-known Puritan families. His grandfather was a civil servant who became owner and for a time editor of the *Athenaeum*, a periodical later absorbed into the *Nation*, which was itself absorbed into the *New Statesman*. His father founded the *Gardeners' Chronicle* and the *Agricultural Gazette*, ran the great Exhibition of 1851, and received a baronetcy for his services to the Prince Consort's activities. The grandfather, father and Dilke himself lived in the same house and frequently entertained literary men (including Dickens and Thackeray). The grandfather, who had been a close friend of Keats, took charge of Dilke's education, and encouraged him to read widely. In Cambridge, Dilke's closest friends were two young dons of Trinity Hall, Henry Fawcett (the economist, afterwards Postmaster-General in Gladstone's Government) and Leslie Stephen (afterwards Sir Leslie and editor of the *Dictionary of National Biography*).[2] Though he rowed in the Mays and at Henley, he was a voracious reader and a fluent writer, was first in the University in Law, and became President of the Union. He read a great deal on politics and was particularly impressed by John Stuart Mill: but he reviewed Alexandre Dumas for the *Athenaeum* and in 1864 placed among his favourite books the Bible, Shakespeare, Homer, Tennyson and Longfellow. On going down he made a long tour of the English-speaking world and wrote a book, to which our attention must later be directed because it was influential in the development of 'Radical imperialism',[3] called *GreaterBritain*.

---

[1] *Life of Sir Charles Dilke*, I, pp. 1–73.
[2] See Leslie Stephen's *Life of Fawcett*, and F. W. Maitland's *Life of Leslie Stephen*.
[3] Volume III.

This is, of course, an exceptional case, quite unlike that of his friend and Radical colleague (until 1886), Joseph Chamberlain.[1] A different case, too, could be presented for the early life of his political chief, Gladstone,[2] yet a case fundamentally similar in the conclusions to be drawn from it. The example shows, in a particular case, the intimate connexions of general literature, political literature, and politics. It is exceptional only in its concentration. With a politician who was not so well-read, like Joseph Chamberlain, we should not find the same concentration, but the influence of literature upon the ideas which he formulated was considerable. Nor must we think in terms only of the education of politicians. Since politicians have to win elections, they must formulate policies acceptable to a large section, if not the whole, of the population, and they must express those policies in a manner and form which accord with the prejudices of the electors.

The influence of political literature is obvious, and among political literature must be classed any literature which is either designed to influence or does in fact directly influence governmental policy. This can hardly be a definition, for directness is a matter of degree. For instance, nationalism is primarily a literary movement because it is primarily emotional. It is possible, and later we shall make the attempt,[3] to trace from the political literature the rise and fall of that brand of nationalism which was called 'imperialism': but fiction, poetry and the drama or at least some fiction, poetry and drama, are read more widely and have more influence than political literature. To trace the influence of general literature on nationalism would be the labour of a lifetime.[4] It would begin with some of the earliest printed books, the romances which idealised the past. Shakespeare would take a very prominent place in the story, and it would be necessary to consider not only his immediate influence but the successive stages in his popularity.[5] How far Milton came into the story would have to be discovered. In the eighteenth century we should turn to prose, but with the Romantic

[1] *Life of Chamberlain*, I, pp. 1–79.
[2] *Life of Gladstone*, I, pp. 1–88.   [3] Volume III.
[4] The best attempt, so far, is E. Wingfield-Stratford, *History of English Patriotism*.
[5] Charles Whibley, writing when imperialism was under attack, evidently thought that Shakespeare was the first Conservative propagandist: Whibley, *Political Portraits*, pp. 20–46.

Movement we should be back to poetry. The swelling tide of the nineteenth century would presumably end with Kipling. It would, however, be wrong to concentrate on the great names. Shakespeare is continually relevant, but to the last generation Marie Corelli, Rider Haggard and other popular novelists were more important because their books had such large circulations. It is probable, too, that Sexton Blake and Billy Bunter had more influence on the older generation now living than Hamlet and Macbeth, though what that influence was and whether they had any effect on nationalism would require a good deal of imaginative research. Nor must one forget the penny novelette and the magazine serial in which sin was triumphant until the last chapter or the soapy lord married the silly shop-girl after many frustrations. There can be little doubt that what the press agents call the 'build-up' of Queen Victoria was actively assisted by the romantic novelists, or that the novelettes and the women's magazines have helped to create the mawkish sentimentalism and intrusive curiosity which surround, and no doubt embarrass, Queen Elizabeth and Princess Margaret: and both developments have important political implications.

There is, however, a distinction between the literature which records changing ideas and emotions and the literature which helps to change them. The writer is the child of his own generation and the prophet of the future. Much of the best literature is written by the 'angry young men' of each generation, who have imagination but not experience, and whose efforts at self-assertion involve reaction against current ideas, those of the older generation. This, perhaps, is the cause of the curious three-generation cycle, so obvious in the history of political ideas. The young rebels become the middle-aged orthodox and finish their careers as the antiquated old-stagers. This is not necessarily progress, because there is no settled scale of values. The generation which enfranchised women, socially, sartorially and politically, was also cynical, irreligious and given to divorce and birth control. This, of course, was the generation influenced by Ibsen, Bernard Shaw and H. G. Wells. The next generation is, presumably, that of James Joyce, D. H. Lawrence and T. S. Eliot.

The literature of rebellion—or, if that is too harsh a word, of political change—is headed by the authorised version of the Bible, which put the Testaments before the educated middle class in language which it could more or less understand. Read and believed literally, they denied the pretensions of the Church of Rome and even of the reformed Church of England. There was, no doubt, a strong economic motivation, as Professor Tawney has pointed out;[1] but the emotions of the Civil War and the Commonwealth were far stronger than economic history can explain. In due course the churches caught up with the movement and over large areas of opinion established their own interpretation, now modified to suit a generation which could and did read the Bible, just as, a couple of centuries later, all the churches produced new interpretations to satisfy those, or some of those, who had read something of geology, astronomy, physics, and biology. They were of course helped by the rebellious tendency of each generation of young men, for rebellion often takes the form of teaching grandmother, by means of the intellectual equipment in great-grandfather's library, to suck eggs.

Though literature is one of the instigators of political change, it is also one of the mainstays of stability. Though most of the products of one generation go into the furnace of the next, a portion remains, and that portion usually has a sedative and conservative effect upon subsequent generations. Nevertheless, each generation produces its own 'escapist' literature. The high life of the novelettes kept people below stairs from bloody revolution, while the revolt of the middle classes is now being suppressed by detective stories. Literature is thus admirably adapted to the two-party system. It stimulates the emotions of the reformers and adds to the self-satisfaction of the conservatives.

3. BROADCASTING AND TELEVISION

Broadcasting and television, though new instruments of propaganda, have become the most effective, other than newspapers, because like newspapers they have entered the homes of the great majority of the people of the United Kingdom. The number of such homes is known because of the legal requirement that a licence be taken out either for a broadcasting (sound) receiver, or for both broadcasting (sound) and

[1] *Religion and the Rise of Capitalism.*

television. The number of licences current on 31 December 1957 was 6,904,000 for sound and 7,782,000 for sound and television. The increases in the numbers are shown in Tables 20 and 21.[1] Table 20 shows only sound licences, and Table 21 includes sound and television.

Year	Licences	Year	Licences
1922	35,774	1934	6,780,569
1923	595,496	1935	7,403,109
1924	1,129,578	1936	7,960,573
1925	1,645,207	1937	8,479,600
1926	2,178,259	1938	8,908,900
1927	2,395,183	1939	8,947,570
1928	2,628,392	1940	8,904,177
1929	2,956,736	1941	8,625,579
1930	3,411,910	1942	9,139,426
1931	4,330,735	1943	9,435,617
1932	5,263,017	1944	9,649,475
1933	5,973,758	1945	9,987,276

TABLE 20

	Licences		
Year	Sound	Television	Total
1946	10,762,490	7,467	10,769,957
1947	11,021,292	32,994	11,054,286
1948	11,367,458	92,784	11,460,242
1949	11,930,934	239,345	12,170,279
1950	11,875,766	343,882	12,219,648
1951	11,605,086	763,941	12,369,027
1952	11,304,246	1,449,260	12,753,506
1953	10,749,779	2,142,452	12,892,231
1954	10,187,901	3,248,892	13,436,393
1955	9,476,730	5,503,766	13,980,496
1956	8,521,958	5,739,593	14,261,551
1957	6,904,096	7,782,042	14,686,138

TABLE 21

It was said in 1949[2] that at any one time on a winter evening about one in four of the adult population of Great Britain and Northern Ireland (that is to say those aged sixteen and upwards) might be

[1] *Report of the Broadcasting Committee,* 1949 (Cmd. 8116), p. 18; brought up to date by reference to *B.B.C. Yearbook,* 1957.
[2] *Ibid.* p. 20.

expected to be listening. In the summer months the proportion fell to about one in five. With the addition of television and the increase in the number of licence-holders, the proportions are not likely to have fallen, and it may be assumed that some ten million adults will look or listen on a winter evening and some eight million adults on a summer evening. There is of course competition among the two television programmes and the three sound programmes. There are also variations among the different regions of England and between England on the one hand and Wales, Scotland and Northern Ireland on the other.

It is immaterial for our purpose that few of the programmes have any direct connexion with politics. As the Beveridge Committee said in 1949:[1]

Broadcasting is the most pervasive, and therefore one of the most powerful of agents for influencing men's thoughts and actions, for giving them a picture, true or false, of their fellows and of the world in which they live, for appealing to their intellect, their emotions and their appetites, for filling their minds with beauty or ugliness, ideas or idleness, laughter or terror, love or hate.

In what their author, Mr Selwyn Lloyd, described as 'less striking words',[2] 'broadcasting is a very fine medium for the oral and visual transmission of information, education and entertainment'.

Whether the conclusion is clothed in Lord Beveridge's purple or Mr Lloyd's sub-fusc, however, it cannot be doubted that broadcasting and television do affect the minds of the people who listen and look. The British Broadcasting Corporation taught one generation to listen with increasingly critical minds: and it deliberately set out to raise the standard of criticism. The Corporation has been deprived of its monopoly of television, and it is not yet possible to assess the consequences of having 'independent television'[3] which is most successful when it attracts the largest audience and must therefore be pitched as near as possible to the median of popular taste. It is probable that that median

---

[1] *Report of the Broadcasting Committee*, 1949 (Cmd. 8116), pp. 163–4.

[2] *Ibid.* p. 201.

[3] 'Independent television' is the euphemism for television provided at advertisers' expense by a body called the Independent Television Authority (I.T.V.). The B.B.C. is 'more independent', because it is not dependent even on advertisers.

will shift nearer to the higher B.B.C. standard, because people will get bored with constant repetition of inferior stuff and will tend to switch to the B.B.C. circuit unless—as is almost certain—the I.T.V. shifts its emphasis with the median. This assumption may of course be falsified by experience. The B.B.C. itself thought differently in 1949:

So far as the part that broadcasting can play in the life of the community is concerned, the crucial test is that of standards. By this is not meant merely the technical or professional quality of the broadcasts.... The most brilliant broadcast technically and professionally may have the most deplorable standards. By standards is here meant the purpose, taste, cultural aims, range and general sense of responsibility of the broadcasting service as a whole.

Under any system of competitive broadcasting all these things would be at the mercy of Gresham's law. For, at the present stage of the nation's general educational progress, it operates as remorselessly in broadcasting as it did in currency. The good, in the long run, will inescapably be driven out by the bad. It is inevitable that any national educational pyramid shall have a base immeasurably broader than its upper levels. The truth of this can be seen by comparing those national newspapers which have circulations of over four millions with those whose circulations are counted in hundred-thousands. And because competition in broadcasting must in the long run descend to a fight for the greatest possible number of listeners, it would be the lower forms of mass appetite which would be more and more catered for in programmes. Any effort to see whether some of that appetite could appreciate something better would be a hostage to fortune. It would be too dangerous: the winner in *that* race being the loser in competition.[1]

It is doubtful if this argument would apply even if the B.B.C. felt it necessary to compete with the I.T.V. at the latter's own level; there is no evidence that taste would degenerate through such competition, though no doubt both services would be deplorably bad. Television is not normally sampled in small lots; it is expected to provide an evening's entertainment—perhaps a day's entertainment—seven days a week. The effect of such an intake must be to improve standards rather than to cause them to deteriorate. It is true that the demand for better programmes would not make itself felt very quickly or very easily,

[1] *Report of the Broadcasting Committee*, 1949. Appendix H (Cmd. 8117), p. 197.

because nobody can know very efficiently, even by a sampling process, how many switch off and how soon: but it would be felt eventually. In fact, however, there is not much competition in nastiness. No doubt the success of the I.T.V. in obtaining a large audience where its programmes are available has caused the B.B.C. to lower its own standards: it is not, however, B.B.C. policy to do so; and the fact that the viewer can, if he pleases, switch to a programme which is not designed to sell detergents or cigarettes does something to encourage the I.T.V. to improve its standards. The I.T.V. would fail if it did not regularly get a mass audience; the B.B.C. would fail if it did; but it seems probable that the I.T.V. will continually run the risk of the B.B.C.'s becoming too popular, and be forced to put up its standards to meet the popular demand for slightly better trash. In short, there is no doubt more trash than there would be if the B.B.C. had the monopoly, but there does not seem to be any justification for assuming that Gresham's law is applying.

There are, of course, other arguments for and against monopoly, but they are not the concern of this book. Indeed, the general standard of taste is relevant only so far as it affects political attitudes. If it be true, as experience seems to suggest, that political attitudes are so strongly impregnated with emotion that they may almost be described as irrational, the most potent instrument for developing both ideas and emotions must play a fundamental part in politics. Speaking generally, the early influence of the B.B.C. was conservative in general and therefore Conservative in politics. Lord Reith, who was Director-General from 1922 to 1938, had a strong and impressive personality—based on strong and mostly irrational opinions—which necessarily impressed itself on a new and experimental form of public service. He used 'the brute force of monopoly'[1] to apply 'a policy of moral responsibility'. 'The exploitation and development of Broadcasting were (haply) under control from the outset: and in the public interest: without prejudice to entertainment functions, under a *feeling of moral responsibility*: moral in the broadest sense—*intellectual and ethical*: with determination that the greatest benefit possible would accrue from its output.'[2] The ingenuous

[1] Cmd. 8117, p. 364; and see Lord Reith, *Into the Wind*, pp. 99–101.
[2] Cmd. 8117, p. 363. Present writer's italics.

self-assurance of this passage is supported by Lord Reith's autobio-
graphy, *Into the Wind*. Lord Reith's 'feeling of moral responsibility',
which was both 'intellectual and ethical' indicates a scale of ethical
values based on *a priori* assumptions. There were self-evident truths
which the B.B.C. was required to support. This was especially so in the
field of religion, where the 'B.B.C. Sunday' was before 1939 a Calvinist
Sunday enlivened by broadcasts by other religious bodies. Though
many switched off and many switched to Radio Luxemburg, the
B.B.C.'s Sunday audience was probably large enough to justify, in the
mind of its creator, this attempt to force a pattern of behaviour on
listeners. In 1949 the B.B.C. was able to say that one in three of the
adult population heard at least one religious broadcast on a Sunday, and
that there was substantial agreement that 'religious broadcasts have
contributed to maintaining the "religious consciousness" of large
sections of the population'.[1] By this time Lord Reith's personal
influence had been removed, the Sunday broadcasts had been liberal-
ised, and Radio Luxemburg was not a competitor. Also, too much
emphasis must not be placed on the figures, because 'listening' would
vary from using hymns as background music to close attention
to sermons and prayers. Nevertheless, religious propaganda by the
B.B.C. has clearly had a fair measure of success. Since there has been
a swing away from the scepticism of the twenties and thirties to
an acceptance not of religion as a rational structure on a few simple *a
priori* assumptions but of conformity in forms and ceremonies for
the sake of emotional satisfaction, it is probable that the B.B.C. has
helped.

There are no doubt circumstances in which Christianity could be
politically radical as it was in the Roman Empire and in the form of
Puritanism and the Nonconformist conscience. What the B.B.C. seeks
to effect, however, is conformity with one of the churches 'in the main
stream of historic Christianity',[2] one of the main arms being 'evan-
gelistic, in the sense that the audience addressed consists largely of
non-churchgoers'.[3] It is, in other words, deliberate propaganda
directed towards conformity with the churchgoing minority, i.e. the
Church of England and the Free Churches in England, the Church of

[1] *Ibid.* p. 23.   [2] *Ibid.* p. 22.   [3] *Ibid.*

Scotland in Scotland, and the Free Churches in Wales. Except probably in Wales, and more doubtfully in Scotland, this would be propaganda for the Conservative party, though not deliberately so. Speakers are 'expected to concern themselves with the moral and religious principles and criteria by which political and economic questions should be decided, and not to engage in party political controversy'.[1] This, of course, makes the Conservative propaganda more insidious, for a parson or minister who engages in 'party political' controversy is recognised as a politician, sets up a reaction against his political doctrines, and even evokes the old anti-clerical tradition. 'Non-party' propaganda urging conformity with a politically biased Church on the ground of eternal truth is much more effective.

There is evident bias in some other directions, but it is less important because it has no great influence on party politics. That the B.B.C. is against fascism and communism merely means that it repeats an almost solid British opinion. If it were merely against atheism its attitude to religion would be identical: it differs in supporting the churches and the minority of churchgoers against the majority of more or less sceptical and indifferent non-churchgoers. There is, however, a general bias in favour of established institutions, such as royalty, the ancient universities, and the Establishment,[2] in the broadest sense. On the other hand, broadcasting and television would fail to retain an audience if they did not partake of the general movement of ideas. We are not at the moment concerned with matters which are politically controversial. If it be true that political attitudes depend more on personal and emotional factors than on political controversy, a comedian may be more important than a politician, and a joke more important than an argument. In these fields, unlike that of religion, the broadcasting authorities cannot afford to be always in the dull, safe right-centre. The extremes may be avoided as dangerous, probably unconsciously, but a broad band of opinion must be represented, particularly in art, literature and music, because they are superficially non-political. This quite lively interest in novelty probably induces the frequent accusation of leftward political bias. For the average Conservative his ideas are

[1] Cmd. 8117, p. 22.
[2] For the Establishment, see Chapter IX.

sensible and non-political; it is the other fellow who insists on being 'party political'.

Usually this accusation does not extend to news broadcasts, though occasions have arisen. The exceptions are usually due, as the B.B.C. suggests, to the occasional 'preponderance of items on one side of a vexed issue'.[1] The simplest case is a run of by-elections in which the Conservative vote falls heavily. Clearly that is news, which a good Conservative newspaper can seek to explain away by appropriate notes written by 'Our Political Correspondent' and by a soothing leading article. The B.B.C. does not and may not indulge in such explanations, and the bare facts, taken from the reports of the press agencies, tell their own story without assistance from political notes in Liberal and Labour newspapers. Sometimes, however, this is only part of the explanation. That kind of problem did arise in the Suez crisis of 1956. Not only Opposition leaders and private persons of importance but also Commonwealth and foreign statesmen in a large part of the world criticised the actions of the British and French Governments. All these statements were news, which were properly reported by the broadcasting and television system, again without comment. There were of course statements by British and French Ministers, but they tended to cancel each other out through lack of a consistent line of propaganda. Hence the news as such annoyed many Conservatives who felt that a good case was being swamped by 'pro-Nasser' statements.[2] There was, however, a second explanation for this attitude. Conservative thought —or perhaps emotion—assumes that when British troops are engaged everybody should support them; and inevitably this implies supporting the Government which gives them orders. Criticism is 'unpatriotic' and news of criticism almost subversive, since it gives aid and comfort to the enemy. Some Conservatives, however, went even further by suggesting that overseas broadcasts should be used as instruments of policy. This would mean either that critical or adverse news should be suppressed in all programmes, in which case all news bulletins would be suspect as bits of Government propaganda, or different news bulletins would give different versions of the same events. On the effects of the latter practice the B.B.C. expressed itself in 1949: 'Nothing would so

[1] Cmd. 8117, p. 5.   [2] 560 H.C.Deb., 5 s. 1023–1102.

damage the B.B.C.'s reputation for honest reporting as that in one programme service it was heard to say one thing and, in another, something else.'[1] It may be added that nothing would so damage the Government's reputation as a serious divergence between a news bulletin under its control, telling the official story, and a different news bulletin not under its control, telling what appeared to be the truth.[2]

Controversial broadcasting began in March 1928 and has been expanded over a broad range of subjects. Except in religion, where the B.B.C. is frankly propagandist, the object is to achieve impartiality by getting 'the best available spokesmen for the points of view to be represented'.[3] All controversy, even over art, literature and music, indirectly affects politics, though the influence of controversy is greatest in respect of social conditions. Since politicians are concerned with politics, and often with very little else, they tend to assume that discussion of matters in current political controversy is more important. This is, probably, an example of the politicians' exaggeration of their own importance. Except where difficult moral issues are raised, such as the Hoare–Laval proposal for Abyssinia, the Spanish Civil War, and the attack on the Suez Canal, it is unlikely that any speech, broadcast, or television programme has much effect on the electors' minds. Political discussions over a long period, like other discussions, do form opinion; but the real effect of an individual political speech is to

Cmd. 8117, p. 6; and see the quotation from the White Paper on Broadcasting Policy there noted.

[2] The present writer was in an Arab country during the Middle East troubles of 1958 (when United States troops were landed in the Lebanon and British troops in Jordan). He took his news initially from the General Overseas Service but corrected it by reading a couple of English newspapers next day. It seemed to him that the B.B.C. news bulletins gave a biased version because of their emphasis on official statements, due perhaps to the difficulty of getting much else into the ridiculously short time of nine minutes. The news commentaries were even worse, except when they included reports of parliamentary debates. These reports did show that, as usual, British opinion was divided. One could also correct the bias by listening to the broadcast of excerpts from the newspaper editorials—which, unlike the news, came only once on the same wavelength. Probably the bias would not affect political attitudes in Britain, since opinion in other countries would be founded mainly on local newspapers which would (at least in the Arab countries) stress the criticism more than the official story. Hence one would not get a reaction in British opinion based on false impressions of foreign opinion.

[3] Cmd. 8117, p. 11.

convince the speaker himself that there is no case for the other side—an attitude which the viewer, listener or reader can seldom share.

The Ullswater Committee[1] of 1935 made the following comment on political broadcasts:

It must be recognized as inevitable that more prominence is given to the leaders of the political party in power than to the Opposition. There are numbers of occasions on which Ministers of State are called upon to make important pronouncements. These necessarily have some political flavour and tend naturally to stress the beneficence of Government activities. There is an equally inevitable tendency in the general programmes of the Corporation to devote more time to the expression of new ideas and the advocacy of change, in social and other spheres, than to the defence of orthodoxy and stability, since the reiteration of what exists and is familiar is not so interesting as the exposition of what might be.

The Committee emphasised that 'broadcasting should look towards Parliament as the focal point of political thought', that parliamentary proceedings should be reported by a special reporter giving an objective account rather than a personal impression and that there should be special arrangements for general elections.

At other times, though we are far from implying that all broadcast treatment of political questions should be controlled by the political party organizations, we recommend that on the major political issues of the day there should be close cooperation and consultation between the B.B.C. and the authorized spokesmen of the recognized political parties. The B.B.C. must, of course, continue to be the judge of the amount of political broadcasting which the programme will stand, and while recognizing in the allotment of time, according to correct Parliamentary practice, the preponderating position of the main political parties, should allow adequate expression to minority views, however unpopular.[2]

Applying these recommendations, the B.B.C. negotiated an agreement with the political parties which was thus recorded in 1949:[3]

(a) In view of their responsibilities for the care of the nation, the Government should be able to use the wireless from time to time for Ministerial broadcasts which, for example, are purely factual, or explanatory of

---

[1] *Report of the Broadcasting Committee*, 1935 (Cmd. 5091), p. 28.
[2] Cmd. 5091, p. 29.   [3] Cmd. 8117, pp. 9–10.

legislation or administrative policies approved by Parliament; or in the nature of appeals to the nation to cooperate in national policies.

(b) A limited number of controversial party political broadcasts is allocated to the leading parties in accordance with their polls at the last general election.[1] ... The subjects of the broadcasts and the speakers are chosen by the parties and either side is free, if it wishes, to use one of its quota for the, purpose of replying to a previous broadcast. The B.B.C. reserves the right, after consultation with the party leaders, to invite to the microphone a member of either House of outstanding national eminence who may have become detached from any party.

(c) Apart from these limited broadcasts on major policy, the B.B.C. is free to invite members of either House to take part in controversial broadcasts of a round-table character, in which political questions are dealt with.

(d) No discussions or statements may be broadcast on any issue, which is within a fortnight of debate in either House. M.P.s may not be used in discussions on matters while they are the subject of legislation.

The official explanation of the fourteen-day rule in paragraph (d) was 'to ensure that the B.B.C. at no time becomes an alternative debating forum to Parliament'.[2] The B.B.C. accepted it in 1947, but ten years' experience showed that it was rather stupid. In 1956 the B.B.C. asked that it be either waived or issued as a formal instruction. The Government decided to do the latter, but advised the House of Commons to appoint a Select Committee to examine the question. The Committee advised[3] that the period be reduced to seven days; and this is the present rule. The notion that the House of Commons needs to maintain its prestige as a forum of debate may be correct, for in fact few read the debates even in summary form. Nor do Ministers and Opposition leaders reserve their arguments for the House of Commons. They have to win elections and therefore to use all instruments of propaganda; speeches at public meetings, statements at press conferences, official 'handouts', interviews, newspaper articles, and 'inspired' commentaries, are all used for political attack and defence. The newspapers and the weeklies put the case before it gets into Parliament. Any intelligent student could, in fact, draft the briefs on

---

[1] In 1949 there were twelve—Labour Government six, Conservative Opposition five, Liberal Opposition one.
[2] Cmd. 8117, p. 10.   [3] H.C. 288 of 1956.

which the proponents and opponents base their parliamentary speeches, and hardly ever is anything new said in Parliament. Though there are many fluent speakers in the House of Commons, few of them have the imagination or the command of language to make an unusual speech on a theme which has become well-worn by the second reading and stale by the third reading. The notion that Parliament is the forum of debate derives from the age of Gladstone and Disraeli, when other methods of propaganda had not fully developed, the major political conflict was in Parliament, and the newspapers printed columns of parliamentary speeches. In any case, broadcasting and television are not the most efficient instruments for current political controversy because, in the main, they have to entertain and politics is not entertainment. For the politicians to try to stop discussion of current political matters outside Parliament is pretentious; and to stop one of the least important media because, in this respect, it is under Government control, is slightly ridiculous also.

There is, it appears, no published evidence of the effectiveness of 'party political' broadcasts and addresses *via* television. Newspaper comment and personal impressions suggest that, except at elections, they are nearly always unimportant and frequently a bore. It is not at all difficult for a politician to make a bad impression, especially on television. He is usually a fairly ordinary person who has achieved a 'build-up' through the nature of his office and persistent press propaganda. Broadcasting to some extent, and television very quickly, discloses that he is Tom, Dick or Harry and not a great statesman. Probably the viewer begins to wonder why Sir Mortimer Wheeler[1] is not Prime Minister and Dr Bronowski[1] Leader of the Opposition. Moreover the politician is inhibited by his medium. The political speaker is accustomed to make his points at length, whereas broadcasting and television require him to be short and succinct; he is used to the cut-and-thrust of debate and the purple of platform oratory, not the quiet, reasonable, persuasive methods of the loudspeaker and the screen. The way to make certain that the whigs have the worst of it is to admit that there is much to be said for their point of view, but that the balance of advantage lies with the tories for reasons which can be

[1] Current television 'personalities'.

put rationally and coolly: but that is not the way of political controversy. British political conventions do not require the Opposition to
shout 'assassin', but they do assume that the political doctrines of the
other side are obnoxious to all right-thinking citizens and a danger to
something tangible called 'the country'; but these assumptions appear
very doubtful to listeners and viewers.

The difference lies in the environment. The politician speaks in an
emotionally charged atmosphere. In the House he has around him (or
hopes to have) a bevy of friends and he faces a bevy of opponents.
Friends and opponents alike, being politicians, assume that what he is
saying is important, at about the level of importance of a League football
match. To make a point is like kicking a goal; it justifies a rousing
cheer from his own side and a shocked silence from the other. Outside
the House he expects that the party agent has gathered a sympathetic
audience upon whose emotions he can play with the tricks of mob
oratory, and that his most banal ideas, if conventionally expressed, will
in due course lead his audience to sing 'For he's a jolly good fellow'.
Mob oratory, in short, is pep talk for the converted. But the broadcasting or television audience is in its own homes, where politics has to
compete with ordinary domestic life and popular newspapers. If father
is interested in politics he is not likely to listen or look without inter-
ruption; and father cannot be kicked out for breaking up the meeting.
If mother can keep her mind on the speaker she is exceptional; for
politics is usually at the bottom of her schedule of interesting subjects.
If the kids are silent they must be up to mischief. In any case, father is
quite likely to destroy the value of the effort by his closing remark:
'All b—— nonsense.' The successful broadcaster is usually the cross-
bench man who interests his audience in the problem and leads it to
sympathise with his hesitant solution of a problem which, as he admits,
has no perfect solution. Cross-benchers, are however, rare in politics,
where all the colours are primary and pastel shades are discouraged.
If this is so, political broadcasts tend to discourage the mock heroics of
party warfare and to keep the enthusiasts on both sides to the middle of
the road. They also do exactly what the professional politicians do not
want; they diminish the authority of Parliament as the 'forum of
debate' and reduce the stature of the politician as against the actual or

fictitious 'expert'. On the other hand, broadcasting like political oratory is a form of histrionics; we are in danger of substituting one form of actor for another, the slick and superficial 'authority' for the orator.

The danger is perhaps increased by the decision to leave 'party political' broadcasts to the hard-faced professionals in the central offices. The opportunity is inevitably seized to 'build up' the leader. Usually the human material is unpromising, because the leader has succeeded in another field of histrionics, that of parliamentary debate. There is no evidence that a 'good House of Commons man' can be easily converted into a 'television star'. Efforts have clearly been made to produce good scripts; but they must state the party orthodoxies, whereas heresy is always more interesting. The B.B.C. has reserved to itself the right to invite 'a member of either House of outstanding national eminence who may have become detached from any party'. The formula betrays its origin, for it clearly refers to Winston Churchill as the heretic of the thirties. Such parliamentary heretics are rare because few heretics get selected by constituency parties and the House of Commons gets rid of most of its heretics by killing them politically. The parliamentary parties are the temples of conformity and the whips are the high priests of orthodoxy.

4. SCHOOLS AND COLLEGES

'Catch 'em young' is a slogan which the political parties ought to have learned from the churches and chapels long ago. Every year 700,000 young men and women are given the right to vote; and so at every election something like 2,800,000 electors, or seven per cent of the electorate, are new electors. If it be true, as will be suggested, that most votes are determined by long-standing attitudes, it is obvious that these attitudes are generally established in youth. Only recently, however, have the political parties been involved in youth movements, and their efforts have been slight and indeed slightly ludicrous. The explanation, no doubt, is that there is something comic in the spectacle of hard-boiled professionals from the Conservative Central Office and Transport House running youth clubs: and the sort of people who can gain the confidence of young men and women are not those who run 'Junior Imps' or their more modern successors and competitors.

The work is done, however, at home and at school, in the universities and in the factories. This does not mean that any school or university in Great Britain[1] sets out to impress a particular political ideology on its pupils. On the contrary, in a Protestant democracy the greatest care is taken to prevent bias in the teaching. Young men and women are, however, susceptible to pressure towards conformity. They often rebel against it, particularly if the pressure is unusually heavy; but even the rebellion is apt to take conventional forms. Those who seek to think things out for themselves are comparatively few, and they invariably argue from inarticulate major premises, not from first principles. Accordingly, though there is often a divergence between one generation and the next, a divergence based mainly on differences in environment, it is never very great. Since the conditions of the sixties differ from those of the thirties, a similar line of thought produces different conclusions for fathers and sons, even when they are following in their fathers' footsteps: but there is often a reaction against father's ideas which may, in extreme cases, send the son into the Communist party or the Church of Rome. For the most part, however, young men and women conform with conventional pressures; and accordingly their experience at school and afterwards is important.

In the eighteenth century Oxford had the reputation of being tory and Cambridge of being whig. The tradition may have been established in the seventeenth century, for Cambridge made the martyrs and Oxford burned them—though 'Bloody Mary's' Lord Chancellor, Stephen Gardiner, was Master of Trinity Hall. Moreover Oxford was solid for King Charles, while Oliver Cromwell and John Milton were Cambridge men. In the eighteenth century the Walpoles, the Pelhams, the Cavendishes and the Russells were Cambridge families. On the other hand, John Locke at the beginning of the century and Adam Smith towards the end derived from Oxford. Moreover William Pitt was at Cambridge and Charles James Fox at Oxford. In the nineteenth century, however, Cambridge became

[1] Except Roman Catholic schools, where religion impinges closely on politics.

almost as Conservative as Oxford. Both drew their undergraduates almost exclusively from the wealthier classes; both were strongholds of the Church of England; and, though Cambridge was rather more liberal than Oxford in its general outlook, that liberalism tended to express itself more in ideas about the structure of the universe than in ordinary political controversy. Oxford was, and still is, the main centre for the production of professional politicians.

What matters for present purposes is, however, not who produces the politicians but what effect education has upon electors. The removal of religious tests did not itself alter the situation. The dissenters could then matriculate, even in Oxford, and take degrees: but the Church of England has nevertheless kept a remarkably firm hold on both universities. The Colleges have their chapels and their chaplains; the universities have their churches, sermons and professors of theology, who are almost invariably Anglicans. Nobody is obliged to conform, and the influence of the Church varies according to the prevailing sentiment in the world outside. In politics, too, there is considerable variation among the young men. In the thirties of the present century there was a movement leftward; in the sixties there is a movement rightward. But these are minority movements. The median is right of centre, as in the Church of England itself. Oxford and Cambridge have since the Reform Act been centres of moderate conservatism, with occasional movements either way.

This is another aspect of the class structure. The wealthier families have for a hundred years sent their sons to boarding schools called 'public schools'. Eton and Winchester are ancient collegiate schools; but most of the public schools are either ancient grammar schools whose endowments have been diverted for the benefit of the wealthier classes or new foundations designed to meet the middle-class demand for boarding-school education. There are, however, many grammar schools, i.e. day schools, of essentially the same type. Whether ancient or modern foundations they provide education mainly for the sons and daughters of the middle class. In both cases the education is directed towards Oxford and Cambridge. Indeed, in the technical sense a 'public school' is not a boarding school but an independent school,[1]

[1] That is, a school not maintained by a local education authority.

whether boarding or day, which regularly sends a batch of young men or women to Oxford and Cambridge.

The grammar schools and the older universities have never been socially exclusive. On the contrary, they have been anxious to receive, and provide scholarships for, the ablest of each generation. In the present century their opportunities for so doing have been enhanced by the use of public funds. Nevertheless, there is still a class distinction. The 'cream' of each working-class generation finds its way to Oxford and Cambridge by means of the scholarship ladder, which is much wider now than it was a generation ago; but those who come from the public schools include more than the 'cream'. Because their parents can afford to pay, the commoners or pensioners tend to come from the more expensive public schools. At a lower economic level, this is equally true in the grammar schools. The result is that the public schools, both boarding and day, are predominantly middle-class. Oxford and Cambridge are rather less so; but the working-class element is peculiar because it has been selected for its intellectual ability, or at least its examination skill. It tends, therefore, to produce scientists, scholars in the humanities, civil servants, teachers and other professional men, many of whom have no great interest in politics or simply conform, without much thought, with the general moderately conservative, Anglican attitudes of the mass. There are Nonconformist and Roman Catholic public schools, but speaking generally the public schools and the ancient universities are strongholds of a moderate Anglicanism in religion and a moderate Conservatism in politics.

These observations do not apply to Scotland, where class distinctions in education have been less noticeable. Nor do they apply to the smaller grammar schools and the other universities in England and Wales. The smaller grammar schools have, however, until very recently stopped education at the age of sixteen; and it is generally agreed that attitudes tend to be set at a somewhat later age. Nor have the modern universities of England and Wales had much influence on political attitudes, partly because they were until recently mere teaching centres without the intense social and intellectual life of Oxford and Cambridge, and partly because the prestige of the ancient universities has enabled the latter to skim the 'cream'. In any case, most of the graduates of all universities go into middle-class jobs and most of their undergraduates look forward to such jobs. Except in periods of unusual intellectual excitement, as in the thirties, the public schools, grammar schools and universities as a whole tend towards a moderate conservatism.

In the working class and at the lower economic levels in the middle class, the essential characteristic of education is that it usually stops at fifteen or sixteen. No doubt that education helps to determine attitudes, especially because, though the schools do not teach politics, they do teach religion. In the case of the comparatively few Roman Catholic schools, religion stretches far into politics: but even the Church of England and Nonconformist schools give something of a political bias. Most schools are, however, maintained by local authorities, where the bias is due mainly to the fact that the teachers are members of the middle class trained in training colleges and universities with a generally conservative tendency. Where education ends at the age of fifteen or sixteen, however, this bias is less important than that which comes from adult education and the working environment.

Since adult education started in the mechanics' institutes in the early years of the nineteenth century, it has generally had a Radical or Labour bias. Adult education in Britain has usually meant, not elementary education for illiterate adults, but general education for literate adults who wanted something more than they had learned at school. For most of the nineteenth century, therefore, it was provided mainly for members of the lower middle class who had learned reading, writing and arithmetic but not much more. In the twentieth century the main emphasis has been upon the further education of those who have had an elementary education but no more; and hence it has become mainly working-class. Much of the work done has been in fields of art and literature which have had no direct political implications. Even so, as we have already seen, literature helps to create attitudes: moreover there was before 1914 much emphasis upon Carlyle, Ruskin and other Victorian writers whose work had strong political influence. On the other hand, history (especially economic history), economics and politics have always been popular subjects, and here there was very often a strong Radical or working-class bias exhibited, for instance, by the publications of the Workers' Educational Association and the teaching of Ruskin College, Oxford.[1] This kind of adult education has been particularly successful in training active politicians for the Radical wing of the Liberal party (before 1914) and for the Labour party.

It is of course obvious, though it needs to be emphasised, that the electorate consists of men and women of all ages, and that changes in the educational structure influence the electorate only very gradually. It is useful to set out the home population in 1955 of the United Kingdom, above the age of nineteen years, and to indicate the years in which they reached the age of sixteen years. The result is shown in Table 22.

Age group	Number	When aged 16
20–24	3,213,000	1951–47
25–29	3,441,000	1946–42
30–34	3,799,000	1941–37
35–39	3,372,000	1936–32
40–44	3,775,000	1931–27
45–49	3,733,000	1926–22
50–54	3,463,000	1921–17
55–59	2,945,000	1916–12
60–64	2,512,000	1911–07
65–69	2,106,000	1906–02
70 upwards	3,659,000	1901 or earlier

TABLE 22

The educational reforms of 1944 have therefore had very little effect on the electorate; nearly half the electorate had completed its education before the reforms of 1918–21 took effect, and more than one-tenth of the electorate had completed its education before the reforms of 1902 took effect. Nor must it be forgotten that the older men and women, as parents and teachers, have a profound influence on the attitudes of youth. Those attitudes change over the generations, but inevitably they change slowly. The propaganda which influences one generation influences the next; that generation influences its children; those children influence their children; and so *ad infinitum*. In spite of its

[1] The W.E.A. was founded in 1903 to bring together the work of the trade unions, co-operative societies and universities. Ruskin College was founded in 1899 to provide residential adult education for working men. It is not part of the University of Oxford.

perpetuation in and through literature, it becomes weaker in each generation. Moreover each generation applies its inherited ideas to its own conditions; and since 1760, at least, conditions have changed at an ever-increasing pace.

5. LOCAL INFLUENCES GENERALLY

With some qualifications, the instruments of propaganda so far considered are national. The parties extend their jurisdiction throughout Great Britain, but there are some modifications in Northern Ireland. There is a local press, particularly in Scotland and Northern Ireland, but the London newspapers circulate throughout the United Kingdom. The churches and chapels are slightly more restricted because (apart from the Church of Rome, which caters for a small minority[1]) England, Wales, Scotland and Northern Ireland have, in the main, separate religious organisations. Broadcasting and television are national, with insignificant regional variations. Literature is national, except for the small but locally important Welsh literature. Many of the schools and all the universities draw students from all parts of the country. There are other national organisations, especially the trade unions, co-operative societies and other pressure groups. The fact that, with the exceptions mentioned, propaganda is broadly national makes the British electorate remarkably homogeneous. There are, of course, other factors. The United Kingdom is a small country densely populated, with a single economy and a remarkably good system of communications. There are no restrictions on movement, or employment, or intermarriage (other than class). There may be genuine Scots and Welshmen, but they must be few, and there are hardly any genuine Englishmen, because migration and intermarriage have been practised for generations.

On the other hand, the most important factors, especially with those who have left school at the age of fourteen, are probably local. Local opinion is in large measure a reflection of national opinion, but much of the national propaganda reaches the individual elector in large measure through local instruments. For the young man or woman at work, the most important local influences are probably the discussions

[1] About nine per cent of the population.

with fellow-workers in office, factory, canteen, club or bus. The political education of the young elector comes mainly from his job. Before we consider the influence of trade unions, therefore, we must consider local influences generally.

The 'typical' agricultural village of the eighteenth century had a squire, a parson, perhaps a dissenting minister, a number of farmers, a few skilled workers like blacksmiths and carpenters, the shopkeepers and innkeepers, the agricultural workers who might also be freehold or copyhold or leasehold tenants, and the domestic servants. Among the landowners, farmers and agricultural workers there was a conflict of interest, which might from time to time lead to opposition. Generally, however, the forty-shilling freeholders, who alone had the vote, were sufficiently subservient to the squire, who generally recognised the obligations as well as the rights of his station. The squire and the parson could, therefore, usually poll the freeholders according to the arrangements made by the squire with those who had 'influence' in the county. The situation did not change after 1832, although the substantial leaseholders and copyholders obtained the vote. 'Influence' declined, but the freeholders, leaseholders and copyholders usually followed the squire, who was usually Conservative. The squires began to disappear in the agricultural depression of the eighties; and it was in that period that the agricultural labourers, and the self-employed people who had not been enfranchised as tenants, obtained the vote. Most of the squires have now disappeared; but in many of the villages there is a comparatively wealthy family in the 'big house', whose influence in the village is quite substantial. The essential point is that the village, unless it is a 'dormitory' for a large town, is a unit in which opinion is apt to be formed by casual conversation as well as by newspapers, broadcasting, and television. The landowners are apt to be influenced by the Country Landowners' Association, the farmers by the National Farmers' Union, and the workers by the Union of Agricultural Workers, if they happen to be members: but local opinion is strong, and in most agricultural villages the Conservative party (which is of course supported by the members of the Country Landowners' Association and the National Farmers' Union) reigns supreme.

The position in a small country town, which might or might not have been a parliamentary borough but is now part of a county division, has been fundamentally the same. There were more shops and inns, which employed more wage-earners; more domestic servants; more self-employed persons, including probably a doctor, a solicitor, a building contractor, a garage proprietor, and so forth. If there was a single large landowner, his influence was formerly considerable; but generally landowners had less influence in the small towns than in the villages; and after 1832 there was a tendency for the smaller freeholders and the leaseholders to vote Liberal. These groups, in common with their fellows elsewhere, tended to be Conservative after 1880. The workers, who were enfranchised in 1884, were in small units, closely associated with the substantial householders, professional men, shop-keepers, innkeepers, and so forth who employed them. The working class was not a unit, even in the public house; most of the workers were not (and are not) members of trade unions; generally local opinion has been comparatively uniform and so Conservative.

It may therefore be postulated as an axiom that a county division which has remained predominantly agricultural ought to have been fairly consistently Conservative since 1884. As it happens, many such divisions were Liberal in 1885. This was believed by many to be due to the proposals for 'three acres and a cow' in the *Radical Programme* of Joseph Chamberlain; but it may be noted that, though the Gladstone Government of 1885 came in on 'three acres and a cow', most of the constituencies went Conservative in 1886 and have remained so. The explanation probably is that local opinion, led by the middle-class people who voted Unionist, began to assert itself on the newly enfranchised householders.

The Conservative bent of the agricultural counties does not imply that there will not be many Labour or Liberal voters, nor that a constituency—especially in East Anglia and Lincolnshire, where the rural worker has always been an independent sort of person and trade unionism is comparatively strong—may not return a Labour candidate. Local influences in villages and small towns are still strong; but national influences have become progressively stronger through education and newspapers, broadcasting and television. There is a conflict of interest between the farmers and the trades associated with agriculture, on the one hand, and the wage-earners on the other: a politically-minded agricultural worker is not likely to vote for the National Farmers' Union.

The number of agricultural constituencies has, however, progressively diminished. In the industrial areas of the North, the Midlands, South Wales, and the Scottish Lowlands many villages and small towns are dominated by the industrial workers, most of whom are trade unionists. In the neighbourhood of the great towns, the villages and small towns contain many urban employees, usually salaried, whose ideas are like those of the people in the suburbs. Sometimes they take an active part in the formation of local opinion, through the churches and chapels, the pubs and the clubs (especially the golf clubs), the village institutes, and so forth. An increasing number of people, living on pensions or small savings, has migrated to the country and the seaside. Ease of transport by road, more land for housing, lower rates, and other factors have led to the establishment of offices and small factories in rural areas. In other words, the distinction between urban and rural is less noticeable than it was even a generation ago.

The industrial areas in the counties are subject to the same influences as the industrial areas in the towns. Opinion is moulded in the mine or factory, the trade union branch and perhaps the co-operative society. The workers are generally organised, and trade union opinion tends to predominate. The effect of the urbanisation of areas which are still predominantly rural is less easy to estimate. Probably local opinion is less important than national opinion, though the immigrants are in most cases middle-class and therefore increase the weight of Conservative opinion, through casual conversation in the streets and shops, and through clubs, societies (including ratepayers' associations) and public houses. The workers are generally in small units and, even if they are members of trade unions, are somewhat remote from general trade union opinion. Generally it may be said that there is a movement towards conservative ideas which generally (but not invariably) benefits the Conservative party. This is, however, one of the consequences of the progressive equalisation of real incomes at a comparatively high level, because of heavy taxation, social services, full employment, and the power of the trade unions.

6. THE TRADE UNIONS

Since this is a book on politics, it is wise to remind the reader that a trade union is not a political organisation but, in the words of the Webbs,[1] 'a continuous association of wage-earners for the purpose of maintaining or improving the conditions of their working lives'. Even the term 'wage-earners' may be doubted, for there are trade unions, registered as such, of salaried employees. Indeed, the official statistics give figures of 'all organisations of employees with head offices in the United Kingdom—including those of salaried and professional workers, as well as those of manual wage-earners—which are known to include among their functions that of negotiating with employers with the object of regulating the conditions of employment of their members.[2] In 1955 there were 666 such unions, containing 9,662,000 members. Not all of them were registered as trade unions so as to secure the benefit of the Trades Unions and Friendly Societies Acts. In Great Britain (i.e. excluding Northern Ireland) in 1955 there were 405 registered unions, with 8,517,000 members.[3]

Nor must it be assumed that, even now, a trade union uses, or seeks to use, political action as one of the means for maintaining or improving working conditions. This was in any case a late development. The Trades Union Congress, which is the main instrument of political action (though it also exercises other functions), was not established until 1868, and not all trade unions are, or have been, represented on it. Moreover, the political instrument of organised labour is not the T.U.C. but the Labour party; and not all trade unions are affiliated to that party. Table 23 gives the figures for 1955. Finally, it must be noticed that 'organised labour' is only a fraction of the total working population, which in 1955 was 23,912,000.[4] Roughly half the male employees and one-fifth of the female employees are members of trade unions.

The Webbs[5] refer 'the ingenious seekers of historical parallels' to the revolt of the Hebrew brickmakers in Egypt against being required

---

[1] Sidney and Beatrice Webb, *History of Trade Unionism* (1920 ed.), p. 1.
[2] *Annual Abstract of Statistics*, 1957, p. 127.   [3] *Ibid.*
[4] *Ibid.* p. 105.   [5] *History of Trade Unionism*, p. 2.

to make bricks without straw. Even in England there are precedents of combinations among journeymen—as distinct from master crafts-men—going back to 1383.[1] The journeyman could hope, however, to become a master craftsman; and the Webbs suggest[2] that trade unionism developed when it became almost impracticable for the journeyman to become a master. It should be noted, however, that from the Tudors to

	Unions[3]	Members
Trade unions (U.K.)	666	9,662,000
Registered trade unions (G.B.)	405	8,517,000
Trades Union Congress	183	8,106,000
Labour party	87	5,605,000

TABLE 23

the Hanoverians Parliament sought to regulate wages and prices. What made trade combination essential, and gave it its peculiar emphasis, was the adoption by Parliament of the *laissez-faire* theory that wages, like prices, must be regulated by the market.[4] Adam Smith himself pointed out that combination among employers to lower wages was easier and more likely to be effective than combination among workers to raise wages.[5] The essential function of a trade union, in modern terms, is collective bargaining. Most early trade unions were also friendly societies, providing benefits for workers who were sick or unemployed and for the widows and orphans of workers.

Political action was, of course, not excluded; but with the early trade unions it was designed to persuade Parliament, upon petition, to alter the law relating to wages or prices or the regulation of apprentice-ships. It was not, and could not be, designed to influence elections, because until 1868 very few wage-earners had the vote.[6] Moreover until the spread of railways and the invention of the penny post, trade

---

[1] *History of Trade Unionism*, p. 2.   [2] *Ibid.* p. 6.

[3] The T.U.C. and the Labour party regard a federation of unions as a single organisa-tion; the Ministry of Labour does not. Hence this column is misleading.

[4] Adam Smith, *Wealth of Nations* (Cannan's 1937 ed.), especially pp. 140-3.

[5] *Ibid.* p. 66.

[6] Except in those freemen boroughs in which journeymen became freemen after apprenticeship; cf. Liverpool where before 1832 the shipwrights combined to sell their votes: Sidney and Beatrice Webb, *op. cit.* p. 39.

unions had to be small local affairs; and even when large-scale amalgamation became possible and, from the political point of view, desirable, it was obstructed by the enormous burden of distributing friendly society benefits among a large membership. The small local societies were run by men working at their trades and undertaking the secretarial work during the evenings. The amalgamated societies had to employ paid secretaries, draw up constitutions, and involve themselves in large-scale administration. The Amalgamated Society of Engineers, which was created in 1881, had 11,000 members and was 'the largest and most powerful union that had ever existed in the engineering trades, and far exceeding in membership, and still more in annual income, any other trade society of the time'.[1] It was the model on which other amalgamations were built: but it became a very conservative body, involved in its responsibilities as a friendly society, more anxious to protect its funds than to take action, whether industrial or political, on behalf of its members.

The example was followed by the carpenters almost immediately: but it was not followed generally until the end of the century. Nevertheless, there were enough professional trade union officials in London to create what the Webbs called a 'cabinet' of the trade union movement.[2] These officials were not merely trade union leaders but also Radical politicians; and, while they were conservative in purely trade matters, they were anxious for political reforms which would benefit the working class, with the result that the London unions began to take an active part in political agitation and this idea gradually spread to the provinces. The agitation was conducted mainly by the trades councils, which were established between 1851 and 1867 as joint committees representing the trade unions or trade union branches in a particular locality. The unions as such were still reluctant to engage in politics, and few of their members had the vote until 1868; but the trades councils provided strength for the Liberal party as soon as the Reform Act of 1867 took effect. It is possible that Disraeli would have 'dished the whigs' in 1868 if there had not been sufficient support from organised labour—small and immature though the organisation was.

[1] *Ibid.* p. 213.   [2] *Ibid.* p. 233.

We are, however, more concerned with the trade union as an instrument of local opinion. That influence is not necessarily direct. What is said at the branch meeting is probably less important than what is said in the factory and the canteen, in the public house in the evening, and on the trek to and from work. As trade unionism developed, loyalty to the union became a fundamental principle among trade unionists, and the social pressure towards political conformity became heavy. On the other hand, the number of persons involved was at first small. The unions represented at the first Trades Union Congress in 1868 had only 118,000 members, and there were still only 256,000 in 1872.[1] There was a very large increase in 1873, and the membership rose to 1,192,000 in 1874: but in 1881, at the bottom of the depression, it was back to 464,000.[2] Many of these members were not electors; in any case the permeation of the unions with the ideas which were so readily acceptable to the bureaucracy in London must have taken a whole generation. What really brought the unions round to 'leftist' politics was the offensive conducted by the employers between 1890 and 1914 in consequence of the 'new unionism'.

Even so, the trade union vote must have had some influence, even in 1874. The Liberal Government had legalised the unions by the Trades Unions Act, 1871, but it had at the same time made strikes illegal by the Criminal Law Amendment Act of the same year. The Webbs remarked that 'it will be a question for the historian of English politics whether the unexpected rout of the Liberal party at the election of 1874 was not due more to the active hostility of the trade unionists than to the sullen abstention of the Nonconformists'.[3] The historian has not pronounced on the subject and probably never will be certain, for it is not a simple choice of alternatives. It is, however, reasonably certain that the antagonism of organised labour to the Liberal Government was one of the factors. Certainly Disraeli thought it politically discreet to change the law in 1875. Moreover a movement for direct labour representation had already begun. In 1874 the miners, the ironworkers and some other societies voted money for parliamentary candidatures, and thirteen

[1] B. C. Roberts, *The Trades Union Congress*, p. 379.
[2] *Ibid.*
[3] Sidney and Beatrice Webb, *History of Trade Unionism*, p. 286.

'Labour' candidates went to the poll. Usually they split the Liberal vote and let the Conservative in; but Alexander Macdonald at Stafford and Thomas Burt at Morpeth were not opposed by Liberals and won the seats.

It must again be emphasised that political action by trade unions, and even Labour representation, were designed to supplement industrial action and collective bargaining. Because most of the Labour historians have been socialists, and because the Labour party became officially socialist in 1918, there has been a tendency to treat trade union history as part of the history of socialism and to exaggerate the influence of socialist societies. The trade unions of the Victorian era, however, had no theory of society or of economics. The task of a trade union was to secure better living conditions for its own members. Collaboration among unions was designed partly to get legal restrictions, in such matters as safety measures, liability for accidents and industrial diseases, and hours of work, imposed upon employers, and partly to get the law so amended that the unions could, without interference by the courts, organise the members of their trades for collective bargaining and, if necessary, strikes. There were no 'party politics' in these matters unless the parties chose to make them 'party political'. In the early seventies the Liberal party, which was still dominated by the manu-facturers or industrial 'bosses', was on the whole unfavourable to trade union action, while the Conservative party was still dominated by landowners, was antagonistic to Liberal 'bosses', and retained some of the patrician sympathy for the industrial worker which has given the seventh Lord Shaftesbury (who succeeded in 1851) a place in industrial history. Moreover Disraeli was too good a politician not to realise that 'dishing the whigs' implied support for organised labour. On the other hand Joseph Chamberlain, though himself a 'boss', saw that a policy must, after 1867, be attractive to the workers. Also, many of the trade union leaders were, as private citizens, active Radicals.

Three great changes occurred in the eighties. Trade unionism flourishes in a boom and weakens in a depression because industrial action for the improvement of working conditions is more effective when employers are making profits and are competing for labour than when employers are going bankrupt and there are masses of unemployed. The depression which began in the late seventies and continued until the late eighties therefore weakened the unions. At the same time unemployment and the fear of unemployment led to the development of more Radical, and even socialist, ideas among the workers. The unemployed standing daily at street corners or seeking poor relief might be against the Government (which was Liberal from 1880 to 1885), or the 'bosses', or the 'system', but certainly became politically conscious and very often even conscious of the necessity for 'working-class solidarity'. It seems probable that not only much un-organised labour—which in the villages and smaller towns has always been under strong Conservative influence—but also some sections of organised labour became Conservative between 1880 and 1886. Since Joseph Chamberlain took many Radicals with him in 1886, the Unionists had enough working-class support to remain in power, except for the interlude of 1892–5, from 1886 to 1905.

Secondly, the great influx of food from North America, combined with the lower demand caused by trade depression, created a great depression in British agriculture and destroyed the preponderance of the landed interest in the Conservative party. In industry, too, the 'bosses' were no longer 'masters' working and living with their men in small units, but large employers and company directors, educated in the public schools and the universities, pillars of the Church of England, and generally typical Conservatives. Those who, for old times' sake, continued to call themselves Liberals, also called themselves Unionists after 1886. Hence after 1886 organised Labour had to be against the Conservative party because that party was dominated by the employers or the 'capitalists'.

Thirdly, in the last years of the decade there was a trade boom and a revival of trade unionism. This time it spread to the unskilled workers, whose numbers swamped the numbers of the ancient and conservative societies of the engineers, miners, carpenters, stonemasons, bricklayers, ironfounders, and so forth. This might have caused a breach between the old craft unions and the new general workers' unions. It did not because new leaders like Tom Mann and John Burns (of the engineers) began attacking their own unions, asking for an aggressive policy, and expressing ideas of working-class solidarity. They were helped by small

but enthusiastic groups of socialists who appealed to the new generation educated (since 1870—elementary education became compulsory
in 1881) in the board schools. Moreover the Trades Union Congress—
established, as we have seen, in 1868—provided a forum in which the
battle could be fought; and the 'new unionism' was bound to win
because the unskilled workers had the votes. From 670,000 in 1887
the membership of the affiliated unions rose to 1,470,000 in 1890.[1] It
fell back to 900,000 in 1893 not because of secession—the number of
societies represented increased from 131 in 1887 to 211 in 1890 and
226 in 1893[2]—but because of trade depression. The skilled workers
remained in and the unskilled came in.

The general effect of these changes was gradually to swing opinion
among trade unionists. The swing of course occurred more slowly than
the changes. In a trade union, as in every large society, decisions are
taken at all levels by the active and enthusiastic, who attend branch
meetings, sit on executive committees, attend conferences as delegates,
and so forth. When a union throws a card vote of 100,000 at a conference it does not imply that 100,000 members are unanimous. The
trade unions have always used the majority vote at a mass meeting at
branch level as the ultimate democratic principle—one of the few
places in British political life in which Athenian democracy operates:
but meetings are attended by proponents and opponents, not by the
apathetic, who need their trade union tickets to keep their jobs but are
more interested in football, dahlias or darts. The 100,000 votes include,
however, not only the proponents but also the opponents and the
apathetic. Nevertheless, if conditions remain the same the decision
becomes accepted opinion. The swing becomes just as evident in the
union as it becomes in, for example, the Conservative party, which is
now virtually unanimous about policies which it would violently have
repudiated in 1911.

The swing was helped by the employers, who began to use the courts
to demonstrate that the legislation of 1871 and 1875 did not give the
powers that the union leaders thought they had. A strike was a civil
conspiracy in respect of which not only the trade unionists but also the
trade union as such could be made liable in damages. What is more, it

[1] B. C. Roberts, *The Trades Union Congress*, p. 379.   [2] *Ibid.*

was unlawful to use trade union funds for political purposes. As the Conservatives know, there is nothing so effective as a war for producing solidarity; and an attack by the employers was even more effective than an attack on the employers. Loyalty to the union became the first article of faith; and the second was loyalty to unionism, which could easily be broadened into working-class solidarity, notwithstanding that, even in 1892, only about four per cent of the population or twenty per cent of the adult manual-working wage-earners were members of trade unions.[1]

The swing was political as well as industrial. Though the cotton operatives were still dominated by Conservatives, most of the trade union leaders were, after 1886, Liberals. On the other hand the Liberal party after 1886 was still not particularly sympathetic to trade unionism. Gladstone, Rosebery and even Harcourt were bred in Victorian liberalism; younger men like Asquith, Haldane, Grey and Morley were either patrician or middle-class. The demand for working-class representation was met reluctantly, and in the constituencies, not in the centre. The miners' lodges could get their men in because nobody else stood a chance. In the two-member constituencies it was sometimes good tactics to let 'Labour' have one seat in order to return two Liberals. Elsewhere the Liberal associations were reluctant to give preference to a working man over the typical middle-class Liberal. Moreover the socialist societies, especially the Independent Labour Party, were intensifying their propaganda; and they had many members in the trade unions. Even so, only forty-one trade unions, with a membership of 353,000, supported the Labour Representation Council in 1900; but by 1906 there were 176 unions, with a membership of 904,000;[2] whereas in 1900 there were 184 unions, with 1,250,000 members, represented at the Trades Union Congress, and in 1906 there were 226 unions, with 1,555,000 members.[3]

The Labour Representation Council from 1900 to 1906, and the Labour party since 1906, have been dominated by the trade unions, but have been separate organisations. Even when a union is affiliated to

[1] Sidney and Beatrice Webb, *History of Trade Unionism*, p. 472.
[2] G. D. H. Cole, *History of the Labour Party from 1914*, p. 480.
[3] B. C. Roberts, *The Trades Union Congress*, p. 379.

the Labour party it does not carry its full membership. Since 1914 each trade union has had a separate political fund into which a member need not pay; from 1914 to 1927 those who did not wish to pay had to 'contract out'; from 1927 to 1946 those who wished to pay had to 'contract in'; and since 1946 those who did not wish to pay have had to 'contract out'. The proportion paying the 'political levy' has been as high as 78 per cent (in 1927)[1] and as low as 36 per cent (in 1944, a wartime year, with many trade unionists in the forces and much 'dilution' in the factories), though percentages are misleading because the raw numbers are affected by economic conditions. In any case, it is clear that some trade unionists vote Conservative; and from time to time there appears the famous 'Conservative working man' who not only votes Conservative but even takes an active part in Conservative party affairs.

Nevertheless, the pressure towards conformity in the mine and the factory has been very considerable since 1886. A swing in political opinion occurs more slowly than a swing in industrial opinion because —though professional politicians often think otherwise—practical issues are far less important in politics than in industrial action. Since electors vote upon tendencies and not upon 'issues', political opinion changes slowly, and is due more to the new electors than to conversions among the older electors. The swing of organised labour to Liberalism did not become really effective until 1906, and by that time another swing towards the nascent Labour party was already in being. That swing to Labour went on developing (in spite of the loss of votes in 1931) until 1951.

Every active trade unionist who is not a communist is, in his own mine or factory, an active political propagandist, whether he is also active in the local Labour party or not. The appeal to union loyalty and working-class solidarity is strong among the older workers and almost irresistible to the young. The union card takes the place of the old school tie, though it is much easier for the old boy to vote Labour than it is for the unionist to vote Conservative, because the old boys fore-gather only once a year while the trade union members meet every day.

[1] It fell to 52 per cent in 1928 because of the change from 'contracting out' to 'contracting in'.

CHAPTER VIII

PARTY PROPAGANDA

The history of party propaganda is part of the history of party and must therefore occupy much space in the second volume. It would, however, be hard on the 'salt of the earth' (as they have been called, though admittedly in the Labour party) who sit on local committees, and positively insulting to the 'back room boys' in the Central Offices who devote their lives to the winning of elections, to suggest even by omission that they do not influence opinion. Much of their propaganda consists in 'mob oratory' and 'literature'. The latter term is defined by the cynical Oxford dictionary-makers as 'literary culture (archaic);... writings whose value lies in beauty of form or emotional effect...; (colloq.) printed matter'. In relation to parties, 'literature' clearly means '(colloq.) printed matter'. It is not unreasonable to suppose that electoral literature was more influential when the literate electors could not afford to buy newspapers or books.[1] Since pamphlets and leaflets are issued in hundreds of thousands, however, it must be thought that they serve a purpose. In any case, 'oratory' and 'literature' are two only of the means of propaganda used by parties. We have already mentioned several others; canvassing and the snob appeal are methods of propaganda of respectable antiquity; whether free liquor can be regarded as a method of persuasion is perhaps arguable, but if publicans have not been party propagandists, parsons have; money and influence have always talked; and so forth. All the methods should be considered together, but it will be convenient to look at the matter both locally and centrally.

[1] This is not fanciful. The author was once chairman of a War Publicity Committee which produced propaganda in English (for the middle class) and two local languages (for the poorer classes). On investigation it was found that most of the English propaganda went straight into waste-paper baskets; but that the propaganda in the local languages was in circulation for months, among people who could read but could not afford to buy anything to read.

I. LOCAL ORGANISATION

The degree to which electors needed persuasion before 1832 depended upon the nature of the constituency. In most there was no contest, either because the 'influence' on one side was too considerable to be challenged or because those with 'influence' did not want to disturb the peace of the county, or to spend much money, and therefore compromised. If there was to be a contested election, the appropriate technique might be to buy up burgage tenements, or to get more freemen created, or to persuade members of corporations. In the counties and many of the boroughs there were enough independent electors to make canvassing the first of the electioneering arts; and two famous canvassers, the Marquis of Wharton and Georgiana, Duchess of Devonshire, have already been mentioned. Very often, however, the person to be canvassed was not the elector but his landlord, employer or spiritual adviser. The implication was not so much that the tenant might have his lease terminated, or the employee be sacked, or the worshipper be threatened with damnation—though all three did happen—as that loyalty to landlord or employer or to church or chapel was expected as a matter of course. Only in the open boroughs and populous counties after John Wilkes, and in some other constituencies after the French Revolution, does one find serious attempts to persuade the electors to support a policy, or to support a candidate on the ground of his opinions or class origin. From 1830 the balance began to change, and from 1832 political propaganda as such became more important: but the period of transition was much longer than is commonly assumed. A Reformer would appeal to political sentiment; and indeed he would probably appeal to the free and independent electors to vote against the landlord's candidate because he was the landlord's candidate; but the Reformer would do his best to have as many as possible of the landlords on his side, would use the snob appeal if he could, would take a reasonable number of the public houses and open them to the free and independent electors, would hire bands and distribute what in many cases were vast quantities of ribands, would present banners, would find out who could be bribed, how much they wanted, and whether they wanted it in cash or in kind, would organise rowdies to abduct opposition electors and defend his own supporters, and generally would use the methods of Eatanswill. There was not much mob oratory until the general election of 1841, when the Anti-Corn Law League took a hand: usually the only speeches were those on the hustings when the candidates were nominated. 'Literature' was usually local, and there was often a good deal of it because the local printers had votes and, like the publicans, expected to profit from the election. The candidate had to have an election address containing the proper sentiments, such as:

I have fortunately claims on your confidence beyond the mere profession of future service. I have laboured under the public cause to the best of my ability....Never, during the longest debates to which [the Reform Bill] gave rise have I in any way quitted my post from fatigue or any other cause, and if I look with honest exultation at the success of a measure to which I gave my humble but hearty support, it is because I am impressed with the full conviction that the valued Institutions of our Country are strengthened by it, and that new vigour is imparted to that form of Government which has been the boast of Englishmen and the admiration of the world....[1]

There might also be open letters to the free and independent electors, signed 'Reformer' or 'Honest Citizen', in which it was not necessary to refer to 'my honourable opponent', but in which it might be permissible to mention 'the lacquey of the noble lord' who, before 1832, owned the constituency. The ballad or squib was very popular, perhaps because it would be read to and repeated by illiterate citizens who probably had no votes but would enjoy repeating a few stanzas in the taproom of the Blue Boar:

> Thus ends the strain, the Tory thought
> That with his acres he had bought,
> Our yet 'Free Voices'!—Is it so?
> Electors! boldly answer NO![2]

There was, too, the local newspaper, whose proprietor and editor (usually the same person) had to choose between the tory landowners

---

[1] William Albey, *Parliamentary History of Horsham*, pp. 269–70. It relates to the general election of 1832.
[2] *Ibid.* p. 385 (election of 1847).

and the whig shopkeepers, but was glad to receive paid contributions and advertisements from both sides. He might (if adequately paid) even print cartoons, copies of which could be exhibited in the privies.

All this required organisation, and it was usually done by a local man, often a solicitor or a man of business for a local landowner, who probably did the job for successive elections. In a small borough it was necessary to know every elector, who was his landlord and his employer, whether he went to church or chapel, what his price was, and so on. A sufficiency of public houses had to be taken over and supplies of free liquor authorised. A band had to be hired, liveries provided, banners embroidered, and 'whiteboys'[1] employed. The whiteboys marched in the procession, protected the candidates and their supporters, distributed ribands, looked after drunkards of the right sort and disposed of drunkards of the wrong sort, abducted voters of the wrong sort, rescued voters of the right sort, cheered or jeered as occasion required, threw rotten eggs, and generally enabled the free and independent electors to exercise their independent choice. A good agent would know roughly how much the election would cost, though much would depend on how much the opponent would spend, and sometimes agreements were made for the limitation of expenditure—for instance by giving chits on the public houses instead of making them free houses. In case there was an election petition, however, the candidate himself must have nothing to do with expenditure except to pay for it. In an extreme case a House of Commons committee might avoid an election for general corruption, but it was undesirable to have a candidate unseated, and his opponent declared elected, for personal corruption.

A new element was introduced when Radicals sought election on the grounds of policy. It then became necessary to organise propaganda of an argumentative kind—local committees, ward meetings, 'literature', and so forth. Francis Place, the famous tailor of Charing Cross, was the first election agent of the new type, and he began his work in Westminster (a scot and lot borough) in 1807. He had an election committee with a warren of sub-committees. His pupil was Joseph

---

[1] A term adapted from Ireland, where in the agrarian disturbances of the eighteenth century agricultural workers in their white smocks roamed the countryside at night, burned ricks, and so forth.

Parkes, who became a professional, though part-time, election agent and virtually taught electioneering to the Anti-Corn Law League and the Liberal party.

Election committees were known even before this new style of electioneering developed. Where an election was not a foregone conclusion, a contest was very good for a borough because a great deal of money was spent in it. Not only the publicans and printers benefited, for free meat and free groceries were sometimes provided. In any case, much money passed in the town through the employment of bands, sempstresses and whiteboys. Besides a local election agent was naturally anxious for a job which might bring him in £500 (and pickings) for six weeks' work. Accordingly, it was not uncommon, in anticipation of an election, to form a committee and look for a rich man whose candidature would bring honour and profit to the borough. Place's committees, on the other hand, were composed of keen local politicians, who would themselves canvass, organise meetings and processions, and produce 'literature'. They might even provide from their own pockets some at least of the expense required for these purposes and for such other electioneering devices as they were prepared to try.

The first Reform Act did not in itself alter the style of electioneering. The division of counties created new spheres of influence and caused the 'peace' of many counties to be disturbed, so that a beginning had to be made at organisation. In the boroughs which continued to be represented the number of electors increased, and the cost of old-style electioneering became heavier. The election of 1832 was often a genuine contest between a Reformer and a moderate Reformer—few Conservative candidates were stupid enough to be anti-Reformers. In the election of 1835 old-style electioneering was more common, and that of 1837 was pretty corrupt. It was difficult to find rich enough candidates for the election of 1841, but that of 1847 proved to be the most profitable for many constituencies. Charles Dickens probably found precedents for Eatanswill in the election of 1835;[1] but by 1847 *Pickwick Papers* was almost an election agents' handbook. These methods continued in use until after 1883, when the Corrupt and Illegal

[1] Mr H. G. Nicholas suggests that his precedent was Sudbury, which was disfranchised for corruption in 1844: H. G. Nicholas, *To the Hustings*, p. 21.

Practices Act made the law much more stringent. In 1884 the Conservative Central Office warned constituency organisations:

After the last general election [1880] nearly thirty Members of Parliament were deprived of their seats in consequence of malpractices having been resorted to at their elections, and several persons of good position underwent long terms of imprisonment for such offences. In many of these instances the elections were upset through acts of enthusiastic supporters, who were ignorant of the stringent law prevailing against corrupt practices [i.e. the Act of 1854]. By the Corrupt Practices Act of 1883, this law has been made much more severe, and it is thought useful to state in concise language the chief provisions of the statutes now in force, in order that members of Conservative associations, clubs and committees, as well as others interested in the success of the party, may be able to avoid the discredit and scandal, as well as the more serious consequences, which will follow a breach of them.[1]

The fact of such a circular is significant, and so is the language employed. By 1884 a corrupt election cast 'discredit and scandal' on the party and on the persons who employed corrupt methods.

There had in fact been a growth of the new-style electioneering introduced by Francis Place, developed by the Reformers from 1830, and by the Conservatives from 1834, electioneering designed to persuade honest voters. Place's organisation at Westminster sought to remain in being during elections, but it was difficult to keep committees together for mere propaganda. The first Reform Act gave such a committee a job to do, because for the first time there were official registers of electors; and Reformers and Conservatives alike had to see that their supporters were on the registers. Application for registration had to be made, and in the boroughs every year; and there was a small charge for registration. Obviously, a good election agent would want to see that his supporters were on the register whether he wanted to convince them or bribe them. He had also to see that the other party did not register persons who were not qualified. A Radical agent, whose candidate might not have as much money as his opponent, would also be suspicious of 'dead names' (i.e. the names of persons who had died or ceased to be qualified) because, as constituencies became large and

[1] *Offences at Elections and their Consequences* (Conservative Central Office, 1884).

electors not known to the polling agents at the hustings, 'polling the dead men' became a feature even of new-style electioneering.

This development produced a crop of 'registration societies' which had a continuous existence, and some of these called themselves 'Reform associations', 'Conservative associations', etc. This arrangement had the further advantages that candidates for election to the new (in 1835) borough councils could be supported every year and that the member of Parliament could, if he pleased, come down frequently to give a dinner to his supporters or make a speech in the town hall. The process of 'nursing' a constituency could thus be permanently employed. The association was usually a small body of keen local politicians, but after 1868 Liberal associations in the great towns tended to organise themselves in depth on the 'Birmingham plan'. This was invented by the Radical, William Harris, to defeat the provision of the Reform Act of 1867 which gave to the great towns three members each but gave the electors only two votes each. By careful organisation and strict discipline it was possible so to organise the voting that three Radical candidates were elected, though if there were no such organisation even a large Liberal majority would find, as the peers intended, that one of the persons elected was Conservative. This 'Birmingham plan' was followed even in constituencies which returned two members: and indeed only in Birmingham was the organisation so efficient that three Radicals could be returned for a three-member constituency. Because Joseph Chamberlain soon became the leader of the Birmingham association and the members were regarded as delegates of the association, the Birmingham plan was known as 'Joe's Caucus'. After his defeat in 1868 Disraeli realised the importance of local organisation and stimulated the development of Conservative organisations, not exactly on the lines of 'Joe's Caucus', in preparation for the general election of 1874. Thus a network of Conservative and Liberal associations was gradually spread throughout the country.

2. CENTRAL ORGANISATION

The ordinary member of Parliament in the eighteenth century was not in any sense a party man. He might call himself a whig or a tory: but he was not elected as a whig or as a tory; and indeed most members had no labels. He might be a local landowner or burgess; what views he had about the Revolution Settlement or Occasional Conformity or the behaviour of Americans had little importance and might have none. His job was to represent the county or borough and see that it received an adequate supply of loaves and fishes. On the other hand, he might be what the nineteenth century called a 'carpet-bagger', a man from outside, acceptable to the people who had influence, or prepared to 'do good to' the county or borough. For the most part, however, the carpet-baggers were members for boroughs. If a patron nominated one, there was a moral obligation to support the patron; and both Walpole and the Duke of Newcastle took great care to secure, through patrons, and through the distribution of loaves and fishes, a sufficient number of supporters. There were, too, family allegiances and personal relationships which, with a modicum of 'politics' (also largely personal) created the 'connexions' of the eighteenth century. Leaders of connexions and their 'men of business', like the First Lord of the Treasury and his henchmen, wanted to maintain and enlarge their influence, but there was no electioneering on a national scale. The London clubs, especially White's and Brooks', were useful places to meet and do business: but most political business, which may almost be described as intrigue, was done in the town houses and, during prorogations, the country houses, of the half-a-dozen peers whose connexions were large enough for them to be described as political leaders.

There was no fundamental change while Pitt and Fox were opposing each other in the House of Commons, but there was a gradual change of emphasis from a purely personal relationship to a relationship which was at least partially political. It is possible to speak of the new connexions as 'parties' because, in some measure, they were based on political principles. Burke's description of parties in *Thoughts on the Causes of the Present Discontents* in 1770 was more an anticipation than an analysis, a hope rather than a description: but it did indicate (and probably helped to produce) the line of development. Though Pitt is commonly regarded as the founder of the Conservative party, the foundations were really laid under Lord Liverpool between 1812 and

1827. Fox is commonly regarded as the founder of the Liberal party, but the real foundation was the formation of the Grey Ministry in 1830, when the relics of the old Opposition and the followers of Canning combined in what was bound to become the Reform Ministry. The need for some central meeting-place for like-minded members and a clearing-house for borough-mongering was soon felt. The Carlton Club was founded in 1832 and the Reform Club in 1836.

These were not party organisations, though a great deal of political work was done at both. Primarily they were social clubs, but based on political association. Central organisation really developed through the whips' offices. The Conservative whips operated from the Carlton Club until the Conservative Central Office was established in 1870, though in fact most of the constituency work was done by a firm of London solicitors. The Liberals used the Reform Club until 1860, when a body originally called the 'Liberal Registration Association' and afterwards the Central Liberal Association, was established. The functions of these bodies were not propaganda but the organisation of constituency associations, the maintenance of lists of candidates, and the control of outvoters.[1]

The Conservative Central Office was one consequence of the Conservative defeat in 1868, but another body had been established in November 1867, when it was decided at a meeting in London to form a federation of Conservative associations under the name of the National Union of Conservative and Constitutional Associations. This was a body of no great importance. From 1872, indeed, it was virtually controlled by the Conservative Central Office. In 1883 Lord Randolph Churchill and his colleagues in the 'Fourth Party' made a determined effort to capture the National Union and to make it an effective body. They failed to do so and, though from time to time reformed, it

[1] Outvoters were persons who were registered in constituencies in which they did not live. Until the Central Offices were established the candidates' agents had to discover them and, if they lived near enough, send carriages (usually driven and escorted by whiteboys) to fetch them. As the railway system developed it became easier to send railway tickets. The Central Office, however, was able to give a voucher for a first-class ticket, which was returned to the Central Office by the railway company and paid. The Central Office then recovered from the candidate's agent: see Ostrogorski, *Democracy and the Organisation of Political Parties*, I, pp. 147–8. Though illegal after 1884, the practice continued *sub rosa* until 1910.

has never played a really important part in the Conservative party, though it has been since 1868 a useful centre of party propaganda.

The corresponding body in the Liberal party, the National Liberal Federation, grew out of a federation of Liberal associations on the 'Birmingham plan', formed by Joseph Chamberlain, with Gladstone's approval, in 1877. In 1886 it remained loyal to Gladstone and its headquarters were moved to London. It then came under the dominance of the Liberal Central Association much as the National Union was dominated by the Conservative Central Office. The Federation published a few pamphlets after 1874, but there was little attempt to produce 'literature' under official party control until 1887, when the Liberal Publication Department was established.

The Labour party was founded in 1900 as the Labour Representation Committee and changed its name in 1906. It was not exactly a federation, but something approaching a confederation, of some of the trade unions and three socialist societies, the Independent Labour Party, the Fabian Society, and the National Democratic Federation. The socialist societies and to some extent the trade unions were already propagandist bodies, and the Labour party initially had little money for propaganda. It was, however, reorganised in 1918 and has since been a very active propaganda body. Its machinery is somewhat different from that of the Conservative party because the centre of its activities is not the parliamentary party but the Labour party itself, an extra-parliamentary body. There is nothing corresponding to the Conservative Central Office, because Labour headquarters in Transport House are under the control of the National Executive Committee, which is responsible to and, in the main, elected by the annual conference.

3. LOCAL PROPAGANDA

The local unit of the Conservative party is the constituency association. The Labour party has a more complicated organisation which is difficult to describe. The basis is the ward committee, i.e. a committee of Labour party members acting for the ward of the borough or district. The next level in a county constituency is the local Labour party, acting for the whole borough (which is, for parliamentary purposes, part of the county division) or district. At this level affiliated bodies such as trade union branches, co-operative societies, branches of the Co-operative party and branches of socialist societies, as well as the local Labour parties, are represented. The constituency is the next unit, and it has a divisional Labour party built up out of local Labour parties and affiliated bodies. In a borough constituency, however, the ward committees are represented directly in the divisional Labour party, there being no local Labour party as such. If the borough has two or more parties, there is usually a central Labour party. Nevertheless, both in the counties and in the parliamentary boroughs the unit for parliamentary elections is the divisional Labour party. We may therefore use a generic term and say that in every constituency there are Conservative and Labour 'constituency parties' (and possibly a Liberal 'constituency party' also) whose essential function is to select a candidate and, if possible, secure his election.

Because of the Queen's prerogative of dissolution, which is usually exercised on the advice of the Prime Minister, nobody knows how soon there will be a general election. The maximum duration of a Parliament is five years, but few Parliaments last much more than four years, and sometimes there have been elections in quick succession, such as 1922, 1923, 1924 and 1950, 1951. It is therefore desirable to select a prospective candidate as soon as possible after the last election. Besides, he is supposed to go through the process of 'nursing' the constituency. As we shall see in a later chapter, there is evidence that the personality of the candidate, his knowledge of the constituency, and the knowledge which the electors have of him, are not very important. Most electors vote for the party and not for the candidate. There are, however, some qualifications to be made. First, though electors generally follow a national pattern, a strong and active constituency party can, over a long term, affect the party balance in the constituency. Every active member becomes a centre of propaganda in himself; good work may be done on the local authorities; in other local affairs party members may be prominent and, if they show ability, politically influential. Since the main purpose of the organisation is parliamentary, however, a series of good members of Parliament or candidates can infuse enthusiasm into the organisation and help to make it influential, not so much by the numbers involved as by the quality of the persons. If a good constituency party persists over a period, it will be less subject to the swing of the pendulum or other national phenomena than a constituency party whose support depends entirely on the national reputation of the party—as we have seen in the Liberal party.

Secondly, though local propaganda and party organisation affect few voters in the short run, it does persuade them to vote. What the constituency parties are trying to do, in the short term, is to 'get out the vote'; and in doing so they have to compete with the weather, television programmes, sports and pastimes, and plain lethargy. This is particularly true when the pendulum is swinging against the party: not very many, probably, change party, but many feel tempted deliberately to abstain and many more cannot be bothered. Again a good local organisation with a good candidate can resist part, at least, of the national pull.

Thirdly, though a good candidate attracts few votes as such, those few may be a few hundred, or even as many as a couple of thousand. In most constituencies, at most elections, this is unimportant. Some constituencies are, however, endemically marginal and some become marginal when the pendulum swings. In extreme cases, as in 1906, 1931 and 1945, the comparatively safe seats become unsafe. Moreover the character of constituencies changes in changing social conditions—for instance, as good middle-class houses turn into tenements or flats replace slums, as industries are established in rural areas or agricultural areas become suburban, as new towns are established or old towns decay. In such cases safe seats become marginal and marginal seats become safe.

It will be seen that this is as much a problem of organisation as of candidates, though the two aspects are related. The problem of organisation may, however, be treated separately. Among those who vote Conservative (or Labour) at an election are three classes of person: active party members, party members, and people who just vote. The function of the constituency party is in the short run to get out all the potential Conservative (or Labour) voters and in the long run to increase their number. Party members as such are no more useful than ordinary voters except—and it is an important exception—that they contribute to party funds. The 'salt of the earth' are the active party members, who run the machine, raise the money, do regular propaganda, and fight the election. Both parties have very complicated local machines. For instance, the Conservative constituency party is advised to have an annual general meeting, an executive council, a finance and general purposes committee, a publicity committee, a political education committee, a council of trade unionists with a trade unionists' committee, a women's advisory committee, a branch of the Young Conservatives, a branch of the Young Britons, and branches in each ward or polling district. The Labour organisation is equally complicated. Moreover the constituency party is but the unit. The Conservative party is organised also in 'Provincial Areas' and the Labour party in 'Area federations' with another warren of committees. All this looks like big business, whereas, except at an election, the whole organisation could be run by one man and a shorthand typist. The explanation is twofold. First, if a person is brought into an organisation and given a job to do he becomes loyal and enthusiastic. Nobody can possibly believe in all the assertions of his party, but the nearest to complete acceptance is found in the local party men. They have a mission in life, to convert the constituency to Conservatism or Socialism, very emphatically with capital letters. Secondly, at election time a large staff of voluntary workers is required. It can be too large, and it is not uncommon to see voluntary workers falling over each other in the committee rooms, begging for jobs. They distract the agent, who is already distracted by the candidate, though the candidate can be sent out to make a speech to somebody, somewhere. Even so, too many cooks are better than too few.

In the long run not the election, but the propaganda machine, is the more important. The best propaganda is the private conversation in the pub or the club, the bus or the railway carriage, the canteen or the luncheon room, the factory or the board room, because Bill Bloggs (unlike Macmillan, Gaitskell, *et al.*) is a sensible sort of chap and anyhow nobody likes to be thought peculiar. The active party man, unless he becomes a bore, is therefore a very good propagandist. 'What the devil is this Government up to?' asked the man in the pin-striped suit, dropping his *Daily Mail.* 'I was talking to Rab Butler about it the other day', begins the man in tweeds, and at once becomes the focus of attention. This is not part of the machine, but the man in tweeds is. The machine has in the first instance its warren of committees, where the converted are taught to be firm in the faith and loyal to the leaders. Their weakness is that they tend to become too firm, propagandists of extreme opinions; having been baptised and confirmed, so to speak, they tend to go over to Rome. Nevertheless they are, politically speaking, the 'salt of the earth'.

Formal propaganda is probably less important. The value of the public meeting diminished with the cinema and has diminished further with television. Nor has great success been obtained with youth movements. The Junior Imperial and Constitutional League was founded by the Conservative party in 1906, but the 'Junior Imps' became Young Conservatives (and Unionists) in 1947. The purpose was to 'catch 'em young'. The objects of the Junior Imps were thus defined in the official handbook in 1933:

To create a practical interest in political work and organisation among the youth of the country by organising Junior Associations in each Parliamentary Division and throughout the Empire, to cooperate with existing Conservative and Unionist Associations in advancing the cause of Imperial Unity, upholding Constitutional principles, and actively furthering the Conservative and Unionist Cause.[1]

The present version is:

1. To encourage all between the ages of 15 and 30 to take an interest in politics and to play their part fully as citizens of the British Commonwealth of Nations.

2. To attract support for the Conservative Party by spreading knowledge of Conservative faith, principles and policy.

3. To form Branches of the Organisation and enrol members in every constituency, and maintain and develop the interest of young people through political and social activities.

4. To provide a forum for members on matters affecting the interests and welfare of youth and a channel within the Conservative Party for the expression of their views.

5. To afford facilities for study and training and encouragement for all wishing to fit themselves for service in Local and National Government.

[1] *Constituency Organisation* (1st ed.), p. 14.

14-2

6. To assist the Conservative Party in every practical way to achieve its declared aim of securing peace in the world through cooperation and improved relationships between all countries; development of trade to mutual advantage, and at home ensuring a minimum standard of life below which none should be allowed to fall, but above which all should be encouraged to rise.[1]

A Young Conservative must, in the elegant language of the Conservative Central Office,[2] 'know his stuff'. This means that 'you must be able to argue the Conservative case with an opponent and more than hold your own'. 'Political education' is provided by the Conservative Political Centre. Debates are important because, though political questions have been argued since Socrates, 'it is typical of the British that they should have evolved a system of arguing according to rules'. In the main, however, the tasks of the Young Conservatives are those of what is called 'political work'—recruiting members, distributing 'literature', acting as stewards at meetings, taking notes at Opposition meetings, and so forth.

Young Conservatives are usually between the ages of fifteen and thirty, and they are given representation at various levels, so that a Conservative schoolboy can eventually graduate to the annual Conference and perhaps even to the Conservative candidature in a safe Labour seat. There are said to be over 150,000 members,[3] but no information is given as to the number under twenty-one.

To provide for those small boys and girls who were unfortunately too small to become Junior Imps, it was decided in 1925 to establish another body called the 'Young Britons', whose ages were between six and sixteen.[4] The Conservative and Unionist Central Office[5] says that the Young Britons were formed 'primarily to counteract the blasphemous and seditious doctrine of the Communists, by extending the teaching of patriotism to boys and girls who were too young to join the Youth Movement [i.e. the Junior Imps] of the Conservative and

---

[1] *The Young Conservative and Unionist Organisation* (1956 ed.), p. 3.
[2] *Ibid.* p. 8.
[3] It was alleged (by Labour propagandists) that in the late forties there were 600,000 members: *sed quaere.*
[4] Now nine and fifteen.
[5] *The Young Britons Organisation* (1952 ed.), p. 1.

Unionist Party'. At first no 'political teaching' was given, and there is no evidence that any religious teaching has ever been given to counteract the blasphemous doctrine of the communists. In 1931, however, the constitution was altered in order to permit the teaching of 'Conservative principles' at Young Britons' meetings. The objects were therefore defined in 1933[1] as 'the instilling into the minds of children good citizenship, love of country, love of Empire, and realisation of simple Conservative principles'. By 1952 the objects had changed to 'to teach patriotism, love of Empire, good citizenship and the basic principles of the Conservative way of life to the children of this country and to set a good example in matters of discipline and behaviour'.[2] What are the 'basic principles of the Conservative way of life' is indicated only by a suggested syllabus for a proficiency test, which is as follows:[3]

1. Satisfy branch officers of regular attendance and good behaviour over a period of six months.
2. Know composition and history of the Union Jack.
3. Be able to take the chair for a visiting speaker.
4. Be able to give a five minute talk on the country from which his 'Dominion' takes its name.[4]
5. Be able to organise and run a team game.
6. Know two verses of the National Anthem and the chorus of Land of Hope and Glory.
7. Produce some article of handiwork useful to the branch.
8. Introduce at least two new members within the six months period of the test.

The Union Jack, the National Anthem, and Land of Hope and Glory presumably being 'patriotism' and giving a talk on a 'Dominion or Colony' being 'love of Empire', it might be assumed that the 'basic principles of the Conservative way of life' consist in organising and running (not playing) team games, producing useful handiwork, presiding at meetings, and creating a succession of Young Britons: and there is something in this, for these are essentially the functions of a

---

[1] *Constituency Organisation* (1st ed.), p. 33.
[2] *The Young Britons Organisation* (1952 ed.), p. 1.   [3] *Ibid.* p. 27.
[4] The children are divided into sections, each of which is given the name of a 'Dominion or Colony': *ibid.* p. 6.

Conservative peer. On the other hand, the team games recommended are not good Conservative games like cricket, Rugby football (Association football is Socialist) and rowing, but extraordinarily odd games dealing with such matters as 'Trade Winds and Empire Products' and asking such questions as 'How many litter baskets are there in the public park?'[1]

The whole document is an extremely interesting demonstration of the fundamentals of Conservative 'philosophy'. What is important for the moment, however, is the way in which imperialist propaganda is pumped into children from the age of nine and developed into formal political activity at the age of fifteen. The use made of the Union Jack and the National Anthem as party symbols, too, is noteworthy. The Conservative Central Office even supplies 'Union Jack envelopes'; and the second verse of the *Young Britons Song* (sung to the tune of *The British Grenadiers*) begins:

> We've talks upon the Empire, our country and our Queen,
> On famous deeds of history and where great men have been.

From the party point of view, the approach is psychologically correct. There is no emphasis on party policies. It simply associates the Conservative party with loyal, patriotic, nationalist and imperialist sentiment. It also associates the Conservative party with fun and games, and probably much of the rather obvious propaganda of the games is dropped in practice. The emphasis on handicrafts is more puzzling; it is probably a relic of the Boer War, like much of the emphasis of the Boy Scout movement. Even here some imperialism is brought in, e.g. 'Dominion' scrapbooks and Empire Day Collective Pictures.[2] However, the general idea is to indicate that the ideal life is that of the country landowner who has retired from the Grenadier Guards and become a scoutmaster, though there is no evidence of emphasis on huntin', shootin' and fishin'.

The Conservative party caters for older people through Conservative clubs. An Association of Conservative Clubs was formed in 1894 with the principal object of promoting co-operation for political

[1] *The Young Britons Organisation* (1952 ed.), pp. 11–14.
[2] Nothing to do with collective farms.

purposes among Conservative and Constitutional Clubs. In 1948 it became a limited company with Articles of Association which include:[1]

(*a*) To assist and encourage the formation and management of such clubs and to promote the knowledge of the principles and policy of the Conservative and Unionist party and to encourage the study of politics and economics by all legal means;[2]

(*b*) to encourage, support and promote the status and general interests of the Party in the principles and practice of Conservatism and Unionism and in all aspects of party organisation, politics, economics, sociology, history, constitutional law and imperial and foreign affairs and kindred subjects;[3]

(*c*) to encourage a wider understanding of the British tradition and way of life among all classes and sections of the community and in particular among the members of the Association and generally to assist the activities of the Party and to further its influence.

There are said to be 1500 such clubs, though the leadership appears to be taken by the London clubs, i.e. the Carlton, Junior Carlton, Constitutional, St Stephens, and Ladies' Carlton. Political activity outside the London clubs (where meetings addressed by Conservative leaders are held) is small, but membership of a club must lead to increased political interest. The working man meets his fellows in the factory and the canteen, the bus and the train. The director, the manager or the professional man works alone or in small groups, and often goes home by car. The pressure of conformity therefore applies more easily to the worker than to the ordinary member of the middle class, unless the latter belongs to a club and makes frequent use of it. Also, the Conservative or Constitutional Club is usually the leading club of a provincial city. In it can be met what in the current cant are described as 'Top People'; the ambitious young man has to become a Conservative (though he is probably one already) in order to promote his career.

Nor must it be forgotten that Conservative associations are advised to organise fêtes, bazaars, sales, dances and whist drives.[4] True, this is

---

[1] Conservative and Unionist Central Office, *The Party Organisation* (1954 ed.), p. 17. The provisions have been a little shortened in the text set out above.

[2] It is not clear how one can study politics and economics by illegal means.

[3] It is equally not clear how it is possible to promote the general interests of the party in all aspects of constitutional law, except perhaps by asking good Conservatives to write it with a Conservative bias.

[4] Conservative and Unionist Central Office, *Constituency Finance* (1954 ed.), p. 14.

primarily for the purpose of raising money, but they can also be used
for propaganda purposes. The Conservative party has almost a monopoly of the large private gardens where fêtes and garden parties can be
held, and of the large private houses suitable for dances and whist
drives. Also, it can utilise its snob appeal by getting along anybody
from a Duchess to a baronet's wife to grace the occasion and preside
over the tea-tables, where tea is provided for half-a-crown instead of
the plebeian shilling customary in the Labour party. Tours to places
of interest, especially ducal houses, are another means both of raising
money and of getting people together in Conservative company.
Indeed, there is (or was) a Conservative travel agency which makes
travel arrangements for Conservative associations and their members
'varying from Conservative cruises to outings at home'.[1] Nor is (or
was) the Conservative party entirely ignorant of culture. The National
Conservative Musical Union began with a Festival of Song organised
by Lady Brittain in 1927. The objects of the Union are to 'encourage
the playing of British music and to make the works of British composers
better known', to arouse musical interest in the constituencies, and to
hold musical competitions among constituencies.[2]

In respect of these kinds of propaganda the Labour party has some
advantages but many disadvantages. The advantages are to be found
mainly in the collection of workers in factories, canteens, trade unions
and the public bars of public houses.[3] Moreover the local trades council
(which also provides accommodation for the local branches of trade
unions) and the local Labour party usually share premises with a
Trades and Labour Club whose atmosphere is, for some, more attractive than that of the Conservative Club: one can, for instance, play
darts. On the other hand, the Labour party has no snob appeal and it
has difficulty in finding suitable places for fêtes and garden parties.
Dances and whist drives in the Trades and Labour Club are much less
attractive than Conservative affairs. There are Labour tours as there are
Conservative tours, and the Workers' Travel Association will be glad
to make arrangements. Labour tours are, of course, less respectable
than Conservative tours, and perhaps, therefore, jollier.

[1] *Constituency Organisation* (1st ed.), p. 21.   [2] *Ibid.* pp. 19–20.
[3] Saloon bars tend to be Conservative.

The main difficulty of the Labour party, however, is to 'catch 'em young'. The decision to form 'Young People's Sections' for boys and girls between the ages of fourteen and twenty-one years was taken by the annual conference of the Labour party in 1924. This was long after the foundation of the Junior Imps: but it should be remembered that young persons could join the Labour party as full members at the age of sixteen. The work of the Young People's Section of 1924 was to be 'mainly educational and recreational'. This meant that there should be 'sports, music, dramatic societies and social intercourse' and also study circles, classes, and an understanding of the conduct of public work, all in association with the local Labour party. Every encouragement would, however, be given for participation in election work. In the following year the name 'Labour Party League of Youth' was adopted, and it was agreed that young people from twenty-one to twenty-five might remain members, provided that they also became members of the Labour party.

From 1929 an annual conference of the League of Youth was summoned, and it was agreed that an advisory committee consisting of members of the League should be appointed; in 1934 it was agreed that the League should be represented at the annual conference of the Labour party, and that its chairman should be a member of the National Executive Committee. These changes did not satisfy the League of Youth, which asked that its advisory committee should be given executive powers and that its annual conference should be empowered to debate and criticise party policy. In the general leftward movement of young people in the thirties the League of Youth had taken a full share. Branches were small and were dominated by persons over twenty-one. There was strong communist influence and agitation for a 'united front'. The Labour party therefore decided in 1936 to make twenty-one the effective age, to disband the advisory committee, and to suspend the annual conference.[1]

New rules were then laid down, setting out the objects of the League of Youth as follows:[2]

(a) To promote the policy and programme of the Labour party. (Under this object branches of the League may engage in propaganda, i.e. propaganda

---

[1] On all this, see *Annual Report of the Labour Party*, 1936, pp. 70–4.
[2] *Ibid.* p. 148.

meetings, literature distribution, debates. Every item of party policy may be expounded by speakers.)

(*b*) To give opportunity for sport, music, dramatic societies and social intercourse.

(*c*) To provide study circles, classes and debates in order to give understanding of the conduct of public work in association with the Labour party. (Under this object, apart from amusement, discussions on party policy, and classes in connection with the same, are not only allowable, but encouraged. In addition, steps may be taken to train young men and women for future public work on behalf of the Labour party.)

(*d*) To assist the Labour party in elections. . . .

(*e*) Generally to promote opportunities for the development of the character, capacity, and knowledge of its members. (The formulation of Labour party policy is the concern of the annual conference of the Labour party, and it is not competent for the League of Youth to deal with policy matters, except as subjects for propaganda and education.)

The reorganisation was not a success. By 1939 the League of Youth was again engaging itself in the policy of the Executive, and was indeed supporting Sir Stafford Cripps in his conflict with the Executive. The advisory committee and the annual conference were again suspended.[1] The League almost disappeared during the war, but was revived in 1946, without an advisory committee or annual conference. Regional conferences are held, and regional councils elect members to a National Consultative Committee of the League of Youth. Not having anything to fight about, however, the League has been singularly unsuccessful.

While admitting, like the Conservative party, that the little children shall lead us, the Labour party has not sought to follow the Conservative example and to make certain that they lead us on the march towards Socialism. There is nothing in the Labour party like the Young Britons. This is not because the Labour party disagrees with the principle of 'catching 'em young'. Probably there are three reasons. First, the Young Britons were due to a newspaper stunt in the course of which it was discovered that there were Communist (or Socialist) Sunday Schools. One of the propaganda devices of the Conservative party and its journalist supporters is—or at least was in the twenties and thirties—

---

[1] G. D. H. Cole, *History of the Labour Party since 1914*, p. 364.

to confuse the Labour party and the Communist party, or socialism and communism. Any attempt to form a body of Young Socialists would forthwith be misrepresented and would perhaps frighten the middle-class vote in the marginal constituencies. Secondly, it would not be so easy to establish a socialist or internationalist boys' and girls' brigade as it was to establish a nationalist brigade. As the Labour party might put it, flag-wagging and drum-beating are childish pursuits whether indulged in by Conservative children or Conservative adults: tub-thumping is not.[1] Thirdly, while it is slightly humorous to find the Conservative Central Office running boys' and girls' clubs, it would be downright hilarious to ask Transport House to do it.

Thus the Labour party has not been very successful in its propaganda among youth. It must be remembered, however, that most young Labour voters have left school at the age of fifteen and have come under trade union influence before reaching the age of twenty-one. Moreover, though Fabian socialism as such has little attraction for youth, being too much associated with the dismal science of economics, the sort of idealism, or ascent to Utopia, or 'Pie in the Sky', which the Independent Labour Party used to foster, has such attraction. Young men and women take a strong line when high moral issues are involved, and, in the cynical world of power politics this benefits the Labour party. In the twenties and thirties young electors were more inclined towards socialism and internationalism than their elders, and this inclination was probably largely responsible for the continuous rise—except in 1931—of the Labour vote. In the fifties, however, there has been some reaction towards mysticism of the religious, if not the nationalist, type,

---

[1] One could produce a proficiency test on the following lines, but it would not be wholly satisfactory:

1. Satisfy branch officers of regular attendance and obedience to majority decisions over a period of six months.
2. Know composition and history of the United Nations.
3. Be able to take the chair at a mass meeting.
4. Be able to give a five-minute talk on a country subject to Colonial Rule.
5. Be able to fill in a football pool coupon.
6. Know two verses of the Internationale and the chorus of the Marseillaise.
7. Do a job of work at the rate for the job, not forgetting overtime.
8. Introduce at least two new Comrades, but not communist ones.

Cf. the Young Britons' effort, *ante*, p. 213.

and the pre-war tendency has been reversed, though it may benefit the Liberal party rather than the Conservative party.

One advantage possessed by the Labour party between the wars was that the adult education movement had a leftward bias. Officially the Workers' Educational Association, and even more obviously the University Extension services, were non-political. The adult education movement was, however, mainly an attempt to give the members of the working class, who had left school at the age of fourteen or earlier, some of the general education which the middle classes obtained at the expense of their parents. It had, however, to be treated rather differently, because the adult student was not working for examinations but was usually anxious for an education which related to his own conditions. He was, for instance, more interested in economic and social history than in political history, in the impact of trade unionism on economic conditions than in economic theory, and in the social implications of literature than literary criticism. Though the tutors tried to be impartial, many of them had Labour sympathies; and in any case the pupils drew their own conclusions from, for instance, the inclosures of the common fields and the manorial wastes, the Industrial Revolution, and the history of trade unionism. The W.E.A. had strong support from the local Labour parties and trade unions, usually not for 'party political' reasons, but simply because their members were anxious for mass education.

The Conservative party was well aware that the adult education movement generally helped the Labour party in the long run, and accordingly the Conservative Central Office laid great stress on 'political education'. The pre-war *Handbook on Constituency Organisation* had a chapter on the subject. As that remarked, 'no party propagandist can be thoroughly efficient without a good knowledge of political and economic science'. Oddly enough, this was thought to be a field in which women's committees could be particularly useful. On the other hand, the sound advice given to the constituency parties by the Central Office might equally have been given by Transport House to local Labour parties, or by the W.E.A. to its local committees. It could of course be assumed that in lectures, study circles, classes, week-end schools and so forth, organised by the Conservative parties, care would be taken to see that the whig dogs did not get the best of it: and the apex of the system was the Bonar Law College at Ashridge, where 'non-party' speakers were welcomed because the discussions could be given a 'party' bias.

There is less emphasis on this subject in the post-war 'literature', partly perhaps because the British Broadcasting Corporation has taken over much of the work of adult education. The draft constitution for a Conservative association still provides for a political education committee; there are area education committees, and a National Advisory Committee on Political Education which 'maintains liaison between the National Union and the political education movement of the party'. The Conservative Political Centre is the 'headquarters of the political education movement of the party', and it is apparently under the control of the Central Office.[1] Its publications 'are designed to explain the nature of political, social and economic problems, to provide factual background material, and suggest solutions in accordance with Conservative principles'.[2] It provides postal study courses and organises a summer school. It provides a link with 'non-party' adult education organisation and maintains contact with the Swinton Conservative College.[3]

From this emphasis on indirect propaganda, it must not be thought that there is no direct propaganda. The Conservative Central Office devotes a whole pamphlet to the organisation of indoor and outdoor meetings and another to the voluntary worker and the party organisation. What the party aims at is a 'canvassers' corps', which works hard not only at elections but also between elections. The ward or polling district is the unit for a corps, working under a 'warden'; but the unit should be divided into 'blocks' each with a canvasser or a pair of canvassers. In his block the canvasser distributes 'literature', spreads verbal propaganda, delivers invitations to meetings and social functions, collects information for the 'marked register' which can be used to 'get out the vote' at elections, and recruits active workers. Canvassers are born and not made. 'Interest in one's fellow creatures and faith in

[1] In C.P.C. *Political Education Handbook*, p. 9, its status is described as 'semi-autonomous'. [2] *The Party Organisation* (1954 ed.), p. 15.
[3] *Political Education Handbook*, p. 27.

our cause are the prime essentials, combined with persistence, tact and unfailing courtesy. These qualities go a very long way to help in the work, and are often as effective as an armoury of facts.'[1] At the same time, a good canvasser must know his facts, and so he ought to attend lectures and classes, read the press carefully, listen to talks on the wireless, and attend meetings. Detailed instructions are given as to what to wear, about eating before canvassing (nothing is said about drinking), shutting the gate, approaching by the back door (sometimes), talking to the elector, and so forth. 'Your first object is to arouse interest. Your second is to persuade and convince. It is most important to leave one or two facts in the mind of the elector, which can be remembered, and are likely to be repeated. All information should be clear and concise, and if possible, backed up by printed material.'[2]

All this (and much more) is of course preliminary to 'getting out the vote' at the election. At this stage not much persuasion can be done, but the canvasser is directed to persuade 'doubtfuls' and to induce those disinclined to vote or indifferent to politics to cast their votes 'if it is likely their votes will be cast in our favour'.[3] The instructions add: 'Do not spend time talking either with pledged supporters or confirmed opponents, except to make sure that the pledged supporters are going to vote.'[4] On polling day itself, however, the one object is to 'see that the maximum number of pledged supporters record their votes';[5] i.e. to get out the vote.

In spite of the opposition of the cinema, broadcasting and television, there is still belief in the value of meetings. As the Conservatives put it: 'A public meeting, large or small, can produce an impression on a far wider circle than those who are present. If it is successful, those who attended will talk about it and, in addition, it will be reported in the press and reach a larger number still. Public meetings are also a source of encouragement to our own people.'[6] They also give the prospective candidate something to do and enable him to meet and encourage the voluntary workers.

[1] *The Voluntary Worker and the Party Organisation* (1950 ed.), p. 7.
[2] *Ibid.* p. 11.   [3] *Ibid.* p. 17.
[4] *Ibid.* p. 19.   [5] *Ibid.* p. 22.
[6] *Organisation of Indoor and Outdoor Meetings* (1954 ed.), p. 1.

How effective is this system of direct propaganda nobody can say because it is impossible to sort out the effects of national propaganda, direct local propaganda, and indirect local propaganda. There is a firm belief among professional politicians that 'organisation' pays dividends, but it may be exaggerated. It is fairly certain, from the experience of the Liberal party, that a well-organised constituency will remain faithful long after the organisation disappears, that a well-organised constituency will remain faithful when the national trend is against it, and that good organisation will enable a constituency to become marginal, or even to swing, when the swing of the pendulum is favourable. On the other hand, 'organisation' will not enable the Labour party to win Bournemouth or the Conservative party to win Merthyr Tydfil.

4. NATIONAL PROPAGANDA

The use of 'Grub Street', and its subsidisation for purposes of propaganda have already been mentioned. Generally, however, most forms of propaganda before 1867 were local. It is significant that Peel, who first realised the real effects of the first Reform Act, used his address to his electors in 1834 as a means of national propaganda. He had it approved by his colleagues and thus used a piece of local propaganda for national propaganda. Pamphlets and leaflets on a national scale were, however, first used by the Anti-Corn Law League, which produced and distributed millions of copies between 1841 and 1846. What is more, the League distributed to non-electors as well as electors. It had learned from the Reform Bill agitation that indirect propaganda was as useful as direct propaganda, and that public opinion among non-electors could bias public opinion among electors. The political parties could not, however, follow the example of the League until they had organisations and funds for the purpose. In effect there was very little until 1868; and the 'pamphlet war' was not a real battle until the eighties.

It is interesting to notice how little political pamphlets have changed in three-quarters of a century. Perhaps they were a little heavier in the eighties. There was, for instance, a collection of Conservative pamphlets showing at length what the Conservatives had done for the working classes, but they were also summarised in a four-page leaflet entitled 'What have the Conservatives done for the People?' We find, for instance, that they had 'Protected Women Against Brutal Husbands' by 'an act giving Magistrates the Power to grant a Judicial Separation to Wives whose Husbands have Committed Aggravated Assaults upon them'. We do not find any claim by the Liberal party to have protected men against brutal wives; but we do find a Liberal leaflet headed 'The Tory Claim to have Carried Popular Legislation' which points out, *inter alia*, that 'the Liberals abolished flogging in the Army and the Navy'. These quotations are of course unfair. The Conservatives stressed their labour legislation and the Liberals retorted that the Conservatives passed Bills which had been drafted by the Liberals. The Liberals had the better of the argument, for it was due to them that 'we secured cheap food in 1846, cheap newspapers in 1861, and the penny postage in 1839'. The claim to have repealed the Corn Law could be made by both parties in the eighties after the death of Disraeli; but the Liberals pointed out that the tories, led by Disraeli, 'harassed and thwarted Sir Robert Peel unceasingly for the rest of his life'. The Conservatives retaliated by reprinting Disraeli's famous speech of 1872, in which he referred to the Liberal leaders as 'extinct volcanoes'.

The accusation against the 'war-mongers' was as useful in 1885 as in 1955, but on the former occasion the Conservatives produced a list of wars since 1834—a more convenient date than 1784—showing that the Liberals had fought twenty-four wars and the Conservatives seven; and for three of the Conservative wars (1843–45) Gladstone was a member of the Government. The Conservatives also made much use of the death of General Gordon, and one leaflet gave a list of the members of Parliament 'who voted to abandon General Gordon'—a device used in *Your M.P.* (not, however, an official Labour party publication) in 1945. Generally, however, the most common pamphlets were verbatim reports ('corrected on authority') of speeches by leading politicians. Presumably it was thought that the newspapers, which in those days published speeches at great length, had not a wide enough distribution. They were of course distributed by railway and had to be collected at the railway stations. Local newspapers were numerous, but the telegraph companies were responsible for the collection of news until

1870, and charges were high. Press rates were low on the Post Office system after 1870 (1s. per hundred words at night) but high for newspapers with small circulations, and the telephone system was still embryonic in the eighties. It is obvious that in 1878 (let us say) there were enough potential readers to justify the publication of a speech on the Afghan War by Viscount Cranbrook (afterwards Marquis of Salisbury). On the other hand, there appears not to be a single speech among the publications of the Labour party since 1918. Nowadays there are more specially written pamphlets; and 'policy statements' have been common since 1918, though more so in the Labour party than in the Conservative party.

Ostrogorski said in 1902[1] that the effect of 'literature' was far less considerable than the parties imagined.

The pamphlets are little read. They are of use rather to second-rate speakers, who take their arguments from them. The leaflets are read a great deal, and some of them are liked. During the election campaign they are distributed by millions. The productions of political iconography brought in during the last few years are also much appreciated, the coloured pictures with political subjects which not only take the eye but appeal directly to the emotions. Of this kind, for instance, are the compositions relating to recent events in Ireland, by means of which the Gladstonians represented the cruel conduct of the police in the pay of the Unionist Government, while the Unionists portrayed, with a similar abundance of chromo-lithography, scenes of assassinations committed by the moonlighters on tenants who had refused to join the Land League. The struggle of labour against capital, against the landlords, also furnishes subjects for pictures. They make a deep impression, especially on women, who know how to pass them on to the men with the naïve and passionate power of persuasion which Michelet has described with his poet's penetration.

Fifty years later this passage becomes less applicable as it comes to an end. Nowadays the posters make clear that it is the struggle of capital against labour: and anybody who suggested that our female fellow-citizens resembled the angry hags of the French Revolution would find his party out of office for a decade. The pamphlets are still used by second-rate speakers, though they also provide whatever there is of substance in first-rate speeches. In the main, however, they are designed

[1] *Democracy and the Organization of Political Parties*, I, p. 408.

to meet the insatiable appetite of semi-professional politicians in the constituencies for more and more 'policies'. Except in confirming the faithful in their faith, they have little electoral value. Most of them are, however, a little better written than their grandfathers, since Transport House discovered a generation ago that people do not read the un-readable, and the staff of the National Union has made a gallant attempt to write English. The leaflets are not quite as numerous. Ostrogorski says that in 1895 the Liberal party distributed twenty-three million; but in 1955 the Conservatives supplied eighteen million and the Labour party supplied fourteen million[1]—with an electorate five times that of 1895. The change is of course due to the enormous circulation of the popular newspapers, which do find some space for elections among more exciting topics. Who reads the leaflets, apart from the Oxford dons who write books about elections, is not known. The posters are declining in popularity. Of large ones for the hoardings the Conservative party supplied only five thousand, and the Labour party only one thousand, in 1951.[2] They make no deep impression on anybody, male or female. Primarily they are intended to remind electors that an election is going on and, if possible, to put a few slogans into circulation. 'It's Full Employment', say the Conservatives (in office in 1955): 'Record High Prices', answers Labour (out of it). 'Full Employment', says Labour (in office in 1950); 'Fight the Rising Cost of Living', answer the Conservatives (out of it).

There are more modern methods of propaganda. The Conservative and Unionist Film Association was founded in 1930. The method usually employed for exhibition was that of the mobile cinema van, hired for the association. 'Experience has shown', says the Conservative handbook of 1933,[3] 'that [films] attract audiences considerably larger than those which attend ordinary open-air meetings, and that the propaganda films shown have a very direct appeal to the voter.' Films could also be hired by Conservative associations which had their own projectors. The Association was still in existence in 1954.[4] By that time, however, broadcasting was more important and television be-

[1] D. E. Butler, *The British General Election of 1955*, p. 111.
[2] *Ibid.* p. 110.　　　[3] *Handbook on Constituency Organisation* (1st ed.), p. 21.
[4] *The Party Organisation*, p. 14.

coming dominant: and accordingly the Conservative Central Office had a Radio and Television Department 'equipped with a studio for training broadcasters on sound radio and television'.[1] The 'party political' broadcasts between elections are a bit of a bore and probably have little effect, though the technique has improved since 1955. The election broadcasts are more important. In 1951 an average of thirty-six per cent of the population listened to sound broadcasts; the percentage came down to fifteen in 1955, but another fourteen per cent watched television.[2] The fall was attributable in part to the climate; but there was also some switching off.

In 1951 . . . the audience for the 9.15 election broadcasts tended to be as large as, if not larger than, for the news which preceded it, whereas in 1955 one in six of the listeners to the news broadcast switched off the politician who followed it. In 1951 after the 10 o'clock news on the Light Programme six-sevenths of the listeners waited for the 10.15 repeat of the election broadcast; in 1955 half of them switched off.[3]

This fall in interest in political broadcasts was part of a fall in interest in elections generally, which appears to have continued until 1955. It may have been due in substantial measure to the development of controversial broadcasting and especially to television. The party organisations have done their best to limit such controversy, and thereby have actually helped the development of the 'cross-bench mind' which finds the sound and fury of electioneering puzzling if not distasteful. Some electioneering is plain nonsense, much of it is distortion, and most of it is gross exaggeration. It may be that, listening to sound broadcasts and watching television programmes in which the difficulties of political problems are made evident, the ordinary elector is beginning to appreciate this fact and to pay little attention to the antics of politicians on both sides. In 1959 all parties tried to show on television that they had sweet reason on their side, though tub-thumping continued in local propaganda.

[1] *Ibid.*
[2] D. E. Butler, *The British General Election of 1955*, pp. 49, 51.
[3] *Ibid.* p. 51.

CHAPTER IX

RANK AND CLASS

The best political propaganda is completely unorganised. It is conducted in the home, the club, the pub, the canteen, the office, the works and the bus. It would be completely false to assume that politics is the normal staple of conversation. The political fanatic, like the religious fanatic, or indeed any fanatic, is a bore. Nevertheless, political ideas are 'put over' by constant iteration within the circle in which the elector moves. He may be a rebel, especially if he is young and is consciously or unconsciously reacting against the dominance of his elders. Nevertheless, in a particular circle there is usually a large measure of conformity. Since the circles overlap there is a tendency to conformity within a particular class. What Bill Bloggs says is neither here nor there; but Bill is a sensible sort of chap and all the sensible chaps are saying much the same sort of thing; they are of course influenced by what they read in the newspapers, see on television, and hear in the church, the chapel or the trade union meeting; but public opinion has a considerable power of resistance to political propaganda, whether it is blatantly open or unconsciously suggestive. The politician or the newspaper editor finds it easier to sail with the wind than to sail against it; and when he or any other propagandist, including the parson, the minister and the professor, says something with which Bill's friends do not agree, they simply beg to differ, in less polite language. Bill's friends have acquired a set of assumptions or postulates by which they test the validity of any political proposition; if the proposition does not follow from the postulate it must be wrong and the propagandist must have an axe to grind.

The postulates are the sediment of experience, especially of recent experience. Bill Bloggs has learned from his father and mother, his teachers, the boys at school, the lads of the village, the mates in the factory, the cronies in the club or the pub, the newspapers, the wireless, television, magazines, books, and so forth. There are inevitable geographical variations, though they have been much diminished by ease of communications. More important are the class variations; and, since 'class' keeps intruding, it is time to examine it.

The sociologists have great fun in attempting to delineate the social classes. They are never very successful—and they admit it—because the notion is imprecise. It has been said that 'in deciding whether an individual belongs to a particular class, we must take into account a wide range of considerations, including income, occupation, accent, spending habits, residence, culture, leisure pursuits, clothes, education, moral attitudes, and relationships with other individuals'.[1] This may be both too wide and too narrow. It may be too wide because, for instance, 'culture', if it means something different from 'education', appears to be irrelevant. It may be too narrow because religious affiliation, trade union membership, and so forth, are important considerations. It is, however, unnecessary to go into niceties of definition because, when the matter is regarded historically,[2] it appears clearly that the only permanent class is the middle class; and it is permanent because there are always groups which stand between whatever other classes there happen to be at any particular time.

The alleged stratification into the 'upper', 'middle' and 'lower' classes was a nineteenth-century idea which, with some qualifications, satisfied conditions in that century tolerably well. The eighteenth century knew of the 'lower orders', and also other classes, such as the landed gentry, the mercantile class, and the peasantry (the last being idealised in the nineteenth century into the 'yeomen of England'). The twentieth century is somewhat embarrassed by its inheritance, has lost its 'upper class', converted the 'lower class' into the 'working class', divided the 'middle class' into the 'upper middle class' and the 'lower middle class', and done its best to satisfy the Marxists by looking for a 'capitalist class' and a 'bourgeoisie', as well as workers who have nothing to lose but their chains.

I. RANK

It is safer to return to history: but history is complicated by the fact that 'class', however defined, is confused with a different system of

[1] Ray Lewis and Angus Maude, *The English Middle Classes* (Penguin ed.), p. 14.
[2] See R. H. Gretton, *The Middle Class.*

classification deriving from the monarchy, i.e. the nobility and the orders of baronets and knights. The Glorious Revolution and the Hanoverian succession lowered the status of the monarchy. Hereditary succession is not by divine right, and everybody knew that the Tudors were *parvenus*. Elizabeth I was too imperious a queen to be much concerned with the fact that the Tudors had a very doubtful claim and that her mother was Anne Boleyn, and in any case Charles I raised the status of the monarchy by becoming a martyr, though perhaps James II lowered it again by being a Roman Catholic. Dutch William was, legally speaking, merely the husband of his wife, who was at least a Stuart; but the Georges were nothing more than the descendants of the youngest female Stuart. Even Victoria was consciously middle-class, in the more derogatory sense, though she lived long enough to see the great landowners lose their prestige in the depression of the eighties.

These factors would have been more important if aristocracy had been a matter of descent and not a matter of prerogative. Rank was a consequence of service to the Crown. There was a connexion between rank and property, because property carried electoral influence; but there was no necessary connexion with ancient lineage. Disraeli spoke of 'the Manners, the Somersets, the Bentincks, the Lowthers, and the Lennoxes'[1] who helped to defeat Sir Robert Peel: but who were they? The Manners were perhaps country gentlemen, but their nobility dates from the Tudors and their dukedom (of Rutland) from Queen Anne. The Somersets were ennobled by Henry VIII and their dukedom (of Beaufort) was conferred by Charles II. The Bentincks came over with William of Orange. The Lonsdales were great borough-mongers who owed their peerages to the Georges. The Lennoxes were Restoration peers. These families were obviously of respectable antiquity, but they could not put their claims very high.

As has been said, there was a connexion between rank and estate, even as late as the later years of Victoria, for no person was ennobled unless he had property to 'support the title': but rank is nevertheless less a hierarchy of property than a hierarchy of service to the Crown. The Prime Minister, if a commoner, becomes an earl and a lesser Minister becomes a viscount; long membership of Parliament, on the

[1] *Life of Bentinck*, p. 216.

right side politically, earns a barony or a baronetcy. Service to the Crown by a peer, whether by putting seats at the disposal of the Government or by serving in the Government, justified a step or two steps in the peerage. The result was, even in the eighteenth century, that rank, though an indication of wealth, was not an indication of relative wealth. The duke might have broad acres, but so might the independent country gentleman, who refused to compromise his independence by supporting Ministers.

In the nineteenth century the system became even more anomalous. As landed property became less important than industrial choses in action, the industrialist commoner was wealthier than the noble lord. The industrialists and their progeny did seep into the peerage, but in the lower ranks. The noble lords revised their ideas of social prestige and often married money. Even so, the social hierarchy bore even less relation to the hierarchy of wealth than in the eighteenth century. In the present century, even the requirement that the peer should have sufficient income to 'support a title' has been relaxed, and many peers of second and subsequent generations have been compelled to take middle-class jobs.

Knighthoods have followed a parallel development at a lower social level. The Garter was, until recently, conferred only on peers of high rank. The Order of the Bath, which was created in 1399 because there was need for an order at slightly lower level than the Garter, has virtually become a perquisite of the civil service. The Order of St Michael and St George, created in 1819, has similarly been appropriated by the foreign and colonial services. The Order of the British Empire, created in 1917, is the order most generally used, with knighthoods bachelor, for awards to private citizens. The knights bachelor were formerly squires who had assisted the Crown, generally in electioneering, or lawyers. With the development of local political associations, however, service on committees for party or public purposes became a qualification; and there was even a not entirely unfounded suggestion that contributions to party funds were helpful.[1] A reasonable income to 'support the title' was expected until recently, but now knights are to be found at nearly all economic levels.

[1] *Cabinet Government* (3rd ed.), ch. XIV.

2. SOCIETY

It will be seen that rank and class are associated but do not coincide. Neither coincides with 'Society' as it has developed since the beginning of the present century, or perhaps even earlier. In the Georgian era, particularly during the Regency, 'Society' was associated with the Court. The peers and country gentlemen came up from their country houses to spend 'the season' in their town houses. Many of them attended the Regent's levees, as well as the House of Lords or the House of Commons. Balls and dinner parties were organised to introduce their daughters into Society, where they met eligible young men, and the daughters were presented at Court. The withdrawal of Queen Victoria from society after the death of the Prince Consort modified the system but did not change it fundamentally, and in due course the Prince of Wales (Edward VII) took his mother's place as a leader of Society. The connexion between Parliament and Society became, however, gradually more tenuous. The whigs and the tories were usually acceptable in Society, though some were careerists and the Radicals were never accepted. Nor were the stern Nonconformists of the Liberal party prepared to countenance the 'conspicuous waste' characteristic of Society—numerous and expensive clothes, jewellery, expensive dinners and balls, carriages with servants in livery, and so forth.[1] After 1886, in fact, Liberals were usually ostracised as being outside the social pale. Moreover, the growth of commercial and industrial property and the agricultural depression of the eighties broke the connexion with rank and landed property. Edwardian Society consisted in large measure of the Court, the officers of the Brigade of Guards, the members of the clubs in St James's, and other men and women whose lives consisted mainly of enjoying, or trying to enjoy, 'conspicuous waste'.

After 1919 these tendencies were accentuated. The 'bright young things' were, on the male side, those expensive young men who had survived the slaughter of the first war and, on the female side, the 'little bits of fluff' emancipated by that war, whose fathers could still keep them in clothes and taxis. The older men in the clubs were generally hard-working professionals who dashed in for lunch and

[1] T. Veblen, *The Theory of the Leisure Class.*

occasionally stayed to dinner. In spite of high taxation and economic difficulties, there were however still wealthy people living in Mayfair, shopping in Bond Street, drinking in the bars of the expensive hotels, and attending the more fashionable race meetings. The social prestige of this 'smart set' had nevertheless diminished, partly because it had a periphery of crime and vice featured in the 'yellow press', and partly because so much of the expenditure came from war profits which many people considered inequitable.

'Society' still has some political importance. It is, of course, wholly Conservative. So far as it retains any social prestige, therefore, it is an encouragement to conformity. It does retain some social prestige, because of the patronage of members of the Royal Family in its more sober manifestations: the Queen is an owner of racehorses and is frequently seen at race meetings; Princess Margaret sometimes dines in fashionable restaurants; the Duke of Kent shares in the activities of the younger officers of the Brigade of Guards; expensively dressed young women were until 1958 presented at Court. On the other hand, the exuberances of the 'bright young things' of this generation now appear in the pictures and gossip columns of the popular newspapers and salacious scandal, where it exists, cannot be hidden. Many readers, probably, have their palates tickled but do not draw political conclusions. On the other hand, the grievances of the surtax payers, the views of captains of industry on the need for increased production, the arguments for reducing consumption in order to increase capital, and indeed most of the case which the Conservative party puts to its working-class and lower middle-class supporters, are answered by the 'conspicuous waste' of this small and unimportant section of the population. On balance, 'Society' is probably an asset in the Labour party's campaign for social equality.

3. THE RULING FEW

'Society' is exceptional only in that its members have money to spend out of inherited wealth or capital gains. Bill Bloggs and his family are just as interested in entertainment, but they have to earn all the money they spend. If he is typical of his class he downs tools just before the whistle blows in order that he may clock out and go home to his real life. This may consist of watching television, or going to the pictures or the dog races, or going to see if one team of professional footballers can score more goals than another, or gardening, or playing darts in the local.[1] This is not 'conspicuous waste', but it takes up a large part of the national income; and Mrs Bloggs insists on keeping up with the Joneses. Bill Bloggs, like Captain Horace Boycott of the Blues, enjoys life when off duty and does not purport to govern the country.

It must however be remembered that both Bill Bloggs and Captain Boycott help to formulate opinion in their respective circles. What Bill says in the local and Boycott says in the club are part of the process of formulating and propagating postulates. The sources of those postulates are however so diverse and diffused that they are difficult to discover. Since the postulates are partly emotional and partly rational, they arise from imaginative literature as well as that classed by the public libraries as neither 'fiction' nor 'poetry'. There is constant interaction between writer and reader, the popular press and the unpopular press, the daily press and the weeklies, the weeklies and the world of less ephemeral literature. There are constant discussions at meetings of boards of directors, co-operative societies, trade unions, political parties, churches and chapels, women's institutes, debating societies, and so forth. There are lectures, classes and conversations at the universities, technical colleges and schools. There are all the casual conversations in canteens, clubs, public houses, railway carriages, parties, and indeed wherever two or three are gathered together. Much of this is non-political; but much is live intellectual discussion which eventually finds its way into public opinion. Those who spend their lives in universities see the gulf beginning to yawn between the generations, as one set of ideas becomes old-fashioned and is replaced by a new, though not very new, set of ideas. The operation of the three-generation cycle has already been mentioned.[2] Victorian ideas are replaced by the Edwardian and the Edwardian by the neo-Georgian; the neo-Elizabethan has a measure of sympathy with the Victorian which his father cannot share.

Though Bill Bloggs and Captain Boycott may be typical in one sense, there are many who take an active part in the process of Government.

[1] A 'local' is a saloon in which alcoholic liquor is sold and consumed.
[2] *Ante*, p. 162.

This must be understood in a broad sense so as to include the whole organisation of social life. If Bill Bloggs helps to run the darts club he is, in this sense, helping to govern the country. Captain Boycott, as a regular officer, is clearly a professional part of the governmental machine; but if he is a committee member of the Life Guards Polo Club he is also an amateur. The strength and stability of the voluntary associations are part of the strength and stability of the British Constitution. They make Britain one of the most highly organised countries in the world, a very large part of the organisation being outside the political field. The explanation is to be found in part in the Protestant character of the British churches and the divisions among them; for when, as in Roman Catholic countries, the Church competes with the Government, in so far as it cannot control it, it seeks to dominate those institutions of social life and action which are not under governmental control. Partly, however, the strength of the voluntary associations derives from the density of population, the degree of urbanisation, and the ease of communications, which combine to make inexpensive voluntary action easy.

To talk of 'the ruling few'[1] is therefore something of a misnomer. Whitaker's *Almanac* devotes nearly forty pages to lists of societies and institutions, research institutes, and trade unions: but these are the national organisations of some importance. There are besides hundreds of other national organisations and thousands, perhaps tens of thousands, of local organisations. There are, too, hundreds of committees in a single composite entity like the University of Cambridge, hundreds of branches of national organisations, and so forth.

Each of these organisations takes part in the process of government, and each helps to form public opinion. Some of them even form pressure groups of considerable public importance.[2] Through them, too, the private individual makes his weight felt. In the end, however, one does reach 'the ruling few' because, though many help to create opinion, decisions are taken by very few and, even in a democracy, are often determined less by principle than by personality. 'I have many times seen purely personal likes or dislikes, personal health, vanity,

[1] See Sir David Kelly, *The Ruling Few*.
[2] See Jennings, *Parliament* (2nd ed.), ch. VII.

prejudice, or just lack of time for proper consideration, decide important issues.'[1] These few, expressed collectively, are the Cabinet Ministers and the senior officers of the civil service, the chiefs of staff and the senior officers of the armed forces, the leading members of the diplomatic and colonial services, the Archbishop of Canterbury, the Governor and the directors of the Bank of England, and such persons as may be consulted by any of these. It is, however, misleading to name them collectively, because they never act collectively. On a particular issue the initiative is taken by a group of senior officials in the department concerned, in consultation with their 'opposite numbers' in other departments likely to be affected. If issues of principle were raised, these 'opposite numbers' would submit them to their own Ministers for decision. The case having then been prepared, it would go to a Minister, and possibly a Cabinet Committee. At this stage it might be thought desirable to consult outside interests or experts, formally and in public, or informally and in private. Ultimately, a Cabinet decision would be taken.

Oxford:	Eton and Christ Church	4	
	Sherborne and Christ Church	1	
	Eton and Balliol	1	
	Harrow and Balliol	1	
	George Watson's and Balliol	1	
	Eton and Magdalen	2	
	Winchester and New College	1	11
Cambridge:	Eastbourne and Jesus	1	
	Marlborough and Pembroke	1	
	Fettes and Magdalene	1	3
Others:	Manchester Grammar School and Manchester University	1	
	Eton	3	4

TABLE 24

It follows that, apart from the Ministry and the public service, 'the ruling few' are not an organised collectivity. Allegations that there is an entity—recently called 'the Establishment'—operating as a sort of conspiracy, are frequently made when a Conservative Government is in power, because most of the persons concerned in a particular decision

[1] Sir David Kelly, *The Ruling Few*, p. 2.

are drawn from a narrow social circle. Table 24 shows how the Cabinet could be classified by school and college when Sir Anthony Eden (Eton and Christ Church) was Prime Minister.

Oxford:	Eton and Balliol	1	
	George Watson's and Balliol	1	
	Marlborough and Balliol	1	
	Eton and Christ Church	2	
	Sherborne and Christ Church	1	
	Winchester and New College	1	
	Merchant Taylors and Merton	1	
	Eton and Magdalen	1	9
Cambridge:	Harrow and Trinity	1	
	Winchester and Trinity	1	
	St Olave's and Trinity	1	
	Fettes and Caius	1	
	Marlborough and Pembroke	1	
	Fettes and Magdalene	1	6
Others:	Eton	2	
	Queen's, Taunton, and King's College, London	1	
	County school	1	4

TABLE 25

Thus, in a Cabinet of eighteen, with a Prime Minister educated at Eton and Oxford, ten were educated at Eton and eleven at Oxford. On the resignation of Sir Anthony Eden, the Queen had a difficult choice between Mr Macmillan (Eton and Balliol) and Mr R. A. Butler (Marlborough and Pembroke, Cambridge). She consulted Sir Winston Churchill (Harrow) and the Marquis of Salisbury (Eton and Christ Church), and Mr Macmillan was appointed. Table 25 shows the composition of the Cabinet a year later. Thus, the appointment of an Oxford Prime Minister had doubled the Cambridge representation, and the appointment of an Old Etonian had reduced the Eton representation from ten to six.

The example does not disprove the theory of the 'Establishment', though it casts some doubt upon it. Indeed, the predominance of Eton and Oxford in the counsels of the Conservative party can be explained more easily. To achieve Cabinet rank lengthy service in the House of Commons is usually required; and most young Conservatives in the

House of Commons have to live on inherited wealth.[1] Wealthy men usually send their sons to the more fashionable public schools and (in the last generation, when there was little competition) the more fashionable Oxford colleges. Moreover, Oxford encourages young politicians, while Cambridge is apt to consider that politics provide suitable careers for Oxford men. The general predominance of the public schools and the older universities can similarly be explained by the 'spread' of wealth in the last generation. Even if the wealth was not considerable, it provided at least for the beginning of a career compatible with membership of the House of Commons. The boy from the county school, as the example in Mr Macmillan's Cabinet shows, had to make a career in commerce or industry and enter politics, if at all, *via* the House of Lords.[2]

There is no doubt that loyalty to school and college does affect appointments. To the person educated in the right place, Trinity Hall should be preferred to Trinity College, Cambridge to Oxford, and Oxford to *hoi polloi*. The preference may be rationalised by claiming that one knows some of the qualities of the article being purchased; and anyhow the candidate is vouched for by the Senior Tutor, whose

[1] See Jennings, *Parliament* (2nd ed.), pp. 44–58.
[2] So far as the Conservative party is concerned, there has been little change in social composition (apart from the substitution of *rentiers* for landowners) since the Reform Act. Professor H. J. Laski, in *Studies in Law and Politics*, pp. 181–201, gave figures relating to the social background of those who have held Cabinet office between 1801 and 1924. If the figures relating to school and university be taken out, and those for 1925–55 (inclusive) be added, the following table is obtained:

Schools and Universities of Cabinet Ministers, 1801–1955

Educated at Eton	104	
Educated at other Public Schools	111	
Others	169	
	——	384
Educated at Oxford	146	
Educated at Cambridge	92	
Educated at other Universities	38	
Others	108	
	——	384

If the figures be taken in periods, following Professor Laski, and the period 1925–55

judgment can be relied upon. Moreover a career is more easily carved
out if one's superiors wear the same tie and therefore speak the same
language. If a particular piece of work has to be done and there are
half-a-dozen people capable of doing it, the name that sticks out is that
of Oliver Twist, who rowed in the boat that 'went head'. Even in the
service with the most rigid hierarchy, that of the Army, red tape can
be ignored if the brigadier was 'up' with the second lieutenant's father.
This does not mean that the so-called 'Establishment' is not open to

be added, but using percentages, the following figures are obtained (if a Minister holds
office in two periods he is counted twice):

	1801–31	1832–66	1867–84	1885–1905	1906–16	1917–24	1925–55
No. of Ministers	71	100	58	69	51	52	102
Percentage at:							
Eton	28·2	27	34·5	36·2	23·3	11·5	22·5
Other Public Schools	31·0	28	24·1	30·4	25·5	36·5	31·3
Others	41·8	45	41·4	33·4	51·2	52·0	46·2
Percentage at:							
Oxford	33·8	38	50·0	50·7	39·2	34·6	33·3
Cambridge	33·8	30	20·7	24·7	31·4	17·3	13·7
Other Universities	9·9	10	5·2	7·2	9·8	7·7	13·7
Others	22·5	22	24·1	17·4	19·6	40·4	39·3

Though (at p. 191) Professor Laski gives figures, divided according to party, for the
period 1868–1924, he does not give the totals, and accordingly it is not possible, without
repeating the research, to give the proportions. The following are the figures for 1925–55
(inclusive), excluding three Liberals in office in 1931–2:

	Conservative	Labour
No. of Cabinet Ministers	57	41
Percentage at:		
Eton	38·0	2·4
Other Public Schools	54·4	26·2
Others	7·6	71·4
Percentage at:		
Oxford	45·6	16·7
Cambridge	17·5	9·5
Other Universities	10·5	19·0
Others	26·4	54·8

the talents; it simply means that it is reached more easily by those who have not only the right talents but also the right ties. Nor must it be forgotten that Oxford and Cambridge are preferred by employers because those universities are preferred by the ablest young men and women of each generation, and vice versa. The number of people of the highest ability in each generation is small, and most of those who receive a university education are to be found among the scholars and exhibitioners of the Oxford and Cambridge colleges. Something more, or something less, than academic ability is required; and indeed in politics it is something of a handicap; but industry, the civil service, the Church and the universities themselves need more of it than they can get. There is plenty of room at the top for those who are prepared to work hard.

4. CLASS

Having disposed of some concepts which are not those of class but which are important in the process of government, we return to class. The word itself, in this context, is modern; but the typical and indeed the classical example of class was the landed interest of the eighteenth century. It attained remarkable stability and power as an unorganised community of interest. There was a simple test of membership, the ownership of land by the head of the family in sufficient quantity to provide for the maintenance of the whole family out of rents, with such adventitious assistance as could be derived from advowsons, marriage portions, places in the public service (preferably sinecures or capable of being performed by deputy) and pensions. As with all classes, its margins were uncertain. The forty-shilling freeholder was a landowner, but he did not belong to the landed interest unless he had sufficient land to justify his assuming the rank of an esquire, which had ceased to have a precise meaning as a rank but had not yet become a synonym for 'master' or 'mister'. His wife was neither a Lady nor a lady, but a mistress or goodwife. Nor was the landed class exclusive. The wealthy merchant who bought land, as all wealthy merchants did, was not at once accepted as socially a member of the landed interest, but there was no great difficulty about social acceptability in the second generation if that generation lost its connexion with trade, particularly if it married into the landed interest; and the landed interest was not socially so exclusive as to refuse to marry money tainted by trade, particularly if the taint had been removed by the purchase of land.

Further, the landed interest was typical of a class in that it was not a community of equals. The hierarchy was not one of wealth, though wealth was important, both politically and otherwise, because it carried influence. Nor was it a hierarchy of rank, because the independent country gentleman who had not curried favour with the King's ministers regarded himself, and was regarded by others, as a more worthy representative of the landed interest than a member of the new nobility. Nor was it a hierarchy based on ancient lineage. The ancient families had some snob appeal; but the newer families which profited from the dissolution of the monasteries, and the still newer families which had come over from trade, were fully accepted. In short, a member of the landed interest, like an elephant, was easily distinguished but not easily defined.

The landed interest occupied all the benches in the House of Lords because all the temporal peers were landowners, while the spiritual peers not only were landowners as bishops but also were bishops because they came from landowning families. Before the Reformation the lowly cleric might aspire to a cardinal's hat, as Wolsey showed just as the Church of Rome was losing control of the Church of England. After the Reformation canonries, deaneries and bishoprics were at the disposal of the King's ministers, while the wealthier parish livings were in the gift of the landowners and were normally filled by younger sons of landowners. The impoverished curate might aspire to one of the poorer rectories or vicarages if he made himself useful, but would go no higher. The more valuable places were perquisites of the politically dominant section of the landed interest.

The county members and most of the borough members of the House of Commons belonged to the landed interest. In the counties, as we have seen, the forty-shilling freeholders deferred to rank, wealth and social esteem: i.e. the landed interest. Most of the boroughs were villages or market towns under the influence of the neighbouring landowners. Similarly local government, outside the greater towns, was in the hands of the landed gentry, acting as lords lieutenant, sheriffs and justices of the peace. Literature and art, too, depended on the patronage of the landed interest. Public opinion on public issues, in so far as there was any, was formulated and expressed when the justices came to sit in quarter sessions, or in the coffee-houses in London where the wits and the gallants met.

As the eighteenth century developed, however, the intrusion of the mercantile interest became more noticeable. Trade and transport developed before capitalist industry because production was mainly in cottage industries. The towns began to develop as industrial centres late in the century with the use of steam power and machinery, and accordingly the industrial middle class did not become important until after the Napoleonic Wars. Meanwhile, however, the towns, and especially the seaports, had been growing as commercial and financial centres. There was no opposition between land and trade. Traders became landowners; landowners speculated in trading ventures; the daughters of wealthy merchants and financiers married into the landed interest; landowners had estates in the West Indies and North America. The concern of the House of Commons with trade, even while still dominated by the landed interest, has often been remarked upon.[1] The West India interest, whose members had plantations in, or commercial contacts with, the West Indies, may have numbered forty in 1761.[2] The East India Company provided one of the major issues for eighteenth-century politics. The East India interest was not so strong in the House of Commons as the West India interest, but its influence was not disdained by governments.[3] On the other hand, the persons concerned were not all merchants. Sir Lewis Namier estimates that there were only fifty merchants in the Parliament of 1761,[4] most of them London merchants sitting for pocket boroughs; with a couple of exceptions, only the members for the City of London and Southwark were genuine representatives of commercial constituents.

Representation is not, however, a fair test either of social importance or of influence on public opinion. A busy merchant would have no

[1] Sir Lewis Namier, *England in the Age of the American Revolution*, pp. 35–40.
[2] *Ibid.* pp. 272–6.
[3] Lucy S. Sutherland, *The East India Company in Eighteenth Century Politics*, p. 19.
[4] *Op. cit.* p. 267.

time for parliamentary work. He might, late in life, seek a borough seat in order to advance his social pretensions; and his sons might leave the business to others in order to live the life of wealthy men, which might include service in Parliament. As other forms of investment became more important than land, the *rentiers*, who supplied most of the members to both parties for most of the nineteenth century, were as interested in *rentes* as in rents. In fact, classifications of members of Parliament based on trade, profession or occupation,[1] though interesting, are not conclusive. Until comparatively recently most members of Parliament lived on inherited wealth. The landed interest was still strong in 1846, but the repeal of the Corn Law cannot be shown as a conflict between the representatives of the landed interest and the representatives of commerce and industry; indeed, the Peelites, whose defection from the old orthodoxy enabled repeal to be carried, were mostly landowners. Already investments were mixed; and the process developed apace as the limited liability company enabled anybody to invest in almost anything without devoting much time and energy to it. In the nineteenth century there is a very clear 'railway interest' and strong evidence of a 'brewers' interest', usually known as 'the Trade': but it would be unrealistic to speak of a mercantile interest or an industrial interest. Most members of Parliament, Liberals and Conservatives alike, had shares in a variety of companies, whether or not they also owned land.

One effect of changing economic conditions in the eighteenth century was a change in the demand for literature, both journalistic and more narrowly literary. The literary set under Queen Anne was concentrated in London and depended mainly on patronage by wealthy landowners, generally peers. It was, therefore, extremely respectable, at least in one sense. Indeed, with Steele and Addison it became respectable in every sense, for it was no longer necessary to be obscene. Journalism, on the other hand, was far from respectable. 'Grub Street' had developed out of the Civil War, and the daily news sheet began at the beginning of the eighteenth century.[2] These

---

[1] J. A. Thomas, *The House of Commons, 1832–1901*; Jennings, *Parliament* (2nd ed.), ch. II.

[2] Sir Leslie Stephen, *English Literature and Society in the Eighteenth Century*, pp. 68–9.

journalistic activities would have been impracticable but for the large reading public which London already provided: but Grub Street paid its way by subsidies from politicians. What was happening, however, was a progressive expansion of the reading public through the development of commerce and industry, so that by Dr Johnson's time the journalist and the author had freed themselves from patronage. They were dependent upon the purchase of their productions by the smaller landowners and the mercantile class. This development proceeded apace through the Napoleonic Wars. Dr Johnson was the last of the great literary proconsuls because the demand for literature had expanded and had been met by a more extensive supply. The literary world could no longer be ruled from the Mitre Tavern or anywhere else.

This was, however, part of another development out of the Industrial Revolution. The expansion of commerce and industry had compelled a great expansion of the financial houses, the professions, the wholesale counting houses and the retail shops. The term 'middle class' is generally used of any class between the dominant class on the one hand and the labouring or working class, 'the lower orders', on the other. Thus the Civil War has been described as the revolt of the middle class because so many of the Commonwealth men were small landowners and it had the support of the City of London. Modern writers[1] also regard the mercantile interest of the eighteenth century as the middle class because in the social hierarchy it was intermediate between the landowners and the lower orders. In the nineteenth century, however, the landed interest and the mercantile interest were fused, and to them were added, in the second and third generations, the families whose wealth came from the mines and factories. The middle class as we now know it is in the main a product of the Industrial Revolution, though it also includes the farmers. Indeed, the 'upper class' has virtually disappeared. Some people are wealthier than others, but not much wealthier. There are still great landowners, but the farmer may be as wealthy as the owner; and indeed the word 'farmer' has lost its etymological meaning because the farmer may be a landowner

[1] For example, R. H. Gretton, *The English Middle Class*; Roy Lewis and Angus Maude, *The English Middle Classes*.

and not a tenant, or both an owner of some land and a tenant of other land. The landowner who has an income from rent will probably farm also. All large enterprises in commerce and industry are statutory corporations or limited companies; the 'captains of industry' are directors, but their wealth depends on the quantity and value of their shares. Many of them are, however, lawyers, accountants and other professional men. In short, it is impossible to find any 'upper class'; the 'middle class' of the nineteenth century has caught up with and swallowed it.

The distinction which now exists is expressed most simply, in purely economic terms, as a distinction between surtax payers and other income tax payers. The one dominates the public schools and the other the grammar schools,[1] though the grammar schools also draw very largely from the working class. Both public schools and grammar schools feed Oxford and Cambridge, and the proportions are roughly equal, though of course the grammar school boys are drawn from a much larger population. The distinction is drawn in words by using the terms 'upper middle class' and 'lower middle class'. The former includes the company directors, the lawyers, the doctors, the higher clergy, the wealthier members of the newer professions, the administrative class and the professional classes of the civil service, the officers of the armed forces, the senior employees of public corporations and the larger companies, and so forth. The lower middle class includes those salaried persons who are not members of the upper middle class—the school teachers, the executive and clerical classes of the civil service and persons of comparable grades in commerce and industry; it also includes self-employed persons who are not members of the upper middle class, such as shopkeepers, insurance agents, commercial travellers, the smaller contractors, the directors of most private companies, and so forth.

Both sections of the so-called 'middle class' have grown enormously since the beginning of the nineteenth century, and the lower middle class has grown particularly fast in the present century. When the secondary schools were established in 1902 it was doubted whether

[1] Some of the grammar schools are, technically, public schools and there is no clear line: but there are no definable boundaries between classes.

there would be suitable employment for their products. The output has been increased many times, but there is still a shortage, particularly of technicians who have had some technical training.

In the eighteenth century the professional classes were closely associated with the landed interest; but as commerce and industry developed they came to be more closely associated, in many cases, with the mercantile and manufacturing interests, and in fact they were numerically swamped by them. Not only they but also the 'lower middle class' were enfranchised by the Reform Act of 1832. Radicalism, which by the end of the century became Liberalism, was predominantly 'middle class', though by the end of the century the upper middle class tended to be Conservative. The connexion between the professional class and the landed interest brought most of it within the Church of England, while the Nonconformist churches were strongest in the lower middle class. The 'Nonconformist Conscience' was essentially middle-class and, by the end of the century, essentially lower middle-class.

The 'lower orders' or the working classes have always included the great mass of the population, though the great growth of the lower middle class in the present century has substantially reduced the numerical superiority of the working class. Neither the cottagers in the villages nor the journeymen and labourers in the towns were of much political importance until John Wilkes captured Middlesex in 1768. Middlesex then included what is now a large part of the County of London and the growth of the capital had given its southern part a large urban population. Though the electors were the forty-shilling freeholders, the popular support for Wilkes helped to sway opinion in his favour. Westminster and Preston were boroughs in which the workers had votes, and in other boroughs (such as Liverpool) there were working-class freemen. It is probably true that the number of working-class electors was diminished by the Reform Act.

The rapid growth of the towns after the factory system developed enabled working-class opinion to be formed out of discussions in the factory and the public house. Its importance was very evident in the struggle for the People's Charter; and popular support was sought by the Anti-Corn Law League, which was essentially a middle-class movement. There were areas, too, especially in the North, in the West and in Wales where Nonconformity was strong among the working class. The urban workers obtained the vote in 1867 and the rural workers in 1884: but the strength of the labour movement was not exhibited until the end of the century, when the trade union movement became strong and turned to politics. Though the disappearance of the Liberal party, as a major political force, was assisted by the conflict between the two wings led by Asquith and Lloyd George after 1922, it was perhaps an inevitable consequence of the class consciousness of the trade union movement. The Liberal party had become lower middle-class when the Whigs and the Chamberlain Radicals seceded in 1886. So long as it had working-class support, as in 1906, it was capable of forming a Government. After 1922 it was necessarily a minority party. On the other hand, it has a chance of revival because the lower middle class is increasing in size and is likely to increase. It has no great sympathy with the Old Etonians and other wearers of 'old school ties' who dominate the Conservative party. On the other hand, it has little sympathy with the Labour party under trade union domination, and would have even less if that party were dominated by the doctrinaire socialists. It shares the enthusiasm of the Labour party for social services; but, within a good system of social security, it has some sympathy with individual enterprise. It is very class-conscious and does not want to be equated with the workers.

The middle class and the working class, like all classes, are hierarchical. To the inhabitant of the west end of an industrial city[1] the streets in the east end are very much alike. In reality, however, the inhabitants of Henry Road look down on those of George Street as being 'common'. In the Edwardian era the houses in Henry Road had bay windows, carefully obscured by lace curtains, and adorned, where the curtains did not quite meet, with a flourishing aspidistra.[2] In George Street there were no bay windows, the curtains were of cotton cloth, and there might not be an aspidistra. The rents were

---

[1] Owing to the wind off the Atlantic, the more expensive houses are usually on the west.

[2] The aspidistra was obtained in exchange for old clothes. In George Street there were no saleable old clothes.

7s. 6d and 5s. a week respectively. Henry Road was in fact on the upper margin of the working class or the lower margin of the lower middle class. Forty years on, these distinctions are becoming blurred. Skilled workers earn more than clerks and school teachers and have moved into a housing estate which has garages, or at least room for a car in the garden. Members of the middle class, finding the houses in Henry Road or even George Street easy to run without servants, have moved there but have shown their individuality and indicated a class distinction by painting the woodwork a bright red. The lavatory in the back has been converted into a perambulator shed, and the small bedroom is now a bathroom. Possibly in the next generation the distinction will disappear, or a new alignment of classes develop: but the skilled worker is still a trade unionist and is thought to be working-class even though his son is now at Cambridge, while the school teacher shows by his clothes and his accent that he does not work with his hands, except on the blackboard. The telescoping of salaries and wages, full employment even in the building trade, good social services, and a broad educational ladder, have led to a state approaching egalitarianism, but the traditional attitudes are likely to remain at least for one generation.

5. CLASS AND POLITICS

These general observations lack precision, but it is difficult to be more precise for several reasons. One is that the concept of class and its importance in politics vary from age to age, as we have tried to indicate. Another reason is that in discussing the influence of 'class' on politics we are apt to change our definition according to the aspect of class under consideration. Let us try to sort out some of the aspects.

First, the impression which electors have of the parties, the 'image' which, as we shall suggest, is the primary factor in choice of party, is a class image. The Labour party, by reason of its origin in and domination by the trade union movement, is the manual workers', or perhaps organised workers', party. It looks after 'people like us'. The Conservative party, on the other hand, originated in the landowners of the country party, became the party of employers generally (the 'bosses') by 1886, is led by professional politicians who are living mainly on inherited wealth and went to expensive public schools, and is supported by all the 'privileged' sections of the community—West End Society, the clubs, the officer class, the professional men, and generally those who do not send their sons and daughters to public elementary schools. It is, therefore, the party of the 'upper class'.

Even in this general description there are differences of classification. The phrase 'people like us' imports a subjective judgment. In 1952 the British Institute of Public Opinion took a sample poll on the question, 'If you had to say what social class you belong to, which would it be?' The replies put fifty per cent into the middle class and forty-six per cent into the working class, the remaining four per cent making no reply. It follows that, if the Labour party is regarded as a working-class party, it cannot appeal to a majority of the people. It has, of course, a wider appeal. It has inherited the idealism of Victorian radicalism and, to a substantial degree, of nineteenth-century evangelism. That it is not a mere 'class' party may be shown by the social composition of the Labour Government of 1951 (Table 26).

Oxford:	Haileybury and University College	1	
	Marlborough and New College	1	
	Winchester and New College	1	
	Wellington and Christ Church	1	4
Cambridge:	Eton and King's	1	
	Downside and Trinity College	1	
	Grammar school and Christ's	1	3
Others:	Harrogate College and London University	1	
	Grammar school and Glasgow University	1	
	Dulwich College	1	
	Elementary schools	8	11

TABLE 26

Clearly the Attlee Government was more 'representative' of the people at large than the Eden and Macmillan Governments.

On the other hand, the Conservative party has not obtained the 'image' of a middle-class party. It may have done locally, because its local organisations are often dominated by local business and professional men; and its paid agents, secretaries of Conservative clubs, etc., are so often retired officers from the armed forces. Its atmosphere is thus rather that of the officers' mess than that of the NAAFI canteen. Moreover it continually uses the snob appeal by bringing in 'lords and ladies'; and a Conservative Government is obviously 'upper class'. The image which the Conservative party tries to create is that of a non-class party: but the probable result is to make it look different to different classes of people. To some, as the general description indicates, it is the landowners' party, to some the bosses' party, to some the party of Society, to some the party of the rich, and to many the party of the salaried employees.

In the second place is the concept of 'class solidarity'. In principle this applies to the working class only. It arose in the nineteenth century, mainly through the trade union movement, though it was helped by Karl Marx and socialist propaganda. Before 1868 few great parliamentary debates related to the 'condition of the people', though under the influence of evangelicalism some remedial 'labour' legislation was passed. The agitation for the People's Charter was a demand for such constitutional reform as would, it was thought, enable the 'people' to dominate Parliament: it was, however, a small minority movement. After 1868 politicians from Joseph Chamberlain to Lloyd George sought to convert the Liberal party into a party sympathetic to the workers, but their success was limited by the middle-class ideas of the vast body of active Liberals, both in Parliament and in the constituency associations. In consequence many of the trade union leaders, without breaking from the Liberal party, thought it necessary to have an organisation for working-class representation, and thus set in train the events which led to the foundation of the Labour party. This was another minority movement, for the trade unions have never included more than a minority of the population. Even in 1955 the trade unionists were only forty-three per cent of the employees, though among male employees they were fifty-four per cent.[1] It must not be thought, however, that these figures show the degree of class-consciousness. Of the trade union members only 88·7 per cent belong to unions affiliated

[1] A. M. Carr-Saunders, D. Caradog Jones and C. A. Moser, *Social Conditions in England and Wales*, p. 129. The figures relate to Great Britain.

to the Trades Union Congress,[1] and many of them take the trade union ticket for the sake of getting and keeping employment, not because they are class-conscious. It is probable that not more than one-third of the employees—perhaps forty per cent of the male employees—are class-conscious.

Among the middle class, class-consciousness is entirely unorganised. It exists particularly among salaried employees and especially among income tax payers. It has developed more recently as an almost inarticulate reaction to the success of the trade unions in raising money wages and obtaining wide social services. 'Fair shares for all' is a Labour party slogan, but many members of middle-class families, anxious to live on the plane to which they have become accustomed and to give their children an education as good as, or better than, their own, feel that they have become depressed by economic conditions and that they are not getting 'fair shares'—an obviously ambiguous phrase. Their number cannot be guessed; but in 1951 the salary earners were twenty-two per cent of employed males and the wage earners seventy-eight per cent.[2] It should, however, be noted that whereas the real incomes of the rich, before tax, have undoubtedly fallen since 1938,[3] this seems to apply only to the million people with the largest incomes.[4] The million people with the next largest incomes have, on the average, gained; and the gain increases progressively as one goes down the income scale. However, the statisticians cannot deal with psychological factors; more people of moderate means think that they are worse off than before the war, and many blame the class bias of the Labour party. In this sense they are class-conscious.

In the third place is the factor of so-called 'class-interest'. This is really a question not of class in any subjective or psychological sense, but mainly one of income. The implication is not necessarily that those with small incomes belong to one class and those with large incomes

---

[1] Calculated from *ibid.* pp. 129 and 132.

[2] *Ibid.* p. 114. The figures relate to England and Wales. The corresponding figures in the United Kingdom in 1924 were estimated at thirteen per cent and eighty-seven per cent: Carr-Saunders and Caradog Jones, *Social Structure of England and Wales* (1st ed.), p. 63.

[3] Carr-Saunders, Caradog Jones and Moser, *Social Structure of England and Wales*, p. 151. [4] *Ibid.*

belong to another. When Parliament raises the income tax rates in order to increase the social security benefits it helps—or appears to help—the poorer at the expense of the richer, because everybody gets more social security and only the income tax payers pay for it: and the income tax payers have to show that in the long run nobody benefits because savings, and therefore investment, and therefore potential employment, and therefore wages, are reduced. On the other hand Parliament can, by raising the income tax and paying heavy subsidies to farmers, benefit the landowners by raising rents, the farmers by increasing profits, and perhaps the agricultural labourers by increasing wages, but at the expense of some at least of those engaged in other employments. In other words, class-interests may be divided, in terms of income, either horizontally or vertically. In practice, however, the position is much more complicated. Before the tariff was slipped through in 1932, the Conservative party never could make up its mind whether it was or was not proposing to tax all imports, or all imports except food, or all imports except food and raw materials. It wanted to 'protect' agriculture so as to increase the rural vote, but not to raise the price of food; it wanted to 'protect' all industries, whether or not they used imported materials like cotton or rubber; it wanted to keep imports out for 'protection' of industry but also to let them in subject to a tax to meet the cost of increased social services. We may note, too, the complications involved in 'balancing the Budget' in 1931. If one has to meet a deficit of £170,000,000, how shall the burden be shared among taxpayers, employers, employees and unemployed persons? If taxpayers have to meet £100,000,000 how shall that sum be divided among the various types—surtax, income tax, death duties, customs, excise, purchase tax, and so forth?

With categories so vague it is impossible to give statistics, but indications may be given by three tables. The first (Table 27) was worked out by Professor Cyril Burt and was later revised by him with the assistance of Miss Spielman. It classified male adults, evidently on the basis of the census of 1921, according to intellectual requirements and expressed them as percentages of all occupied male adults.[1]

[1] Carr-Saunders and Caradog Jones, *Social Structure of England and Wales* (1st ed.), p. 58.

Occupational group	Percentage of all occupied male adults
1. Highest professional work (lawyers, doctors, higher administrative posts in State or business, university teachers)	0·1
2. Lower professional and technical work (elementary teachers, clerks holding higher posts)	3·0
3. Clerical and highly skilled (clerks of lower grade and highly skilled labour)	12·0
4. Skilled labour and minor commercial posts (small tradespeople, shop assistants)	26·0
5. Semi-skilled labour and poorest commercial positions	33·0
6. Unskilled labour and coarse manual work	19·0
7. Casual labour	7·0
8. Institutional cases	0·2

TABLE 27

	Social class	Percentage of occupied and retired males in 1951
I.	Professional, etc. occupations	3
II.	Intermediate occupations	15
III.	Skilled occupations	53
IV.	Partly skilled occupations	16
V.	Unskilled occupations	13

TABLE 28

The second table (here, Table 28) has been used in the census reports since 1911.[1] This classification is based on the nature of the occupation, not on the remuneration received, and thus provides for a considerable amount of overlapping in terms of income. Also the very large Class III includes not only the skilled manual workers, many of whom would be 'class-conscious' trade unionists, but also shop assistants, clerks, typists, and so forth, many of whom would be self-consciously 'middle-class'. Nevertheless the classification is

[1] Carr-Saunders, Caradog Jones and Moser, *Social Structure of England and Wales* (1958), p. 116.

253

sometimes used to judge electoral results.[1] Classes I and II and Classes IV and V are then combined so as to divide the working population of England and Wales thus: I and II, 18%; III, 53%; IV and V, 29%. Assuming the Conservative party to be particularly attractive to Classes I and II and the Labour party to be particularly attractive to Classes IV and V, Class III would obviously hold the balance of power. What actually happens, however, is far more complicated.[2]

The third table (Table 29) comes from the census report of 1951 and gives the 'socio-economic groups' into which occupied and retired males may be classified.[3]

This third table is as near as we can get to an objective test of 'class' based on kinds of employment. It ought not to be assumed, however, that each group has a separate 'class-interest', or that the interests of each person in a group are the same. Nor must it be forgotten that there are groups not based on occupation at all. One consists of the owners of houses and another of tenants. According to a survey made in 1953, one in five of the households in Great Britain owned its own house—eighty per cent of the group whose income was over £2000 a year and thirteen per cent of the group whose income was between £200 and £300 a year.[4] Thus, one family in five is interested in local rates and four in five in rents (including rates).

'Class', however defined, tends to affect older people more obviously than it affects young men and women. In terms of class, whether

[1] R. S. Milne and H. C. Mackenzie, *Marginal Seat*, p. 55.

[2] *Ibid.* Mark Benny, A. P. Gray and R. H. Pear in *How People Vote*, p. 102, use a more complicated classification giving a sevenfold division: (1) professional and higher administrative; (2) managerial and executive; (3) inspectional, supervisory and other non-manual, higher grade; (4) inspectional, supervisory and other non-manual, lower grade; (5) skilled manual and routine grades of non-manual; (6) semi-skilled manual; (7) unskilled manual. This comes from John Hall and D. Caradog Jones, 'Social Grading of Occupations', *British Journal of Sociology*, i, pp. 31–55. See also Carr-Saunders, Caradog Jones and Moser, *op. cit.* p. 86. In practice, groups (1), (2) and (3) are combined, and so are groups (6) and (7). For the effect in Greenwich, see Mark Benny, etc., *op. cit.* p. 103.

[3] Quoted from Carr-Saunders, Caradog Jones and Moser, *Social Structure of England and Wales* (1958), p. 118. The original reference is Census of England and Wales, 1951, Occupation Tables: xi, p. 149.

[4] *Ibid.* p. 181.

defined objectively or subjectively, an older person will probably stay
where he is. The class mobility in Britain is considerable, but it affects
mainly the young; and the young man having the world before him
can think of his prospects. The 'inexorable march' of the Labour party
from 1918 to 1950 was not due only to a consolidation of working-class
support. It was due also to a continuous influx of young Labour voters,

Socio-economic group	Percentage of occupied and retired males in 1951
Agricultural	
1. Farmers	2
2. Agricultural workers	5
Non-agricultural	
I Non-manual	
3. Higher administrative, professional, and managerial (inc. large employers)	3
4. Intermediate administrative, professional, and managerial (inc. teachers and salaried staff)	9
5. Shopkeepers and other small employers	4
6. Clerical workers	5
7. Shop assistants	3
8. Personal service	2
II Manual	
9. Foremen	4
10. Skilled workers	36
11. Semi-skilled workers	11
12. Unskilled workers	13
III Others	
13. Armed forces (other ranks)	3

TABLE 29

many of them with secondary-school and even university education.
The causes were no doubt complex—the depression, which created
not only shortage of jobs but also distress among their relatives; the
idealism of youth, especially in respect of social conditions and international affairs; the sense of rushing headlong into a war which would do
no good to anybody; the reading of Ibsen, Bernard Shaw, H. G. Wells
and Galsworthy; and perhaps others. Class-consciousness and class-

interest probably played little part. Today we seem to have a tendency towards Conservatism, partly perhaps because in a troubled world the elementary propositions of Christianity (but not the dogmas of the sects) seem attractive, but mainly because social security, taxation of the fruits of enterprise and initiative, and the close control of a regulated society, discourage the ambitious.

Finally, it should be noticed that, so far as the idea of class is subjective, it is influenced by the local environment. The county and borough divisions which are primarily industrial, and the 'working-class areas' of the great cities, have two characteristics which they do not share with other constituencies. First, making all allowances for 'differentials', there is considerable uniformity of living standards and of ideas, and that uniformity tends to create a uniformity of opinion. Secondly, the workers are generally employed in large units, where trade union influence is strong. These are accordingly the safe Labour seats. At the other extreme are the seaside resorts, residential towns like Bath and Cheltenham, university and cathedral towns, and the residential suburbs of the great cities. In each case the balance is apt to be different. The seaside resorts discourage industries, except on a very small scale, and employment is in small units. The shopkeepers and shop assistants are more numerous than the size of the towns would normally justify, because of the influx of summer visitors. There are numerous small hotels and lodging-houses employing few servants. There is a high proportion of retired people, mainly from socio-economic groups 3 to 6 and perhaps 9 and 10. There is generally a conservative attitude which becomes Conservative in politics. The trade unions are weak, while the Chamber of Commerce and the rate-payers' association tend to be strong. The residential suburbs of the big cities, too, contain substantial numbers drawn from groups 3, 4 and 8, and a more than average representation from groups 5 and 7. Local influence is, however, not so strong because these suburbs are 'dormitories'.

The marginal constituencies are generally of three types:

(1) the inner suburb, where a mixed population is drawn mainly from groups 4 to 10, though many people work in the larger factories and offices;

(2) the smaller borough having one member or two members but no large industries; here the 'differentials' are important and trade-unionism is weak; or

(3) the urbanised or suburbanised county division dominated by small towns and suburban development, and therefore having something of the character of the residential suburb and something of that of the small borough.

CHAPTER X

A PRIMER OF ELECTIONEERING

Although the history of parliamentary elections has been continuous for nearly seven hundred years, electioneering took its present form in the seventies and eighties of the last century. The Liberal Central Association was set up in 1860 and the Conservative Central Office in 1870. The Corrupt and Illegal Practices Act of 1854, as well as a developing public opinion, had discouraged exuberances of the Eatanswill type; the judges took over election petitions in 1868; and the work was completed by the Ballot Act of 1872 and the Corrupt and Illegal Practices Act of 1883. Finally, the Representation of the People Act, 1884, and the ensuing Redistribution of Seats Act abolished the smaller constituencies, increased the number of electors, and made the single-member constituency the rule, though some exceptions continued until after 1945. Meanwhile Gladstone and Disraeli were engaged in single, though verbal, combat.

It is indeed obvious that even in 1880 the great mass of electors was voting for a party as such. In that election there were sixty-seven two-member constituencies in Great Britain in which two Conservative candidates and two Liberal candidates were nominated. In all cases except eight, the two Conservatives or the two Liberals were elected. In two of the eight exceptions the election was avoided for corruption, leaving only six cases to be explained. In all these eight elections the contest was so close that a few votes made a great difference. The maximum variation between two Conservatives or two Liberals was ± 1·35 per cent of the electorate. Though it is true that a pair of candidates always ran in double harness whether they tried to win by bribery or by oratory, the closeness of the voting suggests that few votes were cast for personal reasons. This conclusion is supported by the results of the election in sixty-three constituencies in which one Liberal opposed two Conservatives, or one Conservative opposed two Liberals. In all except nineteen of these constituencies the two Conservatives or the two Liberals won the seats. In sixteen of the nineteen cases the two Liberals or the two Conservatives were at the bottom of the poll, so that only one of them was elected. In two of the other three cases the voting was very close. The third case, Truro, certainly looks very odd: but it is probable that the second Conservative candidate withdrew from the contest.

It does not follow that none of the tricks of Eatanswill was played at the election of 1880, and indeed a pair of candidates could share the cost: it is however plain that most electors were voting for Gladstone or for Disraeli, not for the particular candidates. The modern election is a contest between two parties, represented in that constituency and for that election by a pair of cyphers known as Messrs Dodson and Fogg. As in the Irishmen's fight, anybody can join in, provided he can get eight electors to nominate him: but he will probably get fewer votes than the number of pounds sterling he spends on election literature. The nature of the party battle is sometimes hiden by oddities of nomenclature. At the general election of 1959 most of the Conservative candidates called themselves Conservative; but there were also Conservative and Liberal, Liberal and Conservative, Conservative and National Liberal, National Liberal and Conservative, and even one stalwart who called himself National Liberal but appealed for Conservative votes. This was a relic of 1931, when a section of the Liberal party broke away from Lloyd George's leadership, and of 1932, when that section refused to leave the 'National' Government with Sir Herbert Samuel.

There are, of course, genuine Liberal candidates, competing against both the Conservative and the Labour parties. What is important, however, is that there are three national parties of which two invariably and the third sometimes nominate candidates in nearly all constituencies from Land's End to the Shetland Isles. Being national parties, they have to appeal on national policies, and they are led by national leaders, not by people with only local influence. Candidates do not ignore the vested interests of their constituencies; but they explain how national policy benefits those interests. There may be local 'bosses', too; but they have to be or become the willing instruments of the national parties. The main issue before all the electors of Great Britain is therefore the same, whether the United Kingdom shall be governed by a

Conservative, Labour or (perhaps) Liberal Government. In consequence, it is possible to lay down general propositions about voting behaviour.

The situation in Northern Ireland is different because another issue, the maintenance of the union with Great Britain, dominates Irish politics. The union having become historically the special preserve of the Conservative party, the Ulster Unionist party is in all essentials a branch of the Conservative party; and, since the issue of the union dwarfs all other issues and the Unionists are highly organised in the Orange Lodges, the normal political battle of Great Britain does not extend to Northern Ireland. Accordingly, the propositions about voting behaviour extend only to Great Britain and the statistics quoted refer to Great Britain unless it is expressly stated otherwise.

PROPOSITION 1. *With rare exceptions, the electors vote for parties and not for candidates.*

This may be shown in several different ways:

(1) In the two-member constituencies which existed before 1948, if a party entered two candidates, each of the two had very much the same number of votes. This process began at least as early as 1880, and the differences between two candidates of the same party rarely exceeded a few hundreds. There were, however, a few exceptional cases in which one of the candidates had a strong local connexion;[1] but even then the 'local boy' who had 'made good' could not get more than a couple of thousand votes more than a 'carpet-bagger', unless one party nominated only one candidate.

(2) Candidates successful as 'independents' are very rare. Most of the 'independents' stand as candidates of splinter parties (e.g. Common Wealth, Independent Labour party, Democratic party, Communist party, Welsh Nationalist party, Scottish Nationalist party), though some stand as 'Independent Conservative' (or 'Constitutionalist' or 'National') or 'Independent Labour' or 'Independent Liberal'. That is, nearly all the candidates seek to win the 'official' party vote, and they very rarely win the seat unless either there is no 'official' candidate

---

[1] E.g. Bolton in 1929 and 1931; Derby in 1924 and 1929; Stockport in 1929 and 1931; but in four of the six cases one party put up only one candidate.

of the right persuasion or (as with the I.L.P. members in 1935) the splinter party or 'unofficial' candidate catches the 'official' party vote.

Only fifteen members not belonging to one of the three major parties were elected in the four elections between 1924 and 1935 and only thirteen in the five elections between 1945 and 1959. Of these twenty-seven members, twelve were members of splinter parties and nearly all the others were 'Independent' Conservative, Labour or Liberal, in most cases standing without an 'official' candidate.

(3) A member who loses the whip almost invariably loses the seat. Usually he does not stand, but when he does he has little chance of winning unless no 'official' candidate stands against him. Mr D. N. Pritt was elected in 1945, although he had been deprived of the Labour whip in 1940; but he and all the other Labour 'rebels' were defeated in 1950, though all the seats were won by Labour. On the other hand, four of the former Labour members who stood as Independent Labour in 1935 were elected, in spite of Labour opposition in their constituencies.

(4) A member who changes party carries few votes with him. This may not be so where a party splits, like the Liberal party in 1886 or 1931. The effect of change of party may be studied in the two-member constituencies in 1931. J. H. Thomas, Labour member for Derby in 1929, had 3400 votes more than his Labour colleague, since he took some Liberal votes (there was only one Liberal candidate). In 1931, as 'National Labour' he had 1500 votes more than his Conservative colleague; but in 1935 he had 150 votes less than his Conservative colleague. The 'Liberal National' candidates in Norwich, Oldham, Southampton and Sunderland apparently gained nothing from their 'Liberal' labels; they simply had the straight Conservative vote.

PROPOSITION 2. *The issue at every general election is, which party shall form the Government, and therefore a party which is not likely to be able to form a Government tends to be pushed out.*

The issue might be put differently. Which party leader shall be Prime Minister? The process began after the death of Palmerston in 1865. The elections of 1868, 1874 and 1880 were contests between Gladstone and Disraeli. On the other hand, the 'cult of the individual' varies according to party and personality. Lord Salisbury, the Prime Minister, never sought to be a popular figure, but Joseph Chamberlain did, while never claiming the leadership of the Unionist party; hence the elections of 1886, 1892, 1895 and 1900 were dominated, on the Unionist side, by Chamberlain. Also, after the resignation of Gladstone in 1894 the Liberal party never had a leader who was potentially or actually a popular Prime Minister, except Lloyd George, who split the party in 1916 and widened the split in 1918. The Conservative party returned to the 'cult of the individual' after Baldwin's reputation was built up, i.e. after 1931, and has continued with it under his successors, Churchill, Eden and Macmillan. The Labour party, on the other hand, has always emphasised the Party with a capital P, and indeed it appeared to benefit by playing down Attlee while the Conservatives were playing up Churchill. In other words, the personalities of the party leaders do not necessarily dominate an election (though they may do in the television age), though every elector is well aware that he is helping to determine whether the Government shall or shall not remain in office.

The proposition must be read subject to two qualifications. First, there are always electors concerned with some particular issue which is not in conflict between the major parties. The Labour party was able to get itself established on the theory that there ought to be separate working-class representation and it did not begin to compete for power until 1918. Possibly, too, many Liberal voters since 1935 have believed in the theory of the middle way. Smaller parties, such as the Independent Labour party (between the wars), the Communist party, and the Nationalist parties of Wales and Scotland, have been able to win some votes, and some of them have even been able to win seats, although they were not able to compete for power. Secondly, party loyalty, or disinclination to change political opinions, or both, may enable a party to win votes, and perhaps seats, for a considerable time after it has ceased to compete for office. Much of the Liberal vote between the wars, and even in 1945, could be shown to be a relic of past glory, for most of the Liberal electors were in constituencies which had been strongly Liberal in 1906 and had not come under strong trade union influence.

262

Subject to these qualifications, the proposition can be demonstrated as follows:

(1) The problem was first faced after 1922, when the Labour party formed the 'official' Opposition with 142 members, while the Liberals had only 53 members. There was still a chance of a Liberal Government and in December 1923 the total Liberal vote was almost as large as the total Labour vote. The experience of the Labour Government of 1924 seems to have convinced the electorate that it had to choose between the Conservative party and the Labour party. Table 30 shows the voting in 1923 and 1924 expressed in round figures.

	1923	1924	Difference
Conservative	5,422,000	7,403,000	+1,981,000
Liberal	4,311,000	2,929,000	−1,382,000
Labour	4,439,000	5,489,000	+1,050,000

TABLE 30

The difference can be explained in large part by the number of candidates nominated by each party: but in all the constituencies in which all three parties nominated candidates in 1923 and 1924 the Liberal vote was reduced (except in Dorset East, Swansea West and Peebles South), whereas the Conservative vote was reduced in only one such constituency and the Labour vote in only ten. Indeed, the Liberal vote was reduced in nearly all constituencies in which the Liberal had a straight fight with a Conservative and in most of those in which he had a straight fight with a Labour candidate. It is of course possible to assert that electors objected to the policy of the Liberal party— especially that of putting the Labour Government in and then turning it out—but it is more likely that the experience proved to many electors that they had to take a choice between a Conservative Government and a Labour Government. A Conservative Government took office in 1924 not because of decreased electoral support for the Labour party, but because of decreased electoral support for the Liberal party, which eliminated many seats held by Labour in three-cornered contests.

(2) In 1929 the Liberal party nominated 501 candidates (against 569 Conservative and 567 Labour candidates) with the deliberate intention

of making plain that it could form a Government. It is probable that the electorate was not convinced; for, though the Liberal vote rose to 5,208,000, the Conservative vote was 8,302,000 and the Labour vote 8,390,000. It was in fact plain that the Liberals could not win more than 100 seats, and they actually won only 59. The Liberal vote was large enough to produce a minority Labour Government. What effect this would have had upon the electorate never became plain because of the crisis of 1931, but in 1935 the Liberal vote fell to 1,375,000.

(3) In 1950 the Liberal party made another attempt by nominating 475 candidates. It obtained a total of 2,622,000 votes, or 11·8 per cent of the votes cast, but only nine Liberal members were elected. Even so, the effect of the Liberal 'intervention' was that the Labour majority was reduced to five. Only 109 Liberal candidates were nominated in 1951, and they obtained 14·7 per cent of the votes cast in the constituencies in which they were candidates, or 2·5 per cent of all the votes cast. The former figure is, however, illusory; wherever there were candidates from all three parties both in 1950 and 1951 the Liberal vote was reduced. Once more, it appears, the electors realised that they must choose between a Conservative and a Labour Government.

(4) The most convincing evidence is the failure of all small parties to establish themselves. The great exceptions are the Irish Nationalist party and the Labour party. The former was a revolutionary party, in the sense that it did not intend (after Isaac Butt) to play the party game according to the rules; the Irish electors were induced to support not a Government but a party acting against the Government. The Labour party relied at the outset not only on its purely class appeal but also on Liberal votes. The Liberal party helped it by remaining, under Asquith, a rich man's party like the Conservative party. Hence the class-conscious members of the working class, especially those organised in trade unions, voted for Labour candidates without reference to the question of the formation of a Government. The split in the Liberal party in 1916 enabled the Labour party to become the alternative to the Conservative party. In consequence the Liberal party, and not the Labour party, became the 'intervening' party, i.e. the party which could not hope to form a Government.

PROPOSITION 3. *At each general election the electors arrange themselves according to a pattern, showing a trend of political opinion in all parts of Great Britain.*

This proposition implies that the result of the whole general election can be forecast in general terms as soon as a few returns have been made. In 1951, for instance, the first return announced was at Watford. Table 31 shows how the result may be compared with that of 1950.

	Percentage of electorate		Change
	1950	*1951*	
Conservative	38·5	40·8	+2·3
Labour	41·3	41·7	+0·4
Liberal	7·3	4·6	−2·7
Not voting	12·9	12·9	—

TABLE 31

Our proposition assumes that in the rest of Great Britain there would be a small increase in the Conservative vote, a very small increase in the Labour vote, a substantial decrease in the Liberal vote, and the same sort of poll as in 1950. When all the returns were in that assumption proved to be substantially correct, but subject to three minor qualifications. First, there were, as one might expect, larger increases in both the Conservative and the Labour shares of the electorate where there was a Liberal candidate in 1950 but not in 1951; but the Conservative increase was larger. Secondly, where there was no Liberal candidate either in 1950 or in 1951 the Conservative share usually showed a very small decrease—again as Watford would lead one to expect. Thirdly— and in this respect Watford misled us—there was generally a decrease in the proportion of electors voting.

Lest this example be regarded as a coincidence, let us consider the experience in 1955, when the Billericay division of Essex and Cheltenham were the first constituencies to announce results. Since redistribution had altered the boundaries of the Billericay division, we must examine the position in Cheltenham (Table 32). From this result it could be inferred, correctly, that there had been a low poll throughout Great Britain, and that the Conservative party would obtain a good majority because the fall in the Labour vote was larger than the fall in the Conservative vote. What the commentator could not infer—though some commentators did—were the sizes of the respective abstentions, and the consequent Conservative gain in marginal seats; for this constituency was far from marginal, as the figures show.

	Percentage of electorate		
	1951	1955	Change
Conservative	47·4	47·1	−0·3
Labour	35·7	32·3	−3·4
Not voting	16·9	20·6	+3·7

TABLE 32

The best way to prove the doctrine of the regular trend is, however, to plot graphically all the election results between 1923 and 1935, a period during which there was no redistribution of seats. Some examples are given on pages 266–8 from Chelsea (safe Conservative),

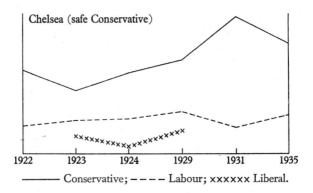

——— Conservative; — — — Labour; xxxxx Liberal.

Battersea S. (Conservative bias), Maryhill (marginal), Islington W. (Labour bias) and Bow and Bromley (safe Labour). They have been chosen because of their regularity and therefore they are not quite typical. The element of irregularity was, however, supplied by the presence or absence of Liberal candidates. There was regularity wherever at successive elections there was a 'straight fight' between Conservative and Labour or a 'three-cornered fight' with Conservative,

Liberal and Labour involved; but the Liberals did not, and indeed could not for financial and other reasons, follow a consistent policy in respect of nominations.

The elections since 1945 have been described in a series of valuable election studies prepared on behalf of Nuffield College, Oxford.[1] The authors and their collaborators not only assume the regularity of election trends, but emphasise one aspect of it, which they call the 'swing'. This takes its origin from the phrase 'the swing of the pendulum',[2] which was used to describe one of the phenomena of the two-party system, the process of changing opinion leading to frequent and almost regular changes of Government. Its nature is studied

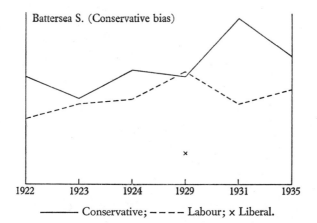

Battersea S. (Conservative bias)

1922   1923   1924   1929   1931   1935

———— Conservative; — — — — Labour; x Liberal.

under a later proposition, but if the two-party system operates and there is a regular process of changing opinion exhibited in a change in the balance of votes it is not unreasonable to speak of a 'swing' of votes from Labour to Conservative or vice versa. The word gives the impression, however, that the changes at elections are due to Labour

[1] R. B. McCallum and Alison Readman, *The British General Election of 1945*; H. G. Nicholas, *The British General Election of 1950*; D. E. Butler, *The British General Election of 1951*; and D. E. Butler, *The British General Election of 1955*. In the Introduction to his volume on the election of 1951, Mr Butler, following Mr McCallum, called the study of elections 'psephology'. Though it hardly seems necessary to give a bad name to an old dog, it will be convenient to refer to the galaxy of authors and collaborators by the collective name 'psephologists'.

[2] See the pictorial representation in Jennings, *The British Constitution* (3rd ed.), facing p. 30. It was adapted from a much older book.

electors voting Conservative or Conservative electors voting Labour. That is too simple an explanation, and it should be said that the psepho-

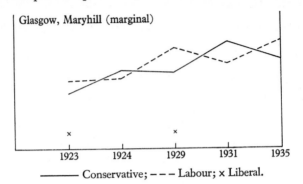

Glasgow, Maryhill (marginal)

——— Conservative; – – – Labour; x Liberal.

logists do not give it. An elector in any constituency in which there are only Conservative and Labour candidates has not two choices but

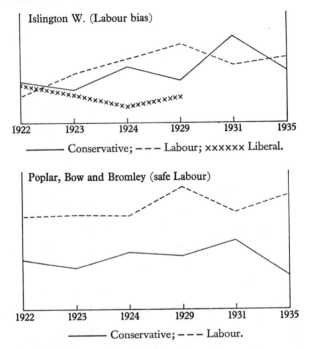

Islington W. (Labour bias)

——— Conservative; – – – Labour; xxxxx Liberal.

Poplar, Bow and Bromley (safe Labour)

——— Conservative; – – – Labour.

three, to vote Conservative, to vote Labour, or to abstain from voting. If a constituency is Conservative in one election and Labour in the next, the explanation may be that a sufficient number of Conservative electors were too bored, or too critical of Conservative policy, to vote Conservative, and therefore abstained from voting. If this phenomenon exists in other constituencies—and the proposition under discussion suggests that it happens in nearly all constituencies if it happens in one—there is, in ordinary language, a 'swing' to abstention and not a swing to Labour. In the psephological formula, however, there is a swing to Labour, because the swing is defined as half the total of the Conservative loss and the Labour gain. The psephological swing is discussed in Appendix I. It is inevitably a very crude method, but the Appendix suggests that no more refined method could be produced.

Whether the method used is the psephological swing or any other, however, there can be no doubt about the existence of a pattern. This does not mean, of course, that the distribution of votes in every constituency will be the same. What it does mean is that any movement will be comparatively uniform, a small or a large increase or decrease in the total poll, the Conservative vote, the Labour vote, and the Liberal vote, in nearly every constituency. Usually the pattern is complex. For instance, if there is a low poll the fall will not be uniform throughout the country. Probably the miners will exhibit their usual solidarity. Though on the national plane the election may be dull and the degree of abstention high, in the marginal seats, and in the towns where there are local newspapers, it may be comparatively low; and Wales and Scotland usually poll more consistently than most parts of England. These are lines in the pattern. If in most constituencies there is a lower poll than in the last election, there must be some explanation of any variation from the norm, and that explanation will usually apply not to the particular constituency, but to the kind of constituency concerned. For instance, in 1951 there was, on the average, a lower poll by 1·5 per cent than in 1950, but it was not so low in Wales (0·5 per cent) and Scotland (0·5 per cent) as in England (1·7 per cent); and it was lower in business and dormitory areas and seaside resorts than in most of the rest of England. Generally, it was lower in the safe seats than in the seats nearer the margin; but there was considerable variation in the great cities, from a decrease of 3·4 per cent in Sheffield (where all the seats are comparatively safe) to an increase of 0·7 per cent in Newcastle upon Tyne (and 1·2 per cent in Edinburgh). The higher poll in Wales and Scotland was not due to the discipline of organised Labour in the industrial areas, for it was higher in rural Wales than in industrial Wales and in the Highlands than in the Lowlands. On the other hand, the actual poll (as distinct from the variation since 1950) was generally higher in the industrial areas. Obviously the explanations are complicated: but our present point is that there is a pattern.

Let us now look at the Conservative vote, which in 1951 increased by 4·5 per cent of the votes cast or 3·4 per cent of the electorate. Apart from six seats in which the Conservatives withdrew to support the Liberals, there were only sixty-seven constituencies in which the Conservative section of the electorate was reduced. The Labour vote increased by 2·7 per cent of the votes cast, or 0·6 per cent of the electorate; but there were many constituencies in which the Labour vote was proportionately reduced. We can see what happened only by more detailed analysis:

(1) There were ninety-five constituencies in which there were 'straight fights' between Conservative and Labour at both elections. In the normal case the balance between Conservative and Labour was altered to the disadvantage of Labour. There were, however, twenty-four constituencies in which this was not so. The phrase 'swing to Conservative' was, in any case, not always appropriate, because in nine constituencies both the Conservative and the Labour vote declined, the latter more than the former; and in those cases the alteration in the balance was more likely to be due to differential abstention.

(2) There were eighty constituencies in which the Conservative, Labour and Liberal parties fought both elections. In only seven constituencies, four in Scotland and three in the West of England, did the Liberal percentage of the electorate increase. In the normal case, the Liberal share decreased and both the Conservative share and the Labour share increased. There were forty-three such cases, but there were also twenty-three cases in which the Conservative vote increased while the Labour vote decreased. The exceptional cases were those in which the percentage vote for all candidates decreased (3), those in which the Labour party gained while the Conservative party lost (2), and those in which both Labour and Conservative gained but Labour gained more (7).

(3) Though at both elections there were candidatures of independents and nominees of small parties, only in two or three cases was it possible for them to have affected the result.

(4) In nearly all other cases there was a Liberal candidate in 1950 but not in 1951. In 284 constituencies both the Conservative and the Labour votes increased, and in 270 of them the Conservative increase was greater than the Labour increase. In twenty-two constituencies the Conservative vote only increased and in one the Labour vote only increased. In two constituencies both the Conservative and the Labour vote decreased. On the other hand, it is not possible to assert as a general principle that when there was no Liberal candidate the proportion of non-voters increased.

It will be seen that there was a pattern but that it was a little complicated. The Labour Government increased its support a little, mainly it appears by the transfer of Liberal votes in constituencies where there was a Liberal candidate in 1950 but not in 1951. The Conservative Opposition increased its support rather more, almost invariably out of the vote which had been Liberal in 1950. There may have been some transfer of Labour votes to Conservative, not offset by the transfer of Conservative votes to Labour, but if so it was on a small scale. In any case, the Labour Government was defeated in those marginal constituencies which it won with narrow pluralities in 1950 and in which, through the withdrawal of the Liberals in 1951, the Conservatives obtained small majorities.

The elections of 1950 and 1951 have been analysed above not only because there was no redistribution but also because the effects of changes in the register were minimised by the short interval between the elections. Those effects are usually considerable, especially through the enfranchisement of young persons. At the census of 1951 the number of persons aged fifteen to nineteen was 3,228,000. The number of electors in 1955 who were too young to vote in 1951 was therefore about 2,500,000, and they replaced some 2,300,000 electors of 1951 who had died before the election of 1955. In addition there were changes due to migration to and from the United Kingdom and within the United Kingdom. The effects are by no means uniform, but in few constituencies could there have been a change in the electorate of less than five per cent, and something like ten per cent would probably be more usual, possibly going up to as much as twenty-five per cent in the newer dormitories.

The task of analysing the results of the general election of 1955 was, however, complicated by the redistribution, which affected all but 398 seats in Great Britain. Table 33 shows the distribution of the electorate as compared with 1951.

	Percentage of electorate		Change
	1951	1955	
Conservative	39·5	37·9	−1·6
Labour	40·8	36·4	−4·4
Liberal	2·1	2·1	—
Others	0·2	0·4	+0·2
Not voting	17·4	23·2	+5·8

TABLE 33

These figures suggest that the Conservative Government won an increased majority in the House of Commons because so many electors, especially potential Labour electors, refrained from voting. One factor was that the election was held in June, when many people would find other things to do. A second was the spread of television since 1951, which provided competition with electioneering as a form of amusement. A third was the very recent redistribution, which not only compelled some local parties to find candidates after the election was announced, but also upset the normally efficient election machines of the parties. There is some evidence, too, that the Conservative party deliberately stepped down the emotional tone, though it may simply have been due to Sir Winston Churchill's resignation and the inability of Sir Anthony Eden and his colleagues to make 'fighting' speeches. Mr Attlee, too, was no forensic gladiator; and Mr Bevan's outbursts of oratory were treated (by Conservatives) as evidence that the tail was wagging the Labour dog. In short, it was a dull election.

In the constituencies which had not been changed since 1951, the Conservatives won ten from Labour and Labour won one (Norfolk

S.W.) from the Conservatives. To these eleven must be added Central
Ayrshire, which had had only a minor boundary revision, and which
the Conservatives won from Labour. Table 34 shows the voting changes
in these twelve constituencies.

	Percentage change				
	Conservative	Labour	Liberal	Others	Not voting
Wandsworth C.	−1·4	−4·7	—	—	+6·1
Carlisle	+7·2	−0·1	−12·3*	—	+5·2
Ealing N.	−4·2	−4·9	+6·5†	—	+2·6
Halifax	−0·4	−3·7	—	—	+4·1
Hornchurch	−1·4	−4·6	+1·8	—	+4·1
Preston S.	−1·8	−2·8	—	—	+4·6
Walthamstow E.	−1·2	−5·9	+2·6	−0·4*	+5·0
Watford	+2·0	−2·1	−4·6*	—	+4·7
Maldon (Essex)	−0·9	−3·2	—	—	+4·1
Norfolk S.W.	−0·7	+0·7	—	—	—
The Wrekin (Salop)	+0·8	−4·0	—	—	+3·0
Central Ayrshire	+0·5	−3·5	—	—	+3·0

TABLE 34

* No candidate in 1955.   † No candidate in 1951.

The pattern so produced is much like the 'national pattern' produced
by considering the total electorate and the total vote. Except in South-
West Norfolk, there was a low poll, for the most part at the expense of
the Labour party (the low Conservative poll in Ealing N. was obviously
due to there being a Liberal candidate in 1955). The Conservative vote
declined slightly, except in Carlisle and Watford (where there were
Liberal candidates in 1951 but not in 1955) and in the Wrekin and
Central Ayrshire (where the increases were very small).

	Percentage of electorate		
	1955	1959	Change
Conservative	37·9	38·5	+0·6
Labour	36·4	35·3	−1·1
Liberal	2·1	4·7	+2·6
Others	0·4	0·5	+0·1
Not voting	23·2	21·0	−2·2

TABLE 35

There was no redistribution between the general election of 1955 and that of 1959. Table 35 shows the distribution of the electorate in the two elections.

	Percentage change				
	Conser-vative	Labour	Liberal	Others	Not voting
Baron's Court	−0·5	−2·5	—	+3·5	−0·5
Holborn and St Pancras	+5·9	+2·9	−2·1†	—	−6·7
Lewisham N.	0	−2·5	+5·6*	—	−3·1
Wandsworth, Clapham	+2·3	−1·4	—	—	−0·9
Acton	+0·6	−1·4	—	—	+0·8
Birmingham					
All Saints	+1·4	−1·2	—	—	−0·2
Sparkbrook	+4·3	−3·9	—	—	−0·4
Yardley	+4·9	−2·8	—	—	−2·1
Bristol N.E.	+2·8	−2·8	+1·1	—	−1·1
Bristol N.W.	+3·3	−1·0	—	—	−2·3
Coventry S.	+3·0	−2·3	—	—	−0·7
Hartlepools	+2·2	−0·8	—	—	−1·4
Keighley	+10·7	+2·6	−14·7†	—	+0·4
Newcastle upon Tyne E.	+4·1	+0·3	—	—	−4·6
Nottingham W.	+0·7	−5·9	—	—	+5·2
Oldham E.	−2·1	+1·9	+2·4	—	−2·3
Reading	+2·9	−4·2	—	—	+1·3
Rochester and Chatham	+2·1	−3·5	—	—	+1·4
Willesden E.	+1·1	−3·9	—	—	+2·8
Derbyshire S.E.	−0·9	−3·7	+7·6*	—	−3·0
Uxbridge (Middlesex)	−0·8	−4·9	+8·3*	—	−2·6
Wellingborough (Northants)	+1·8	−1·1	—	—	−0·7
Brierley Hill (Staffs.)	+5·1	−5·5	—	—	+0·4
Meriden (Warwicks.)	+2·6	+0·4	—	—	−3·0
Rugby (Warwicks.)	−3·3	−7·3	+13·4*	−2·5	−0·3
Cleveland (Yorks.)	+2·4	−0·1	—	—	−2·3
Swansea W.	+4·7	+2·3	—	—	−7·0
Glasgow, Craigton	+0·9	+1·9	—	—	−3·8
Glasgow, Scotstoun	−2·3	+4·6	—	—	−2·3
Central Ayrshire	+0·2	+4·0	—	—	−4·2
Lanark	−0·8	+2·1	—	—	−1·3

TABLE 36

* No candidate in 1955.
† No candidate in 1959.

The increase in the Liberal vote was due in large part to an increase in the number of candidates from 110 to 216. The figures suggest that, on balance, the Liberal party took some votes from Labour and some from the non-voters of 1955, though it must be remembered that there were something approaching three million new voters. Since the register was staler in 1959 than in 1955, there was evidently more interest in the election, which was, however, held in a more suitable month.

The Conservatives gained twenty-eight seats from the Labour party and one from the Liberal party, but lost five seats to the Labour party and one seat to the Liberal party. The figures for these marginal constituencies are given in Table 36.

Again there is close correspondence with the 'national pattern' shown in Table 35. There was almost everywhere a higher poll than in 1959. Most of the exceptions were in the constituencies where the fall in the Labour vote was above the average, thus suggesting that some dissatisfied Labour supporters voted Conservative or Liberal and some abstained from voting. There was usually a small increase in the Conservative vote, and the exceptions were usually due to the 'intervention' of a Liberal candidate. Usually, too, there was a smaller decrease in the Labour vote. The exceptions to the general trend were Holborn and St Pancras N. (where there were special local factors), Acton (where there were population changes), Oldham E. (where the depression of the cotton industry was important), and the industrial area of West Scotland (which was suffering from a high level of unemployment).

PROPOSITION 4. *Between fifteen and twenty-five per cent of the electors do not vote, and a low poll is usually evidence of apathy, or distrust of all parties.*

The size of the poll is determined by several factors, of which, probably, the most important is the imperfections of the register. A person becomes an elector by having his name placed on a register of electors for a particular constituency. For this purpose, he must be qualified on a certain date (which varies as between Great Britain and Northern Ireland), known as the 'qualifying date'. This register becomes operative four months later and remains in operation for twelve months, with the result that an election might be held on a register compiled (in draft) sixteen months before.

The registers are compiled from forms completed by house-holders. Since the population is almost completely literate, British registers show initially a high degree of accuracy: but they become increasingly inaccurate as they become more 'stale', partly because the older electors die off and are not replaced by young electors until new registers come into operation,[1] and partly because removals are frequent.

Other factors affecting turn-out would include the weather. Always a substantial number of electors are ill or apathetic; a wet or cold day makes the sick and the apathetic even more reluctant to vote. Even so, it is plain from the returns that many electors deliberately refrain from voting because they feel unable to vote for any of the candidates—which means, of course, that they are unable to support any of the parties. 'Apathy' is, in most cases, a function of the same elements. A person who does not vote because he is not interested in politics, or cannot be bothered, is only one step removed from the elector who deliberately abstains.

The voting in contested elections in the United Kingdom since 1918 is shown in Table 37.

Election	Electorate	Total vote	Percentage
1918	18,307,404	10,788,657	58·9
1922	19,180,969	14,393,692	75·4
1923	19,619,988	14,548,521	74·1
1924	20,653,641	16,640,279	80·6
1929	28,507,346	22,648,375	79·5
1931	27,130,006	21,656,373	79·8
1935	29,560,811	21,997,054	74·4
1945	32,836,419	24,973,298	77·4
1950	34,269,764	28,769,477	83·8
1951	34,553,197	28,602,323	82·6
1955	34,855,907	26,760,661	76·8
1959	35,388,939	27,862,738	78·7

TABLE 37

[1] This is subject to the qualification that a person under age on the qualifying date (10 October) but coming of age before 17 June next may be put on the register and may vote from 1 October next.

Voting by proxy and by post has been increased since 1945 and has had an appreciable effect on the poll. One of the causes of the decline in voting since 1950, however, is the spread of television, which discourages people from leaving home in the evening. For reasons which will become plain, this reacts more seriously on the Labour party than on the Conservative party. The presence or absence of a Liberal candidate does not affect the size of the poll, as we have seen when the voting at the elections of 1950 and 1951 was discussed, though it may have done so in 1959.

The low poll of 1918 must be discounted, partly because the election was held immediately on the termination of the war and so many electors were absent, but mainly because the continuance of the wartime coalition dampened political controversy. There was a much higher poll in 1945, in spite of the imperfections of the stale registers and of post-war dislocation. The high polls of 1924, 1931 and 1950 followed Labour Governments, and suggest that many of those who do not hold with politics, or cannot be bothered, are Conservative when they do vote. This interpretation is not rendered doubtful by the high poll of 1929. The Liberal party may have brought out some votes which would not have been cast if there had not been over 500 Liberal candidates, but there was also a very large increase in the Labour vote, which was presumably due to the 'flappers' enfranchised by the 1928 Act. The increase in the Conservative vote was comparatively small.

PROPOSITION 5. *In a normal election, the totals of the votes cast for Conservative and Labour candidates respectively differ by a small percentage only.*

The almost equal division of voting strength is one of the most remarkable phenomena of British politics, and it goes back a long way. Table 38 shows the election results since 1880, taking only Conservative and Liberal votes from 1880 to 1900, Conservative and Liberal and Labour votes in 1906 and 1910, and Conservative and Labour votes since 1923, ignoring the elections of 1918 and 1922, when the conditions were peculiar owing to the Coalition.

It will be seen that, apart from 1931, when the circumstances were very exceptional, no party has obtained as many as sixty per cent of the votes cast for the two major parties. The explanation is clearly to be found in the class division of British politics, which is discussed under the next proposition.

	Conservative	Liberal and/or Labour
1880	44·7	*55·3
1885	47·3	*52·7
1886	53·4	*46·6
1892	51·6	*48·4
1895	51·7	*48·3
1900	52·4	*47·6
1906	44·2	†55·8
1910 Jan.	47·8	†52·2
1910 Dec.	47·6	†52·4
1923	56·5	††43·5
1924	58·6	††41·4
1929	50·8	††49·2
1931	66·4	††32·6
1935	58·6	††41·4
1945	45·4	††54·6
1951	49·6	††50·4
1955	51·7	††48·3
1959	52·2	††47·8

TABLE 38

* Liberal.   † Liberal and Labour.   †† Labour.

PROPOSITION 6. *A safe Conservative seat is predominantly middle-class and a safe Labour seat is predominantly working-class.*

Expressed in this form, the proposition is comparatively modern, but the class division of British politics goes back to 1832. The question is discussed in some detail in Appendix II, but the conclusions should be set out here to support the proposition:

(1) From 1832 to 1865 most of the boroughs which were whig, Liberal, etc. might be placed in two groups, great cities and the industrial towns on the one hand, and small boroughs (probably under 'influence') on the other. Most of the Conservative boroughs, too, were in the latter group. Most of the county divisions which were whig, Liberal, etc. were the urbanised or industrialised areas. The rest were usually Conservative. Allowing for 'influence', the distribution between the landed interest and the urban classes is plain, except in Scotland, which was generally Liberal, no doubt because it was Presbyterian.

(2) From 1868 to 1880 the English and Welsh boroughs were generally Liberal and the Scottish burghs were entirely Liberal, though there was a tendency towards Conservatism in England. Some English counties, especially where the urban vote was important, were however becoming more Liberal. This was a transitional period, when the middle-class division between the landed interest and the industrialists was disappearing and a new division (significant because of the household franchise of 1867) developing between capital and labour. It was a differential development, more noticeable in the coal-fields and Yorkshire than in the Midlands and Lancashire, where the small industry was still typical. The lower middle class of clerks, small shopkeepers, etc. was becoming more important and tended to be 'chapel' and accordingly Liberal. But in some areas, notably in the West of England, Yorkshire, Wales and Scotland, the free churches were quite powerful among the poorer householders also.

(3) The elections of 1885 and 1886 were confused by the Liberal split, but the principal effect of the split was the completion of the transfer of the urban middle class to the Conservative party, where it has remained ever since. From 1892 to 1910 all the safe Liberal seats in England were in industrial areas, but Wales and Scotland were still predominantly Liberal in all types of constituencies. London was divided according to class, the residential areas and the commercial areas being Unionist and the rest (i.e. the lower middle-class and working-class areas) being Liberal. The larger towns, except Birmingham and Liverpool (in both of which there were strong organisations controlled respectively by Joseph Chamberlain and Alderman Salvidge), tended to follow the same pattern. The smaller towns, especially the cathedral towns, were generally Unionist. In the counties the industrial areas were generally Liberal or Labour and the rest Unionist; but where Nonconformity was strong, as in the West of England, Yorkshire and Wales, Liberal support was considerable. Scotland, too, remained strongly Liberal.

(4) The Liberal vote continued to be important until 1932, and it seems probable that the development of the Labour vote was due less to 'conversions' than to its strength among the younger electors who had no pre-war Liberal loyalties; and the development was continuous

until 1950, except in 1931. In other words, party loyalty was an important factor. Nevertheless, most of the former Liberal seats turned Labour. Most of the exceptions were in areas which had apparently been Liberal because of religion. Some of these remained Liberal and others went Conservative, while the industrial areas went Labour. This meant that, in London, the residential areas and the commercial areas were generally Conservative, while most of the other areas became Labour strongholds. The Conservative belt was nearer the Thames south of the river because of the North Downs, and the same pheno-menon is evident in the great cities—Cheshire for Manchester, the Derbyshire hills for Sheffield, the moors for Leeds, the Downs for Bristol, and so forth. In other words, the wealthier people who lived in the more attractive areas made them Conservative. The smaller boroughs and the county areas which were not heavily industrialised were also Conservative. There were, however, variations in the normal class structure, due mainly to the continuance of the Liberal tradition in many areas and the strength or weakness of trade unionism. Areas in which organised labour was strong went Labour before areas (especially rural areas) in which it was weak.

(5) There has been no fundamental change since 1945. The Liberal tradition became progressively weaker and trade unionism stronger (experience shows that it is always strong during a boom). The abolition of the business premises qualification converted most of the commercial centres into Labour seats. Better transport facilities have moved populations into residential suburbs which can be classed as Conservative, marginal or Labour according to the sizes and densities of the houses. The movement of factories to small towns and rural areas has made some safe Conservative seats marginal. The only other significant change is a tendency for East Anglia to become more favourable to Labour, perhaps because the agricultural labourers are moving over.

PROPOSITION 7. *The marginal constituencies as between Conservative and Labour are usually those in which the lower middle class predominates, or which are from the point of view of class very mixed.*

A constituency may be described as 'marginal' because it is apt to change allegiance in consecutive elections. A small majority is not necessarily conclusive, for two reasons. First, a constituency which remained Liberal in 1900, Conservative in 1906, Labour in 1931, or Conservative in 1945 was, comparatively speaking, safe. The parties concerned had reached the bottom limit of their popularity, and the constituencies were virtually certain to keep their allegiance in the next election. Secondly, where the normal conflict is between Conservative and Labour, the nomination of a Liberal candidate may shift the balance without any change of opinion among the electorate.

What is 'marginal' is a question of degree. In one sense, all constituencies which are not 'safe' are marginal. In practice, it is convenient to divide constituencies into five classes, sometimes described as safe Conservative, Conservative bias, marginal, Labour bias, and Labour. Here 'Conservative bias' means that the seat is usually Conservative, but that on a more violent swing than usual, as in 1945, it is capable of electing a Labour candidate. It must not be thought that the classes of constituencies can be precisely defined; they shade into each other.

If the election returns from 1923 to 1935 be studied, it is found comparatively simple to give a general description of the marginal constituencies. Looking at the electoral map of London, north of the Thames, and going from west to east, they were Hammersmith N., Kensington N., St Pancras N. and St Pancras S.E., the whole of Islington, Hackney C. and S., and Bethnal Green N.E. and S.W. With these London boroughs must be associated certain other constituencies, namely, Willesden W., Edmonton, the Enfield division of Middlesex, Tottenham (both seats), Walthamstow (both seats), Leyton (both seats) and East Ham (both seats). These could be described as the 'inner suburbs' of Greater London on the west and north-west and both inner and outer suburbs (but not going into Hertfordshire) on the north-east and east. On the west there was a significant barrier formed by Hampstead, though further out Hendon was classed as 'Conservative bias', not a safe seat. Clearly the marginal areas consisted of the constituencies in which the lower middle class predominated.

There were fewer marginal seats in south London because the proximity of the North Downs and the great Surrey commons pushed the margin nearer the centre of London, e.g. Wandsworth C., Battersea N.,

Lambeth N., etc. The great towns, too, show the same phenomenon as London. Thus, Bristol W. was safe Conservative and Bristol E. was safe Labour; but Bristol N. and S. were marginal (and so was Bristol C., but because of the business vote). Similarly, Leeds N. and N.E. (i.e. towards the moors) were safe Conservative and Leeds S. and S.E. were safe Labour, while Leeds W. was marginal.

Many of the smaller towns were marginal, for instance, Reading, Walsall, Wednesbury, Oldham, Rochdale, Carlisle, Darlington, Huddersfield, Norwich, Ipswich. So were many county divisions of the same character, such as Dartford (Kent), Swindon (Berks.), Camborne (Cornwall), Nuneaton (Warwicks.), Cannock (Staffs.), Belper (Derbyshire), Crewe (Cheshire), Widnes (Lancs.), Cleveland (Yorks. N.R.), Pontefract (Yorks. W.R.), Brigg (Lincs.), Romford (Essex). The same phenomenon is to be found in Wales and Scotland, though with some modifications in rural Wales and rural Scotland because of the persistence of the strong Liberal vote.

It is impossible to use a comparable technique for the elections between 1945 and 1959, because of the redistributions of seats. The best examples of marginal seats are those which changed sides between 1950 and 1951. The change was usually due to the Liberal vote; but the Liberal vote could have that effect because, as between Conservative and Labour, the constituencies were marginal. Of the 'inner suburb' type were Battersea S., Dulwich (Camberwell), Blackley (Manchester) and Middlesbrough W. Of the 'small town' type were Bolton E. and W., Darlington, Doncaster, Oldham E., Sutton (Plymouth), Reading N., Rochdale, Buckingham (Bucks.), Wycombe (Bucks.), King's Lynn (Norfolk), Yarmouth (Norfolk), Conway (Caernarvon) and Barry (Glamorgan). The constituencies omitted are Norfolk S.W., Eye (Suffolk) and Anglesey; and the last two had a very strong Liberal tradition.

By 1955 there had been some changes. Greater London had expanded, and among 'inner suburbs' must be classed Willesden E., Acton, Ealing N., Baron's Court, Holborn and St Pancras S., Battersea S., Clapham, Wandsworth C., Woolwich W., and Walthamstow E. Similar constituencies in the great cities were All Saints (Birmingham), Bradford N., Bristol N.E., Hull N., Kirkdale (Liverpool), Gorton (Manchester),

Nottingham C., Oldham E., Devonport (Plymouth), Preston S., Salford W., Sunderland S. In the 'small town' group were Blackburn, Carlisle, Gloucester, Halifax, Keighley, Reading, Rochdale, Watford, York, Buckingham (Bucks.), Stalybridge and Hyde (Cheshire), Eastleigh (Hants), Hitchin (Herts.), Faversham (Kent), Chorley (Lancs.), Uxbridge (Middlesex), King's Lynn (Norfolk), Yarmouth (Norfolk), Wellingborough (Northants), The Wrekin (Salop), Brierly Hill (Staffs.), Leek (Staffs.), Rugby (Warwicks.) and Cleveland (Yorks. N.R.).

By 1959 there had again been changes, due mainly to the movement of population, but partly also to the tendency of the upper 'brackets' of the working class to identify themselves with the middle class. The 'marginal seats' listed in the previous paragraph showed the following results:

Inner suburbs and large towns

Conservative seats which remained Conservative:

Ealing N., Battersea S., Walthamstow E., Wandsworth C., Woolwich W., Bradford N., Hull N., Kirkdale (Liverpool), Nottingham C., Devonport (Plymouth), Preston S., Sunderland S.

Conservative seat which changed to Labour:

Oldham E.

Labour seats which changed to Conservative:

Willesden E., Acton, Baron's Court, Holborn and St Pancras S., Clapham, All Saints (Birmingham), Bristol N.E.

Labour seats which remained Labour:

Gorton (Manchester), Salford W.

Small towns, etc.

Conservative seats which remained Conservative:

Carlisle, Halifax, Watford, York, Buckingham (Bucks.), Eastleigh (Hants), Hitchin (Herts.), King's Lynn (Norfolk), Yarmouth (Norfolk), The Wrekin (Salop).

Labour seats which changed to Conservative:

Keighley, Reading, Uxbridge (Middlesex), Wellingborough (Northants), Brierly Hill (Staffs.), Rugby (Warwicks.), Cleveland (Yorks. N.R.).

Labour seats which remained Labour:

Blackburn, Gloucester, Rochdale, Stalybridge and Hyde (Cheshire), Faversham (Kent), Chorley (Lancs.), Leek (Staffs.).

Apart from the above, the following constituencies changed hands:

Labour to Conservative

Lewisham N., Sparkbrook (Birmingham), Yardley (Birmingham), Coventry S., Hartlepools, Newcastle upon Tyne E., Nottingham W., Rochester and Chatham, Derbyshire S.E., Meriden (Warwicks.), Swansea W.

Conservative to Labour

Craigton (Glasgow), Scotstoun (Glasgow), Central Ayrshire, Lanark.

It is not suggested that the wealthier classes are solidly Conservative, the poorer classes solidly Labour, and the minor salaried classes (clerks, etc.) uncertain of their allegiance. If that were so there would always have been a Labour Government. The idea prevails, nevertheless, that the Conservative party is the rich man's party and the Labour party the poor man's party. That is so historically. The Conservative party led by Disraeli was the landowners' party, while the Liberal party was the party of commerce and industry. As the nineteenth century developed, the landowners moved into trade and industry while the traders and industrialists, if wealthy enough, joined a club, the Church of England, and the Conservative party. The small traders and industrialists, and their clerks and foremen, went to chapel and voted Liberal, though they were uncertain whether the two things were compatible in 1874. Joseph Chamberlain realised that something more than 'temperance and other evils' was required by the new working-class electors and tried to divert the Liberal party from its shopkeeper mentality; but he crossed the floor in 1886 and was never replaced. The working men were therefore not catered for politically, and they were divided until militant trade unionism developed. The Labour party was, in its origin, a workers' party designed purely to put working-class, and especially trade union, representatives into Parliament. At first a wing of the Liberal party, and until 1918 not clearly differentiated from it, in 1918 the Labour party broadened its organisation and appeal. The Liberal party had had a Radical wing, led by Lloyd George and Winston Churchill, in the Parliament of 1906 to 1918; but it failed to catch the working-class vote, and the split between Asquith and Lloyd George ended the experiment. Hence the Labour party became the opposition to the Conservative party, while retaining its working-class sympathies. It is, especially, the party of organised labour, the political equivalent of the Trades Union Congress. Through its political wing it has tried to secure the support of the large and growing middle class, but it is continually being recalled to its origin and is thus leaving the way open for a revived Liberal party, if that party is prepared to accept the Welfare State but to reject nationalisation and militant trade unionism.

The Conservative party is the party of the West End, the City, the professional classes and the public schools; though there are exceptions they seem to be comparatively few. The Labour party is the party of organised labour; but even trade unionists are far from unanimous. There are large Conservative minorities in constituencies which are almost entirely working-class. Many of the manual workers now have incomes exceeding those of shopkeepers, clerks, insurance agents, school teachers, etc., who consider themselves to be middle-class. The former are tending to oust the latter from the inner suburbs and compete with them for houses in the less expensive outer suburbs. This of course works both ways. On the one hand it induces marginal constituencies (e.g. Islington) to become safe seats for Labour; on the other hand it encourages trade unionists to vote Conservative, or at least not to vote Labour. In a small town, particularly outside the industrial areas, the 'aristocracy' will vote Conservative; and, because there is such an 'aristocracy', many if not most of the lower middle class will vote Conservative; but some of the working class will also vote Conservative, especially if the town is not in an area where trade unionism is strong. The story is, however, complicated by the existence of the Liberal party.

PROPOSITION 8. *The Liberal party still derives most of its strength from the lower middle class.*

When the whigs left the Liberal party between 1846 and 1886, the Liberals became the party of the lower middle class, the party of the shopkeepers, clerks, etc. Though between 1945 and 1955 it was a minority party, the constituencies in which it could make a show were (outside Wales) those which were, as between Conservative and Labour, marginal. If we take a Liberal vote of 10,000 as indicating some substantial support, the relevant constituencies in 1945 were: Blackpool N., Bolton, Bournemouth, Bromley, Croydon N., Halifax, Huddersfield, Withington (Manchester), Middlesbrough W., Oldham, Rochdale, Southport, Stockport, Wolverhampton E., Mid Bedford, Aylesbury (Bucks.), Knutsford (Cheshire), The Wirral (Cheshire), North Cornwall, North Cumberland, South Derbyshire, Barnstaple (Devon), Tavistock (Devon), Torquay (Devon), North Dorset, Stroud (Gloucestershire), Thornbury (Gloucestershire), Leominster (Herefordshire), Hemel Hempstead (Herts.), Wood Green (Middlesex), Berwick Upon Tweed (Northumberland), Henley (Oxfordshire), Weston-super-Mare (Somerset), Yeovil (Somerset), Eye (Suffolk), Guildford (Surrey), Chichester (Sussex), Bewdley (Worcestershire), Stourbridge (Worcestershire), Buckrose (Yorks. E.R.), Holderness (Yorks. E.R.), Scarborough and Whitby (Yorks. N.R.), Caernarvon Boroughs, Anglesey, Caernarvonshire, Cardiganshire, Carmarthen, Denbigh, Flint, Llandaff and Barry, Montgomery, Pembroke, Dundee, Kincardine and West Aberdeenshire.

The first characteristic of this list is the strength of the Liberal tradition in the old Nonconformist areas, especially Wales and the western counties of England. The persistence of tradition may also explain the presence of so many seaside resorts, which contain a high proportion of older electors. The small town and the intermediate suburb also figure prominently. Some items in the list are due to the absence of Conservative or Labour candidates, but the fact that the case against the Conservatives or Labour was left to the Liberals indicates that the local party managers believed in the strength of Liberalism.

A gallant attempt to revive the fortunes of the Liberal party was made in 1950. It would be wearisome to read another list; if a lower limit of 8000, 6000 or 5000 electors be taken, however, it will be seen that Liberalism was quite strong in Wales, the western counties of England, the smaller towns, and suburbia, but not strong enough to win more than a handful of seats. This gallant attempt could not be repeated in 1951, and only 109 Liberal candidates were nominated. In almost all constituencies they lost votes; and both in those constituencies and where there were Liberal candidates in 1950 but not in 1951, most of the Liberal votes not cast for Liberals were cast for

Conservatives. The Labour candidates gained some votes from Liberals, but only about one in ten. This does not necessarily mean either that those who were traditionally Liberal went Conservative, or that the lower middle class had for all time turned to the Conservative party. The argument for voting Conservative or Labour in 1951 (apart from the intrinsic merits, if any, of those parties) was that it was necessary to have a Government with a clear majority. The argument persisted in 1955, when the Liberal vote was virtually the same as in 1951.

Another effort was made in 1959 with 216 candidates. This was a peculiar election, particularly favourable to the Liberal party in that the Conservative Government had lost credit and expected to lose votes through the swing of the pendulum, but the Labour party had gained no credit. It was evident from the sample polls that the number of waverers was much higher than usual. The by-elections, too, had been favourable to the Liberal party. In the end, the Liberal party retained six seats, gaining one from the Conservatives and losing one to the Conservatives. Three of the seats were retained with the help of Conservative votes. The Liberal party obtained 8000 votes or more in only sixty-five of the constituencies which they did not win, and of these fifty-three were safe Conservative seats. Two others, Billericay (Essex) and Hitchin (Herts.) were marginal. In seventy other constituencies the Liberals obtained between 6000 and 8000 votes. Only three of these were marginal seats, Gloucester, Oldham E., and Rugby (Warwicks.). Most of the others were safe Conservative seats. The inference to be drawn is that many electors were prepared to vote Liberal, as a protest against the Conservative Government, where that protest would not result in the return of a Labour candidate. In other words, the Liberal party suffered from the fact that it could not form a Government, so that those who disliked the Conservative Government but disliked the prospect of a Labour Government still more could not vote Liberal in a marginal constituency.

It is less easy to show that the Liberal voters tended to be drawn from the lower middle class. There is, however, a general air of suburbia, small town and seaside resort about the constituencies in which the Liberal candidates did best. The Labour constituencies where the

Liberal vote was high were Ipswich, Hull E., Oldbury, Rochdale, Romford, Carmarthen and Greenock (Merioneth is omitted because there was no Conservative candidate). In the suburbs were Hampstead, Beckenham, Finchley, Hornchurch, Southgate, Twickenham, Billericay, Epping, South-West Hertfordshire, Orpington (Kent), Carshalton (Surrey), East Surrey, Epsom (Surrey) and Esher (Surrey). Among seaside resorts and spas were Southend W., Blackpool N., Bournemouth E. and Christchurch, Cheltenham, Poole, Southport, Torquay, several constituencies in Cornwall, Devon and Dorset, Weston-super-Mare (Somerset), Eastbourne (Sussex) and Scarborough (Yorks. N.R.). All this suggests that the Liberals are to be found mainly in 'bijou villas' in housing estates at something like eight or twelve to the acre.

PROPOSITION 9. *Most electors vote not for a party policy but for a party image.*

The term 'image' was applied to parties by Graham Wallas.[1] The proposition means that the average elector has formed concepts of what are the Conservative party or 'the Tories' and the Labour party or 'the Socialists', and that these concepts have no direct connexion with the policies which the parties advocate at a particular election. There is, however, an indirect connexion, because the party must advocate policies which suit its clientele. Though an elector may vote Conservative or Labour and yet disagree with all or most of the specific proposals of the appropriate party at a particular election, there cannot permanently be a divorce between image and policy. The image will gradually become distorted, especially among the younger electors. On the other hand, the image is not devised only out of policy: it is in large measure produced by personalities. The Conservative party looks like, and is, the party of the public schools (especially Eton) and the older universities (especially Oxford). It is associated with the West End, the officers of the Brigade of Guards, the Royal enclosure at Ascot, Rugby football, polo, golf, the B.B.C. accent, cocktail parties, debutantes, the clubs of Pall Mall, etc. The Labour party, on the other hand, is the party of the elementary schools and the trade unions. It is

[1] *Human Nature in Politics* (1929 ed.), p. 84.

associated with the East End, the back streets, the co-operative stores, the cockney accent and its equivalents, association football, the pools, the bathing beaches of the popular and therefore 'unfashionable' resorts. Even though it be led by 'Haileybury and Univ.' or 'Winchester and New College', it is still the party of the 'people' as contrasted with 'Society', or the rich, or the 'lords and ladies'.

The proposition might seem to be controverted by the concentration of parties and candidates on 'issues'. A candidate or a propagandist who has to make thirty set speeches and give a hundred or so little talks has to talk about something; and the comparatively few people who attend meetings[1] ask questions about matters which interest them. Whether there is much discussion in private about such things as the nationalisation, denationalisation or renationalisation of the iron and steel industry may be doubted. Electors often give particular issues as reasons for voting as they do;[2] but this may be, and probably often is,[3] due to an association between the party and the policy. Thus, a lifelong Liberal would probably give 'free trade' as his reason even if he had never seriously considered the matter. Certainly people vote against a party and yet agree with it on some at least of the main issues.[4] The elector's job, as he sees it, is to 'keep out the Socialists' or 'keep out the Tories'.

That rational electioneering and argument about 'issues' or policies are of little importance was laid down by an experienced Radical election agent as long ago as 1841. Joseph Parkes was the father of all election agents (though he learned the technique from Francis Place); and he advised Lord John Russell before the general election of 1841 that 'the action of *political* principle and particular Cabinet policies on the English borough constituencies is much overrated'.[5] He laid emphasis on local circumstances, and the sufficiency and wealth of

---

[1] In Greenwich in 1950 the Conservatives had twenty-seven meetings and the Labour party had eleven. Each candidate addressed about 2200 people: Mark Benney, A. P. Gray and R. H. Pear, *How People Vote*, p. 81. It seems, however, that there were more people at meetings in 1959.

[2] R. S. Milne and H. C. Mackenzie, *Straight Fight*, p. 120; *Marginal Seat*, pp. 120–1.

[3] *Straight Fight*, pp. 136–7; *Marginal Seat*, pp. 121–6.

[4] Mark Benney, etc., *How People Vote*, p. 141.

[5] Norman McCord, *The Anti-Corn Law League*, p. 160.

candidates. Circumstances have since altered, and the most important influences are long-standing prejudices, social conditions, and gradually changing ideas. The tradition of the Labour party, which it perhaps derives from the adult education movement and the 'educational' activities of the socialist societies, that masses of electors can be influenced by policy statements and election programmes, devised *ad hoc*, is misplaced. It has got the votes not because of its socialist objective, nor above all because of its vast array of policy pamphlets and conference decisions, but because it 'favours the working man'. This does not mean that policy statements and electioneering are useless. On the contrary, a party needs the active work not of a few professionals but of a host of enthusiastic amateurs who, if they are Labour supporters, are for the most part convinced socialists, and whose faith has to be kept orthodox by frequent stimulation. This produces an odd differentiation between the more or less articulate ideas of the enthusiastic amateurs and the inarticulate prejudices of the Labour electors. It does not matter in the short run, because the electors vote for the image and not the policy; but it does matter in the long run because the image gets distorted if the average man becomes convinced that Labour politicians are hare-brained doctrinaires. It seems reasonably certain that the Labour party would never have achieved power if it had been merely the successor of the Independent Labour party. The solid support of the trade unions has, however, made it the working man's party; and all the flamboyance of the left wing has been unable to destroy that image.

Electioneering, too, is important, not because people are persuaded by programmes and argument, but for two reasons. First, it turns an election into a sporting contest and encourages the apathetic to vote according to the party image. It 'gets out the vote'. Secondly, it produces a chain reaction in the pubs and the clubs, the shops and the factories, which encourages class conformity. This helps to retard the swing of the pendulum where the party has been in office, and to accelerate it where it has been in Opposition. The election surveys show that many people who are willing, at the beginning of an election, to vote against the party, do in fact vote for it on polling day. Generally speaking, these people have not been convinced by rational argument or party policies; they have simply been persuaded by public opinion that they ought not to be traitors.

The great difficulty of the Liberal party is that, for the new generation, it has no image. It is constantly being accused of not having a policy, not because the accusation is true, but because most electors have only the vaguest ideas about the policy of any party, and no ideas at all about Liberal policy. Its prominent personalities, too, have been dead long enough to get into the history books; only the older generation remembers Asquith and Lloyd George, while nobody remembers Gladstone. It therefore has to rely partly on the Liberal tradition of the older generation, but mainly on distrust and disillusionment with the other parties. A new image is thus being created, that of a party which might be capable of solving international and social problems because, it is alleged, both the other parties have failed. If that 'gets over', it will not need a policy; or it can, as its opponents allege it does, produce a different policy for each constituency.

PROPOSITION 10. *Most electors vote consistently for one party.*

In the language of electioneering, most electors are 'regulars'; but there are also the 'apathetic' and the 'waverers' or 'floaters'. The task of electioneering, therefore, is to poll the apathetic and convince the waverers.

That the 'regulars' are more numerous than the 'apathetic' and the 'waverers' combined is a proposition deriving from the experience of election agents who (in the days when a complete canvass of a constituency was practicable, i.e. between the wars) could check their impressions by comparison on the registers of the canvassers' lists and the polling agents' lists. The proposition is, however, supported by the more recent sampling surveys.[1] Table 39 shows the results at Greenwich in 1945 and 1950.

In the sample panel used by the London School of Economics team,[2] sixty-one per cent of those who voted Conservative, sixty-six per cent of those who voted Labour, and five per cent of those who voted

[1] The surveys cannot, however, be accurate on a matter of this kind: see the warning in Mark Benney, etc., *How People Vote*, pp. 216–19; and John Bonham, *The Middle Class Vote*, p. 176.

[2] Mark Benney, etc., *op. cit.* p. 221.

Liberal in 1950 had voted the same way in 1945 (in the same or a different constituency). Ten per cent of those who voted Conservative had previously voted Labour, and four per cent of those who voted Labour had previously voted Conservative. There was no Liberal candidate in Greenwich in 1945, and that party drew its strength in

	Percentages of electors		
	1945	*1950*	*Change*
Conservative	24·1	29·8	+5·7
Labour	45·9	48·0	+2·1
Liberal	—	5·1	+5·1
Not voting	30·0	17·1	−12·9

TABLE 39

1950 as to forty-five per cent from the Labour voters, as to nineteen per cent from the Conservative voters, and as to thirty-one per cent from those who did not or could not vote in 1945. The increase in the Conservative vote, shown above, was due for the most part to non-voters of 1945 voting in 1950. The increase in the Labour vote was due for the most part to non-voters of 1945, but was small because of the heavy abstention of Labour voters in 1950.

Table 40 gives the results in Stretford[1] in 1945 and 1950.

	Percentages of electors		
	1945	*1950*	*Change*
Conservative	35·4	42·2	+6·8
Labour	43·1	35·1	−8·0
Liberal	—	10·2	+10·2
Not voting	21·5	12·5	−9·0

TABLE 40

Table 41 gives the figures obtained by the Manchester University team[2] in their sample. This means that seventy per cent of the

[1] There was a change of boundary in 1950, which adversely affected the Labour candidate.
[2] A. H. Birch and P. Campbell, 'Voting Behaviour in a Lancashire Constituency', *British Journal of Sociology*, I, p. 200.

Conservative voters and sixty-nine per cent of the Labour voters of 1950 had voted the same way in 1945.

It should be noted, however, that the figures for 1950 were abnormally low because of the low poll in 1945. The 101 'new voters' in Stretford, for instance, included twenty-six persons who found it difficult or

Voted Conservative in 1945 and 1950	145
Voted Labour in 1945 and 1950	112
Changed party	67
New voters	101
Did not vote in 1950	23
Total	448

TABLE 41

impossible to vote in 1945. Fortunately we have one set of figures for 1951: Table 42 gives the results in Bristol N.E. in 1950 and 1951.

	Percentages of electors		
	1950	*1951*	*Change*
Conservative	32·9	38·9	+6·0
Labour	41·8	43·9	+2·1
Liberal	9·9	—	−9·9
Not voting	15·4	17·2	+1·8

TABLE 42

In the sample panels of the Bristol University survey,[1] seventy-one per cent of the Conservatives and eighty-one per cent of the Labour voters voted the same way in 1950 and 1951; seven per cent of the Conservative voters of 1951 voted Labour in 1950 and two per cent of the Labour voters of 1951 voted Conservative in 1950; ten per cent of the Conservatives and four per cent of the Labour voters of 1951 voted Liberal in 1950; and ten per cent of the Conservatives and twelve per cent of the Labour voters did not vote in 1950. It is stated[2] that most of the non-voters of 1950 just mentioned were too young to vote in 1950.

[1] R. S. Milne and H. C. Mackenzie, *Straight Fight*, p. 35.
[2] *Ibid.* p. 35.

This investigation was followed by a second investigation in 1955. The results are given in Table 43.

| | Percentage of electors | | |
	1951	1955	Change
Conservative	38·9	34·9	−4·0
Labour	43·9	36·3	−7·6
Liberal	—	6·7	+6·7
Not voting	17·2	22·1	+4·9

TABLE 43

There had been a small boundary change. This time the Bristol University team[1] gives us not the proportions of the electors in the several parties who voted the same way in 1951 and 1955 (though they do tell us that, taking all groups, 81·7 per cent did so),[2] but the proportions of the electors who had behaved consistently at the general elections of 1945, 1950, 1951, and 1955. The figures of the consistent electors (i.e. the 'regulars') in the several groups in 1955 are shown in Table 44.

	Percentage of electors
Conservative	63·0
Labour	82·1
Liberal	9·3
Not voting	60·4
All electors	65·9

TABLE 44

Bristol N.E. cannot be regarded as typical—indeed, there is no typical constituency. It is a marginal constituency with a population which probably fluctuates a good deal. Though comparatively new as a constituency, its older districts had a strong Liberal tradition; and it is evident from the figures that, in the absence of a Liberal candidate, many possible Liberal electors vote Conservative or Labour, thus giving an impression of wavering. Moreover the degree of consistency varies

[1] R. S. Milne and H. C. Mackenzie, *Marginal Seat*, p. 76.
[2] *Ibid.* p. 85.

considerably with age,[1] with social class,[2] and even with sex.[3] Nor must we forget that the degree of consistency may be exaggerated unconsciously by the persons questioned.[4]

In the Greenwich survey it was found that twenty-two per cent of the sample changed their minds between December 1949 and the date of the election, February 1950.[5] In Bristol S.E. in 1951 the interval was shorter, only 2½ weeks. Those who had made up their minds at the beginning of that period and who had not changed them at the end were seventy-six per cent of the sample;[6] if however we add those who were uncertain about voting but expressed a preference at the end, the proportion rises to eighty-four per cent. Moreover some of those who had voted in 1950 (especially for Labour) and had changed party by the beginning of the period changed it back at the end. In Bristol S.E. in 1955 the period was about sixteen days. It was found that of those who expressed a preference for the Conservatives at the beginning of the campaign, eighty-nine per cent voted Conservative; and the comparable figures for Labour and Liberal were respectively eighty-five per cent and sixty-seven per cent. Three-quarters of those who had expressed an intention to vote differently in 1955 from their 1951 vote in fact voted the same way as in 1951.[7] This one would expect: some 'regulars' would be dissatisfied with their own Government and yet not be able to 'let the party down' when they had to decide. In many cases there must be a conflict between the party image and the party policy, especially when the party has recently been in power. The policy, they agree, has been disastrous and the Government weak and inefficient; at a by-election or at a public opinion poll well before the election this opinion may be expressed by an apparent change of party; but when it comes to helping the Tory, or the Socialist, Opposition into power there is incentive to vote for the disastrous policy and the weak and inefficient Government.

It may be, therefore, that the proportion of 'regulars' is as high as seventy per cent in the Conservative party and eighty per cent in the

[1] *Ibid.* p. 78.   [2] *Ibid.* p. 81.   [3] *Ibid.* p. 83.
[4] Mark Benney, etc., *How People Vote*, pp. 216–19.
[5] Mark Benney, etc., *How People Vote*, p. 168.
[6] Calculated from R. C. Milne and H. C. Mackenzie, *Straight Fight*, p. 27.
[7] R. C. Milne and H. C. Mackenzie, *Marginal Seat*, p. 41.

Labour party. It is, however, safer to claim only that at least half are 'regulars'. Dr Bonham, who used the figures of the Gallup poll, says indeed that less than half the electorate were either regularly Conservative or regularly Labour in the elections of 1945, 1950 and 1951. This is, however, not a fair test. In the first place, many 'regulars' did not vote in 1945 because of wartime dislocation and imperfections in the arrangements. In the second place, a person who voted Labour in 1945 and now intends to vote Conservative for the rest of his life is a 'regular'. In the third place, a person who first voted in 1950 or 1951 and intends to vote the same way for the rest of his life is a 'regular'. In the fourth place, a lifelong Liberal is a 'regular' even if, at half the elections, nobody provides him with a Liberal candidate. A genuine 'floater' may be allowed to mix his metaphors as well as his votes, and may therefore be said to sit on the fence unless and until he decides to slip off.

PROPOSITION 11. *The most important determinants of party are class, sex and age.*

In what it excludes, this proposition follows from earlier propositions. We refer to determinants of party because the personalities of the candidates are almost irrelevant. This has been demonstrated as Proposition 1, and the assertion is supported by the surveys.[1] It has been shown under Proposition 3 that throughout Great Britain the electors arrange themselves according to a pattern. Incidentally under that proposition and elsewhere it has been suggested that geographical factors, which may also be associated with religion, sometimes have appreciable effects, but they are not very important. This is, too, the assumption of the surveys. Greenwich, Stretford, Droylsden and Bristol N.E. were studied because it was thought that the results would be generally valuable; and the fact that teams from three universities, working in London, Bristol and Lancashire, are in substantial agreement is itself significant.[2] That the pattern is in large measure deter-

---

[1] Mark Benney, etc., *How People Vote*, pp. 158–9; R. S. Milne and H. C. Mackenzie, *Straight Fight*, pp. 120, 121; *Marginal Seat*, pp. 51–61.

[2] The demonstration would be better if Wales and Scotland had been included. The 'strong Liberal tradition' of Bristol N.E. (Milne and Mackenzie, *Straight Fight*, p. 90) is probably part of a general Liberal tradition in the West of England.

mined by the class distribution is evident from the discussion on Propositions 6, 7 and 8.

First, however, we must consider the effect of age on party support. In Greenwich the classes were divided for this purpose into two, which we may distinguish very roughly as 'middle class' and 'working class'. Table 45 shows the age and class distribution in Greenwich in 1950.[1]

	Middle class		Working class	
	Aged 21–49	Aged 50 and over	Aged 21–49	Aged 50 and over
Percentage voting				
Conservative	63	67	18	42
Labour	24	23	79	53
Liberal	13	10	3	5

TABLE 45

Similar figures for Bristol N.E. in 1951 are given in Table 46.[2]

	Middle class		Working class	
	Aged 21–49	Aged 50 and over	Aged 21–49	Aged 50 and over
Percentage voting				
Conservative	70·6	79·1	24·5	44·7
Labour	29·4	20·9	75·5	55·3

TABLE 46

[1] Mark Benney, etc., *How People Vote*, p. 105.
[2] R. S. Milne and H. C. Mackenzie, *Straight Fight*, p. 57. In *Marginal Seat*, p. 60, Messrs Milne and Mackenzie give a different classification for 1955. They used the objective test of the Census returns to distinguish class, giving the percentages voting Conservative according to class and age-group as follows:

Class	Percentage under 50	Percentage 50 and over
I and II	59·2	69·4
III	43·2	50·9
IV and V	28·9	40·5

For this test, see *ante*, p. 255.

In the Lancashire surveys age and class were not correlated, but in Table 47 the age figures for all classes are put in a comparable form.[1]

	Age group percentages	
	21–49	50 upwards
Greenwich 1950		
Conservative voters	53	47
Labour voters	74	26
Stretford 1950		
Conservative voters	59	41
Labour voters	69	31
Droylsden 1950		
Conservative voters	52	48
Labour voters	64	36
Droylsden 1951		
Conservative voters	58	42
Labour voters	66	34
Bristol N.E. 1951		
Conservative voters	49	51
Labour voters	65	35
Bristol N.E. 1955		
Conservative voters	58	42
Labour voters	66	34
Liberal voters	51	49

TABLE 47

These figures seem to suggest that, on the average, people get more Conservative as they grow older. There are, however, other possible explanations. First, there is still a differentiation in the expectation of life of the middle and the working classes. Secondly, the Labour party was still suffering from the time-lag due to its novelty as a party. There were in 1950 and 1951 still electors who had voted Conservative in 1900, Liberal in 1906, or Coalition in 1918, and a great many who had voted Liberal in 1929. If it be true, as the evidence quoted under Proposition 10 suggests, that 'regulars' do not easily change party, there must have been many electors of 1950 and 1951 who regarded the mild socialism of the Labour party as new-fangled non-

[1] Lancashire figures from P. Campbell, D. Downison and A. Potter, 'Voting Behaviour in Droylsden in October 1951', *Manchester School*, pp. 57, 60, 61.

sense. Thirdly, the 'over 50' group contains a larger proportion of women,[1] and we shall see that more women than men vote Conservative.

In the population aged twenty and over in the United Kingdom at the census of 1951[2] the proportion of men to women was 47 to 53; and the proportion of men to women among the electors would not be very different. The proportion of men to women in the Conservative party, as shown by the Lancashire surveys, was 41 to 59 (Stretford, 1950), 42 to 58 (Droylsden, 1950) and 44 to 56 (Droylsden, 1951). In the Labour party, on the other hand, it was 54 to 46 (Stretford, 1950), 49 to 51 (Droylsden, 1950) and 47 to 53 (Droylsden, 1951). In Bristol N.E. in 1951 it was 47 to 53 in the Conservative party and 53 to 47 in the Labour party.[3] A more complex analysis was made in Bristol N.E. in 1955[4] (Table 48).

	Aged 21–49		Aged 50 and over	
	Men	Women	Men	Women
Percentage voting				
Conservative	44	47	50	53
Labour	50	44	36	38
Liberal	6	9	14	9
	100	100	100	100

TABLE 48

Table 49 shows an even more complex analysis which was made in Greenwich in 1950.[5]

For statistical reasons it would be wise to ignore the Liberal figures, though they do show the party's middle-class support and may suggest that few women vote Liberal. The combination of figures from four constituencies shows, however, a definite bias towards Conservatism among the women, especially among working-class women. The

[1] The difference in the general population was 1,961,000 in 1951.
[2] The census figures are, for statistical reasons, given in quinquennia.
[3] Milne and Mackenzie, *Straight Fight*, p. 38.
[4] Milne and Mackenzie, *Marginal Seat*, p. 54.
[5] Mark Benney, etc., *How People Vote*, p. 107.

Greenwich survey[1] shows that it is stronger among single women of fifty and over than among married women of that age, thus suggesting that husbands affect their wives' votes. The difference between men

	Middle class				Working class			
	Aged 21–49		Aged 50 and over		Aged 21–49		Aged 50 and over	
	Men	Women	Men	Women	Men	Women	Men	Women
Percentage voting								
Conservative	58	67	68	68	15	21	34	47
Labour	31	22	17	23	83	75	57	50
Liberal	11	11	15	9	2	4	9	3
	100	100	100	100	100	100	100	100

TABLE 49

and women, in respect of politics, is that fewer of the women have contacts outside the home, especially in the factory or trade union.[2] Possibly the newspapers and the wireless (and now television) have a greater influence with women voters than pressure to social conformity.

The influence of class has appeared incidentally. It may, however, be convenient to reproduce the summaries from the Lancashire surveys (Table 50).

	Percentage of voters		
	Middle class	Lower middle class	Working class
Stretford 1950			
Conservative	55	13	27
Labour	24	7	64
Droylsden 1951			
Conservative	24	23	48
Labour	10	13	74

TABLE 50

[1] Mark Benney, etc., *How People Vote*, p. 110.
[2] *Ibid*. p. 108.

Table 51 gives the figures for Bristol N.E. expressed not as percentages of voters in each class, but as percentages of each class who voted for the respective parties.[1]

	Middle class		Lower middle class		Working class	
	1951	*1955*	*1951*	*1955*	*1951*	*1955*
Conservative	76·7	66·6	57·8	59·6	31·3	36·1
Labour	23·3	25·0	42·2	24·7	68·7	56·5
Liberal	—	8·4	—	15·7	—	7·4
	100	100	100	100	100	100

TABLE 51

Here the classification is 'subjective', i.e. the persons answering the question decided to what classes they belonged.

In the Greenwich survey a four-point scale was used, based on income, apparent standard of living, accent, and general bearing. This meant in fact that what is usually called the middle class and what is normally called the working class were both divided into two. Of the lowest class, 78 per cent voted Labour and 18 per cent Conservative; and of the other manual workers, 69 per cent voted Labour while 27 per cent voted Conservative. At the upper level of the middle class, 82 per cent voted Conservative and 12 per cent voted Labour, while at the lower level of that class (i.e. what is normally called the lower middle class) 64 per cent voted Conservative and 24 per cent voted Labour. The balance, i.e. 4 per cent in the working class, 6 per cent at the upper level of the middle class, and 12 per cent in the lower middle class, voted Liberal.[2]

It must be remembered that the Conservatives in the working class contain substantial proportions of women and older men. Moreover, the figures seem to show[3] that a member of the middle class who inclined to Labour or a member of the working class who inclined to Conservative was quite likely to change his mind before the election. The

[1] Milne and Mackenzie, *Marginal Seat*, p. 56.
[2] Mark Benney, etc., *How People Vote*, p. 103.
[3] A. H. Birch and P. Campbell, *op. cit.* p. 202; Mark Benney, *op. cit.* p. 180.

'Conservative working man' is not a mythical creature, but he is probably quite a rare bird.[1] The Labour working man who sometimes votes Conservative is not so rare. On the other hand, it must be remembered that the elections of 1950 and 1951, when these figures were collected,

	Percentage in each party		
	Con-servative	Labour	Neither
1945			
Middle class	50	18	27
Manual wage class	46	77	64
1950			
Middle class	48	14	31
Manual wage class	48	80	64
1951			
Middle class	48	14	31
Manual wage class	46	81	66

TABLE 52

	Percentage in each party		
	Con-servative	Labour	Neither
1945			
Middle class	47	21	32
Manual wage class	20	42	38
1950			
Middle class	56	18	26
Manual wage class	26	48	26
1951			
Middle class	62	18	20
Manual wage class	28	52	20

TABLE 53

were marginal elections, producing respectively a small Labour majority and a small Conservative majority. The pendulum was almost perpendicular. Different results would have been obtained in 1945, 1955 and 1959.

[1] When found he is put on show; cf. Bob Bulbrook of the Old Kent Road: Mark Benney, etc., *How People Vote*, pp. 68–9.

Dr Bonham[1] has a different class criterion, and in particular he omits a small 'intermediate class' consisting mainly of white-collar workers with low incomes. If his estimates of the class structure of the total vote be put into percentages, however, the class composition of the Conservative and Labour vote can be shown as in Table 52. On this basis, about half the Conservative voters are middle class and four-fifths of the Labour voters are working class. The same figures may be shown as percentages of the total electorate in each of the classes (Table 53).

In these tables, the last column includes non-voters, Liberals and persons voting for other candidates. Since owing to practical difficulties the poll was very low in 1945, the extent of the 'swing' is exaggerated.

PROPOSITION 12. *Direct 'conversions' from Labour to Conservative or vice versa are comparatively few and may consist mainly of persons who voted out of their class.*

The first part of this proposition means that most of the electors who appear to be 'floaters' are persons who (*a*) vote Liberal when there is a Liberal candidate, or (*b*) do not always vote. In neither case are they necessarily 'floaters' in the true sense. Obviously a Liberal 'regular' has to 'float' if there is no Liberal candidate. Nor is non-voting necessarily the consequence of a political decision. The non-voter may be a 'regular' who is deterred by the rain, or sickness in the house, or temporary absence from the constituency, or a birthday party or wireless programme. The second part of the proposition means that where an elector changes from Conservative to Labour he probably belongs to the working class, and where an elector changes from Labour to Conservative he probably belongs to the middle class; in other words, his change of opinion is a change from nonconformity with class opinion to conformity.

The proof of the proposition is not easy because of the inadequacy of the surveys in this respect. Of those in the Greenwich sample in 1950, only nine per cent changed party from 1945.[2] But the low poll of 1945 makes this analysis less representative than usual. In the samples

[1] *The Middle Class Vote*, p. 168.
[2] Mark Benney, etc., *How People Vote*, p. 220.

in Bristol S.E. in 1951 there were 186 apparent 'floaters', but of these only thirty-three changed from Labour to Conservative or vice versa, while fifty-two had voted Liberal in 1950, eighty-three had not voted in 1950, and eighteen did not vote in 1951. A 'conversion' is however important because it counts twice in the net gain as between Conservative and Labour. The net gain of the Conservative candidate in this sample was fifty-seven, of which forty-two were due to 'conversion' (fifty-four less twelve, i.e. twenty-seven from Labour to Conservative and six from Conservative to Labour).[1] For the 1955 election Messrs Milne and Mackenzie produced a useful table in percentages, but it is even more useful when expressed in raw numbers as in Table 54.[2]

Classification according to 1951 vote	1955 vote (numbers)				
	Cons.	Lab.	Lib.	Did not vote	Total
Conservative	190	12	17	5	224
Labour	14	175	17	17	223
Did not vote:					
too young	9	6	3	4	22
other reasons	14	10	5	21	50
Total	227	203	42	47	519
Actual total[3]	(226)	(204)	(42)	(48)	(520)

TABLE 54

It will be noticed that in this sample the Conservatives won the election both in 1951 and in 1955. In point of fact they lost both elections.[4] In any case the numbers involved are so small that the sample may be quite unrepresentative. Taking the sample as a 'little election' in its own right, however, it will be seen that only twenty-six out of 519 electors changed from Conservative to Labour or vice versa.

The second part of the proposition must be put tentatively because the samples in the surveys were small. The Greenwich team found,

[1] R. S. Milne and H. C. Mackenzie, *Straight Fight*, p. 33.
[2] Milne and Mackenzie, *Marginal Seat*, p. 42.
[3] The errors in the totals are due to conversion into percentages and reconversion.
[4] The authors draw attention to the main error, that the sample did not contain enough non-voters: *op. cit.* pp. 202-3.

however, that those who changed their voting intention between December 1949 and February 1950 were more often 'among those whose original vote intention diverged from that of the majority of their social group'. Some of these, however, may have been discontented 'regulars' who eventually followed the party line.[1] The Bristol team did not produce a similar conclusion, but drew attention to the large proportion of women under fifty and men over fifty.[2] This is, however, very much the same thing: for the people concerned were working-class, and in that class women of all ages and men over fifty more often vote Conservative than men under fifty. Of the six Conservatives of 1950 who changed to Labour in 1951 in Bristol N.E., three were middle-class; and of the twenty-seven Labour voters of 1950 who changed to Conservative in 1951, eighteen were middle-class.[3] So far as they go these figures support the proposition; but they do not go very far.

PROPOSITION 13. *The 'swing of the pendulum' is caused mainly by the new voters and the non-voters.*

There may of course be an apparent 'swing of the pendulum' without a real one. The main cause of the apparent 'swing' in 1951 was, as we have seen, that the great Liberal effort of 1950 was not repeated in 1951, and that most of the Liberal votes went to the Conservative party. On the other hand, there seems also to have been an increase in non-voting in both the major parties.

The number of new electors every year is approximately 700,000[4] or two per cent of the electorate of the United Kingdom. Thus, some eight per cent of the electorate changes if the interval between elections is in the region of four years. Since the Labour party is stronger than the Conservative party among the younger voters, the former tends to gain, and this gain may not be offset by increasing Conservatism among the middle-aged. The trend might, however, be reversed, and there is some evidence, though of a fragmentary and empirical kind, that it is being reversed. The young men in the universities are showing signs of

[1] Mark Benney, etc., *op. cit.* p. 216.
[2] Milne and Mackenzie, *Straight Fight,* p. 46.
[3] *Ibid.*
[4] Including immigrants from the Commonwealth.

giving up politics and taking to religion. Both indicate a trend towards Conservatism.[1] Undergraduates are, of course, not representative of their age-group; but movements of opinion in universities generally precede similar movements outside.

Assuming that there is an interval of four years between elections, that twenty-five per cent of the new electors vote Liberal or do not vote, a shift of five per cent of the new voters from Labour to Conservative would produce a net gain to the Conservative party of some 210,000 votes, taking the United Kingdom as a whole. In 1951 the Conservative gain exceeded the Labour gain by 533,000 votes, and in 1955 the Labour loss exceeded the Conservative loss by 1,112,000 votes. Moreover, any such shift of opinion would be cumulative, since a large proportion would become 'regulars'.

Even so, the new voters are not so important, except cumulatively, as the non-voters. In the four most recent elections their number was as follows:

1950:	5,500,287
1951:	5,950,874
1955:	8,095,246
1959:	7,526,201

In the 1951 election they were not so important a factor as the shift of the Liberal vote, partly because of the shortage of Liberal candidates, and partly because nearly all Liberal candidates in 1951 lost votes. In 1955, however, the increase in the non-voters was the major factor. Of the loss of two million votes in that year the Conservative party suffered 431,000 and the Labour party 1,544,000. Unfortunately for our present purpose, most of the changes in representation occurred in constituencies subjected to redistribution. Only in twelve constituencies which were not altered, or not altered much, was there a gain by Conservative from Labour or by Labour from Conservative. Table 55 shows the fall in the total vote expressed as a percentage of the electorate, and the parallel fall in the Conservative and Labour vote, also expressed as percentages of the electorate.

[1] As to religion, see Mark Benney, etc., *How People Vote*, p. 111. Roman Catholics tend to vote Labour, but that is a class distinction. It did not, for instance, occur in Bristol N.E. in 1955: Milne and Mackenzie, *Marginal Constituency*, p. 65. They divided equally between Conservative and Labour, but there were few Liberals.

If these changes were due primarily to a differential increase in abstentions, we should have to regard seven of these twelve cases as

	Fall in percentage of electorate in 1951 and 1955		
	Total vote	Conservative vote	Labour vote
Wandsworth C.	6·1	1·4	4·8
Carlisle	5·1	−7·2	0·1
Walthamstow E.	5·0	1·2	5·8
Watford	4·8	−2·0	2·2
Preston S.	4·6	1·8	2·8
Halifax	4·1	0·6	3·5
Hornchurch	4·1	1·4	4·6
Maldon (Essex)	3·9	0·9	3·0
Wrekin (Salop)	3·0	−1·1	4·0
Ayrshire C.	3·0	−0.5	3·5
Ealing N.	2·6	4·2	4·9
Norfolk S.W.	0·0	0·8	−0·8

TABLE 55

normal. Can we find any explanation of the 'abnormality' of the other five? Apparently we can, as follows:

Carlisle. Here there was a Liberal candidate (who secured the support of 12·3 per cent of the electorate) in 1951 but not in 1955. Most of his votes went to the Conservative in 1955, though some went to the Labour candidate, with the result that there was an increase in the Conservative support and virtually no change in the Labour support.

Ealing N. There was a Liberal candidate in 1955, but not in 1951, and he obtained the support of 6·5 per cent of the electorate. He drew most of that support from those who had voted Conservative in 1951, and so the Conservative vote fell more than the Labour vote.

Watford. The explanation is the same as for Carlisle.

Norfolk S.W. This was one of the rare cases where the candidate's personality was of importance. The Labour candidate had been Labour member for the constituency from 1945 to 1951. He had been defeated in 1951 by the transfer of Liberal votes to the Conservative. He was a farmer who had been a farm labourer and thus cut across the class line in an agricultural constituency. He gained only 253 votes, but his opponent lost 382 votes: i.e. the margin was so very small that personality counted.

20-2

The Wrekin. The change may have been due to personality combined with abstention. Both candidates were 'carpet-baggers', but the Labour candidate (a trade union official from S. Wales) had sat from 1945 to 1955. He lost 1568 votes and the Conservative gained 714 votes.

Ayrshire C. There was a small change of boundaries which may have operated against the Labour candidate.

In the 1959 election there was, in general, an increase in the total poll. In the thirty-two constituencies which changed representation, however, seven showed a decrease in the total poll and must be separated from the others. It will also be convenient to ignore constituencies in which there was a Liberal or other minority candidate in 1955 or 1959 but not in both. Table 56 shows what happened where the total poll decreased.

	Fall in percentage of electorate in 1955 and 1959		
	Total vote	Conservative	Labour
Acton	0·8	−0·6	1·4
Nottingham W.	5·2	−0·7	5·9
Reading	1·3	−2·9	4·2
Rochester and Chatham	1·4	−2·1	3·5
Willesden E.	2·8	−1·1	3·9
Brierly Hill (Staffs.)	0·4	−5·1	5·5

TABLE 56

It will be seen that, except in Reading and Brierly Hill, more than half the fall in the Labour vote can be accounted for by an increase in the non-voters.

Table 57 shows what happened in the more numerous constituencies in which the total poll increased. It will be seen that the rise in the total poll was the major factor in eight of these nineteen constituencies and was of some importance in the others.

These facts are sufficient to demonstrate the importance of the non-voters, but not enough to demonstrate that they sway an election. We know from the sampling surveys that the proportion of voters who change sides between elections may be somewhere in the region of ten per cent of the electorate.[1] They tend to cancel out: on the other hand, the Government in power tends to lose popularity between elections (though the Conservative Government gained in 1955 and 1959), and so the Opposition usually has a net gain from 'conversions', though it is generally small. Theoretically it could be twenty per cent (e.g. Conservative + 10 per cent, Labour − 10 per cent), though it is more likely to be four per cent, except in a khaki election or a 'crisis' election like 1931.

	Rise in percentage of electorate in 1955 and 1959		
	Total vote	Conser- vative	Labour
Clapham (Wandsworth)	0·9	2·3	−1·4
All Saints (Birmingham)	0·2	1·4	−1·2
Sparkbrook (Birmingham)	0·4	4·3	−3·9
Yardley (Birmingham)	2·1	4·9	−2·8
Bristol N.E.	1·1	2·8	−2·8
Bristol N.W.	2·3	3·3	−1·0
Coventry S.	0·7	3·0	−2·3
Hartlepools	1·4	2·2	−0·8
Newcastle upon Tyne E.	4·6	4·1	0·5
Wellingborough (Northants)	0·7	1·8	−1·1
Lowestoft (Suffolk)	2·0	4·1	−2·0
Meriden (Warwicks.)	3·0	2·6	0·4
Cleveland (Yorks. N.R.)	2·3	2·4	−0·1
Swansea W.	7·0	4·7	2·3
Oldham E.	2·3	−2·1	1·9
Craigton (Glasgow)	3·8	0·9	2·9
Scotstoun (Glasgow)	2·3	−2·3	4·6
Central Ayrshire	4·2	0·2	4·0
Lanark	1·3	−0·8	2·1

TABLE 57

The non-voters are generally between fifteen and twenty-five per cent of the electorate, but they are made up of

(1) Electors who have died since the register was completed. The

[1] Mark Benney, etc., *How People Vote*, p. 220; R. S. Milne and H. C. Mackenzie, *Straight Fight*, p. 33, where it was only four per cent as between 1950 and 1951 and might be ten per cent over a longer period. Changes to and from Liberals are excluded; R. S. Milne and H. C. Mackenzie, *Marginal Seat*, p. 42. The table on p. 43 is, however, misleading: twenty-six out of 520, i.e. five per cent, changed sides, and they almost cancelled out.

variation, as between one election and another, may be as much as three per cent of the electorate.

(2) Electors who have moved too far to make voting convenient. A stale register will affect the number, but the possible variation cannot be estimated.

(3) Electors who are temporarily absent on polling day. There will be more in summer than in winter, but nobody knows by how much.

(4) Electors who are too ill to vote. Their proportion must be quite large, especially in winter. On the other hand there have been polls of over 90 per cent, and in Fermanagh and South Tyrone in 1951 no less than 93·4 per cent of the electorate voted. There is no reason to believe that the conflicts of Ulster cause the local parties either to 'poll the dead men' or to force the sick to take up their beds and walk.

(5) 'Regular' non-voters who 'don't 'old with politics' or disdain all parties.

(6) Genuine 'floaters' who sometimes vote and sometimes do not, according to the degree of excitement, indignation or gratitude inspired by the parties, the presence or absence of Liberal candidates, the weather, and so forth.

It is impossible, from the information available, to guess at the size of the sixth group. The fall in the percentage of voters from the 84 per cent of 1950 to the 82·5 per cent of 1951 and the 76·8 per cent of 1955 shows, however, how important it can be. Also, it is a differential fall;

Election	Non-voters	Conservative	Labour	Liberal
1923	25·9	28·2	22·6	21·9
1924	19·4	38·0	26·5	14·2
1929	20·5	30·4	29·3	18·6
1931	20·2	43·9	24·5	8·6
1935	25·6	39·9	28·2	4·9

TABLE 58

that is, there are variations due to Conservative and Labour voters respectively becoming apathetic. Possibly this was so between the wars; but it is difficult to use the figures because of the number of uncontested elections, the variation in the number of Liberal candidates, and the different attitudes of the Liberal party towards other parties in

1923, 1924, 1929 and 1931. The figures in Table 58 relate only to contested elections, i.e. the percentages of the non-voters and Conservative, Liberal and Labour voters in contested constituencies in the United Kingdom. The fact that uncontested elections are ignored is offset by the fact that Northern Ireland is included.

The changes in the Liberal vote are misleading, since the number of candidates varied. Also, the Liberal Nationals are regarded as Liberals in 1931 and Conservatives in 1935. Another change of importance, not brought out in the table, is the increase of the electorate by some eight million, mostly 'flappers', in 1929. Nevertheless, it is easy to see what happened. Owing to a light poll and a Radical bias in 1923 (a reaction from the 'hard-faced men' of 1918) a Labour Government came into office in 1924. The Liberals were stupid enough[1] to turn it out before it had become really unpopular; and so at the election of 1924 the Labour party increased its vote, but the right-wing Liberals and the apathetic Conservatives voted Conservative. After five years of Conservative rule the pendulum had swung; and in 1929 one would expect a low poll (due to apathetic Conservatives) and an increase in the Labour vote. The emancipation of the 'flappers', however, resulted in a poll almost as high as in 1924; and both the Labour party and the Liberal party (which had put up more candidates) gained at the expense of the Conservative party. The economic crisis of 1931 altered the normal trend. Oddly enough there was not a higher poll, though at the time we thought there was; and the great Conservative majority was due mainly to Liberal electors. Then the pendulum began to swing normally again; in 1935 there was an increase in non-voters and Labour voters, and a decrease in Conservative and Liberal voters. The pendulum would have completed its swing in 1939 or 1940; but the war delayed it.

Table 59 shows the post-war figures. The low poll of 1945, due to wartime dislocation, has distorted these figures, but the trend is clear. The Labour Government of 1945 received its majority on a low poll. With a very high poll in 1950 it increased its electoral support, but the Conservative vote took the greater part of the increased poll. In 1951 both parties increased their vote at the expense of the Liberal party, but the Conservative increase was greater; and, as we have seen,

---

[1] And the Conservatives clever enough.

the swing of most of the marginal seats was due to the Liberal vote. Though the Conservative party increased its parliamentary majority in 1955, it actually lost votes, mainly through abstentions; but the Labour party suffered worse from abstentions. In 1959 there was an increase in the total poll, but on balance the Labour party lost votes.

Election	Non-voters	Conservative	Labour	Liberal
1945	24·0	30·3	36·5	6·8
1950	16·0	36·5	38·7	7·6
1951	17·5	39·6	40·3	2·1
1955	23·2	38·1	35·6	2·7
1959	21·3	38·8	34·7	4·8

TABLE 59

It must be emphasised that there is never a simple explanation of a change of Government. The Conservative vote at a particular election is compounded of (a) 'regulars' who voted Conservative last time, (b) 'converts' from the Labour and Liberal parties, (c) new voters and (d) persons who did not vote last time. The additions are offset by (e) 'converts' to the Labour and Liberal parties, (f) dead Conservatives and (g) persons who voted Conservative last time but abstained this time. The Labour vote is similarly compounded. It is impossible to say that any addition or subtraction is the 'cause' of a swing. Where there is a normal interval (four to five years) between elections, however, the new voters are important; and, since there is usually a greater increase or decrease in the non-voters than there is in the vote of either party, those non-voters are obviously important, though the 'converts' count twice because they increase the Conservative (or Labour) vote and also decrease the Labour (or Conservative) vote.

On the other hand, elections are won not by 'swings' in the total vote but by changes in the marginal constituencies. The 'swing' in the total vote, whatever it is—probably it is not the 'psephological swing' —is relevant only because the British electors in general vote (and refrain from voting) according to a pattern. In the words of the old music-hall song, when father turns we all turn, or at least a certain number of us.

APPENDIX I

THE PSEPHOLOGICAL SWING

Though Oxford has converted 'electoral arithmetic' into 'psephology', there is no suggestion that there is anything wrong with Oxford arithmetic. The psephological swing was invented by Mr D. E. Butler for a specific purpose, to enable an estimate to be made of the effect of a changed balance of opinion, as estimated at a public opinion poll taken immediately before a general election. It should be noted at the outset that an error is introduced if the poll is taken before nomination day, because electors will indicate an intention to vote, say, Liberal, but may not be able to do so because no Liberal candidates are nominated in their constituencies. If, however, the poll is taken after nomination day, it is reasonable to assume that the distribution of votes at the election, taking the country as a whole, will be approximately the same as that shown by the poll.

The figures produced by the poll have to be expressed in percentages, and a complete poll would produce something like Conservative 33%, Labour 33%, Liberal 3%, Others 1%, Will not Vote 20%, Don't Know 10%. In fact, however, it is not practicable to ascertain with any accuracy how many will not vote; and the 'Don't Know' category has to be omitted because, apart from other considerations, there is nothing about 'Don't Know' on the ballot paper.[1] Hence the poll is published in the form Conservative 48%, Labour 47%, Liberal 4%, Others 1%. The comparable figures for the last general election are the respective percentages of the votes cast for the three main parties, amended to allow for any constituencies in which candidates were elected without opposition: but this is presumably too complicated, for the psephologists use the respective percentages of the votes actually cast, e.g. in 1955[2] the figures were Conservative 49·7%, Labour 46·4%, Liberal 2·7%, Communist 0·1%, Others 1·1%.

---

[1] It would be an interesting experiment to put it in, especially in countries where adult franchise has been given to educationally backward people, and with compulsory voting.
[2] D. E. Butler, *The British General Election of 1955*, p. 171.

The problem is to estimate how the change in the balance of opinion since 1955, as shown by the poll, is likely to alter the distribution of seats among the parties. This is not at all easy because:

(*a*) Though Great Britain is electorally a very homogeneous country, there may well be regional differences; e.g. opinion tends to change less quickly in Wales and Scotland than in England; and, further, Northern Ireland is very peculiar.

(*b*) There may be local factors, such as the candidature of a popular local man or a dispute in the local party machine or heavy unemployment.

(*c*) Many people may not vote, and this may operate differentially; e.g. the number of apathetic Conservatives may be larger, and the number of apathetic Labour supporters smaller, than in 1955.

(*d*) In some constituencies in which there were Liberal or Communist candidates in 1955 there may be none this time, or vice versa.

(*e*) In the marginal constituencies, where the gains and losses will be made and incurred, the fierceness of the contest may produce less of a change than in the safe seats.

(*f*) There is no reason why the changes should be in percentages: an increase of 25 per cent in the Conservative vote in a safe Labour seat may be equal to an increase of 12 per cent in a safe Conservative seat.[1]

(*g*) The changes due to deaths, coming of age and immigration may be very important, especially in individual constituencies.

The psephologists are of course aware of these difficulties.[2] If our purpose is only to discover whether there will be a change of Govern-

---

[1] Also, an all-round increase produces differential percentages, thus:

		Conservative	Labour	Liberal	Total
1951 election	No.	40,000	30,000	10,000	80,000
	%	50	37·5	12·5	100
1955 election	No.	50,000	40,000	20,000	110,000
	%	45·5	36·4	18·2	100
Change	%	−4·5	−1·1	+5·7	

There is thus, in psephological terms, a 'Conservative swing to Labour' of 1·7%.

[2] See McCallum and Readman, *The British General Election of 1945*, p. 278; H. G. Nicholas, *The British General Election of 1950*, pp. 315–16; D. E. Butler, *The British General Election of 1951*, pp. 267–75; D. E. Butler, *The British General Election of 1955*, pp. 207–8.

ment they probably will not vitiate the result, and some of the errors may cancel out. At any rate it is reasonable for a first approximation to assume that the changes will be uniform and to ignore the votes of the Liberal party and the splinter groups. Table 60 gives figures calculated on this basis.

	1955 vote (%)	Poll (%)	Change (%)
Conservative	49·7	48	−1·7
Labour	46·4	47	+0·6

TABLE 60

We may now assume that every constituency in which there was in 1955 a Conservative majority over Labour of less than 2·3 per cent will be won by Labour; and by finding out the number of such constituencies we ascertain whether there will probably be a Labour Government.

Unfortunately, the psephologists expressed the change by saying that there was a 'swing' from Conservative to Labour of one-half 2·3 per cent, i.e. 1·15 per cent, and thus led people to assume that the 'swing' was brought about by people who voted Conservative in one election voting Labour in the next. Even if it is put in such a way as to allow for the changes in the registers, such as dead men going off and young men coming on, it may give a false impression. Thus, after comparing 1935 and 1945 the authors of *The British General Election of 1945* spoke of the 'movement of opinion from Conservative to Labour'.[1] But this may not be the reason for a change: possibly the Conservatives are apathetic and cannot be bothered to vote in sufficient number; or the Liberals, who put up 200 candidates in one election, might put up 500 at the next and take more votes from Conservatives than from Labour. In other words, the 'swing' is a purely artificial concept, useful for the purpose for which it was invented, but not necessarily useful for other purposes.

Nevertheless, the psephologists appeared on television in 1955 and, having worked out the 'swing' for one constituency, at once estimated

[1] Page 264.

the number of Conservative gains by means of an empirical formula. Even given that the formula is a rough approximation, a single constituency cannot produce a 'swing' because any of the difficulties already mentioned may apply to it. The 'swing' is a hypothetical formulation of a national phenomenon which is useful because it is a rough average. Other commentators have gone even further: they have thought to calculate a national 'swing' at a general election from a 'swing' at a by-election or local authority election, where factors not yet mentioned are involved.

Table 61 takes the simplest possible case of two elections in a single constituency, without any change in the electorate.

	Voters				Percentage change
	1st election		2nd election		
	No.	%	No.	%	
Conservative	36,000	51·4	33,000	49·3	+2·1
Labour	34,000	48·6	34,000	50·7	−2·1
Not voting	20,000	22·2	23,000	25·5	+3·3

TABLE 61

We see clearly that 3000 Conservative electors have decided not to vote, while the Labour vote has remained steady. There is a psephological swing to Labour of 2·1 per cent, though not a single vote has swung to Labour. Clearly the result of the elections ought to have been expressed as in Table 62.

	Electors				Percentage change
	1st election		2nd election		
	No.	%	No.	%	
Conservative	36,000	40	33,000	36·7	−3·3
Labour	34,000	37·8	34,000	37·8	—
Not voting	20,000	22·2	23,000	25·5	+3·3

TABLE 62

This shows what has really happened—a swing from Conservative to Not Voting of 3·3 per cent.

So simple a case never occurs. An example of a simple situation is that of the Broxtowe division of Nottinghamshire in 1950 and 1951. Table 63 gives the figures expressed in psephological terms.

	Voters				Percentage change
	1950		1951		
	No.	%	No.	%	
Conservative	13,445	27·5	13,274	27·3	−0·2
Labour	35,471	72·5	35,317	72·7	+0·2
Not voting	7,999	14·0	8,994	15·8	+1·8

TABLE 63

There was thus a psephological swing to Labour of 0·2 per cent, whereas what probably happened was that the Conservative vote dropped a little more in number, but a little less in percentage, than the Labour vote. This is shown clearly by Table 64.

	Electors				Percentage change
	1950		1951		
	No.	%	No.	%	
Conservative	13,445	23·6	13,274	23·1	−0·5
Labour	35,471	62·4	35,317	61·1	−1·3
Not voting	7,999	14·0	8,994	15·8	+1·8

TABLE 64

A more complicated situation arises where there are three candidates at both elections. To be fair, we ought first to take a normal case, and so we will take Bournemouth East and Christchurch in 1950 and 1951. Table 65 shows the result in psephological terms.

	Voters				Percentage change
	1950		1951		
	No.	%	No.	%	
Conservative	27,677	58·8	29,138	63·3	+4·5
Labour	12,790	27·2	11,550	25·1	−2·1
Liberal	6,594	14·0	5,338	11·6	−2·4
Not voting	8,317	15·0	10,910	19·0	+4·0

TABLE 65

317

There was thus a psephological swing from Labour to Conservative. It is however plain that, though there was a 'swing' to Conservative, there was also a 'swing' to non-voting; and though there was a 'swing' from Labour there was also a 'swing' from Liberal. Who swung from what to what cannot be guessed from this analysis because, above the line, only voters and not all electors are considered. Table 66 gives a clearer picture, since it takes the percentages of electors.

	Electors				Percentage change
	1950		1951		
	No.	%	No.	%	
Conservative	27,677	50·0	29,138	51·2	+1·2
Labour	12,790	23·1	11,550	20·3	−2·8
Liberal	6,594	11·9	5,338	9·5	−2·4
Not voting	8,317	15·0	10,910	19·0	+4·0

TABLE 66

This is a very different kettle of fish, though even here (this being a safe Conservative seat) we notice how percentages distort the picture. The Conservative vote went up by 1500 and the Labour vote went down by 1200, though the one is an increase of 1·2 per cent and the other a decrease of 2·8 per cent.

Let us now take an extreme case, that of the Berwick Upon Tweed division of Northumberland in 1950 and 1951, and it is as well to mention that Sir William Beveridge was Liberal candidate in 1950 but not in 1951. The psephological results are shown in Table 67.

	Voters				Percentage change
	1950		1951		
	No.	%	No.	%	
Conservative	14,804	43·9	17,632	52·7	+8·8
Labour	8,651	25·1	11,069	33·1	+8·0
Liberal	10,260	31·0	4,759	14·2	−16·8
Not voting	8,360	20·0	8,978	21·2	+1·2

TABLE 67

The psephological swing is half the Conservative gain *plus* half the

Labour loss; but there was no Labour loss, so presumably in this instance the swing ought to be half the Conservative gain *minus* half the Labour gain, i.e. 0·4 per cent. It is however plain that the dominant factor was the division of Sir William Beveridge's personal (as distinct from party) vote between the Conservative and Labour candidates. The position becomes plainer if we take percentages of electors and not of voters (Table 68).

| | Electors | | | | Percentage change |
| | 1950 | | 1951 | | |
	No.	%	No.	%	
Conservative	14,804	35·2	17,632	41·5	+6·3
Labour	8,651	20·5	11,069	26·1	+5·6
Liberal	10,260	24·3	4,759	11·2	−13·1
Not voting	8,360	20·0	8,978	21·2	+1·2

TABLE 68

We can now see what happened to Sir William Beveridge's personal vote, which was something like 13 per cent of the electorate.

Again, there were in 1950 and 1951 many constituencies of which Henley-on-Thames was typical, i.e. constituencies in which there was a Liberal candidate in 1950 but not in 1951. Table 69 shows the results in psephological terms.

| | Voters | | | | Percentage change |
| | 1950 | | 1951 | | |
	No.	%	No.	%	
Conservative	20,488	49·4	23,621	58·0	+8·6
Labour	14,709	35·5	17,090	42·0	+6·5
Liberal	6,255	15·1	—	—	−15·1
Not voting	9,297	18·3	11,261	21·6	+3·3

TABLE 69

Calculating psephological swing as for Berwick Upon Tweed we have a swing from Labour to Conservative of 1·05 per cent, though obviously the dominant factor was the distribution of the Liberal voters of 1950 in 1951. We get a better view if we consider electors instead of voters (Table 70).

	Electors				Percentage change
	1950		1951		
	No.	%	No.	%	
Conservative	20,488	40·4	23,621	45·5	+5·1
Labour	14,709	29·0	17,090	32·9	+3·9
Liberal	6,255	12·3	—	—	−12·3
Not voting	9,297	18·3	11,261	21·6	+3·3

TABLE 70

When the results in a single constituency in successive elections are compared, the important factors are:

(1) *Changes in the Registers.* These include the addition of the young electors, the deletion of deceased electors, and removals to and from the constituency. The last factor may be very important owing to rehousing or new development (e.g. new towns or factories or building estates). These factors are less important where the interval between elections is short, and for that reason (and the absence of redistribution changes) the elections of 1950 and 1951 have been taken in the examples above. There is, however, no means of judging what effect the changes have upon voting. On the national plane internal immigration cancels out, except so far as some of the migrants vote for Liberals and splinter parties: but in a single constituency it may be very important. The changes due to lapse of time are also important: and when one talks about 'swing' it is wise to remember that it may be due, in whole or in part, to the young voters.

(2) *Local factors.* These may be such matters as a strong candidate (e.g. Sir William Beveridge at Berwick Upon Tweed in 1950), a dispute in a local party, a weak organisation or lack of money.

(3) *The intervention of third parties.* The fundamental assumption of psephology is the two-party system: but there may be 200 Liberal candidates at one election and 500 at another: and in a particular

constituency there may be a splinter candidate, perhaps (as on Clydeside in 1935) a strong one.

(4) *Genuine national trends.* These may be an increase or decrease in the popularity of the Conservative party, or the Labour party or the Liberal party, or any two of them, or all of them. There are in fact four main 'parties', Conservative, Labour, Liberal and Non-voters. Between the wars the Labour vote increased at every election except that of 1931, whether or not the Conservative vote increased. In 1950 both the Conservative party and the Labour party increased their votes. Since 1950 the 'non-voter's party' has become increasingly important though it declined in 1959.

It is, however, easier to criticise the psephological swing than to produce a better. What one would like is a more refined technique which would allow for variations in the Liberal vote and the non-voters. It should however be said that in 'straight fights' the variations in the non-voters are irrelevant, provided that the 'swing to Conservative' is, as the psephologists intended, a purely artificial formulation and does *not* mean necessarily that more people have voted Conservative (it may mean that more Labour supporters have watched television). Nor would the Liberal vote matter if there was a Liberal candidate in each constituency and his vote stayed at $\pm 10\%$, as it tended to do in 1951 and 1955. What confuses prognostication is that the Liberals keep popping in and out, and some of them make 'pacts' with Conservative associations so as to win on the combined Liberal and Conservative vote.

In using the sample polls a more refined technique is impracticable. We have not, and cannot have, the proportion of non-voters, because some are dead, some sick or bed-ridden, some intended to vote but forgot, some found the television programme too interesting, some decided at the last moment that they 'had no clothes fit to wear', some, probably, got annoyed with candidates who kept driving up and down with their loudspeakers blaring, and so forth. Since one knows the number of Liberal candidates, it is possible to determine the average vote in each constituency. In 1955, for instance, 2·1 per cent of the electors voted Liberal; but in three-cornered contests (Conservative–

Labour–Liberal) 10·4 per cent of the electors voted Liberal on the average. Even if one could get that figure, however, one cannot judge how the Conservative and Labour votes will be affected by a Liberal intervention. We do know that in 1955 the percentages of electors were as in Table 71.

	Conservative	Labour	Liberal	Non-voters
All contests	37·8	36·4	2·1	23·2
Straight fights	38·1	38·0	—	23·5
Three-cornered	38·4	29·1	10·4	21·8

TABLE 71

We must not, however, jump to the conclusion that when a 'straight fight' in one election is followed by a 'three-cornered contest', the Liberal votes will be gained mainly at the expense of the Labour candidate. The fact is that the Liberal party has a not unexpected fondness for suburbia, small towns, semi-rural county constituencies, and the Celtic fringe, in which (except in Wales) the Conservative vote is usually higher than the Labour vote. In other words, the third line contains selected constituencies. If there is a very large increase in the number of Liberal candidates we should expect the Conservative and Labour votes to be nearer the proportion in the top line (though both would be reduced): and this proportion is exactly what the psephologist uses for his 'swing'.

Even so, the potential inaccuracy of the public opinion poll, on which the swing is based, should be recognised. An error of +1 per cent in the Conservative vote probably means an error of −1 per cent in the Labour vote: and in a constituency with 50,000 votes this would mean an error of 1000 votes, which in 1955 would have affected twenty-one seats. An equal error the other way would have affected nineteen seats.

An attempt to estimate from the early returns is almost certainly doomed to failure, though those returns do show which way the wind is blowing. In 1955 the first return in an unchanged constituency was that at Cheltenham, which gave a psephological swing of 2·2 per cent, whereas the national swing was 1·6 per cent. The present writer produced a more refined alternative (Table 72), bringing in the non-voters.

	Conservative	Labour	Non-voters
Prediction	40·0	38·9	21·0
Actual	38·1	38·0	23·5

TABLE 72

In other words, the estimate of non-voters was 2·5 per cent in error, and (as with the psephologists) the Conservative vote was exaggerated. An estimate for three-cornered contests, based on Finchley, was even more unsuccessful. The psephologists gave a swing of 1·0 per cent as against a national swing of 1·6 per cent—which was not unreasonable: but the more refined method gave the figures in Table 73.

	Conservative	Labour	Liberal	Non-voters
Prediction	34·1	29·7	11·6	27·0
Actual	38·4	29·1	10·4	21·8

TABLE 73

Another attempt, made with Poole, was more successful. The psephologist swing was 1·1 per cent, against the national swing of 1·6 per cent. Table 74 gives the refined estimate.

	Conservative	Labour	Liberal	Non-voters
Prediction	37·0	30·5	11·0	19·9
Actual	38·4	29·1	10·4	21·8

TABLE 74

That was better; but clearly one has to choose the right constituency; and who knows which is the right one?

In any case, refinement completely breaks down where a Liberal candidate appears only at the second election. Consider, for instance, Table 75, which represents the psephologists' own constituency, Oxford, in 1951 and 1955.

21-2

This gave a psephological swing of 1·4 per cent,[1] which compared favourably with the national swing of 1·6 per cent: but it was a pure accident. But how can one extend the whole range of figures to other constituencies where the Liberal vote may be greater or less and the balance of profit and loss, as between Conservative and Labour, quite different? A similar problem would arise where there was a Liberal candidate in 1951, but not in 1955.

	Percentages of electors			
	Conservative	Labour	Liberal	Non-voters
1951	45·9	36·1	—	18
1955	40·9	29·4	7·9	21·8
Changes	−5·0	−6·7	+7·9	+3·8

TABLE 75

On the other hand, a useful scheme can be worked out for by-elections. It is based on two assumptions, that the general election figures will be distorted in a by-election, and that by-elections exhibit a trend of their own. The method involves using percentages of electors, comparing with the previous general election, and taking the median. For instance, in Table 76 the Conservative vote in straight fights in 1957–8 is compared with that in the general election of 1955.

	(%)		(%)
Leicestershire S.E.	−16·1	Newcastle N.	−10·7
Islington N.	−15·2	Warwick	−10·1
Hornsey	−13·6	Lewisham N.	− 9·2
Bristol W.	−13·2	Dorsetshire N.	− 8·6
East Ham N.	−13·2	Wednesbury	− 7·5
Beckenham	−12·5	Wigan	− 7·4
Kelvingrove	−12·2	St Helens	− 7·2

TABLE 76

The median is −11 per cent. If the Conservative vote in the constituency was, at the general election, 47 per cent of the electorate, one assumes that the Conservative vote in the by-election will be 36 per cent of the electorate. For the Labour party the median is −1·1 per

[1] It will be appreciated that the swing works on the percentage of *voters*, not of *electors*.

cent, and if the Labour vote at the general election was 31 per cent of the electorate, in the by-election it will be 29·9 per cent of the electorate. Other lists are necessary for (*a*) three-cornered contests at both elections, and (*b*) three-cornered contest at the by-election but not at the general election: and in both cases the Liberal vote is similarly treated. This method was used at a series of by-elections in June 1958, with the results given in Table 77.

		Forecast	Actual
Argyll	Conservative	10,900	12,541
	Liberal	7,800	7,375
	Labour	6,800	6,884
	Majority	3,100	5,166
Ealing S.	Conservative	18,700	17,417
	Labour	11,300	11,258
	Liberal	10,600	5,956
	Majority	7,400	6,159
St Helens	Labour	34,200	26,405
	Conservative	10,600	14,411
	Majority	23,600	11,904
Weston-super-Mare	Conservative	16,200	21,271
	Labour	14,300	11,295
	Liberal	11,100	10,588
	Majority	1,900	9,976
Wigan	Labour	27,900	27,415
	Conservative	7,800	10,248
	Communist	?	972
	Majority	20,100	17,167

TABLE 77

Obviously no claim to accuracy can be made. The method excludes local factors. For instance, Sir Hartley Shawcross, who was the Labour candidate for St Helens at the general election, no doubt had a substantial personal support which his successor did not receive. Moreover there was conflict over the succession—it was alleged that the selection committee had been 'packed' by the Roman Catholics.[1] In

---

[1] The gross over-estimation of the Liberal vote at Ealing S. was, however, due to defect of technique. There was only one previous by-election at which there had been a Liberal candidate at both elections, and so the list for change from straight fight to three-cornered was used. This put up the Liberal estimate.

any event, the choice of the median minimises the national trend. A nearer approach to accuracy might be obtained by taking only the by-elections since the previous first of January; but the shorter the list the more important becomes a 'freak'. Nor can one avoid distortion due to having a substantial number of by-elections in constituencies of a particular type, e.g. safe Conservative seats.

It should be added that the technique cannot be used for forecasting the result of the next general election. At a by-election the elector is not voting for a Government, and the poll is generally low. In 1957–8 three by-elections showed an increased poll and twenty-one a decreased poll. The largest decrease was 29·1 per cent of the electorate.

THE CLASS DIVISION IN BRITISH POLITICS

The summary account of the class division in British politics, given in Chapter x, needs to be supported by more detailed evidence. The subject must be studied in periods, since there was some change after each alteration in the franchise.

I. FROM 1832 TO 1865

Examination of the English boroughs which were wholly or predominantly whig, Radical, or Liberal or Peelite from 1832 to 1865, shows that they fell almost exclusively into two groups. First, there were most of the great cities and the industrial towns, including all the London boroughs, Birmingham, Manchester, Bristol (especially after 1847), Coventry, Wolverhampton, Walsall (after 1835), Northampton, Peterborough, Derby, Grimsby, Chester, Stockport, Salford, Ashton-under-Lyne, Oldham, Bury, Sheffield, Huddersfield and Halifax. Secondly, there were many small boroughs, which clearly remained under 'influence' until 1868. Most of the boroughs which were wholly or predominantly Conservative also fell into this latter class.

Most of the English county divisions which were wholly or predominantly Liberal were the urbanised or industrialised divisions, like Middlesex, East Surrey, South Staffordshire, North Derbyshire, East Cumberland, the West Riding and Durham (not, however, Lancashire). Most of the other English county divisions tended to be Conservative, though often the two seats were divided between the parties, usually without a contest.

Wales followed England in these respects; but Scotland was almost exclusively Liberal in the burghs and more Conservative than Liberal in the counties.

Allowing for 'influence', the distribution between the landed interest and the urban classes is plain, though allowance must be made in Scotland for the Liberal influence of Presbyterianism.

2. FROM 1868 TO 1880

After 1865, London became rather more Conservative, especially in Westminster and the City. In the southern boroughs there was no great change, except that some seats under 'influence' disappeared. In most of the Midland boroughs the Liberals predominated. The Lancashire boroughs, on the other hand, became more Conservative, whereas Yorkshire and Durham became predominantly Liberal. The Welsh boroughs did the same and (except for four seats in 1874) the Scottish burghs were entirely Liberal.

The English counties became predominantly Conservative, except Middlesex, Cornwall, Bedfordshire, Derbyshire, the West Riding and Durham. The Liberals gained considerably in the Welsh counties and in most of the Scottish counties.

These changes, though evident, were perhaps not as marked as might have been anticipated. The class structure was of course changing, the wealthier industrialists tending to become Victorian 'gentlemen' and a larger professional element developing in the towns, while the landowners were becoming more and more interested in mines, railways and industry generally. Simultaneously and consequentially, a class division was developing between 'masters' and men, and more in Yorkshire than in Lancashire, where the small, family textile factory continued. The first 'class-conscious' working men were the miners. On the other hand, this did not at first make the Conservative party the party of the landowners and the 'bosses' and the Liberal party the party of the workers. First, there was a religious element. Though eventually most of the 'bosses' transferred from Nonconformity to the Church of England, they did not do so forthwith, and indeed the change was generally effected by their sons and grandsons. Also, where Nonconformity was strong among the working class, as in the 'Celtic fringe'—Cornwall, Devon, Wales and Scotland[1]—and in Yorkshire, the Liberals stood to gain by the enfranchisement of the urban householders. Elsewhere, as Disraeli recognised, the Conservative party stood to gain, partly because of opposition to 'bosses' (though this

[1] It is of course appreciated that Presbyterianism is 'conformity' and not 'nonconformity' in Scotland.

was offset by the movement of the 'bosses' to the Conservative party), and partly because of exactly the opposite, the lack of 'class consciousness' and the deference to social superiors. In the result, southern England and Lancashire tended to become more Conservative and the rest of industrial England more Liberal.

3. FROM 1885 TO 1910

The election of 1885 must be considered separately because the defection of the Liberal Unionists over Home Rule in 1886 considerably altered the party distribution. The redistribution of seats in 1885 was so considerable that comparison with 1880 is not easy, except in the boroughs which continued to return one member or two members. There the general picture was of a swing to Conservatism in the southern boroughs and Lancashire, while the rest of the northern boroughs, together with Wales and Scotland, remained Liberal. In the larger boroughs, including London, there was a general swing to Conservatism, but an obvious tendency towards differentiation according to class. In London the West End and the suburbs tended to be Conservative, while the East End tended to be Liberal. In the larger towns, the results were as shown in Table 78.

Bristol	Three Liberal, one Conservative (W.)
Birmingham	All Liberal
Wolverhampton	Two Liberal, one Conservative (W.)
Nottingham	Two Liberal, one Conservative (E.)
Manchester	Five Conservative, one Liberal (S.)
Salford	Two Liberal, one Conservative (W.)
Liverpool	Seven Conservative, one Liberal (Exchange)
Sheffield	Three Conservative, two Liberal (Attercliffe and Brightside)
Bradford	All Liberal
Leeds	Three Conservative, two Liberal (W. & S.)
Hull	Two Liberal, one Conservative (C.)
Glasgow	All Liberal
Edinburgh	All Liberal

TABLE 78

The most remarkable phenomenon of the election of 1885 was, however, that so many of the English county divisions went Liberal.

Middlesex, Surrey, Kent, Hertfordshire, Berkshire, Sussex, the East Riding and Westmoreland were strictly Conservative; but Cornwall, Herefordshire, Suffolk, Bedfordshire, Northumberland and Durham were entirely Liberal; and all other counties except Hampshire, Lincolnshire and Lancashire had at least half the divisions Liberal. Even Lancashire had eleven Liberal seats to twelve Conservative seats. Wales and Scotland, too, were almost entirely Liberal. Wales had only four Conservative seats, and Scotland had only seven.

For the interpretation of these results, three factors have to be considered. The first is 'organisation'. The evidence available is not very considerable, but Liberal organisation (on the 'Birmingham plan') was apparently most effective in the Home Counties and the smaller towns of the south. The second factor was Nonconformity, including Presbyterianism in Scotland. This was the dominant factor in Wales, Scotland, the West of England, some of the Midland counties, and perhaps Lancashire, Yorkshire and Durham. The third factor was class, though that was an aspect of Nonconformity, for the free churches were powerful among the working class precisely in the areas named above. There were, however, other factors. If the election of 1885 is considered alone, it would point to the conclusion that a great many rural householders voted against the landlords. We shall see, however, that from 1886 most of the rural divisions went Conservative; and it is impossible to believe that the rural householders changed their minds about their landlords within a year. The probable explanation is that pressure towards conformity had not yet begun to operate with sufficient force, so that Joseph Chamberlain's 'three acres and a cow' proved temporarily attractive. In 1886 Chamberlain was on the same side as the landlords, the landlords and all the 'best people' were Unionist, and the farm labourer had no interest whatever in Home Rule.

It is impossible to draw useful conclusions from the election of 1886 by itself. The Liberal organisations were split; many candidates could not find the money for a second election within a year; candidates had to be withdrawn to avoid splitting the Unionist vote; and the confusion among the electorate must have been considerable. On the other hand, many constituencies which were Liberal in 1885 were Unionist in 1886,

1892 and 1895. They included Chelsea, Clapham, two seats in St Pancras, two in Islington, Stepney, Hastings, Hythe, Bristol S., Salisbury, the whole of Birmingham and several other Midland constituencies, two seats in Salford, Bury, Barrow-in-Furness, three divisions of Essex, two of Dorset, three of Cornwall, two of Devon, two of Somerset, three of Wiltshire, sixteen county seats in the Midlands, four in East Anglia, five in the North-West, and two in Yorkshire. Many seats were, however, marginal, being Liberal in 1885 and 1892 but Unionist in 1886 and 1895. Moreover, only eleven seats in the whole of Great Britain were Unionist in 1886 but otherwise consistently Liberal from 1885 to 1910.

If we add these eleven seats to the other seats consistently Liberal from 1886 to 1910, we obtain a total of 112, of which sixty-six were in England, twenty-three in Wales and twenty-three in Scotland. Of the English seats, all except two in the boroughs (both in Southampton) and five in the counties were in industrial areas. In other words, nearly all the safe Liberal seats were in industrial areas, except in Wales and Scotland, where religion still played a part.

With the single exception of Edinburgh West, all the ninety-seven seats consistently Unionist from 1886 to 1910 were in England. There were fourteen in London, and they fall into two groups, residential areas like Hammersmith, Hampstead, Wandsworth, Clapham and Norwood, and business centres like Holborn, Strand and the City of London. In the boroughs were thirty safe Unionist seats. They included six cathedral towns and some other smallish towns like Croydon, Gravesend, Hythe, Taunton, Dover and Windsor. Some of the great towns (Bristol, Sheffield and Hull) tended to follow the London example; but the Chamberlains controlled Birmingham (seven seats) and Alderman Salvidge kept five seats in Liverpool for well-behaved Conservatives who followed Chamberlain.

In the counties there were fifty-two safe Unionist seats. Of these, twenty-three were in the southern counties from Essex to Hampshire. There were none in Cornwall or Wiltshire and only six in Dorset, Devon, Somerset and Gloucestershire. The Midlands provided thirteen, nine of which were in Worcestershire, Shropshire and Lincolnshire. Lancashire provided five, but the West Riding of Yorkshire only one,

THE CLASS DIVISION IN BRITISH POLITICS

though there were four in the other Ridings. The far north provided one only, in Cumberland.

Excluding Scotland and Wales, where no Unionist could claim a safe seat (except, as has been said, in the residential part of Edinburgh), and excluding also Birmingham and Liverpool, where 'Joe's Caucus' was triumphant, there are clearly two factors. The 'Celtic fringe' was not really Celtic—though perhaps Devon, Dorset, Wiltshire, Somerset, Gloucestershire and Herefordshire were less well colonised by the Anglo-Saxons, or better colonised by the Welsh; the Nonconformist tradition was, however, very strong in the West. It had been strong in Lancashire and Yorkshire, too, but it grew appreciably weaker. Lancashire continued its generally Conservative tradition, but otherwise most of the industrial areas were Liberal, and the main strength of Conservatism was in the small towns, the residential areas, and the rural county divisions.

'Class-consciousness' developed among the working class late in the nineteenth century. It began with the miners, so that the mining areas were solidly Liberal until they became Labour. It then spread to the West Riding generally and to the East End of London. Lancashire and the Midlands, where the small industry was more common—the Chamberlains, it will be remembered, were manufacturers of screws—followed much more slowly. But this brings us to the next period.

4. FROM 1923 TO 1935

The Labour party came into the picture in 1906, but in competition with the Liberal party, and so in the comments above seats which were won by Labour in 1906 and 1910 were regarded as Liberal seats. The party was reorganised and broadened in 1918, but it did not become the alternative to the Conservative party until 1924. In spite of the growth of the Labour party, the consequences of the wartime split between Lloyd George's faction and Asquith's faction, the extension of the franchise, and the redistribution of 1918, many of the former Liberal seats were Liberal in 1923—for instance, Islington E., Stoke Newington, Hackney C., Bethnal Green S.W., Bristol S., Wolverhampton E., one Stockport seat, several Manchester seats, one Oldham seat, Rochdale, one Blackburn seat, Dewsbury, Halifax, Middlesbrough (now two seats), Stockton, Hartlepool, all the seats in Cornwall and most of those in Devonshire, Somersetshire and Wiltshire, Tewkesbury and Stroud in Gloucestershire, Rugby in Warwickshire, Mid Bedford, three seats in Leicestershire, Louth in Lincolnshire, Heywood and Lancaster in Lancashire, four seats in Yorkshire, and Hexham in Northumberland. These were by no means all the Liberal seats, but they show the persistence of the political tradition. In fact, if allowance be made for redistribution, most of the seats which were Liberal in 1923 were also Liberal in 1906. Of the 114 Liberal constituencies in 1923 which can be identified as existing in 1906, only twenty were not Liberal in 1906. Three were Labour, two were Liberal Unionist, and fifteen were Conservative.

The great majority of the constituencies which were Liberal in 1923 were, however, marginal both in the Edwardian period and in the inter-war period. A few—three in London, eleven in the English boroughs, and about forty in the English counties, became safe Conservative seats. Of such safe Conservative seats there were twenty-five in London, fifty-two in the English boroughs, 131 in the English counties, one in Wales, and nineteen in Scotland.

To obtain comparable figures for the Labour party it is necessary to ignore the general election of 1931, when so many famous safe seats toppled over and decimated the Labour party. Accepting that that election was a slaughter and not a normal election, the Labour party had 109 safe seats, of which fifteen were in London, thirty-three in English boroughs, thirty-four in English counties, sixteen in Wales, and twenty-one in Scotland.

In London, the Conservative safe seats included all the southern suburbs from Putney to Woolwich W.; all west London except the extreme west, Hammersmith and Fulham W. (Fulham E. went Labour at a famous by-election in 1934; but the by-election was famous because Fulham E. was a 'safe' Conservative seat); a pocket in the northern suburbs consisting of Stoke Newington and Hackney N.; and the commercial area, Westminster, Holborn and the City of London. One section of the safer Labour seats stretched along the south bank of the river from Battersea N. to Rotherhithe, but neither Lambeth seat was quite safe, nor was Southwark N. (though Southwark C. and S.E. were).

The other section was north of the river and east and north of the City, but not including Bethnal Green.

Conservative	Labour
Bristol W.	Bristol E.
Birmingham, Edgbaston	
Hockley	
Handsworth	
Sparkbrook	
Moseley	
Nottingham C.	Nottingham W.
Manchester, Rusholme	Manchester, Gorton
Moss-side	Ardwick
Exchange	Clayton
	Platting
Liverpool, Wavertree	Liverpool, Scotland
East Toxteth	
Fairfield	
West Derby	
Walton	
Exchange	
Sheffield, Hallam	Sheffield, Attercliffe
Eccleshall	Brightside
	Hillsborough
Leeds, N. and N.E.	Leeds, S. and S.E.
Glasgow, Cathcart	Glasgow, Bridgeton
Central	Camlachie
Hillsend	Gorbals
Kelvingrove	Govan
Pollok	St Rollox
	Shettleston
	Springburn
	Tradeston

TABLE 79

Greater London was similarly divided. All the county divisions of Middlesex except Acton and Enfield were solidly Conservative, as were the boroughs of Ealing and Willesden E., while the boroughs of Willesden W., Edmonton and Tottenham N. were safe Labour seats. All the county seats of Surrey and the borough seats of Croydon, Kingston, Wimbledon and Richmond were safe Conservative seats. Among Kent's eleven county seats eight were classifiable as safe, and so was the borough of Hythe. There were no safe Labour seats either in Surrey or in Kent. Essex was generally marginal, with only four

safe Conservative seats, while the borough seat of East Ham S. was a
safe Labour seat.

In the great provincial cities, the safe seats were as shown in
Table 79.

Conservative	Labour
Lancashire, Stretford	Newton
Middleton	West Houghton
Royton	Farnworth
Waterloo	Ince
Chorley	Wigan
Clitheroe	Leigh
Fylde	Rochdale
Lancaster	St Helens
Lonsdale	Burnley
Bury	Nelson and Colne
Blackpool	
Southport	
Yorkshire, Pudsey and Otley	Rother Valley
Barkston Ash	Penistone
Ripon	Colne Valley
Skipton	Wentworth
Howdenshire	Doncaster
Holderness	Don Valley
Buckrose	Hemsworth
Thirsk and Malton	Pontefract
Scarborough and Whitby	Normanton
Richmond	Rothwell
	Shipley
	Keighley
	Rotherham
	Barnsley
	Dewsbury

TABLE 80

In the other counties south of the Thames and the Bristol Avon there
were thirty-four county seats and ten borough seats which were safe
Conservative seats, but not a single safe Labour seat. The counties of
Buckingham, Oxford, Gloucester, Hereford, Worcester and Salop
provided nineteen safe Conservative seats (including four borough

seats) and only one safe Labour seat (Forest of Dean). East Anglia provided seven safe Conservative seats and no safe Labour seat. In the rest of the Midlands the count was more nearly equal, nineteen county seats and two borough seats being Conservative, while eight county seats and seven borough seats were Labour, all the Labour seats being in industrial areas. In Lancashire and Yorkshire the division was as shown in Table 80.

Cheshire was mainly Conservative and Westmoreland safely Conservative. Cumberland was sufficiently impartial to give Penrith and Cockermouth to the Conservatives and Workington to Labour, and Hexham in Northumberland was Conservative.

In Wales (or, strictly speaking, in or near it) the Conservatives could claim only Monmouth, but there were sixteen safe Labour seats over and near the coalfields. In Scotland, the heart of Conservatism was in the Highlands, but the Lowlands (plus Aberdeen) gave the Labour party twenty-one seats, of which eight have already been mentioned because they were in Glasgow.

The class division is so obvious that it needs no emphasis to those who know their Britain. In London the West End, the City (in the wider, metaphorical sense) and the wealthy suburbs were Conservative, but the East End was Labour. Transpose that to the big towns according to geography (e.g. in Leeds the northern suburbs look on to the moors, in Sheffield wealth prefers the approach to the Peak of Derbyshire, in Manchester it moves south towards Cheshire), and the verdict is the same. Wealth and poverty are not, however, the whole answer. Wales would not worship Mammon, not even in the little England of Pembrokeshire. In Scotland religion qualified affection for bawbees. Lancashire's industry was less solidly Labour than Yorkshire's. Moreover the enormous strength of the Conservative party in the English counties cannot be explained on a purely class basis, for they were not inhabited only by people in big houses and imitation country cottages, but also by the lowest-paid workers in Britain. Besides 'class', two other factors are important. One is tradition. It is evident from the slowness with which constituencies change their allegiance, as well as from other evidence, that many electors, having chosen a party, stick to it for a very long time. The Liberalism of Wales and the West of England, the Conservatism of Birmingham, Lancashire and the agricultural counties (except in East Anglia), and perhaps even the Labour Radicalism of the coalfields, may be explained, in part at least, as an inheritance. In part it is an inheritance from the Non-conformist conscience, and in part an inheritance from the regime of the small manufacturer who worked with and even lived with his men. The successors of the Chamberlains, the Baldwins, the Cobdens and the Brights are company directors living in labour-saving houses near the golf courses, but it has taken a long time for the political consequences of their removal from the 'works' to become evident.

Secondly, a most important factor is the efficiency and militancy of the trade unions, which in Britain were formerly almost solidly Liberal and now are almost solidly Labour. The growth of the trade union movement has already been described. Politically its influence was first obvious in the mining areas, then in London and Yorkshire, and only later in Lancashire and the Midlands. It has never been strong in the rural areas, though it was and is stronger in East Anglia (which also has a Radical tradition) than elsewhere.

5. FROM 1945 TO 1959

The redistribution effected in 1945, 1950 and 1955 renders impossible the method of analysis used in the earlier periods. The only convenient method appears to be to consider the Conservative seats in 1945, when the Labour vote was at its highest, and the Labour seats in 1959, when the Conservative vote was at its highest, in both cases ignoring constituencies with small majorities. Most of the 1945 constituencies will now have disappeared or have different boundaries; and the abolition of the business premises qualification for the franchise will have reduced the Conservative preference in some areas; neither change, however, affects the question under discussion.

Population has been moving out of the County of London to the 'dormitories'. In 1945 only eleven London seats could be classed as safely Conservative. They included three seats in the City and Westminster, now replaced by one seat. Otherwise, the seats were in two blocks, the West End (including Chelsea) and Putney and Streatham. Outside the county area, however, there were eleven safe Conservative seats in the dormitory towns, and twenty county seats which were mainly dormitories. Most of these seats were to the south and west of London, where the environment is more attractive and land values high.

The Labour party in 1959 could regard twenty-two London seats as safe, including the whole of the East End, a band south of the river from Battersea N. to Woolwich E., and a suburban band, from Hammersmith N. to Islington, which has been descending in the social scale. With these areas must be associated such 'dormitories' as Barking, East and West Ham, Dagenham, Enfield E., Tottenham, Walthamstow W., Willesden W., Leyton, Romford, Feltham, and Eton and Slough.

This is clearly a class division, and the large towns follow suit. The safe Conservative seats were Edgbaston and Handsworth in Birmingham; Bristol W.; East Toxteth, Wavertree and West Derby in Liverpool; Withington in Manchester; Newcastle upon Tyne N.; Ecclesall and Hallam in Sheffield; Edinburgh S. and W.; and Cathcart, Partick and Pollok in Glasgow. Fourteen years later, Labour had four safe seats in Birmingham, two in Bradford, three in Bristol, four in Leeds, three in Leicester, three in Stoke, two in Liverpool, four in Manchester, two in Newcastle upon Tyne, one in Nottingham, four in Sheffield, two in Cardiff, two in Edinburgh, and seven in Glasgow.

The division was according to what the Victorians regarded as 'quality', and there was the same division in the smaller towns. Altrincham, Bath, Blackpool, Bournemouth, Brighton, Cheltenham, Exeter, Hastings, Hythe, Oxford (but not Cambridge), Southport and Wallasey were safe Conservative seats. The list of safe Labour seats is too long to be quoted; but if we take one in five we get Barnsley, Blyth, Derby, Gateshead, Jarrow, Lincoln, Stockton on Tees, Northampton, Swindon and Warrington. In fact, the list contains nearly all the smaller industrial towns.

Labour had made some inroad into the counties in 1945, but every seat in Berkshire, Devon, Herefordshire, Surrey, Sussex and the East Riding was safely Conservative. There were also six seats in Cheshire, three in Dorset, six in Hants and the Isle of Wight, and seven in Kent. The industrial counties provided very few, except in those parts

338

(e.g. Solihull, Sutton Coldfield and Warwick and Leamington in Warwickshire; Pudsey and Otley; Ripon and Skipton in the West Riding; and Fylde, Lancaster and Lonsdale in Lancashire) which were residential or truly rural. Fourteen years later, the Labour party swept only one county, Durham. On the other hand, it has many safe seats in the industrial areas, especially of Derbyshire, Lancashire, Nottinghamshire, Staffordshire and the West Riding.

Wales in 1945 provided only one safe Conservative seat, that of Denbigh, but this was because so many rural constituencies were Liberal. In 1959 most of South Wales was solidly Labour, and there were a few other seats, notably Anglesey, Brecon and Radnor, Caernarvon, and Pembroke. Scotland, too, was essentially Conservative only in the rural counties and in residential districts like Montrose, Fife East, Renfrew East, and Midlothian and Peebles North.

GROWTH OF THE CONSTITUENCIES

SUMMARY

Reign	Method of creation	Counties	Boroughs	Uni-versities	Pro-gressive total
	In existence in 1509	74	222	—	296
Henry VIII	Prerogative Charters	—	14⎫	—	341
	Acts of Parliament	16	15⎭		
Edward VI	Prerogative Charters	—	34	—	375
Mary I	Prerogative Charters	—	23	—	398
Elizabeth I	Prerogative Charters	—	62	—	460
James I	Prerogative Charters	—	11	4⎫	487
	Resolutions of the House of Commons	—	12	⎬	
Charles I	Resolutions of the House of Commons	—	20	—	507
	Long Parliament	90	413	4	507
Charles II	Act of Parliament	2	2⎫	—	513
	Prerogative Charter	—	2⎭		
Anne	Union with Scotland	30	15	—	558
George IV	Union with Ireland	64	35	1⎫	658
	Act of Parliament	2	−2	—⎭	
William IV	Parliament of 1831	188	465	5	658
	England	82	403	4	489
	Wales	12	12	—	24
	Scotland	30	15	—	45
	Ireland	64	35	1	100
William IV and Victoria	Parliaments, 1832–65	253	399*	6	658*
	England	144	323*	4	471*
	Wales	15	14	—	29
	Scotland	30	23	—	53
	Ireland	64	39	2	105

* Reduced by two in 1844 and by another two in 1852 by the disfranchisement of Sudbury and St Albans.

Victoria	Parliaments, 1868–84	283	366*	9	658
	England	172	285*	5	463
	Wales	15	15	—	30
	Scotland	32	26	2	60
	Ireland	64	39*	2	105

* Reduced in 1870 by the disfranchisement of Beverley (two seats), Bridgwater (two seats), Cashel (one seat) and Sligo (one seat).

Victoria,	Parliaments, 1885–1917	377	284	9	670
Edward VII,	England	234	226	5	465
George V	Wales	19	11	—	30
	Scotland	39	31	2	72
	Ireland	85	16	2	103
George V	Parliament of 1918–22	372	320	15	707
	England	230	255	7	492
	Wales and Monmouth	24	11	1	36
	Scotland	38	33	3	74
	Ireland	80	21	4	105
George V,	Parliaments, 1922–45	300	303	12	615
Edward VIII,	England	230	255	7	492
George VI	Wales and Monmouth	24	11	1	36
	Scotland	38	33	3	74
	Northern Ireland	8	4	1	13
George VI	Parliament of 1945–50	302	326	12	640
	England	232	278	7	517
	Wales and Monmouth	24	11	1	36
	Scotland	38	33	3	74
	Northern Ireland	8	4	1	13
George VI and	Parliaments of 1950–5	288	337	—	625
Elizabeth II	England	215	291	—	506
	Wales and Monmouth	26	10	—	36
	Scotland	39	32	—	71
	Northern Ireland	8	4	—	12
Elizabeth II	Parliaments since 1955	295	335	—	630
	England	222	289	—	511
	Wales and Monmouth	26	10	—	36
	Scotland	39	32	—	71
	Northern Ireland	8	4	—	12

A. ENGLISH BOROUGHS ENTITLED TO REPRESENTATION IN 1509[1]

Appleby (Westmorland)	2*	Bridgwater (Somerset)	2
Arundel (Sussex)	2†	Bridport (Dorset)	2
Barnstaple (Devon)	2	Bristol (Gloucs.)	2
Bath (Somerset)	2	Calne (Wilts.)	2*
Bedford (Beds.)	2	Cambridge (Cambs.)	2
Bletchingley (Surrey)	2*	Canterbury (Kent)	2
Bodmin (Cornwall)	2	Carlisle (Cumberland)	2
Bramber (Sussex)	2*	Chichester (Sussex)	2
Bridgnorth (Salop)	2	Chippenham (Wilts.)	2

[1] Boroughs disfranchised in 1832 are marked *; those whose representation was reduced in 1832 are marked †.

Chipping Wycombe (Bucks.)	2	Much Wenlock (Salop)	2
Colchester (Essex)	2	Newcastle upon Tyne	2
Coventry (Warwicks.)	2	(Northumberland)	
Cricklade (Wilts.)	2	Newcastle under Lyme (Staffs.)	2
Dartmouth (Devon)	2†	New Romney (Kent)	2*
Derby (Derbyshire)	2	New Windsor (Berks.)	2
Devizes (Wilts.)	2	Northampton (Northants)	2
Dorchester (Dorset)	2	Norwich (Norfolk)	2
Dover (Kent)	2	Nottingham (Notts.)	2
Downton (Wilts.)	2*	Old Sarum (Wilts.)	2*
Dunwich (Suffolk)	2*	Oxford (Oxon.)	2
East Grinstead (Sussex)	2*	Plymouth (Devon)	2
Exeter (Devon)	2	Plympton Earl (Devon)	2*
Gatton (Surrey)	2*	Poole (Dorset)	2
Gloucester (Gloucs.)	2	Portsmouth (Hants)	2
Grantham (Lincs.)	2	Reading (Berks.)	2
Great Bedwin (Wilts.)	2*	Reigate (Surrey)	2†
Great Yarmouth (Norfolk)	2	Rochester (Kent)	2
Grimsby (Lincs.)	2	Rye (Sussex)	2†
Guildford (Surrey)	2	Salisbury (Wilts.)	2
Hastings (Sussex)	2	Sandwich (Kent)	2
Helston (Cornwall)	2†	Scarborough (Yorks.)	2
Hereford (Herefordshire)	2	Shoreham (Sussex)	2
Heytesbury (Wilts.)	2*	Shrewsbury (Salop)	2
Hindon (Wilts.)	2*	Southampton (Hants)	2
Horsham (Sussex)	2†	Southwark (Surrey)	2
Hull (Yorks.)	2	Stafford (Staffs.)	2
Huntingdon (Hunts.)	2	Stamford (Lincs.)	2
Hythe (Kent)	2†	Steyning (Sussex)	2*
Ipswich (Suffolk)	2	Taunton (Somerset)	2
King's Lynn (Norfolk)	2	Tavistock (Devon)	2
Launceston (Cornwall)	2†	Totnes (Devon)	2
Leicester (Leics.)	2	Truro (Cornwall)	2
Leominster (Herefordshire)	2	Wallingford (Berks.)	2†
Lewes (Sussex)	2	Wareham (Dorset)	2†
Lincoln (Lincs.)	2	Warwick (Warwicks.)	2
Liskeard (Cornwall)	2†	Wells (Somerset)	2
London (Middx.)	4	Westbury (Wilts.)	2†
Lostwithiel (Cornwall)	2*	Weymouth and Malcombe	4†
Ludgershall (Wilts.)	2*	Regis (Dorset)	
Ludlow (Salop)	2	Wilton (Wilts.)	2†
Lyme Regis (Dorset)	2†	Winchelsea (Sussex)	2*
Maidstone (Kent)	2	Winchester (Hants)	2
Maldon (Essex)	2	Wootton Bassett (Wilts.)	2*
Malmesbury (Wilts.)	2†	Worcester (Worcs.)	2
Marlborough (Wilts.)	2	York (Yorks.)	2
Midhurst (Sussex)	2†		

Total in 1509   222

APPENDIX III

B. BOROUGHS ENFRANCHISED UNDER HENRY VIII

Berwick Upon Tweed	2	Monmouth (Mon.)	1
(Northumberland)		Newport (Cornwall)	2
Buckingham (Bucks.)	2	Orford (Suffolk)	2*
Chester (Cheshire)	2	Preston (Lancs.)	2
Lancaster (Lancs.)	2	Thetford (Norfolk)	2

Total in 1547   239

C. BOROUGHS ENFRANCHISED UNDER EDWARD VI

Boston (Lincs.)	2*	Penryn (Cornwall)	2
Bossiney (Cornwall)	2*	Peterborough (Northants)	2
Brackley (Northants)	2*	Petersfield (Hants)	2†
Camelford (Cornwall)	2*	Saltash (Cornwall)	2*
Grampound (Cornwall)	2**	Thirsk (Yorks.)	2
Heydon (Yorks.)	2*	West Looe (Cornwall)	2*
Lichfield (Staffs.)	2	Westminster (Middx.)	2
Liverpool (Lancs.)	2	Wigan (Lancs.)	2
Mitchell (Cornwall)[1]	2*		

Total in 1553   273

[1] Also known as St Michael's and Midshall.

D. BOROUGHS ENFRANCHISED UNDER MARY I

Abingdon (Berks.)	1	Knaresborough (Yorks.)	2
Aldborough (Yorks.)	2*	Morpeth (Northumberland)	2†
Aylesbury (Bucks.)	2	Ripon (Yorks.)	2
Banbury (Oxon.)	1	St Albans (Herts.)	2
Boroughbridge (Yorks.)	2*	St Ives (Cornwall)	2†
Castle Rising (Norfolk)	2*	Woodstock (Oxon.)	2†
Droitwich (Worcs.)	2†	Less two members for	
Higham Ferrers (Northants)	1*	Maidstone, disfranchised	

Total in 1558   296

E. BOROUGHS ENFRANCHISED UNDER ELIZABETH I

Aldeburgh (Suffolk)	2*	Maidstone (Kent)	2
Andover (Hants)	2	Minehead (Somerset)	2*
Berealston (Devon)	2*	Newport (Isle of Wight)	2*
Beverley (Yorks.)	2	Newton (Lancs.)	2*
Bishop's Castle (Salop)	2*	Newtown (Isle of Wight)	2*
Callington (Cornwall)	2*	Queenborough (Kent)	2*
Christchurch (Hants)	2†	Richmond (Yorks.)	2
Cirencester (Gloucs.)	2	St Germains (Cornwall)	2*
Clitheroe (Lancs.)	2†	St Mawes (Cornwall)	2*
Corfe Castle (Dorset)	2*	Stockbridge (Hants)	2*
East Looe (Cornwall)	2*	Sudbury (Suffolk)	2
East Retford (Notts.)	2	Tamworth (Warwicks.)	2
Eye (Suffolk)	2†	Tregony (Cornwall)	2*
Fowey (Cornwall)	2*	Whitchurch (Hants)	2*
Haslemere (Surrey)	2*	Yarmouth (Isle of Wight)	2*
Lymington (Hants)	2		

Total in 1603   358

F. BOROUGHS ENFRANCHISED UNDER JAMES I

Amersham (Bucks.)	2*	Ilchester (Somerset)	2*
Bewdley (Worcs.)	1	Marlow (Bucks.)	2
Bury St Edmunds (Suffolk)	2	Pontefract (Yorks.)	2
Evesham (Worcs.)	2	Tewkesbury (Gloucs.)	2
Harwich (Essex)	2	Tiverton (Devon)	2
Hertford (Herts.)	2	Wendover (Bucks.)	2*

Total in 1625   381

G. BOROUGHS ENFRANCHISED UNDER CHARLES I

Ashburton (Devon)	2†	Northallerton (Yorks.)	2†
Cockermouth (Cumberland)	2	Okehampton (Devon)	2*
Honiton (Devon)	2	Seaford (Sussex)	2*
Milbourne Port (Somerset)	2*	Shaftesbury (Dorset)	2†
New Milton (Yorks.)	2	Weobley (Herefordshire)	2*

Total in 1640   401

H. ENGLISH BOROUGHS DISFRANCHISED BY THE REPRESENTATION OF THE PEOPLE ACT, 1832[1]

Aldborough (Yorks.)	D	Lostwithiel (Cornwall)	A
Aldeburgh (Suffolk)	E	Ludgershall (Wilts.)	A
Amersham (Bucks.)	F	Milbourne Port (Somerset)	G
Appleby (Westmorland)	A	Minehead (Somerset)	E
Berealston (Devon)	E	Newport (Cornwall)	B
Bishop's Castle (Salop)	E	New Romney (Kent)	A
Bletchingley (Surrey)	A	Newton (Lancs.)	E
Boroughbridge (Yorks.)	D	Newtown (Hants)	E
Bossiney (Cornwall)	C	Okehampton (Devon)	G
Brackley (Northants)	C	Old Sarum (Wilts.)	A
Bramber (Sussex)	A	Orford (Suffolk)	B
Callington (Cornwall)	E	Plympton (Devon)	A
Camelford (Cornwall)	C	Queenborough (Kent)	E
Castle Rising (Norfolk)	D	St Germains (Cornwall)	E
Corfe Castle (Dorset)	E	St Mawes (Cornwall)	E
Downton (Wilts.)	A	St Michaels (Cornwall)	C
Dunwich (Suffolk)	A	Saltash (Cornwall)	C
East Grinstead (Sussex)	A	Seaford (Sussex)	G
East Looe (Cornwall)	E	Steyning (Sussex)	A
Fowey (Cornwall)	E	Stockbridge (Hants)	E
Gatton (Surrey)	A	Tregony (Cornwall)	E
Great Bedwin (Wilts.)	A	Wendover (Bucks.)	F
Haslemere (Surrey)	E	Weobley (Herefordshire)	G
Heydon (Yorks.)	C	West Looe (Cornwall)	C
Heytesbury (Wilts.)	A	Whitchurch (Hants)	E
Higham Ferrars (Northants)	D	Winchelsea (Sussex)	A
Hindon (Wilts.)	A	Wootton Bassett (Wilts.)	A
Ilchester (Somerset)	F	Yarmouth (Hants)	E

[1] References are to preceding sections of this Appendix.

J. BOROUGHS WHOSE REPRESENTATION WAS REDUCED IN 1832[1]

Arundel (Sussex)	A	Midhurst (Sussex)	A
Ashburton (Devon)	G	Morpeth (Northumberland)	D
Calne (Wilts.)	A	Northallerton (Yorks.)	G
Christchurch (Hants)	E	Petersfield (Hants)	C
Clitheroe (Lancs.)	E	Reigate (Surrey)	A
Dartmouth (Devon)	A	Rye (Sussex)	A
Droitwich (Worcs.)	D	St Ives (Cornwall)	D
Eye (Suffolk)	E	Shaftesbury (Dorset)	G
Great Grimsby (Lincs.)	A	Thirsk (Yorks.)	C
Helston (Cornwall)	A	Wallingford (Berks.)	A
Horsham (Sussex)	A	Wareham (Dorset)	A
Hythe (Kent)	A	Westbury (Wilts.)	A
Launceston (Cornwall)	A	Weymouth and Melcombe	A
Liskeard (Cornwall)	A	Regis (Dorset)	
Lyme Regis (Dorset)	A	Wilton (Wilts.)	A
Malmesbury (Wilts.)	A	Woodstock (Oxon.)	D

[1] Reduced to one except in the case of Weymouth and Melcombe Regis, reduced from four to two. References are to preceding sections of the Appendix.

K. BOROUGHS ENFRANCHISED IN 1832

Ashton Under Lyne (Lancs.)	1	Manchester (Lancs.)	2
Birmingham (Warwicks.)	2	Marylebone (Middx.)	2
Blackburn (Lancs.)	2	Oldham (Lancs.)	2
Bolton (Lancs.)	2	Rochdale (Lancs.)	1
Bradford (Yorks.)	2	Salford (Lancs.)	1
Brighton (Sussex)	2	Sheffield (Yorks.)	2
Bury (Lancs.)	1	South Shields (Durham)	1
Chatham (Kent)	1	Stockport (Cheshire)	2
Cheltenham (Gloucs.)	1	Stoke on Trent (Staffs.)	2
Devonport (Devon)	2	Stroud (Gloucs.)	2
Dudley (Worcs.)	1	Sunderland (Durham)	2
Finsbury (Middx.)	2	Tower Hamlets (Middx.)	2
Frome (Somerset)	1	Tynemouth (Northumberland)	1
Gateshead (Durham)	1	Wakefield (Yorks.)	1
Greenwich (Kent)	2	Walsall (Lancs.)	1
Halifax (Yorks.)	2	Warrington (Lancs.)	1
Huddersfield (Yorks.)	1	Whitby (Yorks.)	1
Kendal (Westmorland)	1	Whitehaven (Cumberland)	1
Kidderminster (Worcs.)	1	Wolverhampton (Staffs.)	2
Lambeth (Surrey)	2		
Leeds (Yorks.)	2	Merthyr Tydfil	1
Macclesfield (Lancs.)	2	Swansea	1

L. ADDITIONAL SEATS FOR COUNTIES IN 1832

Berkshire	1	Cheshire	2
Buckinghamshire	1	Cornwall	2
Cambridgeshire	1	Cumberland	2

Derbyshire	2	Nottinghamshire	2
Devonshire	2	Oxfordshire	1
Dorsetshire	1	Shropshire	2
Durham	2	Somersetshire	2
Essex	2	Staffordshire	2
Gloucestershire	2	Suffolk	2
Hampshire	3	Surrey	2
Herefordshire	1	Sussex	2
Hertfordshire	1	Warwickshire	2
Kent	2	Wiltshire	2
Lancashire	2	Worcestershire	2
Leicestershire	2	Yorkshire	2*
Lincolnshire	2		
Norfolk	2	Carmarthenshire	1
Northamptonshire	2	Denbighshire	1
Northumberland	2	Glamorganshire	1

* Yorkshire's representation had been raised from two to four in 1821 by the Act which disfranchised Grampound.

DISTRIBUTION OF THE CONSTITUENCIES, 1509–1885

A. CONSTITUENCIES IN ENGLAND

The references to Tudor and Stuart monarchs indicate the reigns in which constituencies were created (or restored) if not in existence in 1509.

	1509	1831	1832	1869	1885
Bedfordshire	2	2	2	2	2
Bedford	2	2	2	2	1
County total	4	4	4	4	3
Berkshire	2	2	3	3	3
Abingdon (Mary I)	—	1	1	1	—
Reading	2	2	2	2	1
Wallingford	2	2	1	1	—
Windsor	2	2	2	1	1
County total	8	9	9	8	5
Buckinghamshire	2	2	3	3	3
Amersham (James I)	—	2	—	—	—
Aylesbury (Mary I)	—	2	2	2	—
Buckingham (Henry VIII)	—	2	2	1	—
Marlow (James I)	—	2	2	1	—
Wendover (James I)	—	2	—	—	—
Chipping Wycombe	2	2	2	1	—
County total	4	14	11	8	3
Cambridgeshire	2	2	3	3	3
Cambridge	2	2	2	2	1
County total	4	4	5	5	4
Cheshire (Henry VIII)	—	2	4	6	8
Birkenhead	—	—	—	1[1]	1
Chester (Henry VIII)	—	2	2	2	1
Stalybridge	—	—	—	1	1
Stockport	—	—	2	2	2
County total	—	4	8	12	13

[1] Enfranchised in 1861.

347

	1509	1831	1832	1869	1885
Cornwall	2	2	4	4	6
Bodmin	2	2	2	1	—
Bossiney (Edward VI)	—	2	—	—	—
Callington (Elizabeth I)	—	2	—	—	—
Camelford (Edward VI)	—	2	—	—	—
Fowey (Elizabeth I)	—	2	—	—	—
Grampound (Edward VI)	—	—[1]	—	—	—
Helston	2	2	1	1	—
Launceston	2	2	1	1	—
Liskeard	2	2	1	1	—
East Looe (Elizabeth I)	—	2	—	—	—
West Looe (Edward VI)	—	2	—	—	—
Lostwithiel	2	2	—	—	—
Newport (Henry VIII)	—	2	—	—	—
Penryn[2] (Edward VI)	—	2	2	2	1
St Germains (Elizabeth I)	—	2	—	—	—
St Ives (Mary I)	—	2	1	1	—
St Mawes (Elizabeth I)	—	2	—	—	—
St Michaels (Edward VI)	—	2	—	—	—
Saltash (Edward VI)	—	2	—	—	—
Tregony (Elizabeth I)	—	2	—	—	—
Truro	2	2	2	2	—
County total	14	42	14	13	7
Cumberland	2	2	4	4	4
Carlisle	2	2	2	2	1
Cockermouth (Charles I)	—	2	2	1	—
Whitehaven	—	—	1	1	1
County total	4	6	9	8	6
Derbyshire	2	2	4	6	7
Derby	2	2	2	2	2
County total	4	4	6	8	9
Devonshire	2	2	4	6	8
Ashburton (Charles I)	—	2	1	—	—
Barnstaple	2	2	2	2	—
Berealston (Elizabeth I)	—	2	—	—	—
Dartmouth	2	2	1	—	—
Devonport	—	—	2	2	2
Exeter	2	2	2	2	1
Honiton (Charles I)	—	2	2	—	—
Okehampton (Charles I)	—	2	—	—	—
Plymouth	2	2	2	2	2
Plympton	2	2	—	—	—

[1] Disfranchised in 1821 for corruption.
[2] Afterwards Penryn and Falmouth.

	1509	*1831*	*1832*	*1869*	*1885*
Tavistock	2	2	2	1	—
Tiverton (James I)	—	2	2	2	—
Totnes	2	2	2	—[1]	—
County total	16	26	22	17	13
Dorsetshire	2	2	3	3	4
Bridport	2	2	2	1	—
Corfe Castle (Elizabeth I)	—	2	—	—	—
Dorchester	2	2	2	1	—
Lyme Regis	2	2	1	—	—
Poole	2	2	2	1	—
Shaftesbury (Charles I)	—	2	1	1	—
Wareham	2	2	1	1	—
Weymouth and Melcombe Regis	4	4	2	2	—
County total	16	20	14	10	4
Durham County (Charles II)	—	2	4	4	8
Darlington	—	—	—	1	1
Durham City (Charles II)	—	2	2	2	1
Gateshead	—	—	1	1	1
Hartlepools	—	—	—	1	1
South Shields	—	—	1	1	1
Stockton	—	—	—	1	1
Sunderland	—	—	2	2	2
County total	—	4	10	13	16
Essex	2	2	4	6	8
Colchester	2	2	2	2	1
Harwich (James I)	—	2	2	1	—
Maldon	2	2	2	1	—
West Ham	—	—	—	—	2
County total	6	8	10	10	11
Gloucestershire	2	2	4	4	5
Bristol[2]	2	2	2	2	4
Cheltenham	—	—	1	1	1
Cirencester (Elizabeth I)	—	2	2	1	—
Gloucester	2	2	2	2	1
Stroud	—	—	2	2	—
Tewkesbury (James I)	—	2	2	1	—
County total	6	10	15	13	11

[1] Disfranchised in 1867 for corruption.
[2] City and County of Bristol, included here for convenience.

349

	1509	1831	1832	1869	1885
Hampshire	2	2	4	4	5
Andover (Elizabeth I)	—	2	2	1	—
Christchurch (Elizabeth I)	—	2	1	1	1
Lymington (Elizabeth I)	—	2	2	1	—
Newport (Elizabeth I)	—	2	—[1]	—	—
Newtown (Elizabeth I)	—	2	—	—	—
Petersfield (Edward VI)	—	2	1	1	—
Portsmouth	2	2	2	2	2
Southampton	2	2	2	2	2
Stockbridge (Elizabeth I)	—	2	—	—	—
Whitchurch (Elizabeth I)	—	2	—	—	—
Winchester	2	2	2	2	1
Yarmouth (Elizabeth I)	—	2	—	—	—
County total	8	26	16	14	11
Herefordshire	2	2	3	3	2
Hereford	2	2	2	2	1
Leominster	2	2	2	1	—
Weobley (Charles I)	—	2	—	—	—
County total	6	8	7	6	3
Hertfordshire	2	2	3	3	4
Hertford (James I)	—	2	2	1	—
St Albans (Mary I)	—	2	2[2]	—	—
County total	2	6	7	4	4
Huntingdonshire	2	2	2	2	2
Huntingdon	2	2	2	1	—
County total	4	4	4	3	2
Kent	2	2	4	6	8
Canterbury	2	2	2	2	1
Chatham	—	—	1	1	1
Deptford	—	—	—	—	1
Dover	2	2	2	2	1
Gravesend	—	—	—	1	1
Greenwich	—	—	2	2	1
Hythe	2	2	1	1	1
Lewisham	—	—	—	—	1
Maidstone	2	2	2	2	1
New Romney	2	2	—	—	—
Queenborough (Elizabeth I)	—	2	—	—	—
Rochester	2	2	2	2	1
Sandwich	2	2	2	2	—[3]
Woolwich	—	—	—	—	1
County total	16	18	18	21	19

[1] See Wight, Isle of. [2] Disfranchised in 1852 for corruption.
[3] Disfranchised in 1885 for corruption.

	1509	1831	1832	1869	1885
Lancashire	2	2	4	8	23
Ashton under Lyne	—	—	1	1	1
Barrow in Furness	—	—	—	—	1
Blackburn	—	—	2	2	2
Bolton	—	—	2	2	2
Burnley	—	—	—	1	1
Bury	—	—	1	1	1
Clitheroe (Elizabeth I)	—	2	1	1	—
Lancaster (Henry VIII)	—	2	2	—[1]	—
Liverpool (Edward VI)	—	2	2	3	9
Macclesfield	—	—	2	2	—[2]
Manchester	—	—	2	3	6
Newton (Elizabeth I)	—	2	—	—	—
Oldham	—	—	2	2	2
Preston (Henry VIII)	—	2	2	2	2
Rochdale	—	—	1	1	1
St Helens	—	—	—	—	1
Salford	—	—	1	2	3
Warrington	—	—	1	1	1
Wigan (Edward VI)	—	2	2	2	1
County total	2	14	28	34	57
Leicestershire	2	2	4	4	4
Leicester	2	2	2	2	2
County total	4	4	6	6	6
Lincolnshire	2	2	4	6	7
Boston (Edward VI)	—	2	2	2	1
Grantham	2	2	2	2	1
Grimsby	2	2	1	1	1
Lincoln	2	2	2	2	1
Stamford	2	2	2	1	—
County total	10	12	13	14	11
Middlesex	2	2	2	2	7
Bethnal Green	—	—	—	—	2
Chelsea	—	—	—	2	1
City of London	4	4	4	4	2
Finsbury	—	—	2	2	3
Fulham	—	—	—	—	1
Hackney	—	—	—	2	3
Hammersmith	—	—	—	—	1
Hampstead	—	—	—	—	1
Islington	—	—	—	—	4
Kensington	—	—	—	—	2

[1] Disfranchised in 1867 for corruption.
[2] Disfranchised in 1885 for corruption.

	1509	1831	1832	1869	1885
Marylebone	—	—	2	2	2
Paddington	—	—	—	—	2
St George, Hanover Square	—	—	—	—	1
St Pancras	—	—	—	—	4
Shoreditch	—	—	—	—	2
Strand	—	—	—	—	1
Tower Hamlets	—	—	2	2	7
Westminster (Edward VI)	—	2	2	2	1
County total	6	8	14	18	47
Monmouthshire (Henry VIII)	—	2	2	2	3
Monmouth (Henry VIII)	—	1	1	1	1
County total	—	3	3	3	4
Norfolk	2	2	4	6	6
Castle Rising (Mary I)	—	2	—	—	—
King's Lynn	2	2	2	2	1
Norwich	2	2	2	2	2
Thetford (Henry VIII)	—	2	2	—	—
Great Yarmouth	2	2	2	—[1]	1
County total	8	12	12	10	10
Northamptonshire	2	2	4	4	4
Brackley (Edward VI)	—	2	—	—	—
Higham Ferrars (Mary I)	—	1	—	—	—
Northampton	2	2	2	2	2
Peterborough (Edward VI)	—	2	2	2	1
County total	4	9	8	8	7
Northumberland	2	2	4	4	4
Berwick (Henry VIII)	—	2	2	2	—
Morpeth (Mary I)	—	2	1	1	1
Newcastle upon Tyne	2	2	2	2	2
Tynemouth	—	—	1	1	1
County total	4	8	10	10	8
Nottinghamshire	2	2	4	4	4
Newark (Charles II)	—	2	2	2	—
Nottingham	2	2	2	2	3
East Retford (Elizabeth I)	—	2	2	2	—
County total	4	8	10	10	7

[1] Disfranchised in 1867 for corruption.

	1509	1831	1832	1869	1885
Oxfordshire	2	2	3	3	3
Banbury (Mary I)	—	1	1	1	—
Oxford	2	2	2	2	1
Woodstock (Mary I)	—	2	1	1	—
County total	4	7	7	7	4
Rutlandshire	2	2	2	2	1
Shropshire	2	2	4	4	4
Bishop's Castle (Elizabeth I)	—	2	—	—	—
Bridgnorth	2	2	2	1	—
Ludlow	2	2	2	1	—
Shrewsbury	2	2	2	2	1
Much Wenlock	2	2	2	2	—
County total	10	12	12	10	5
Somersetshire	2	2	4	6	7
Bath	2	2	2	2	2
Bridgwater	2	2	2	2[1]	—
Frome	—	—	1	1	—
Ilchester (James I)	—	2	—	—	—
Melbourne Port (Charles I)	—	2	—	—	—
Minehead (Elizabeth I)	—	2	—	—	—
Taunton	2	2	2	2	1
Wells	2	2	2	—	—
County total	10	16	13	13	10
Staffordshire	2	2	4	6	7
Hanley	—	—	—	—	1
Lichfield (Edward VI)	—	2	2	1	—
Newcastle under Lyme	2	2	2	2	1
Stafford	2	2	2	2	1
Stoke on Trent	—	—	2	2	1
Tamworth (Elizabeth I)	—	2	2	2	—
Walsall	—	—	1	1	1
Wednesbury	—	—	—	1	1
West Bromwich	—	—	—	—	1
Wolverhampton	—	—	2	2	3
County total	6	10	17	19	17
Suffolk	2	2	4	4	5
Aldeburgh (Elizabeth I)	—	2	—	—	—
Bury St Edmunds (James I)	—	2	2	2	1
Dunwich	2	2	—	—	—
Eye (Elizabeth I)	—	2	1	1	—

[1] Disfranchised in 1870 for corruption.

	1509	1831	1832	1869	1885
Ipswich	2	2	2	2	2
Orford (Henry VIII)	—	2	—		
Sudbury (Elizabeth I)	—	2	2[1]	—	—
County total	6	16	11	9	8
Surrey	2	2	4	6	6
Battersea and Clapham	—	—	—	—	2
Bletchingley	2	2	—	—	—
Camberwell	—	—	—	—	3
Croydon	—	—	—	—	1
Gatton	2	2	—	—	—
Guildford	2	2	2	1	—
Haslemere (Elizabeth I)	—	2	—	—	—
Lambeth	—	—	2	2	4
Newington	—	—	—	—	2
Reigate	2	2	1	—[2]	—
Southwark	2	2	2	2	3
Wandsworth	—	—	—	—	1
County total	12	14	11	11	22
Sussex	2	2	4	4	6
Arundel	2	2	1	—	—
Bramber	2	2	—	—	—
Brighton	—	—	2	2	2
Chichester	2	2	2	1	—
East Grinstead	2	2	—	—	—
Hastings	2	2	2	2	1
Horsham	2	2	1	1	—
Lewes	2	2	2	1	—
Midhurst	2	2	1	1	—
Rye	2	2	1	1	—
Seaford (Charles I)	—	2	—	—	—
Shoreham	2	2	2	2	—
Steyning	2	2	—	—	—
Winchelsea	2	2	—	—	—
County total	26	28	18	15	9
Warwickshire	2	2	4	4	4
Aston Manor	—	—	—	—	1
Birmingham	—	—	2	3	7
Coventry	2	2	2	2	1
Warwick	2	2	2	2	1
County total	6	6	10	11	14

[1] Disfranchised in 1844 for corruption.
[2] Disfranchised in 1867 for corruption.

	1509	*1831*	*1832*	*1869*	*1885*
Westmorland	2	2	2	2	2
Appleby	2	2	—	—	—
Kendal	—	—	1	1	—
County total	4	4	3	3	2
Wight, Isle of	—	—	1	1	1
Newport[1]	—	—	2	1	—
County total	—	—	3	2	1
Wiltshire	2	2	4	4	5
Great Bedwin	2	2	—	—	—
Calne	2	2	1	1	—
Chippenham	2	2	2	1	—
Cricklade	2	2	2	2	—
Devizes	2	2	2	1	—
Downton	2	2	—	—	—
Heytesbury	2	2	—	—	—
Hindon	2	2	—	—	—
Ludgeshall	2	2	—	—	—
Malmesbury	2	2	1	1	—
Marlborough	2	2	2	1	—
Old Sarum	2	2	—	—	—
Salisbury	2	2	2	2	1
Westbury	2	2	1	1	—
Wilton	2	2	1	1	—
Wootton Bassett	2	2	—	—	—
County total	34	34	18	15	6
Worcestershire	2	2	4	4	5
Bewdley (James I)	—	1	1	1	—
Droitwich (Mary I)	—	2	1	1	—
Dudley	—	—	1	1	1
Evesham (James I)	—	2	2	1	—
Kidderminster	—	—	1	1	1
Worcester	2	2	2	2	1
County total	4	9	12	11	8
Yorkshire	2	4	6	10	26
Aldbrough (Mary I)	—	2	—	—	—
Beverley (Elizabeth I)	—	2	2	2	—[2]
Boroughbridge (Mary I)	—	2	—	—	—
Bradford	—	—	2	2	3
Dewsbury	—	—	—	1	1
Halifax	—	—	2	2	2

[1] In Hampshire before 1832, when the Isle of Wight became a separate county.
[2] Disfranchised in 1870 for corruption.

23-2

	1509	1831	1832	1869	1885
Hedon (Edward VI)	—	2	—	—	—
Huddersfield	—	—	1	1	1
Kingston Upon Hull	2	2	2	2	3
Knaresborough (Mary I)	—	2	2	1	—
Leeds	—	—	2	3	5
Middlesbrough	—	—	—	1	1
New Malton (Charles I)	—	2	2	1	—
Northallerton (Charles I)	—	2	1	1	—
Pontefract (James I)	—	2	2	2	1
Richmond (Elizabeth I)	—	2	2	1	—
Ripon (Mary I)	—	2	2	1	—
Scarborough	2	2	2	2	1
Sheffield	—	—	2	2	5
Thirsk (Edward VI)	—	2	1	1	—
Wakefield	—	—	1	1	1
Whitby	—	—	1	1	—
York	2	2	2	2	2
County total	8	32	37	40	52

B. CONSTITUENCIES IN WALES

All constituencies in existence before the Representation of the People Act, 1832, were created under Henry VIII (i.e. 1535).

	1831	1832	1869	1885
Anglesey	1	1	1	1
Beaumaris District	1	1	1	1
Breconshire	1	1	1	1
Brecon	1	1	1	—
Caernarvonshire	1	1	1	1
Caernarvon Boroughs	1	1	1	1
Cardiganshire	1	1	1	1
Cardigan District	1	1	1	—
Carmarthen	1	2	2	2
Carmarthen District	1	1	1	1
Denbighshire	1	2	2	2
Denbigh District	1	1	1	1
Flintshire	1	1	1	1
Flint District	1	1	1	1
Glamorganshire	1	2	2	5
Cardiff	1	1	1	1
Merthyr Tydfil	—	1	2	2
Swansea District	—	1	1	2
Merionethshire	1	1	1	1
Montgomeryshire	1	1	1	1
Montgomery District	1	1	1	1
Pembrokeshire	1	1	1	1
Haverfordwest District	1	1	1	—
Pembroke District	1	1	1	1

	1831	*1832*	*1869*	*1885*
Radnorshire	1	1	1	1
Radnor District	1	1	1	—
Total for Wales	24	29	30	30

C. CONSTITUENCIES IN SCOTLAND

All constituencies in existence in 1831 were created by Act of the Parliament of Scotland in 1706.

(1) *Counties*	*1831*	*1832*	*1869*	*1885*
Aberdeen	1	1	2	2
Argyll	1	1	2	1
Ayr	1	1	1	2
Banff	1	1	1	1
Berwick	1	1	1	1
Bute	$\frac{1}{2}$*	1	1	1
Caithness	$\frac{1}{2}$*	1	1	1
Clackmannan	$\frac{1}{2}$*	$\frac{1}{2}$†	$\frac{1}{2}$**	$\frac{1}{2}$**
Cromarty	$\frac{1}{2}$*	$\frac{1}{2}$†	$\frac{1}{2}$**	$\frac{1}{2}$**
Dumbarton	1	1	1	1
Dumfries	1	1	1	1
Edinburgh	1	1	1	1
Elgin	1	$\frac{1}{2}$†	$\frac{1}{2}$**	$\frac{1}{2}$**
Fife	1	1	1	1
Forfar	1	1	1	1
Haddington	1	1	1	1
Inverness	1	1	1	1
Kincardine	1	1	1	1
Kinross	$\frac{1}{2}$*	$\frac{1}{2}$†	$\frac{1}{2}$**	$\frac{1}{2}$**
Kirkcudbright	1	1	1	1
Lanark	1	1	2	6
Linlithgow	1	1	1	1
Nairn	$\frac{1}{2}$*	$\frac{1}{2}$†	$\frac{1}{2}$**	$\frac{1}{2}$**
Orkney and Shetland	1	1	1	1
Peebles	1	1	$\frac{1}{2}$**	$\frac{1}{2}$**
Perth	1	1	1	2
Renfrew	1	1	1	2
Ross	1	$\frac{1}{2}$†	$\frac{1}{2}$**	$\frac{1}{2}$**
Roxburgh	1	1	1	1
Selkirk	1	1	$\frac{1}{2}$**	$\frac{1}{2}$**
Stirling	1	1	1	1

* Two-county constituencies (electing alternately), 1706–1831: Bute and Caithness; Nairn and Cromarty; Clackmannan and Kinross.

† Two-county constituencies (electing jointly), 1832–1866: Elgin and Nairn, Ross and Cromarty, Clackmannan and Kinross.

** Two-county constituencies (electing jointly), 1869–1884, as for 1832–1866 with the addition of Selkirk and Peebles.

	1831	1832	1869	1885
Sutherland	I	I	I	I
Wigtown	I	I	I	I
Total	30	30	32	38

(2) *Burghs*	1831	1832	1869	1885
Aberdeen	—	I	I	2
Dundee	—	I	2	2
Edinburgh	I	2	2	4
Glasgow	—	2	3	7
Greenock	—	I	I	I
Paisley	—	I	I	I
Perth	—	I	I	I
	I	9	11	18

(3) *Burgh Districts**	1831	1832	1869	1885
Ayr District	I	I	I	I
Crail District	I	—	—	—
Dumfries District	I	I	I	I
Elgin District	I	I	I	I
Falkirk District	—	I	I	I
Haddington District	I	I	—	—
Hawick District	—	—	I	I
Inverness Burghs	I	I	I	I
†Kilmarnock District	I	I	I	I
Kirkcaldy District	I	I	I	I
Leith District	—	I	I	I
Montrose District	I	I	I	I
St Andrews District	I	I	I	I
Selkirk District	I	—	—	—
Stirling District	I	I	I	I
Wick District	I	I	I	I
Wigtown District	I	I	—	—
	14	14	?13	13

* The Districts are given the names by which they were known in 1885, except where already abolished before that date.

† Formerly the Glasgow District; Kilmarnock was added to the burghs in the district in 1832.

D. CONSTITUENCIES IN IRELAND

	1800	1832	1869	1885
Co. Antrim	2	2	2	4
Belfast	I	I	I	4
Carrickfergus	I	I	I	—
Lisburn	I	I	I	—
Co. Armagh	2	2	2	3
Armagh	I	I	I	—

	1800	*1832*	*1869*	*1885*
Co. Carlow	2	2	2	1
Carlow	1	1	1	—
Co. Cavan	2	2	2	2
Co. Clare	2	2	2	2
Ennis	1	1	1	—
Co. Cork	2	2	2	7
Bandon	1	1	1	—
Cork	2	2	2	2
Kensale	1	1	1	—
Youghal	1	1	1	—
Co. Donegal	2	2	2	4
Co. Down	2	2	2	4
Downpatrick	1	1	1	—
Newry	1	1	1	1
Co. Dublin	2	2	2	2
Dublin	2	2	2	4
Co. Fermanagh	2	2	2	2
Enniskillin	1	1	1	—
Co. Galway	2	2	2	4
Galway	1	2	2	1
Co. Kerry	2	2	2	4
Tralee	1	1	1	—
Co. Kildare	2	2	2	2
Co. Kilkenny	2	2	2	2
Kilkenny	1	1	1	1
King's County	2	2	2	2
Co. Leitrim	2	2	2	2
Co. Limerick	2	2	2	2
Limerick	1	2	2	1
Co. Londonderry	2	2	2	2
Coleraine	1	1	1	—
Londonderry	1	1	1	1
Co. Longford	2	2	2	2
Co. Louth	2	2	2	2
Drogheda	1	1	1	—
Dundalk	1	1	1	—
Co. Mayo	2	2	2	4
Co. Meath	2	2	2	2
Co. Monaghan	2	2	2	2
Queen's County	2	2	2	2
Portarlington	1	1	1	—
Co. Roscommon	2	2	2	2
Co. Sligo	2	2	2	2
Sligo	1	1	1[1]	—
Co. Tipperary	2	2	2	4
Cashel	1	1	1[1]	—
Clonmel	1	1	1	—

[1] Disfranchised in 1870 for corruption.

	1800	1832	1869	1885
Co. Tyrone	2	2	2	4
Dungannon	1	1	1	—
Co. Waterford	2	2	2	2
Dungarvon	1	1	1	—
Waterford	1	2	2	1
Co. Westneath	2	2	2	2
Athlone	1	1	1	—
Co. Wexford	2	2	2	2
Ross	1	1	1	—
Wexford	1	1	1	—
Co. Wicklow	2	2	2	2
	98	101	101	101

DISTRIBUTION OF THE CONSTITUENCIES, 1885–1955

A. CONSTITUENCIES IN ENGLAND

	1885	1918	1945	1950	1955
Bedfordshire	2	3	3	3	3
Bedford	1	—	—	—	—
Luton	—	—	—	1	1
County total	3	3	3	4	4
Berkshire	3	3	3	4	4
Reading	1	1	1	2	1
Windsor	1	—	—	—	—
County total	5	4	4	6	5
Buckinghamshire	3	3	4	4	4
Eton and Slough	—	—	—	1	1
County total	3	3	4	5	5
Cambridgeshire	3	1	1	1	1
Cambridge	1	1	1	1	1
County total	4	2	2	2	2
Cheshire	8	9	9	9	10
Altrincham and Sale	—	—	1	1	1
Bebington	—	—	—	1	1
Birkenhead	1	2	2	1	1
Chester	1	—	—	—	—
Stalybridge	1	—	—	—	—
Stockport	2	2	2	2	2
Wallasey	—	1	1	1	1
County total	13	14	15	15	16
Cornwall	6	5	5	5	5
Penryn and Falmouth	1	—	—	—	—
County total	7	5	5	5	5

	1885	1918	1945	1950	1955
Cumberland	4	4	4	3	3
Carlisle	1	1	1	1	1
Whitehaven	1	—	—	—	—
County total	6	5	5	4	4
Derbyshire	7	8	8	7	7
Chesterfield	—	—	—	1	1
Derby	2	2	2	2	2
County total	9	10	10	10	10
Devonshire	8	7	7	6	6
Devonport	2	—	—	—	—
Exeter	1	1	1	1	1
Plymouth	2	3	3	2	2
Torquay	—	—	—	1	1
County total	13	11	11	10	10
Dorsetshire	4	4	4	3	3
Poole	—	—	—	1	1
County total	4	4	4	4	4
Durham	8	11	11	10	9
Darlington	1	1	1	1	1
Durham	1	—	—	—	—
Gateshead	1	1	1	2	2
Hartlepools	1	1	1	1	1
Jarrow	—	—	—	—	1
South Shields	1	1	1	1	1
Stockton	1	1	1	1	1
Sunderland	2	2	2	2	2
County total	16	18	18	18	18
Ely, Isle of	—	1	1	1	1
Essex	8	8	9	8	10
Barking	—	—	1	1	1
Colchester	1	—	—	—	—
Dagenham	—	—	1	1	1
East Ham	—	2	2	2	2
Hornchurch	—	—	—	1	1
Ilford	—	1	2	2	2
Leyton	—	2	2	1	1
Romford	—	—	1	1	1
Southend	—	1	1	2	2
Walthamstow	—	2	2	2	2

	1885	*1918*	*1945*	*1950*	*1955*
West Ham	2	4	4	2	2
Woodford	—	—	1	1	1
County total	11	20	26	24	26
Gloucestershire	5	4	4	4	4
Bristol[1]	4	5	5	6	6
Cheltenham	1	1	1	1	1
Gloucester	1	1	1	1	1
County total	11	11	11	12	12
Hampshire	5	6	6	5	6
Bournemouth	—	1	1	2	2
Christchurch	1	—	—	—	—
Gosport and Fareham	—	—	—	1	1
Portsmouth	2	3	3	3	3
Southampton	2	2	2	2	2
Winchester	1	—	—	—	—
County total	11	12	12	13	14
Herefordshire	2	2	2	2	2
Hereford	1	—	—	—	—
County total	3	2	2	2	2
Hertfordshire	4	5	6	6	7
Watford	—	—	—	1	1
County total	4	5	6	7	8
Huntingdonshire	2	1	1	1	1
Kent	8	11	11	12	13
Beckenham	—	—	—	1	1
Bexley	—	—	1	1	1
Bromley	—	1	1	1	1
Canterbury	1	—	—	—	—
Chatham[2]	1	—	—	—	—
Dartford	—	—	1	1	—
Deptford[3]	1	—	—	—	—
Dover	1	—	—	—	—
Erith and Crayford	—	—	—	—	1
Gillingham	—	—	—	1	1
Gravesend	1	—	—	—	—
Greenwich[3]	1	—	—	—	—
Hythe	1	1	1	—	—
Lewisham[3]	1	—	—	—	—

[1] City and County of Bristol, included here for convenience.
[2] Combined from 1918.
[3] Included in London from 1918.

	1885	1918	1945	1950	1955
Maidstone	1	—	—	—	—
Rochester[1]	1	2	2	1	1
Woolwich[2]	1	—	—	—	—
County total	19	15	17	18	19
Lancashire	23	18	18	16	16
Accrington	—	1	1	1	1
Ashton Under Lyne	1	1	1	1	1
Barrow in Furness	1	1	1	1	1
Blackburn	2	2	2	2	1
Blackpool	—	1	2	2	2
Bolton	2	2	2	2	2
Bootle	—	1	1	1	1
Burnley	1	1	1	1	1
Bury[3]	1	1	1	1	1
Crosby	—	—	—	1	1
Droylsden	—	—	—	1	—
Eccles	—	1	1	1	1
Leigh	—	1	1	1	1
Liverpool	9	11	11	9	9
Manchester	6	10	10	9	9
Nelson and Colne	—	1	1	1	1
Oldham	2	2	2	2	2
Preston	2	2	2	2	2
Rochdale	1	1	1	1	1
Rossendale	—	1	1	1	1
St Helens	1	1	1	1	1
Salford	3	3	3	2	2
Southport	—	1	1	1	1
Stretford	—	—	—	1	1
Warrington	1	1	1	1	1
Wigan	1	1	1	1	1
County total	57	66	67	64	62
Leicestershire	4	4	4	4	4
Leicester	2	3	3	4	4
County total	6	7	7	8	8
Lincolnshire[4]	7	7	7	7	7
Boston	1	—	—	—	—
Grantham	1	—	—	—	—
Grimsby	1	1	1	1	1
Lincoln	1	1	1	1	1
County total	11	9	9	9	9

[1] Combined from 1918. [2] Included in London from 1918.
[3] Combined with Radcliffe from 1918. [4] Combined with Rutlandshire from 1918.

London Boroughs[1]	1885	1918	1945	1950	1955
Barons Court	—	—	—	—	1
Battersea[2]	—	2	2	2	2
Bermondsey	—	2	2	1	1
Bethnal Green[3]	—	2	2	1	1
Camberwell[2]	—	4	4	2	2
Chelsea[3]	—	1	1	1	1
City of London[3,4]	—	2	2	1	1
Deptford[5]	—	1	1	1	1
Finsbury[6]	—	1	1	—	—
Fulham[3]	—	2	2	2	1
Greenwich[5]	—	1	1	1	1
Hackney[3,7]	—	3	3	1	1
Hammersmith[3]	—	2	2	2	1
Hampstead[3]	—	1	1	1	1
Holborn[8]	—	1	1	1	1
Islington[3]	—	4	4	3	3
Kensington[3]	—	2	2	2	2
Lambeth[2]	—	4	4	3	3
Lewisham[5]	—	2	2	3	3
Paddington[3]	—	2	2	2	2
Poplar[6]	—	2	2	1	1
St Marylebone[3]	—	1	1	1	1
St Pancras[3,8]	—	3	3	1	1
Shoreditch[3,6]	—	1	1	1	1
Southwark[2]	—	3	3	1	1
Stepney	—	3	3	1	1
Stoke Newington[7]	—	1	1	1	1
Wandsworth[2]	—	5	5	4	4
Westminster[3,10]	—	2	2	—	—
Woolwich[5]	—	2	2	2	2
County total	—	62	62	43	42
Middlesex	7	10	7	2	2
Acton	—	—	—	1	1
Bethnal Green[9]	2	—	—	—	—
Brentford and Chiswick	—	—	—	1	1

[1] The County of London was created in 1889 but it has no county seats, since it is divided into boroughs.

[2] Transferred from Surrey in 1918.   [3] Transferred from Middlesex in 1918.

[4] The City of London and Westminster were combined into a single borough in 1955.

[5] Transferred from Kent in 1918.

[6] Finsbury and Shoreditch were combined in 1955.

[7] Hackney North and Stoke Newington were combined in 1955, leaving a constituency called Hackney Central.

[8] Holborn and St Pancras South were combined in 1955, leaving a constituency called St Pancras North.   [9] Transferred to London in 1918.

[10] Area transferred to London in 1918, but constituency extinguished as such.

	1885	1918	1945	1950	1955
Chelsea[1]	1	—	—	—	—
City of London[1]	2	—	—	—	—
Ealing	—	1	2	2	2
Edmonton	—	1	1	1	1
Enfield	—	—	—	—	2
Feltham	—	—	—	—	1
Finchley	—	—	—	1	1
Finsbury[1]	3	—	—	—	—
Fulham[1]	1	—	—	—	—
Hackney[1]	3	—	—	—	—
Hammersmith[1]	1	—	—	—	—
Hampstead[1]	1	—	—	—	—
Harrow	—	—	2	3	3
Hayes and Harlington	—	—	—	1	1
Hendon	—	—	2	2	2
Heston and Isleworth	—	—	1	1	1
Hornsey	—	1	1	1	1
Islington[1]	4	—	—	—	—
Kensington[1]	2	—	—	—	—
Marylebone[1]	2	—	—	—	—
Paddington[1]	2	—	—	—	—
Ruislip and Northwood	—	—	—	1	1
St George, Hanover Square[2]	1	—	—	—	—
St Pancras[1]	4	—	—	—	—
Shoreditch[1]	2	—	—	—	—
Southall	—	—	1	1	1
Southgate	—	—	—	1	1
Strand[2]	1	—	—	—	—
Tottenham	—	2	2	1	1
Tower Hamlets[2]	7	—	—	—	—
Twickenham	—	—	1	1	1
Wembley	—	—	2	2	2
Westminster[1]	1	—	—	—	—
Willesden	—	2	2	2	2
Wood Green	—	—	—	1	1
County total	47	17	24	26	29
Monmouthshire	3	5	5	5	5
Monmouth	1	—	—	—	—
Newport	—	1	1	1	1
County total	4	6	6	6	6
Norfolk	6	5	5	6	6
King's Lynn	1	—	—	—	—
Norwich	2	2	2	2	2
Great Yarmouth	1	1	1	—	—
County total	10	8	8	8	8

[1] Transferred to London in 1918.
[2] Area transferred to London in 1918, but constituency extinguished as such.

	1885	1918	1945	1950	1955
Northamptonshire	4	4	4	4	4
Northampton	2	1	1	1	1
Peterborough	1	—	—	—	—
County total	7	5	5	5	5
Northumberland	4	3	3	3	3
Blyth	—	—	—	1	1
Morpeth	1	1	1	—	—
Newcastle upon Tyne	2	4	4	4	4
Tynemouth	1	1	1	1	1
Wallsend	—	1	1	1	1
County total	8	10	10	10	10
Nottinghamshire	4	5	5	6	6
Nottingham	3	4	4	4	4
County total	7	9	9	10	10
Oxfordshire	3	2	2	2	2
Oxford	1	1	1	1	1
County total	4	3	3	3	3
Rutlandshire[1]	1	—	—	—	—
Shropshire	4	4	4	4	4
Shrewsbury	1	—	—	—	—
County total	5	4	4	4	4
Somersetshire	7	6	6	6	6
Bath	2	1	1	1	1
Taunton	1	—	—	—	—
County total	10	7	7	7	7
Staffordshire	7	7	7	6	6
Bilston	—	—	—	1	1
Hanley	1	—	—	—	—
Newcastle under Lyme	1	1	1	1	1
Rowley Regis and Tipton	—	—	—	1	1
Smethwick	—	1	1	1	1
Stafford	1	—	—	—	—
Stoke on Trent	1	3	3	3	3
Walsall	1	1	1	1	2
Wednesbury	1	1	1	1	1
West Bromwich	1	1	1	1	1
Wolverhampton	3	3	3	2	2
County total	17	18	18	18	19

[1] Combined with Lincolnshire from 1918.

	1885	1918	1945	1950	1955
Suffolk	5	5	5	4	4
Bury St Edmunds	1	—	—	—	—
Ipswich	2	1	1	1	1
County total	8	6	6	5	5
Surrey	6	7	7	10	10
Battersea and Clapham[1]	2	—	—	—	—
Camberwell[1]	3	—	—	—	—
Croydon	—	2	2	3	3
Kingston Upon Thames	—	1	1	1	1
Lambeth[1]	4	—	—	—	—
Merton and Morden	—	—	—	1	1
Mitcham	—	—	1	1	1
Newington[2]	2	—	—	—	—
Richmond	—	1	1	1	1
Southwark[1]	3	—	—	—	—
Surbiton	—	—	—	—	1
Sutton and Cheam	—	—	1	1	1
Wandsworth[1]	1	—	—	—	—
Wimbledon	—	1	1	1	1
County total	21	12	14	19	20
Sussex	6	6	7	6	7
Brighton	2	2	2	2	2
Hastings	1	1	1	1	1
Hove	—	—	—	1	1
Worthing	—	—	—	1	1
County total	9	9	10	11	12
Warwickshire	4	4	5	6	6
Aston Manor	1	—	—	—	—
Birmingham	7	12	13	13	13
Coventry	1	1	2	3	3
Sutton Coldfield	—	—	—	—	1
Warwick	1	—	—	—	—
County total	14	17	20	22	23
Westmorland	2	1	1	1	1
Wight, Isle of	1	1	1	1	1
Wiltshire	5	5	5	4	4
Salisbury	1	—	—	—	—
Swindon	—	—	—	1	1
County total	6	5	5	5	5

[1] Transferred to London in 1918.　　　[2] Area transferred to London in 1918.

	1885	*1918*	*1945*	*1950*	*1955*
Worcestershire	5	4	4	3	3
Dudley	1	1	1	1	1
Kidderminster	1	—	—	—	—
Oldbury and Halesowen	—	—	—	1	1
Worcester	1	1	1	1	1
County total	8	6	6	6	6
Yorkshire	26	26	26	20	21
Barnsley	—	1	1	1	1
Batley and Morley	—	1	1	1	1
Bradford	3	4	4	4	4
Brighouse and Spenborough	—	—	—	1	1
Dewsbury	1	1	1	1	1
Doncaster	—	—	—	1	1
Halifax	2	1	1	1	1
Huddersfield	1	1	1	2	2
Keighley	—	—	—	1	1
Kingston Upon Hull	3	4	4	4	3
Leeds	5	6	6	7	6
Middlesbrough	1	2	2	2	2
Pontefract	1	—	—	1	1
Pudsey	—	—	—	1	1
Rotherham	—	1	1	1	1
Scarborough	1	—	—	—	—
Sheffield	5	7	7	7	6
Wakefield	1	1	1	1	1
York	2	1	1	1	1
County total	52	·57	57	58	56

B. CONSTITUENCIES IN WALES

	1885	*1918*	*1945*	*1950*	*1955*
Anglesey	1	1	1	1	1
Breconshire[1]	1	1	1	1	1
Caernarvonshire	1	1	1	2	2
Caernarvon Boroughs	1	1	1	—	—
Cardiganshire	1	1	1	1	1
Carmarthenshire	2	2	2	2	2
Carmarthen District	1	—	—	—	—
Denbighshire	2	2	2	2	2
Denbigh District	1	—	—	—	—
Flintshire	1	1	1	2	2
Flint District	1	—	—	—	—
Glamorganshire	5	7	7	7	7
Aberdare	—	—	—	1	1
Cardiff	2	3	3	3	3

[1] Breconshire and Radnorshire were combined from 1918.

	1885	1918	1945	1950	1955
Merthyr Tydfil	2	2	2	1	1
Rhondda	—	2	2	2	2
Swansea	2	2	2	2	2
Merionethshire	1	1	1	1	1
Montgomeryshire	1	1	1	1	1
Montgomery District	1	—	—	—	—
Pembrokeshire	1	1	1	1	1
Pembroke and Haverfordwest	1	—	—	—	—
Radnorshire[1]	1	—	—	—	—
	30	29	29	30	30

C. CONSTITUENCIES IN SCOTLAND

(1) *Counties*	1885	1918	1945	1950	1955
Aberdeen	2	—	—	2	2
Aberdeen and Kincardine	—	3	3	—	—
Angus and Kincardine	—	—	—	2	2
Argyll	1	1	1	1	1
Ayr	2	—	—	—	—
Ayr and Bute	—	3	3	5	5
Banff	1	1	1	1	1
Berwick	1	—	—	—	—
Berwick and East Lothian	—	—	—	1	1
Berwick and Haddington	—	1	1	—	—
Caithness	1	—	—	—	—
Caithness and Sutherland	—	1	1	1	1
Clackmannan and Kinross	1	—	—	—	—
Dumbarton	1	1	1	2	2
Dumfries	1	1	1	1	1
Edinburgh	1	—	—	—	—
Elgin and Nairn	1	—	—	—	—
Fife	1	2	2	2	2
Forfar	1	1	1	—	—
Galloway	—	1	1	—	—
Haddington	1	—	—	—	—
Inverness	1	—	—	—	—
Inverness, Ross and Cromarty	—	3	3	3	2
Kincardine	1	—	—	—	—
Kirkcudbright	1	—	—	—	—
Kirkcudbright and Wigtown	—	—	—	1	1
Lanark	6	7	7	6	6
Linlithgow	1	1	1	—	—
Midlothian	—	—	—	—	1
Midlothian and Peebles	—	2	2	1	—
Moray and Nairn	—	1	1	1	1
Orkney and Shetland	1	1	1	1	1
Perth	2	—	—	—	—

[1] Breconshire and Radnorshire were combined from 1918.

	1885	1918	1945	1950	1955
Perth and Kinross	—	2	2	2	2
Renfrew	2	2	2	2	2
Ross and Cromarty	1	—	—	—	—
Roxburgh	1	—	—	—	—
Roxburgh and Selkirk	—	1	1	1	—
Roxburgh, Selkirk and Peebles	—	—	—	—	1
Selkirk and Peebles	1	—	—	—	—
Stirling	1	—	—	—	—
Stirling and Clackmannan	—	2	2	2	2
Sutherland	1	—	—	—	—
West Lothian	—	—	—	1	1
Western Isles	—	—	—	—	1

(2) *Burghs and Burgh Districts*	1885	1918	1945	1950	1955
Aberdeen	2	2	2	2	2
Ayr District	1	1	1	—	—
Dumfries District	1	—	—	—	—
Dundee	2	2	2	2	2
Edinburgh	4	5	5	7	7
Elgin District	1	—	—	—	—
Falkirk District	1	—	—	—	—
Glasgow	7	15	15	15	15
Greenock	1	1	1	1	1
Hawick District	1	—	—	—	—
Inverness Burghs	1	—	—	—	—
Kilmarnock District	1	—	—	—	—
Kirkcaldy District	1	1	1	1	1
Leith District	1	1	1	—	—
Montrose District	1	1	1	—	—
Paisley	1	1	1	1	1
Perth	1	—	—	—	—
St Andrews District	1	—	—	—	—
Stirling District	1	—	—	—	—
Wick District	1	—	—	—	—
Dumbarton District	—	1	1	—	1
Dunfermline District	—	1	1	1	—
Stirling and Falkirk District	—	1	1	1	1
Coatbridge and Airdrie	—	—	—	1	1

24-2

INDEX

Joyce, James, 165
Junior Carlton Club, 215
Junior Imperial and Constitutional League,
  211
Junius, Letters of, 144

Kidnapping, electioneering device, 105–6
Kipling, Rudyard, 165

Labouchere, Henry, 110
Labour clubs, 216
Labour party
  ages of supporters of, 297–9
  bias towards, in adult education, 183–4
  classes of supporters of, 297–303, 333–7
  clubs, 216
  complications in organisation, 210
  conversion to and from, 303–5
  election programmes of, 290
  emphasis on party, 262
  enthusiastic amateurs, 290
  foundation of, 207
  fun and games, 216, 218
  growth of, 219, 279–80
  idealism of, 219
  'image' of, 248, 288–9
  industrial areas and, 188
  'inexorable march' of, xxx–xxxii, 219,
    255, 279–80
  justification for, 262
  Labour and the New Social Order,
    xxxi
  League of Youth, 217–19
  local parties of, 207–8
  local propaganda, 210–11
  majority principle and, 132
  Pie in the Sky, 219
  policy statements, 290
  safe seats, 256
  schools and universities of Cabinet
    Ministers, 239
  sexes of supporters of, 299–300
  strength of, 279–80
  support of, by electorate, 277–8
  swing to, 197
  trade unions and, 196–7
  Transport House, 220
  Workers' Educational Association, 220
  workers' party, as, 248, 284
  Workers' Travel Agency, 216
  Young Peoples' Section, 217
Labour, representation of miners, 192–3
Labour Representation Council
  deal with Liberal Party, xxxi
  establishment of, xxxi, 207
  trade unions supporting, 196

Ladies' Carlton Club, 215
Lancashire, representation of, 26
Lancaster, Duchy of, representation of, 3
Landed Interest, *see* Agricultural Interest
Lansdowne, Marquis of, 102
Laski, Professor H. J., 238, 239
Lawrence, D. H., 165
League of Youth, 217–19
Liberal Central Association, xxvii, 258
Liberal party
  Birmingham Plan, xxviii, 124–5, 207
  Central Liberal Association, xxvii, 206,
    258
  constituencies, where strong, 286
  deal with Labour Representation Coun-
    cil, xxxi
  decline of, 263–4
  difficulties of, 291
  foundation of, 205–6
  justification for, 262
  Liberal Registration Association, 206
  literature of, 223–6
  local organisation, xxviii
  lower middle classes and, 279, 285–8
  loyalty in, 279–80
  middle classes and, 246, 279, 285–8
  National Liberal Federation, xxix, xxx,
    207
  Nonconformity and, 160, 286
  parliamentary reform and, 23–4
  proportional representation and, 30
  Reform Club, 206
  revival of, 247
  right and justice on the side of,
    156
  safe seats, 1892 to 1910, 279
  seaside resorts and, 286, 287
  small towns and, 286, 287
  split in 1886, 187, 279, 285, 329
  split in 1916, 332
  strength of in Ireland after 1832, 55
  strength of in Scotland after 1832,
    54
  suburbia and, 286, 287
  traditional Liberal seats, 332–3
  whigs' departure, effect of, 285
  working class and, 247
Liberal Registration Association, 206
Lievin, Princess, 115–16
Literature
  political: of Anti-Corn Law League,
    223; ballads, 200; definition of, 198;
    election addresses, 200; flood of, after
    1815, 100; local newspapers, 200–1;
    pamphlet war, 223–6; parties' use of,
    125, 207

Shires, *see* Counties
Six Acts, xxi, 100
Small towns, Liberal party and, 287
Smith, Adam, 180, 190
Smollett, Tobias, 146
Snob appeal, xxix, 125, 216, 250
Society
 Conservatism of, 233
 conspicuous waste in, 232
 Court of St James and, 232
 Liberals ostracised by, 232
 Parliament and, 232
 smart set, 233
Socio-economic groups, 254–5
Speaker's Conference of 1917, 28–9; 1944,
 34, 61
Spender, J. A., 149
Spielman, Miss, 252
Stair, Lord, 96
Star Chamber, 135
Steele, Sir Richard, 136, 243
Stephen, Sir Leslie, 163
Suburbia, Liberal party and, 286, 287
Sudbury
 corruption in, xxv, 202
 and see Eatanswill
Suez adventure, 91, 173
Swift, Jonathan, 135
Swing
 crudity of device, 269
 generally, 290, 305–26
 origin of, 267
Swinton Conservative College, 221

Talents, Ministry of all the, xx
Tamworth Manifesto, xxvii, 223
Taverns, newspapers in, 145
Teaching, bias in, 180
Television
 conservative tendencies in, 172–4
 election of 1955, 272
 leftward tendencies in, 172–3
 political importance of, 166–74
 public meetings and, 123
 standards in, 168–70
 viewers, number of, 167
Ten-pound householders, influence after
 1832, 15–16
Thackeray, W. M., 163
Thomas, J. H., 261
Three-generation cycle, 162, 165, 234
Tories
 honest men, 92
 independent gentry, 92
 ladies unattractive, 115
 political unions, frightened by, 123

split by Roman Catholic Relief, xxii,
 xxiii
 strength of, in 1827, 93
 and see Conservative party
Trade unions
 cabinet of, 191
 class-consciousness in, 250–1
 counter-attack by employers, 195–6
 Labour party and, 196–7
 loyalty to, 192
 majority principle in, 195
 nature of, 189
 new unionism, 194–5
 number of, 189
 origin of, 189–90
 political action by, 190–1, 193
 political levy, 197
 political swing of, in eighties, 196
 solidarity in, 196
 unskilled workers, 194–5
 working-class representation, 196
Trades and Labour Clubs, 216
Trades Union Congress
 establishment of, 189
 foundation of Labour party by, xxxi
 growth of, 192
 unions affiliated to, 250–1
Transport House, 219, 220, 226
Treasury boroughs, 99
Treating, at elections, 83–4, 88, 105, 108
Two-member boroughs, 31–2, 34
Two-party system, 27, 267

Undue influence, at elections, 73, 104,
 107–8
Universities
 Cabinet Ministers at, 236, 237
 Conservatism of, 181, 182–3
 religious tests at, 181
 representation of, 6, 7
 scholarship ladder, 182
Unnatural Coalition, xviii, 90, 91
Upper class, disappearance of, 229
Upper middle class, 245

Victoria, Queen, 165
Volcanoes, extinct, 130
Voluntary associations, importance of,
 235
Voters, *see* Electors
Voting, *see* Elections
Voting behaviour
 age and, 296–303
 apathy, 276, 291
 balance of parties, 277–80
 candidate's personality and, 208–9, 260–1